Jost Dülffer, Robert Frank (Eds.)
Peace, War and Gender from Antiquity to the Present

KLARTEXT

Frieden und Krieg
Beiträge zur Historischen Friedensforschung
Band 14

Für den Arbeitskreis Historische Friedensforschung
herausgegeben von
Detlef Bald, Jost Dülffer, Andreas Gestrich, Christian Jansen,
Thomas Kühne, Wolfram Wette, Benjamin Ziemann

Peace, War and Gender from Antiquity to the Present
Cross-Cultural Perspectives

Edited by Jost Dülffer, Robert Frank

Essen. Klartext Verlag 2009

Titelbilder:
Weibliche Offiziere der 6. Gardearmee, o. O., 8. März 1944,
© Foto: Boris Vdovenko, Sammlung Museum Berlin-Karlshorst e. V.
(mit freundlicher Genehmigung)
Exekias, Aiax und Achill beim Brettspiel während einer Kampfpause,
6. Jahrhundert v. Chr., Vatikanisches Museum, Rom

1. Auflage Oktober 2009
Satz und Gestaltung: Klartext Medienwerkstatt GmbH, Essen,
Druck: Majuskel Medienproduktion GmbH, Wetzlar
© Klartext Verlag, Essen 2009
ISBN 978-3-8375-0214-5
Alle Rechte vorbehalten

www.klartext-verlag.de
www.akhf.de

Table of Contents

Peace and War – Contributions to Historical Peace Research 7

Joan Beaumont, Jost Dülffer, Robert Frank
General Introduction 9

Concepts of Just Wars and Lasting Peace

Jost Dülffer
Conditions of Just Wars and Lasting Peace – An Introduction 15

Hans van Wees
Peace and the Society of States in Antiquity 25

Yvonne Friedman
Christian-Muslim Peacemaking in the Medieval Latin East 45

Arno Strohmeyer
Ideas of Peace in Early Modern Models of International Order:
Universal Monarchy and Balance of Power in Comparison 65

Gottfried Niedhart
Liberal and Democratic Peace as a Concept in
19th and 20th Century International Relations 81

Alfredo Canavero
Popes and Peace. The 'Just War' Doctrine and
Humanitarian Intervention in the 20th Century 97

Sumit Sarkar
Gandhi, Hindu Traditions,
and Twentieth-Century Indian Political Culture 115

Pierre Boilley
Practices of Peace and Resolutions of Conflicts in Contemporary Africa:
Borders, States, Minorities 127

Gender and Violence

JOANNA BOURKE/PENNY SUMMERFIELD
War, Violence and Gender – An Introduction 147

DIANNE HALL/ELIZABETH MALCOLM
Beyond the Pale: Gender and Violence in Ireland, 1169–1603 155

PIETER LAGROU
Irregular Warfare and the Norms of Legitimate Violence
in Twentieth Century Europe 169

BARBARA POTTHAST
Female Soldiers and National Heroes in Latin America 181

TAMMY PROCTOR
Between the Lines: Female Auxiliaries, Resistors, and Spies
in the First World War 205

JEAN H. QUATAERT
Gendered Medical Services in Red Cross Field Hospitals
during the First Balkan War and World War I 219

ROGER MARKWICK
Women, War and 'Totalitarianism':
the Soviet and the Nazi Experiences Compared 235

CHARLES S. MAIER
Targeting the City: Debates and Silences over Aerial Bombing
since World War II 253

Conclusion

ROBERT FRANK
Conclusion 267

Authors 275
Index of Names 277
Veröffentlichungen des Arbeitskreises Historische Friedensforschung 281

Peace and War

Contributions to Historical Peace Research

Historical Peace Research analyzes the prospects and limits for the realization of peace in all its historical dimensions. It is orientated towards peace as a key value, and considers the question if modern societies are able to achieve peace as its key driving force and point of reference for scholarly work. This endeavor is not based on any political commitment to a specific concept of peace. With regard to conceptional clarification, peace is basically defined as an effort for the institutional limitation and reduction of the collective use of physical violence against human beings. In the age of an emerging world society, with new hopes and at the same time new threats for mankind, peace has become a universal matter of concern.

Peace as the limitation and reduction of collective violence and war as the organized use of collective violence are the poles between which the work of Historical Peace Research is situated. This approach seeks to take up ideas from other scientific disciplines, both in terms of methodology and in terms of research areas. Historical Peace Research is particularly indebted to research objectives of social, political and cultural history. Peace movements, peace efforts and peace processes are part of its field of enquiry, but also the history of the military and the use of violence in wartime. Not least, it includes a reflection on the idea of a progress towards a non-violent modernity, in terms of both an intellectual history and a history of scientific concepts.

The series *Peace and War. Contributions to Historical Peace Research* is connected to earlier publications of the *Arbeitskreis Historische Friedensforschung (Working Group for Historical Peace Research)*. It is designed to document the proceedings of the academic conferences of the group, but is also open for monographic studies into the topics of Historical Peace Research.

Detlef Bald – Jost Dülffer – Andreas Gestrich – Christian Jansen
Thomas Kühne – Wolfram Wette – Benjamin Ziemann

General Introduction

JOAN BEAUMONT, JOST DÜLFFER, ROBERT FRANK

War has been central to the history of humanity. From the earliest times, human beings have dreamed of peace while continuing to wage war. In 1900, many believed in progress and thought that "Civilisation" — or at least, the European version — would generate peace for the coming century. Great, however, was the disillusion. In 1914, Europe set the world on the path to the worst war ever known — and an even more dreadful one was to follow some twenty years later. The twentieth century was not, then, a century of peace, but of wars: of massacres, atrocities and genocide, with, from time to time, some periods of renewed optimism and hope.

After the two major global conflicts, Woodrow Wilson, in 1918-1920, and Franklin Roosevelt, in 1944-1945, attempted to reform the international order and to promote democracy as a basis of lasting peace through the creation of new international organisations. However, the League of Nations, weakened by the absence of the US, failed to respond to Japanese aggression against Manchuria and China and to the Italian attack on Ethiopia, and the democracies, haunted by the desire for peace, were unable to contain Hitler's expansion in the late 1930s. War resulted again.

The victory of the democracies and the totalitarian USSR in 1945 provided new prospects for peace, but the United Nations' capacity for action was almost immediately neutralised by the hostility between the two superpowers. Even if the UN performed better than the League, and was able to back the armed response to the North Korean attack on South Korea in 1950, the postwar world order was determined by Cold War, by the balance between Washington and Moscow, and not by the international organisation.

After the collapse of the USSR and the fall of the Berlin Wall in 1989, there was again hope, verging on triumphalism in the US, for a new international order based on democracy. When Saddam Hussein attacked Kuwait in August 1990, the democracies seemed united, and Arab governments joined the coalition to halt aggression. Alas, it was soon clear that there was not a "new world order". Many armed conflicts broke out after 1991, even in Europe where war had been avoided since 1945, while the rise of radical Islam generated new challenges to the West, most notably in the terrorist attacks on New York and Washington on 11 September 2001.

In this context, the second Iraq war of 2003 provoked intense debate throughout the world about the notions of just war, just peace, unjust war, and unjust peace. The Western states were divided, transatlantic relations were damaged, and the legitimacy and efficacy of military intervention in defence of democracy were seriously contested.

Hence, despite continuing attempts in the twentieth century to build a peaceful international system, and to develop international norms and legal regimes protecting the victims of war, armed conflict remains endemic. The search for peace is perpetual, but the prospect of achieving "perpetual peace" — to appropriate the term of Immanuel Kant — is difficult. Peace, it seems, has always to be founded anew ("gestiftet").

Assuredly, then, in the first decade of the twenty-first century, there are few issues of greater importance than the meaning of "war" and "peace". That is the reason why the International Committee of the Historical Sciences chose this subject as a "major theme" for its 2005 world congress in Sydney. This book presents the results of this research. The authors, as historians of different periods from antiquity to the twentieth century, seek to provide a better understanding of the nature of war and peace in the light of long-term historical trends. The critical questions about the violence of war, the right to resort to war, and the preconditions of peace, are not new, and it is important to understand how different cultures have dealt with these issues through the ages and in different continents.

Three questions

The first question is one of universality and/or diversity: while war and peace are universal concerns for all humanity and all cultures, they also raise profound questions of historical and cultural relativism. How did the universality of the need for peace manifest itself in the Greek cities, in the conflicts and peace-making processes of the Crusades or the Hundred Years War, in the peace-building ideas of modern Europe, or in the concept of democratic peace during the nineteenth and twentieth centuries ? What can be learned about war and peace from the experiences of Europe, Latin America, India and Africa? The first aim of this book is to cover a range of historical periods, and case studies from Western and non-Western cultures.

The second goal is to conceptualise war and peace as being in a close relationship historically. In wartime, people are obsessed by peace, yet in peace time they fear and/or prepare for war (*si vis pacem, para bellum*). Moreover, war and peace are interdependent. One cannot be defined without referring to the other. War is an armed conflict between political entities, each of them trying, by the use of force, to impose its will on the other or to resist the other's will. In this respect, to appropriate Clausewitz's famous definition, "war is the continuation of politics by other means", or the pursuit of political aims considered as important and vital enough to achieve them by exceptional means rather than the usual peaceful ones.

Traditionally war is thought as something abnormal, something extraordinary, while peace is the normal and ordinary state. But, paradoxically, peace is more difficult to define. Often it is constructed negatively, simply as the absence of war, or something that occurs between wars — an interwar period — which, in turn, affirms war as being the normality. Sometimes peace is seen not as a state but rather a *momentum*, the end of a war characterised by a treaty: for example, the Peace of Amiens in 1802, or the Peace of Versailles in 1919. Of course, many have aspired to see peace as more than the mere absence of war. From Plato to Spinoza, from Kant to Habermas, the task has been to determine if it might be possible to create a positive "state of peace" that would render war impossible. This necessitates our reflecting historically on the concept of a "culture of peace", in connection with studies of "war culture".

The third goal is to link political and international history with a social and cultural historical approach. This is essential, because war, peace and world order are intrinsically linked with ideas, ideologies, poverty, social inequality, marginalisation of indigenous peoples, and oppression on the grounds of gender, religious conviction and ethnicity. Acknowledging this, the present book covers a range of issues that are at the forefront of contemporary historical debate: for example, *jihad*, sexual violence, relations between ethnic minorities and the State. Indeed, there is a symbiotic connection between war, peace and order, both within societies and in the system of relations between societies.

These three questions inform the two parts of this book. The first part, covering antiquity to the present, explores the possibility of a lasting peace when war was not only a reality of life, but also, in the case of a "just war", legitimised by religious or secular motives. The various chapters focus on the Western tradition from ancient Greece and Rome through the Middle Ages to a modern Eurocentric world, on Muslim traditions of the Middle Ages, and Indian and African approaches in recent times. By moving beyond ethnocentric views, we widen the debate to a global perspective on issues of war and peace.

While this first part of the volume concentrates more on political thought, the second part, "Gender and violence", focuses on social situations in which violence has played a central role and on the gendered dimension of war. Again the temporal and spatial range is wide: from the Middle Ages to the world wars of the last century, from Latin America to the Soviet Union. Do men and women construct and experience war and peace differently? The answer is far from simple. Warriors are not found exclusively on one side of the gender line, and peace lovers, on the other. Aristophanes invented *Lysistrata* who organised a sex strike, convincing

Athenian, Spartan and Boeotian wives to refrain from sex with their husbands until the latter put an end to the Peloponnesian war. But, comedy is not history. It does not express the complexity of reality, even the gender one. And history is more often tragedy, with sexual violence perpetrated on women, and women drawn into fighting, inflicting armed violence for various reasons and motivations. In wartime as in peace time, gender has to be seen — as it is in this book — as a relationship and not as a fixed state.

The chapters of this book hope to raise more questions than they can answer. They form an attempt to consider the interconnections between war, peace, society and international order, across various cultures and different periods of history, with one aim: historians may help us to understand the armed conflicts and peace processes of the present time in the light of the past. In the world chaos that we know today, historical dealing with peace must be of interest to the current actors of peace making.

Acknowledgments

This book originated from the XXth International Congress of Historical Sciences in Sydney, Australia in 2005, where the Commission of the History of International Relations and the International Committee for the History of the Second World War cooperated in organizing one of the three major themes, "War, peace and violence". The theme was chaired by Joan Beaumont and Robert Frank, while Charles S. Maier was the convenor of the first section, on "*Bellum Justum:* Just wars, Unjust Peace? Ideas and Discourses". Jost Dülffer was responsible for the second section ""Changing Concepts and Conditions of Peace in History"; and Joanna Bourke, for the third, "War, Violence and Gender".

Many persons have assisted in this publication. We must thank especially, for their scholarly engagement, constructive critique, translation and editorial support, Roderick Fisher, Andreas Gestrich, Sönke Kunkel, Helen Lenihan, Gottfried Niedhart, Barbara Potthast, Claire Sanderson, Simone Schulz, Hillard von Thiessen and Benjamin Ziemann.

Concepts of Just Wars
and Lasting Peace

Conditions of Just Wars and Lasting Peace – An Introduction

Jost Dülffer

Has "Peace" been the normal state of relations between states and societies throughout history, or is a state of "War" more typical? This question as such is not very fruitful for historians, because the answer depends on definitions and the importance attributed to particular historical circumstances. Suffice it to say that in most historical cases "War" has required legitimization, has been viewed as a morally good affair whose character may change according to time and circumstances. This may result in a relationship in which arms, but also other factors play a changing role. In this book "Peace," on the other hand, is regarded as a very complex relationship within societies and states as well between states in an international system. In most cases it is highly esteemed as a positive value connected with other values and ideas. It has dynamic connotations, as is embodied in the notion of a "peace process." In most cases, however, these dynamics are said to aim at a more or less stable or permanent condition, which is qualified by the notion of peace.

The underlying assumption of this book is that the notion of and the dealing with "peace" differed over time and space. The chapters presented here encompass, from a European perspective, ancient, medieval, early modern and modern times. They cover a core region of the European or transatlantic world, but they also include, for different periods of time, the Middle East, India and Africa. Religious connotations of cultures: Christian, Muslim, Hindu and African traditions and values, are touched upon.

Some questions seemed especially fruitful for a common framework. The chapters of this book seek to answer these questions:
- How important was or is the idea of peace to the whole system of values of a given period, state or society? How is it connected to other core beliefs and values influencing external and/or internal behaviour?
- How did concepts of peace deal with the 'self' and the 'other' ("we" and "they"); were they intended to create structural similarities or convergence? Or could they only build bridges between different entities?

- Is peace related to certain political systems or forms of societal or state organization? Especially, to what extent have free societies (in a modern sense) contributed to a state of peace? Were there other basic features of societies closely related to peace?
- In what cultural context was the idea of peace embedded? Were there cultural mechanisms such as rites, symbols, myths or public images which formed public manifestations of peace and created some permanence?
- Did concepts of peace achieve a permanent position within newly structured societies, or to what extent did they form only temporary experiments for certain situations? Under what circumstances could efforts to achieve peace be regarded as failed and war as justified?
- Does the notion of peace have gendered connotations? Is it intended to have a universal validity independent of time, state or society? With all reservations as to the fixed identity of "cultures," were there differences between intercultural and transcultural relations as regards war?[1]
- Given the limited space of their papers, the contributors to this volume had to select aspects of their subjects to which they attached the greatest importance. I have grouped their papers according to the categories listed in the research questions mentioned above. If peace as well as war is not seen as a stable condition, but rather as a process, which is the view of most of the authors, then it is relevant to ask in which parts of the world it was accepted as a valid principle.

Universal or Partial Claims to Peace?

The conclusions here of course do not neatly fit into this framework, but nevertheless they offer important comparative results.

In most cases notions of peace are formulated as general principles. This is especially the case if they are embedded in religious cultures, as in the Latin West and its Christendom in the Middle Ages, or in the Arab states of that time with their Islamic basis. It cannot be said with the same certainty regarding Hindu thought, and especially not of Gandhi, whose notion of peace was developed in a particular situation, i.e. in the Indian struggle for independence. One of the most contentious issues is the question whether the liberal and democratic peace model includes universal claims. In a historical perspective the notion was propagated only in a limited way during the 19th and 20th centuries and especially after the two world wars. There are good reasons to assume that notions of peace, at least those discussed here, were framed in a universal language but were in fact distinctly European, as was their practical application. This holds true for secular "international" relations as well as the Roman Catholic Church.

---

[1] A good overview: Hans-Henning Kortüm (ed.), *Transcultural Wars from the Middle Ages to the 21st Century*, Berlin, 2006.

The "self" and the "other"

A second problem concerns relations with the outside world, with an "other". In antiquity in general, van Wees argues, there was no natural state of war, but "even the most expansionist powers, such as the Persian and Roman empires, felt the need to justify their wars as means to restore international peace and order." That meant wars were frequent, but the possibility also existed of treaty relations and the exchange of envoys to establish permanent contacts. If for ancient Greeks all people who did not speak Greek were "barbaroi," that meant an exclusion from Greek kinship, rites and common culture which made peace a possibility, but not certain. At least the murder of Persian envoys by Greeks was an extraordinary event which attracted great attention.

In Christian-Muslim relations war, as a *crusade* or *jihad*, was basically considered by both sides to be the normal state of relations. However, in Byzantine times, beginning in the 8th century, the exchange of prisoners became a first step for a truce, as Friedman shows. It was not war that required explanation; peace had to be justified as a sort of (temporary) necessity. In the time of the crusades between 1097 to 1291 she counts ca. 120 treaties between both sides. In the beginning, most of them were concluded as oral agreements which ended a siege by compensation. Later such agreements were generally written. It became customary that the side threatened with defeat asked for a cessation of hostilities, but later a kind of agreement seems to have been concluded even in relatively undecided military situations. All this involved more (temporary) truces than lasting peace. In the course of time, elements of stability came into play, as when Sultan al-Kamil ceded Jerusalem to Frederick II because he had "promised" to do so. And a kind of "common cultural language" with the exchange of gifts or handshakes was used. Images of peacemaking seem to derive more from Western than from Oriental cultural sources, but Friedman contends that there may have been more mutual influence in those years. Especially the confirmation of oaths caused problems, which sometimes could be solved by the invocation of God – for instance when a treaty between Muslims and Christians declared that "God" should bless "all the prophets and have peace upon them".

The idea of a (universal) Christendom was kept alive in early modern Europe, but during the 17th century it developed more and more into simply the notion of Europe, without religious connotations, as Strohmeyer demonstrates. He does not specifically address peaceful relations with other regions of the globe, but other authors (such as Jörg Fisch[2]) have shown that treaty relations were possible and worked on a basis of mutual obligations, which were taken seriously and created

---

2   Jörg Fisch, *Krieg und Frieden im Friedensvertrag. Eine universalgeschichtliche Studie über Grundlagen und Formelemente des Friedensschlusses*, Stuttgart, 1979; id., *Die europäische Expansion und das Völkerrecht: die Auseinandersetzungen um den Status der überseeischen Gebiete vom 15. Jahrhundert bis zur Gegenwart*, Stuttgart, 1984

trust as a kind of symbolic capital, as was also the case with regard to Ottoman expansion in Europe. There is, however, the impression that formulas of friendship and invocations of God were common (Karl-Heinz Ziegler[3]). In early modern times, conflicts between various empires were sometimes aggravated by universal claims.

In the last two centuries the great powers developed the technology that enabled them to compete in expanding their physical domination over large parts of the globe. This was accompanied by new invocations of/references to peace as a universal principle, as Niedhart shows: "The 'invention of peace' (Michael Howard)[4] happened when the modern Western world began to take shape with its main features: a liberal market economy, the transnational division of labour, parliamentary politics, an open society and democracy." This development offered no clear prescript for dealing with the non-European world, because it was meant to be potentially universal, but it opened numerous possibilities, from incentives to conviction and forced conversion. Quite different, i. e. more traditional or universal motives, can be seen in the motivation of the Roman Catholic Church in promoting peace – the topic of Canavero's paper.

One of the consequences of this potential universality was the spread of Western concepts to other parts of the world. As Boilley aptly shows, during the second half of the 20th century, concepts of mainly European origin were applied in various peace processes. It is not primarily a question of how African peace notions dealt with the outside world, but more how the penetration of African states by originally European or Western standards of peace left room or opportunities for genuine or traditional strategies of peace. Suffice it to say, that the liberal, democratic concept of peace can only serve as a rough guideline for peace processes in Africa. The political reality there was and is much more complex. Mahatma Gandhi, as Sarkar emphasizes, was grounded in Hindu tradition but also developed his philosophy of peaceful resistance in part from Western thought. That meant that he internalized to some extent these Western ideas and created a kind of hybrid peace culture. It is my assumption that such superstructures or notions of peace can be found in many parts of the world in the past as well as the present. The question of transfer in these cases thus becomes more significant. In the case of Gandhi, Sarkar shows that his posthumous influence also went in the opposite direction; to some extent his notions were incorporated into Western pacifism. The conclusion can only be that a wide panorama of "connected histories" or "histoires croisées" opens a broad and highly promising perspective and a large area for research.

---

3   Karl Heinz Ziegler *Fata iuris gentium. Kleine Schriften zur Geschichte des europäischen Völkerrechts*, Baden-Baden, 2008.
4   Michael Howard, *The Invention of Peace*, London 2000 (German version: Die Erfindung des Friedens, Lüneburg, 2001).

Peace and its Coherence or Conflict with Other Values and Ideas

How important were concepts of peace to a whole system of values? It is striking that all authors in this volume stress the importance of a notion of "peace" as a positive value, but in most cases it is seen in context with other values which also made the opposite, war and violence, more or less acceptable or even justified modes of societal strategies. It is especially difficult to generalize regarding this problem, but some hints in the papers presented here may be useful.

In Greek antiquity the conviction of a special role for all Greeks was built not so much on a peace concept with a specific set of values – as is shown by the fact that war was a legitimate act – but more on the trustworthyness with which alliances of "great mutual friendship and closeness" or "peace and alliance" (Thucydides) were concluded. While the defense of justice and the gods was a positive motivation for war, peace meant the restoration of these values. Below these alliances there was the conviction of closeness (*oikeios*) or harmony. In the Middle Ages that changed completely. Although Friedman's paper is devoted to relations between Christianity and Islam, and thus to a transcultural perspective, she provides important first results. In Christian as well as Muslim tradition peace might have been equated with victory in a *crusade* or a *jihad*. But for inner cohesion of their respective cultures, the notion of the "Peace of God" meant that real peace could exist only on the common religious basis of Christianity; the *Peace of God* meant a limitation of legitimate war to fellow Christians. The *Peace of God* had among others the function to promote and facilitate crusades. On the Muslim side things were similar: a true peace, *sulh* could only be concluded between co-religionists, while war, too, was a legitimate means of politics, although not linked to the value of *jihad* and thus not fought with the same intensity.

Under the Emperor Charles V in European early modern times Christian cohesion as a common value still played a central role when he stressed the legitimacy, going back to Dante Alighieri, of furthering Christendom as a necessary means of achieving world dominion. That is one part of Strohmeyer's argument. No clear distinction was made between general peace, universal peace and the reign of Christendom. But in the 18th and 19th centuries, the idea of a universal monarchy did not necessarily include a common set of values but rather a set of different bonds and linkage to this unifying and peace-providing institution. Under the heading of a European "balance of power," too, a wide range of possibilities for attaining peace can be distinguished. In both cases law and justice were closely connected with peace, as was the combination of these values with public welfare, the general prevention of war, and the unity and protection of Christendom. All these values provided the formulae of peace treaties. Indeed, as Strohmeyer insists, vague public speeches with propagandistic effects stood in sharp contrast to political reality, a gap which was increasingly criticised in public.

In the 19th and 20th centuries it is even evident, as the title of Niedhart's paper indicates, that the notion of peace was connected with liberalism and democracy.

Compared to the subjects of other papers in this volume, this seems to be a rather recent development: individuals and their secular well-being acquired a central importance; states were seen as providers of these political goods of participation as well as of material wellbeing. Here again not practical application but the teleological connection to a future notion of a kind of stable peace was addressed. In the last decades some politicians, but even more so political scientists tended to define peace as a superior value to all other goods, in the notion of "positive peace" (Johan Galtung[5]) even as an all-including aim for human well-being. In 20th century Africa, Boilley's subject, universal Western notions of democracy and self-determination played a large rhetorical role in official political language. United Nations institutions and special United Nations missions for many African conflicts served as organisations that could be used as external participants and as a forum for intra-African debates on these principles as well as for resolving conflicts. This author discusses a broad range of civil as well as inter-state wars in Africa after the gaining of formal independence. In ending them the notion of self-determination played an important role, as did the argument that it was the task of Africans themselves to conclude peace. Collective African action by the *Organisation of African Unity* (OAU, since 2000 reorganized as *African Union*), but also regional or national self-awareness developed into an important factor for peace. For example, a recent strategy document of the *African Union* (May 2004) argues, the " the scourge of conflicts in Africa constitutes a major impediment to the social and economic development of the continent and of the need to promote peace, security and stability." To a large extent, peace is embedded in a synthesis with security and stability and defines socio-economic well-being as a major aim. Seen in this way, the inner-African debate is not very different from the idea of liberal peace which Niedhart addresses. The popes on the other hand made increasing attempts to allow also intervention for humanitarian reasons, a prerequisite for "real peace," as Canavero shows.

In the various political systems of the Indian subcontinent Sarkar distinguishes genuine Hindu ways of resolving conflicts. But Mahatma Gandhi, who regarded himself as a devout Hindu, must not be considered solely in light of his religious beliefs. In the author's opinion that would mean a kind of *orientalism* – to use Edward Said's illuminating term.[6] He has to be seen in a much broader context. Gandhi himself developed his strategies largely under the influence of Christian beliefs, but he also drew on Leo Tolstoi, Ralph Waldo Emerson and David Henri Thoreau, thinkers who had modern, rationalist and individualistic ideas. Gandhi's views, as well as those of V. D. Savarkar, were based on Hindu approaches that reflected the strong influence of modern nationalism. It was the practical application of nonviolence that divided these two Indian ways of thinking. Gandhian

---

5   Johan Galtung, *Peace by Peaceful Means. Peace and Conflict, Development and Civilization*, Oslo, 2006.
6   Edward W. Said, *Orientalism*, New York, 1978.

nationalism thus could become effective against British rule. Sarkar argues that in practice Gandhi's method of non-violence (*ahisma*) – could promote in reality a stabilisation of the existing order of society though his programme was aimed at overcoming traditional hierarchies. Non-violence as a method used against a modernizing colonial rule could bring about violence in parts of multifaceted Indian society.

Symbols, Rites and Performances of Peace

Peace worked and was furthered in a set of political or philosophical values, but these were often programmatic and did not necessarily have anything to do with the practice of conciliation. The gap or even the opposition between social reality and ideals could be bridged to some extent by social practise, i.e. a set of forms of behaviour, standardized rites, exchanges of symbols or by other means. These facilitated the development of mutual trust or were a part of a whole process that in many cases was called peace. In almost all cases, peace agreements or treaties were embedded in standardized behaviour. Peace was sometimes based on old, common traditions, but in other cases peace procedures were developed through a kind of trial and error, testing which rites or symbols could work and were commonly understood by both sides.

In the case of ancient Greece common blood and religious bonds were maintained. Hans van Wees: "Blood relations involved shared religious rites. Just as all Greeks took part in Panhellenic games and cults, so their ethnic subdivisions and 'family' clusters each had common festivals and rituals. Even at the height of their power and at their most 'tyrannical,' the Athenians went to much trouble to forge religious bonds, most spectacularly through their repeated ritual purifications of the sanctuary of Apollo on Delos, a common cult centre for all Ionians." But this did not prevent frequent wars among the Greeks and was only a prerequisite for peace. Friendship in this regard was the central category which was valid in individual life as well as among states. "We win friends by doing rather than receiving favours … and we are unique in fearlessly helping others, motivated less by calculations of expediency than by faith in generosity," Pericles said in his funeral oration for the war-dead, according to Thucydides. This basis for military pacts as well as for peace processes could be underlined by arbitrated compensation which might be promised in religious ceremonies. "A positive sense of goodwill and an active exchange of services and favours" (van Wees) were part of the process. Truces for shorter or longer periods and peace promises "for all time" formed two extreme positions in a continuum of possibilities for pacification.

In the medieval Middle East two symbolic traditions of peace, Muslim and Christian, had to find common ground. For Christians there was a tradition – in Friedman's words: "the sign of peace was an act of friendly association – eating and drinking with the other party – and one consequence was the return of the letter of *diffidatio*." While mutual kisses were not part of the ceremonies between the two sides, public notaries and witnesses were. During the crusades, "a process of mutual acculturation [developed], exemplified by the employment of the western ceremony of extending the right hand and the eastern use of gifts. Both cases reflect cultural mediation via outside intervention. In a treaty of 1098, a captive Christian wife of the Muslim ruler teaches him western mores. She instructs him to give Godfrey his right hand rather than to use his preferred eastern method of messengers bringing gifts", but later the Christian victor also brought gifts as a sign of lordship and supremacy. In 1167 the Western tradition of shaking bare hands was practiced, which seemed to chroniclers to be an even the greater victory than the material clauses of a treaty. In addition to this adoption of Western customs by the Muslim world, Friedman finds reasons for an even stronger acceptance of "Eastern usage in the Latin east". That is the point where the already mentioned oaths came in to the play, which required a way of acceptance of religious collaboration with infidels. This acculturation facilitated an increasing tradition of written peace treaties instead of only the more volatile oral agreements.

In the Latin West, another example of Friedman's Christian-Muslim relations, a different picture evolved in the *Reconquista* in Spain. While in the East captive women could only act as cultural mediators, "in Europe we have the additional phenomenon of political matrimony as part of peace treaties. Because of the religious divide, such political marriages were ruled out in the East." An exception, according to Friedman, was the idea of a marriage of Richard the Lionheart's sister to Saladin's brother (which, as it turned out, never materialized). Such intermarriage is not explicitly addressed in the other papers of the volume but nevertheless formed an important part of peace building after the conclusion of peace in most of the cases mentioned here. One could contend that only in modern Western tradition did this custom fall into disuse during the 19th century and was largely abandoned in the 20th century. Arguably that had to do with republican traditions which made monarchical representation of states more or less obsolete, but also with the individualisation of marriages. That notwithstanding, examples to the contrary can easily be found down to the present day.

That the conclusion of peace meant a major ceremonial performance is evident from Strohmeyer's paper as well. Friedman provides descriptions of celebrations of the moment of peace, which were quite common in early modern Europe. But there was a difference, when a monarch with universal claims granted peace or when a bilateral peace was concluded in a balance of power system. Thus victory and peace could coincide, as when Charles V celebrated his triumph after his successful Tunis campaign and assumed the role of an imperial peace-maker. In other portraits, such as an allegory by Parmigiano, he is presented clad in armour and holds the staff of command, which was fixed to the top of a globe as a sign of universal power. "A winged victory with her left hand puts a palm leaf as a sign of victory on the emperor's head and with her right hand an olive branch as a symbol peace on the globe." Strohmeyer rightly points out that a certain blurring of the exact meaning of peace can be observed. The symbolic or iconic presentation of peace may have contributed to this intended effect. For the 19th and 20th centuries it is sufficient here to mention that Adolf Hitler's monumental architecture was strongly influenced by symbols of world dominion. Today, we would see that as a symbol of the opposite of peace, or a peace of the graveyard, to which Immanuel Kant alluded in his "Perpetual Peace". Prior to World War II, building was begun in Berlin of a huge people's hall for 300,000 persons, with a dome crowned by a (German) eagle sitting on a globe: universal domination of a racist ideology was one of these visions. In general, it can be argued, that peace had to be visible, and the visibility for all sides in an agreement as well as third parties could best be achieved by rituals and symbols when concluding relevant treaties and popularizing them in the media of the time.

In the case of India, Sarkar does not address the role of peace or treaty making but the process which Gandhi as a person followed. He explains that the tradition of *ahisma* and *satyagraha* had aspects of ritual demonstration of an attitude of peace, which exerted pressure in many ways on the British colonial establishment. The African examples which Boilley presents leave no doubt that ceremonies were of very great importance for a relaxation of tensions. Examples of external mediation with the use of modern techniques can be found, but, as he explicitly shows for Mali in the 1990s: "Africa has started using its own methods of conflict resolution, which mix classical mediation with original efforts based on older, endogenous methods. One of the most recent examples is the Panel of the Wise. With no equivalent in other international institutions, this panel clearly stems from an ancestral philosophy of mediation specific to Africa. Might this not be a reason to have hope in the continent's future?" These methods also include the integration of former fighters of both sides in a conflict into the military or other functions of a pacified state.

Permanent or temporary peace?

Peace was a common value or had a positive notion in almost all the cases presented here. But in many cases it was not regarded as the normal status of relations between states or other political entities. In Greek city states there were frequent wars, which were legitimate and part of politic struggles for power. In the Christian West the same observation holds true. And sultans often waged wars against other Muslim states. In a strict sense peace between Christians and Muslims could only be regarded as a truce, but one increasingly endowed with insignia of peace. In the reality of international relations in early modern Europe, it was quite common to wage war either to achieve a balance of power or to prevent the establishment of a universal monarchy. Hindu thought in the 20th century included a large amount of violence, as, according to Sarkar, V. D. Savarkar has shown, especially where ideas of peace do not seem to have had greater importance. African struggles for independence and wars after achieving sovereignty were frequent. They even came to be considered normal. This met with criticism more or less from the application of traditional values and external principles in the UN system. That agrees to some extent with the diagnosis of European and worldwide expansion in the two last centuries, which brought about not only the two world wars of the 20th century. What is described here in the paper on the ideas of liberal (economic) peace and democratic (participatory) peace demonstrates the utility of peace for the well-being of the peoples and states involved. It was accompanied by a growing legal and even moral condemnation of war as means to create conditions for peace. The ideas of Roman Catholic popes in this regard differed only superficially. Canavero maintains that they continued to argue that in secular societies peace could only be a temporary affair, whereas real peace rested only in God and thus in the true faith.

That would not have seemed strange to people in earlier times, but some individuals now maintain that international organisations of the world state system, grouped around the United Nations and its affiliated or regional organisations in many parts of the world, may be able progressively to develop an effective peace strategy.[7] These organisations should trust not only in the normative power of peace, which allows for war only in self-defense, but also bridge the gap between political reality and the values of peace. This applies not only to contemporary history and for our times but is also based on observations of other periods and non-European regions of the world. The concept of peace as a positive value is regarded by some contributors of this section as very vague and even ambiguous. That may have to do with the often too easily invoked unifying character of the notion of peace. Peace as a final aim could justify virtually any measure of violence and war as necessary and expedient for achieving a later, final state of true peace. But peace can also be seen, from ancient Greece to Gandhian efforts of decolonization to modern African strategies of reconciliation, as a mode of daily practice and symbolic dealing with war, conflicts and various emergency situations. This is demonstrated not least by present-day developments in a globalizing world. Both notions of peace, the stable state in a better future as well as the patient application of everyday improvements, can be found in many different historical contexts. This volume can offer only a broad range of typical examples. Finding the right combination of both is still a great challenge, and not only for historians.

---

7   Paul M. Kennedy, *The Parliament of Men. The United Nations and the Quest for World Government*, New York, 2006.

Peace and the Society of States in Antiquity

Hans van Wees

After inflicting a defeat on the Libyans, Merneptah, Pharaoh of Egypt (1224–1214 BC), proclaimed his achievement in a monumental inscription which glorified not only the king's warlike deeds but also the perfect peace which he had brought to his country:

> Sit down and chatter happily, or walk out on your way: there is no fear people's hearts. Fortresses are left to themselves, wells are open for the messengers' use. The battlements of the walls are becalmed, only sunlight wakes the watchmen. Medjai troops are stretched out asleep, Nau and Tekten patrols are in the fields they love. The cattle of the field are left to roam, crossing the river's flood without herdsmen… People sing as they come and go; they do not lament or mourn. The towns are settled once again. He who tends his crop will eat it.[1]

These charming images are representative of ancient attitudes to peace. As well as the fundamental criterion of an absence of violence, they stress its economic and psychological benefits: peace brings prosperity because people can tend their fields and flocks undisturbed, and peace brings joy to people's daily lives. The threat of violence was never far away, however, and it is equally typical of ancient attitudes that Merneptah's little ode to peace was part of a hymn which otherwise celebrated the crushing defeat of an enemy in war.

If peace is defined as the absence of violence in relations between communities, it can exist in three situations. First, when there is no threat of violence at all, a condition which we may call 'natural' peace. Secondly, when the threat of violence has been suspended by agreement between two or more parties, a condition of 'formal' peace. And thirdly, when the threat of violence from one party is so great that it deters others from resorting to violence, a condition of 'imperial' peace. Many

---

[1] Translation adapted from the versions in Lichtheim 1976, 77, and Liverani 2001, 85.

students of international relations from Thucydides onwards, and many students of state government from Hobbes onwards, recognise only the second and third types of peace. In their view, international relations and social relations fundamentally consist of a war of all against all, and accordingly the threat of violence is ever-present and no such thing as 'natural' peace can exist. For the ancient world in particular, it has often been argued that, in the absence of effective international law or supranational institutions, peace was never more than a brief interruption of a pervasive state of conflict. What is more, it is said that the ancients themselves saw things in precisely this way – that they regarded themselves as by default at war with everyone else, and at peace only if a cessation of hostilities had been formally agreed or imposed.

This conventional picture greatly underestimates the efforts of ancient communities to create a condition of peace for themselves, and the importance of peace in ancient systems of values. There can be no doubt that throughout antiquity wars were very common, but ancient international relations featured a wide range of means designed to inhibit and avoid violence. Beyond the treaties, truces and diplomatic protocols familiar to the modern world, these included bonds such as collective 'kinship' and friendship, less familiar and therefore too often ignored. It is no exaggeration to describe the ancient world as forming a 'society of states' rather than a mere collection of strictly autonomous entities – a conflict-ridden society, certainly, but a society all the same. Within this society of states, political, military and diplomatic activity reveal remarkably ambitious programmes for the creation of 'formal' and 'imperial' forms of peace, while 'natural' peace, not a war of all against all, was widely regarded as the default state of international relations.

'Only sunlight wakes the watchmen': natural peace in the ancient world

The *Iliad* twice refers to days 'in the past, in time of peace [*ep' eirênês*], before the Greeks came', when the city of Troy enjoyed great wealth and its women could safely venture beyond the town walls to wash clothes in 'the beautiful broad stone basins' (9.401–3; 22.153–6). The implication is clear. Until and unless an enemy appeared, a community perceived itself as at peace: not in a state of undeclared war, nor at peace with anyone in particular, but simply and absolutely at peace. The early Greek poet, Hesiod, imagined that a community which treated 'strangers and locals' with justice at all times would be spared war altogether: 'Peace who nurtures youths will prevail thoughout the land and all-seeing Zeus will never cause harsh war to appear among them' (*Works and Days* 225–9). For Hesiod, Peace was a daughter of the supreme god Zeus, and Justice and Good Order were her sisters (*Theogony* 901–3).

This is all the more remarkable because Greek communities at the time of the composition of these poems, c. 700 BC, were not much more than chiefdoms, characterised by a low level of state-formation; small-scale private raids and other forms of violence between communities were common. If any people might have regarded themselves as living in a permanent state of war, it would have been these early Greeks, yet even for them peace was the norm.

When an early Greek town was raided, its inhabitants did not regard this as confirmation of an existing state of war, nor as a provocation which called for immediate violent retaliation. Instead, their first reaction was to send envoys to the raiders' home to try to negotiate a settlement and avoid escalation of the conflict. As Homer told the story of the Trojan War, the Greeks had mobilised only when the Trojans had sent away their envoys empty-handed, with death threats ringing in their ears (*Iliad* 3.205–24; 11.139–41).[2] The same story told from a non-Greek perspective, by the historian Herodotus a few centuries later, reflected the same attitude to international relations. The mythical first contacts between Greece and Asia, according to this version of events, were a series of abductions of women by both sides. Peaceful settlement would have been an option, but the Greeks rejected this. Thus a relationship was established which allowed small-scale acts of violence and retaliation, but still fell short of war. Next, when the Trojans abducted Helen from Sparta, the Greeks upped the stakes again and mounted a full-scale assault on Troy. Only then did Asia finally regard itself as at war with Greece, and it remained so ever after (1.1–5). As in Homer's version, the Trojan war is here the result of repeated provocation, a refusal to negotiate, and deliberate escalation. Just as the Trojans are cursed as gluttons for war in the *Iliad* (13.633–9), so the Greeks are held 'greatly to blame' for their actions in Herodotus' version (1.4): in Greek eyes there was nothing 'natural' or inevitable about this legendary war, or any historical war.[3]

If international relations had been seen in terms of a permanent war of all against all, then it would have followed that 'every war was justified, unless in waging it one broke a treaty',[4] yet this was clearly not the case. Even the most expansionist ancient states never declared war without feeling compelled to offer a justification for doing so. A striking example is the ritual declaration of war employed in early Rome, which took the form of a 'demand for reparations' and thus by definition cast the Romans as victims of previous aggression. A priest, the so-called *fetialis*, went to the border of enemy territory where he uttered a formula proclaiming that the Roman case was 'righteous and pious' (*iustus, pius*), followed by a curse upon himself if his claim should ever prove untrue, and finally a statement of Roman demands. The priest repeated all this on crossing the border, on meeting the first person within enemy territory, on entering the town, and finally on entering the town square. When his demands were not met, he gave the enemy 30 days' notice

---

2   See van Wees 1992, 168–82; Raaflaub 1997.
3   Van Wees 2004, 3–5.
4   Loenen 1953, 80–1; cf. Finley 1985, 67–71; Hanson 1999, 18. This view goes back to Keil 1916, 7–10. Contra e.g. Bravo 1980, 981–2; Baltrusch 1994, 92–4.

of war, and at the end of this period returned in the presence of witnesses to cast a javelin across their border and thereby open hostilities.⁵

The Romans may have been exceptional in observing such scrupulous procedures – one Greek author thought that it was the secret of their success, because it ensured that the gods were always on their side in war (Dionysius of Halicarnassus 2.72.4) – but they were by no means unusual in insisting that they fought justified wars of retaliation, not aggression. The Greeks constantly claimed to fight for the sake of revenge and punishment. The Persian invasions of Greece in the early fifth century BC, for example, were cited for a century-and-a-half afterwards as the justification for Greek and Macedonian campaigns of 'retaliation', up to and including Alexander's conquest of the Persian Empire.⁶ Other reasons for war frequently cited by Greeks and Romans included the obligation to help an ally threatened or harmed by a third party, and to 'liberate' unjustly subjected states. The 'liberation of the Greeks' from the oppression of fellow-Greeks and 'barbarians' was a slogan guaranteed to win support from the start of the Ionian Revolt in 499 BC to the final reduction of Greece to the status of Roman province in 146 BC, and Cicero could say of the Romans that 'our nation gained control of the whole earth by defending its allies' (*De Re Publica* 3.35).⁷

The rulers of ancient empires generally presented themselves as charged by their gods to rule over the entire world, and therefore tended to justify their campaigns as directed against 'rebels': people who defied legitimate imperial authority and a divinely ordained cosmic order. The kings of Persia routinely claimed that some part of the world was 'in commotion' and that by the order of the supreme god Ahuramazda they 'smote that country and put it down in its place'; Assyrian kings made much the same claims in the name of their god Asshur.⁸

The major ancient empires required little or no actual provocation to spot and attack a troublemaker: 'the most paradoxical boast of the king [of Egypt] is to have been able to discover rebels in lands so distant that nobody previously suspected their existence' (Liverani 2001, 87). In a couple of revealing letters sent in the mid-thirteenth century BC, two Hittite kings encourage their younger colleagues, the kings of Babylon and Assyria, to pick some vulnerable opponent almost at random, in order to chalk up an easy victory:

> They have said that my brother is a king whose weapons have been stowed away and who just sits around … Do not keep sitting around, my brother, but go against an enemy land and defeat the enemy! Against which land

---

5   Livy 1.32.5–14; Dionysius of Halicarnassus 2.72.6–9; cf. Cicero, *De Re Publica* 3.35.
6   See e.g. Lendon 2000; Gehrke 1987. On Greeks and Persians: Hornblower 2001.
7   Helping allies: e.g. Rich 2001, 67–8. Liberation of Greeks: Raaflaub 2004, 58–202.
8   Kuhrt 1995, 505–19 (Neo-Assyrians), 676–82 (Persians, citing Kent 1953, *DNa*; *XPh*). In more detail: e.g. Oded 1992 (Assyria); Liverani 2001, esp. 23–37, 96–96 (Late Bronze Age Near East and Egypt).

should my brother go out? Go against a land over which you enjoy three- or fourfold numerical superiority.[9]

Such cynical advice shows clearly that the prestige – and wealth – to be won through military success and conquest might make war a more attractive option than peace, regardless of whether it could be formally justified. Official reasons such as retaliation, liberation, and restoration of order therefore never told the whole story. But we should not conclude that all such justifications were specious and any notion of peace a sham. Speeches and documents for public consumption would not have stated the official reasons for war again and again unless such reasons mattered, and unless it was war, not peace, which needed explaining.

How sincere anyone was in citing justification for their wars is as difficult to tell for the ancient world as it is for the modern world, but for at least some of the people some of the time it was genuinely important to have valid reasons to fight. According to one of the Hittite letters, one of Assyria's most expansionist rulers, Tukulti-Ninurta I, 'keeps saying this: "I want to accomplish something! If the foreign kings became hostile to me, they would come against me, and I could make a name for myself."'.[10] Keen as he was to start a war, the young king evidently felt that he could not do so without provocation. Similarly, according to Thucydides, the Spartans started the Peloponnesian War primarily for nakedly power-political reasons, but they nevertheless felt obliged to engage in a series of diplomatic manoeuvres designed to give them the greatest possible justification – and even then, says Thucydides, their war-efforts were hamstrung because they could not shake the feeling that they were really in the wrong.[11]

Despite occasional flashes of a Realist perspective, then, the normal view in antiquity was that peace was the default state of international relations. Plato had a speaker in one of his philosophical dialogues say that 'every city-state is at all times, by nature, in a condition of undeclared war with every other city-state' (*Laws* 626a), but he made it clear that this was an intellectual position which was not widely shared, and which he himself rejected. Expressions of the opposite view are easily found in ancient literature:

> If it really has been fated by the gods that mankind must wage wars, then it is up to us to be as slow as possible to start any, and, if a war does break out, to end it as soon as we possibly can. (Xenophon, *Hellenica* 6.3.6)

---

9   Beckman 1996, no. 23; cf. no. 24C.
10 Beckman 1996, no. 24C.
11 Thucydides 1.23.6, 33.3, 86.5, 88, 118.2–3 (power politics); 1.126–127, 139.1–3 (justification); 7.18.2 (guilt).

An entire compendium of such sentiments featured in a speech composed by the historian Timaeus in third century BC, mockingly cited by his successor Polybius for its banality:

> Sleepers are woken by trumpets in war, by birdsong in peace. War is like illness and peace is like health, for peace cures even the infirm and war kills even the fit. In peace, the old are buried by the young, in accordance with nature, but it is the reverse in war … and lots of other things like that. (12.26.1, 6–8)

Polybius condemned these phrases as typical of trite 'schoolboy' exercises and unworthy of a serious historian (12.25.11, 26.9), but this makes them all the more important as evidence for popular thought – which clearly saw war as perverse and peace as part of the natural order.[12]

'From the beginning of time and forever': formal peace

The earliest surviving formal treaty was concluded between two Mesopotamian city-states in c. 2450 BC.[13] This document, inscribed on the so-called Vulture Stela, predates the earliest surviving law codes by almost four centuries: a sign that the formalisation of international relations was an integral and prominent part of the process of state-formation.

By the late Bronze Age, treaties had become complex and ambitious agreements. A spectacular example is the treaty concluded in 1270 BC between the Hittite king Hattushili III and the Egyptian pharaoh Ramsesses II 'in order to establish great peace and great brotherhood between them forever'. The preamble insisted that the agreement would 'bring about the relationship which the Sun-god and the Storm-god established for Egypt with Hatti', namely that 'from the beginning of time and forever … the god has not allowed the making of war between them'. In other words, the many years of warfare over domination of the Levant which had just come to an end were now renounced as a mistaken departure from the divine order. For the future, the kings promised that they and their descendants would maintain a relation of 'brotherhood and peace forever', that this would be 'better than the former brotherhood and peace of Egypt with Hatti', and that they would never begin hostilities against one another, again in accordance with the gods' 'eternal regulation for their countries' (Beckman 1996, no. 15, A1–27). The point could not have been more emphatically made: peace was to last for all eternity and should never have been broken at all.

---

12 See further Van Wees 2004, 3–5 (Greeks); Sidebottom 1993 (Romans). On ancient attitudes towards peace, see also Spiegel 1990; Arnould 1981; Zampaglioni 1973; Romilly 1968.
13 Bederman 2001, 137–54; Kuhrt 1995, 36–44.

At the same time, the two kings contracted a defensive military alliance, which required them to send one another 'infantry and chariotry' not only in case of attack by an external enemy but also in case of internal rebellion (when subjects who 'offended' against the king were to be 'destroyed') and Ramesses also promised intervene if Hattushili's heir's succession to the throne should be disputed. Finally, the kings promised to return to one another all deserters, refugees and migrant populations, and to return such people unharmed: 'they shall not tear out their tongues or eyes, and they shall not mutilate their ears or feet'. In short, intense and close co-operation, not just non-aggression, was demanded by the terms of the agreement (Beckman 1996, no. 15, A.28–70). It was capped by a dynastic marriage, to which we shall return.

Strictly reciprocal and equal treaties of this kind were less common in the Near East than hierarchical treaties in which one ruler imposed terms on another, usually a defeated enemy. The major difference was that unequal alliances included not only a reciprocal defensive military obligation, but also a unilateral obligation on the part of the subordinate state to contribute troops to offensive military campaigns waged by the dominant state. 'He shall be at peace with my friend and hostile to my enemy' and when called upon must 'mobilise wholeheartedly' and 'fight wholeheartedly', is a common clause in treaties imposed by Hittite kings on subject rulers. Sometimes the military obligation is more closely specified: in one case, 100 chariots and 1,000 infantry, plus necessary provisions, in the case of an especially favoured vassal, no chariots, only 100 or 200 infantry, and exemption from garrison duty.[14]

Further clauses of unequal treaties, in addition to the provisions made in equal treaties, covered tribute payments, requirements to make personal visits to the superior ruler, the obligation to report rumours of hostile activity, and above all a detailed definition of the boundaries of the subordinate's territories. Special conditions might be added: in one instance, a 'barbaric' ally was made to swear that he would in future adopt Hittite sexual mores.[15] Although unequal treaties focused more on the obligations of the weaker partner than on the maintenance of peace as such, they were implicitly or explicitly conceived of permanent peace agreements. The ruler of Ugarit is instructed thus: 'in the future observe the peace treaty of the king of Hatti, of the sons of the king, of the grandsons of the king, and of Hatti'.[16]

Similar patterns occur in the treaties of the Iron Age Near East, Greece and Rome. 'Perfect peace and friendship' were formally established between Assyria and several other major powers on a basis of equality, while 'peace and vassalage'

---

14 'Wholeheartedly': e.g. Beckman 1996, no. 5 ii.9'-24'; no. 7, A ii 6–32 (Suppiluliuma I, c. 1370–1342 BC). Precise obligations: e.g. Beckman 1996, no. 2, A iv.19–24 (c. 1400 BC) ; no. 18C, iii 32–42 (c. 1250 BC).
15 Beckman 1996, no. 3, A iii 40'-83' (c. 1370–1342 BC).
16 Beckman 1996, no. 9, 1–12 (c. 1330 BC); for 'peace', see also e.g. no. 4, A re. 8'-15' (c. 1370–1342 BC); no. 14, A obv. 15–18 (c. 1330 BC). Cf. Karavites 1992, 194–7.

on a range of conditions much like those of the Hittite treaties were established when minor powers offered their submission to Neo-Assyrian kings, for example. A genuine concern to conclude lasting and effective treaties is nicely illustrated by the query put to an oracle on behalf of Esarhaddon of Assyria (680–669 BC) regarding a diplomatic approach by a Scythian ruler: 'Will Prothothyes, king of Scythia, ... speak true and honest words of peace with Esarhaddon, will he keep the treaty of Esarhaddon, king of Assyria, and do whatever is good to Esarhaddon?'[17]

In Greece and Rome, too, a distinction between equal and unequal treaties was an important feature of international relations. Equals normally accepted only defensive military obligations, whereas in unequal alliances the subordinate was also obliged to 'have the same friend and enemy' as the dominant state and join its offensive campaigns. The obligation might be no more specific than to 'help in the most vigorous manner possible', or it might be precisely defined in terms of soldiers and provisions required. Equal treaties might also define rights to positions of leadership and shares of booty in joint campaigns. The power of Sparta in southern Greece and Rome in Italy, much like the power of the larger Near Eastern kingdoms, was based on extensive networks of unequal alliances. The so-called Delian League dominated by Athens was unusual in being based on a set of alliances which were formally equal yet also imposed offensive obligations on all parties. This system in practice allowed Athens to mobilise its allies in much the same way as Sparta and Rome did theirs.[18]

Unlike in the Near East, however, not all treaties made in Greece and Italy included a military alliance, and not all Greek treaties were meant to last forever. Before the first formal military alliance (*symmachia*) is attested in Greece, we already hear of the sworn treaty of 'friendship' (*philotês*) which the Greeks and Trojans concluded in the *Iliad* in a doomed attempt to end the Trojan War. In one of the earliest surviving historical treaties, the Greeks of Sybaris in Southern Italy 'and their allies' collectively concluded with the Serdaeans, not another alliance, but 'friendship, faithful and without deceit, forever'. In classical Greece, many treaties included both 'friendship *and* alliance', but friendship did remain a distinct category of international relations. The Romans likewise distinguished between 'allies' (*socii*) and 'friends' (*amici*), including not only peers but also weaker states treated as 'clients'.[19] Friendship evidently entailed only a broad moral obligation to the other party, rather than the contractual obligation imposed on allies, but the precise nature of the relationship is difficult to define. It amounted to more than mere non-hostility, at any rate, and indeed seems to have carried quite a emotional charge. Sybaris, for example, not only made 'friends' in southern Italy, but was also

---

17 Parpola and Watanabe 1988, esp. xv–xxv (quotation p. xix); Bederman 2001, 141–6.
18 Van Wees 2004, 12–15.
19 *Iliad* 3.73, 94, 256, 268–301, 323; 4.158–9. Sybaris: Bauslaugh 1991, 57 (and see discussion of distinction ibid. 56–64, 88–91; cf. Van Wees 2004, 10–12; Baltrusch 1994, 3–15). Rome: Bederman 1991.

'more closely bound together by friendship than any cities we know' with Miletus at the other end of the Mediterranean; when Sybaris was sacked in 510 BC, the Milesians shaved their heads and went into collective mourning (Herodotus 6.21).

A peculiar feature of Greek international relations was the use of extended truces (*spondai*). Short truces and armistices were undoubtedly widely used in the ancient world, but classical Greek states regularly agreed on a cessation of hostilities for periods of thirty, fifty or even a hundred years, thereby turning truces into *de facto* peace treaties. Such *spondai* might be followed by the conclusion of friendship and alliance of the same duration, but they could equally stand on their own as non-aggression pacts which did not entail further obligations.[20] The existence of treaties of peace and alliance of limited duration has traditionally been cited as evidence that the Greeks could only conceive of peace as a brief interruption of an enduring state of war, but this is highly misleading. Even if it were true that 'formal peace' agreed by treaty was always temporary in Greece, it would not follow that the Greeks could not conceive of 'natural' peace as a lasting state of affairs. But in any case it is simply not true that the Greeks knew only fixed-term treaties. Plenty of international agreements featured no limitation in time – like the sworn 'friendship' between Homer's Trojans and Greeks and the unequal alliances imposed by Sparta – or were explicity made to last 'forever' – like the friendship of the Sybarites and the Serdaeans and the military alliances of Athens' Delian League, to which member states swore loyalty until the day that iron would float.[21]

Rather than see *spondai* as short-lived peace treaties, we should see them for what they are: spectacularly long-lived truces. Alongside permanent treaties, *spondai* offered the Greeks an additional means to create peace, for up to a century, when a permanent military or diplomatic solution to the issues which had caused war proved to be out of reach. The decision of some Greek states, and Rome, to treat others as 'friends' without also making them 'allies', may similarly be seen, not as a sign of reluctance to engage in closer international co-operation, but as an attempt to improve the prospect of peace by avoiding an accumulation of military obligations. After all, 'an alliance does not mean peace, but a change of war', as one Greek diplomat put it (Xenophon, *Hellenica* 7.4.10). Accordingly, the Greeks in the fourth century BC developed a new type of treaty: a multilateral defensive permanent alliance which obliged all states to join forces against any one of their number who interfered with the autonomy of another. A series of such treaties was established from 386 BC onwards, each collapsing quite soon as powerful states manipulated them in their own interests. But more remarkable than their rapid failure in practice is what these treaties tried to do in principle: their hugely ambitious goal was a lasting end to all war in Greece and a so-called 'common peace'.[22]

---

20 van Wees 2004, 17; cf. Baltrusch 1994, 5–11, 192–3.
21 For this oath, see pseudo-Aristotle, *Athenian Constitution* 23.5; Plutarch, *Aristides* 25.1.
22 *Koinê eirênê*: see Jehne 1994; Ryder 1965.

The Greeks could attempt to set up an international system of this kind because they formed a more or less closed community of small city-states bordering on the territories of greater powers, first the Persian empire and later the Macedonian kingdom, which took it upon themselves to enforce compliance with the terms of treaty. Outside the framework of common peace, too, Greek city-states frequently tried to avoid war by appealing to greater powers, such as the Hellenistic kingdoms or Rome, to arbitrate between them.[23] But usually the only greater powers available were the gods, and these were cited as witnesses to, and enforcers of, the oaths which throughout antiquity accompanied treaties of peace and alliance.

Hittite treaties, for example, concluded with an invocation of 'the Thousand Gods of Hatti' and the local gods of the other country, many of whom were listed by name and title in a long, awe-inspiring roll-call of divine witnesses. These gods, both sides were reminded, would eradicate the family and property of anyone who broke the oath, but protect until 'a good old age' those who kept faith. Assyrian treaties invoked a similar array of deities who would inflict a staggering variety of maladies and misfortunes on the oath-breakers, from insomnia and malaria to venereal disease and famine-induced cannibalism ('instead of grain may your sons and daughters grind your bones'). The Roman ritual was a model of restraint by comparison: the state's official representative swore that the Romans would not be the first to break their oath, or else 'you, Jupiter, must strike the Roman people, just as I here and now strike this pig, and you must strike harder in proportion to your greater might and power' (Livy 1.24.7–9). It is easy to be cynical about the efficacy of such supernatural sanctions, but for most people throughout ancient history the gods were very real and fearsome, and not to be taken lightly.[24]

Some secular guarantees were put in place as well. It was not uncommon to demand hostages from a treaty partner as a sign of good faith and guarantee of loyalty, and any danger of dispute or carelessness about the terms of treaties was minimised by keeping and displaying copies of the written text, having not only divine but numerous human witnesses present, and sometimes requiring that the text of the treaty should be regularly read out as a reminder.[25] It must be conceded that all the supporting measures and sanctions and good intentions combined were rarely enough to ensure long periods of peace or unbroken alliance between neighbouring states, but it must also be said that ancient states could not have done much more to *try*.

---

23 See Ager 1996; Piccirilli 1973.
24 Bederman 2001, 51–73. Assyria: Parpola and Watanabe 1988, e.g. no. 6, 414–663. Hittites: Beckman 1996.
25 Some Hitttite examples: human witnesses: Beckman 1996, nos. 14, A rev. 17–22 (c. 1330 BC); 18B, rev. 28–32 (c. 1275–1260 BC); 18C, iv.30–43 (c. 1260–1220 BC); reading of treaty: Beckman 1996, nos. 11, I iv.1'-8' (c. 1340–1310 BC); 13, A iii.73–83 (c. 1300 BC).

Imperial peace: 'second sun' or 'wasteland'?

Lasting peace was established only when one state grew powerful enough to force others to refrain from violence – which was by no means always the case even within what we tend to call 'empires' in the ancient world. Small states often continued to fight with one another even when both were bound by an unequal alliance to the same great power, as the history of the city-states and petty kingdoms of the Bronze Age Levant and of the Greek city-states in the Hellenistic age illustrates all too clearly.[26] But when dominant powers began to consolidate their conquests and centralise their administration, they usually took steps to end violent conflict within their sphere of influence and began to justify their power as a god-given means to bring peace and prosperity to previously wretched parts of the world. The Pax Romana is well-known example, and has served as a model for modern imperial enterprises, but it had illustrious predecessors from the Bronze Age onwards.

Rome began reducing some defeated opponents to the status of directly administered territories, 'provinces', rather than subordinate allies or friends, when it first expanded overseas in the mid-third century BC, and soon began to see itself as a bringer of peace to these subjects. This self-image was not merely a propagandistic projection, but something in which members of the governing elite of Rome – and no doubt of many another empire, ancient and modern – genuinely believed. In one of his posthumously published private letters, the senator and former consul Cicero reminded his brother, governor of Asia Minor, why he need have no qualms about levying taxes on the population of his province:

> Asia ought to consider this, too: it would never be without the calamity of foreign war and domestic discord if it were not controlled by this imperial government. Since there is no way to maintain that *imperium* without revenues, let Asia be content to buy for itself, with some part of its produce, permanent peace and leisure (*Letter to Quintus* 1.1.34)

A generation later, when Augustus was undertaking a major consolidation and reform of imperial government, Virgil's epic *Aeneid* told the nation that bringing peace and order to the world was Rome's supreme gift and destiny: Greece and the Hellenistic kingdoms might well produce superior sculptors, orators, and astronomers, but 'you, Roman, must remember to govern nations with the power of empire; these will be your arts – to impose order on peace, to spare the conquered, to fight the arrogant aggressor' (6.847–53).

The rhetoric of empire stressed the prosperity which resulted from a lack of internal violence, the suppression of banditry and piracy, and the absence of a significant threat from outside the boundaries of the empire, imagined as set close

---

26 For the Levant, see the evidence of the so-called Amarna Letters: Moran 1992. For city-state warfare in Hellenistic Greece, see Chaniotis 2005, 18–43; Ma 2000.

to edge of the world. Ease of travel was a favourite theme, and the scientifically-minded elder Pliny even sang the praises of the 'awesome majesty of Roman peace' for making accessible species of plants from all over the world. 'May this divine blessing last forever, I pray. Thus have the Romans been given to the world as a second sun to shine light on human affairs' (*Natural History* 27.1).[27]

The blessings of living without any threat of violence were very much part of Near Eastern imperial discourse as well, as illustrated by the hymn to peace composed to mark Merneptah's victories which opened this paper. The kings of Egypt, Assyria and Persia all presented themselves as legitimate rulers of the entire world, who would maintain harmony, justice and security throughout their territories for the benefit of all their loyal subjects. A Middle-Assyrian formula urged the king: 'By your right sceptre enlarge your land! May Asshur give you authority and obedience, justice and peace'.[28] In 492 BC, more than half a century after their original conquest, the Persians banned all Greek cities under their control from resorting to force and imposed diplomatic means of settling disputes (Herodotus 6.42); just over a century later, what the rest of the Greeks saw as a freely chosen 'common peace' agreement backed by the Persian king will have been interpreted by the king himself as a submission to his authority in order to win a share in the benefits of this long-established Pax Persica.

It goes almost without saying that not all subjects accepted that submission was a price worth paying for peace, or that imperial powers really delivered the peace they promised. Those threatened with incorporation into an empire might protest, as Tacitus imagined a British chieftain doing, that 'plundering, butchering, pillaging go under the false name of "imperial government", and they speak of "peace" where they leave nothing but a wasteland' (*Agricola* 30). Internal and external pressures made most ancient empires much more fragile than they claimed to be, yet some succeeded in persuading enough people of the advantages of submitting to central control to ensure a relatively peaceful existence for many. The longevity and scale of the Roman empire even inspired some to dream that the whole world would eventually be pacified and that, one day, soldiers would no longer be needed.[29]

'I and you, we are brothers': the society of states

The high imperial perception of the world as containing in effect only a single legitimate state, surrounded by a few savage tribes ultimately destined to be absorbed as well, was only one particular variation on the ancient view that the world was,

---

27 On Roman peace, see e.g. Woolf 1993; Sidebottom 1993; Zampaglione 1973, 135–84.
28 Liverani 2001, 32; see also ibid. 17–37, 79–100; Oded 1992; Kuhrt 1995, 676–701.
29 As predicted by the emperor Probus (276–82), according to the *Life of Probus* 20 (*Historia Augusta*); Eutropius, *Breviarium* 9.17; Aurelius Victor, *On the Caesars* 37: see Zampaglione 1973, 135.

or should be, an ordered place rather than an arena full of violent contests. Apart from a few Realist intellectuals, no-one in antiquity saw the world as an anarchic system of states pulled apart by incessant competition for power and held together by nothing but fragile treaties. Instead, people tended to regard the world as a society of states, modelled on the societies in which they lived.

One crucial concept was that of international kinship. In the Near East fellow-kings called one another 'brother' (or, if there was a marked age difference, 'father' and 'son'). A letter sent by the king of Amurru to the king of Ugarit shows that this was no empty phrase:

> My brother, look: I and you, we are brothers. Sons of a single man, we are brothers. Why should we not be on good terms with each other? Whatever desire you will communicate to me, I will satisfy it, and you will satisfy my desires. We form a unit.[30]

Brotherhood between kings extended to their subjects as well. Thus, the treaty between Hattushili III and Ramsesses II was made 'in order likewise to establish good peace and good brotherhood of Egypt with Hatti forever' (Beckman 1996, no. 15). Brotherhood was often reinforced by intermarriage between royal families: many letters survive in which one king asks another to send him a daughter or sister as wife, or, failing that, a woman who could pass for a princess ('Who could say: "She is not the king's daughter"?'). Again, the closeness created between royal families was envisaged as involving the whole population: with a Hittte-Egyptian dynastic marriage 'two great countries became a single country', and after another royal wedding 'the people of Assyria and Babylon mingled with each other'.[31]

Kings, members of royal families, and high officials continually sent messengers to 'enquire after the health' of their counterparts in other kingdoms and to present gifts. Often such messengers had business to despatch, but equally often their chief purpose was to offer reassurances of continuing friendship. 'Our messengers will travel continuously between us forever, fostering brotherhood and peace', Ramesses II wrote to his 'sister', the queen of Hatti, adding: 'I have sent a very nice present to my sister'. The same queen's husband wrote to the king of Babylon to complain of his failure to send messengers regularly – 'only if two kings are hostile do their messengers not travel continually between them' – and that his gifts were too mean: the horses too small, the lapis lazuli of inferior quality. Conversely, the Hittites considered themselves 'at peace from afar' with remote Wilusa (possibly Troy) just because it sent messengers.[32] A measure of the intensity of diplomatic contacts was the adoption of a lingua franca – Akkadian, later Aramaic – throughout the Near East.

---

30 Cited Liverani 2001, 137; cf. discussion of brotherhood, ibid. 135–8.
31 Liverani 2001, 190–5, esp. 195. Pretend princess: Moran 1992, no. 3.
32 Beckman 1996, no 22F, 26–9, 76–9; no 23, obv. 50–4, rev. 62–83; and no.13, B i.2–14.

Among the steady flow of generic good-will messages and gifts, 'friends' and 'brothers' also exchanged more specific goods and services. Requests for specialists such as physicians, priests and sculptors, and for specific commodities such as gold from Egypt are common in the surviving letters, always accompanied with an invitation to ask for anything at all in return. The result was the development of an in some respects common material culture across a large part of the Near East, although in otherways local and regional styles remained distinct.[33]

In the world of the city-states of Greece and Italy, where kingship was not the dominant form of political organisation, a similar range of relationships existed in a less centralised and more collective form. Kinship was traced from collective mythical ancestors and shared places of origin, so that for example the Spartans, Athenians and Romans regarded themselves as representing the chief branch of a wider family of communities, the Dorians, Ionians and Latins, respectively. Kinship between communities was also often based on a claim that one had founded the other, whether in the historical or the legendary past. Appeals to kinship were a prominent feature of Greek and Hellenistic diplomacy, and led to some credulity-stretching inventions, such as the idea that the Persians were descended from Perses, founder of the Greek city of Argos (Herodotus 7.150), or that the Jews shared an ancestor with the Spartans (1 *Maccabees* 12.7.19–23). Yet some of the major forms of international kinship were given expression through shared rituals and festivals, and were clearly taken very seriously. Kindred states were supposed to help rather than fight one another, and even the sceptical Thucydides accepted that at least some alliances were genuinely based on a sense of kinship.[34]

As we have seen, Greeks and Romans could also conceive of other states as 'friends'. Even without a formal treaty of friendship, Greek states might regard one another as informal friends, or 'close' (*oikeios*) or 'in harmony' (*arthmios*), a relationship which involved the reciprocal exchange of gifts and favours. Thus the Corinthians once let the Athenians have twenty state-of-the-art warships for a token sum of money, a favour which was still recalled two generations later and used as an argument why Athens ought in turn to lend military aid to Corinth. Athens took particular pride in citing its own legendary and historical record of making friends by helping others, and both Sparta and Athens were known to go so far as to give away conquered land to loyal allies who had lost their own territories.[35]

Instead of the continual traffic of royal messengers, we find that many members of local elites travelled frequently and maintained extensive private contacts abroad. One Greek poet's definition of happiness was the possession of sons, horses, hounds, and 'a guest-friend abroad' (Solon, fr. 23). 'Guest-friends' (*xeinoi*) in other communities provided hospitality and gifts, and looked after one's interests abroad. Intermarriage across community boundaries was common (except in classical Ath-

---

33 Liverani 2001, esp. 146–59; for sources see esp. the so-called Amarna letters: Moran 1992.
34 See Hornblower 1996, 61–80; Jones 1999; Hall 2002; van Wees 2004, 8–10.
35 Van Wees 2004, 10–12; Bauslaugh 1991, 59–62. On reciprocity, see also Missiou 1998.

ens), and there were international religious festivals – above all the Olympic Games, of course – to which crowds of people travelled from far and wide and which accordingly functioned as international social events. For the major festivals truces were proclaimed which forbade any attack on the organising city; it is probably a myth that such truces forbade all warfare for the duration of the festival. The manifold personal contacts cultivated in this way served as a channel for public communication between communities as well, alongside more formal channels such as sacrosanct heralds and public embassies.[36]

The society of states throughout antiquity was shaped not only by egalitarian ties of kinship and friendship, but also by internal hierarchies. In the Late Bronze Age Near East, a handful of 'great' kings who regarded one another as peers stood far above the crowd of 'small' kings who were their 'servants'. In a treaty of c. 1250 BC, the Hittite king listed as 'the kings who are my equals in rank' the rulers of Egypt, Babylonia, Assyria and Ahhiyawa, but the last name was later erased: the ranking order was not fixed, and other lists show that at one time or another the kings of Mitanni and Aleppo also ranked among the peers. The hierarchy of kings was based on the relative status of their countries: 'If you should say: "The king of Babylon is not a great king", then my brother does not know the country of Babylon, what rank it is'.[37]

Differences in status were expressed in a variety of protocols. Equals exchanged good wishes ('I am well; may you be well'), but inferiors abased themselves before greater kings ('I am the dirt under the sandals of the king, my lord'). The gifts of great kings were to be paraded separately from the tribute of inferiors. Lesser kings received graded forms of respect, so that the Hittite king could, for instance, award the ruler of Tarhuntassa the privilege of having everyone but the crown prince rise when he entered the court, and otherwise 'whatever royal ceremonial is allowed [also] to the king of the land of Carchemish'.[38]

Less elaborate but no less significant ranking systems existed among the city-states of Greece and Italy, in which each community saw itself as having superiors to be treated with deference, inferiors to be treated with moderation, and equals who should be treated as such (Thucydides 5.111.4). International standing, and especially positions of 'leadership' at regional and higher levels, were an object of constant competition. Leading states enjoyed privileges such as precedence at international festivals and sanctuaries and the right to take the most prestigious battle stations and positions of command in coalition armies, hotly disputed by Sparta and Athens as rivals for the leadership (*hêgemonia* or *archê*) of all Greece, who fought over the right of first consultation of the oracle at Delphi, and argued

---

36   Guest-friends: Herman 1987; Mitchell 1997. Diplomatic relations: Adcock and Mosley 1975. On festival truces, see esp.

37   Quotations: Beckman 1996, no. 17, A iii 42-iv 18; 22E obv. 53'-56'. See Liverani 2001, 38–45.

38   For greetings formulae, see again the Amarna letters (Moran 1992). Gifts versus tribute: Moran 1992, no.1. Protocols: Beckman 1996, no. 2, A i 38–44; 18C, ii 78–83; cf. Liverani 2001, 197–8.

about who should hold the left and the right wing, or the relative prestige of commanding the army versus the navy. States which claimed an unrealistically high place in the ranking order were mocked for their pretensions. The inhabitants of a small city, who after a minor victory asked the Delphic oracle 'Who are the best?', were told that they, at any rate, ranked nowhere, 'not even twelfth'.[39]

Except when a single power became so overwhelming that it claimed to be the only source of legitimate authority and aimed to turn the whole world into a single society under its imperial control, people in antiquity thus saw the world as a society of states ordered by principles of kinship, friendship and hierarchy. Within this international society, just as in ordinary society, kinsmen and friends could fall out over perceived breaches of the rules of proper behaviour and differences in status could be a source of contention as much as a source of order. The perception of international relations as modelled on social relations certainly never guaranteed peace, and indeed it created a range of causes of war, but it did mean that justice and peace were supposed to prevail and that non-violent settlement of disputes was the norm.

The principle is perhaps best illustrated by an early Roman oath, in use when Rome's ambitions of domination did not yet stretch beyond the cities of their Latin kinsmen. This archaic oath to 'Stone Jupiter' invoked the following curse on those who broke a treaty:

> while all other people live safely in their own countries, under their own laws, in possession of their own properties, temples and tombs, may I alone be cast out – just as this stone is now (Polybius 3.25.7–9).

The worst punishment for those who failed to abide by the rules of international relations, in other words, was nothing more and nothing less than ostracism from the society of states.

Conclusion: peace, war and international order in antiquity

Polybius, writing in an age when city-states, federations and kingdoms were constantly at war with one another when they were not fighting the ever-expanding Roman empire, spoke with great conviction of

> the thing which we all pray the gods may give us, which we desire so much that we will put up with anything in order to have it; the only incontestable blessing among the so-called good things in life – I mean peace. (4.74.3).

---

39 See van Wees 2004, 22–6; Lendon 2000.

He admitted, however, that peace was never the *only* goal in international relations:

> War is terrible, but not so terrible that we should put up with *anything* to avoid it ... For peace with justice and propriety is the most beautiful and advantageous of assets, but peace with inferiority and shameful cowardice is the ugliest and most harmful of all things (4.31.3, 8)

If war was common in antiquity, then, it was not because the ancient concept of peace was deficient, or because commitment to the ideal was half-hearted, but simply because a multitude of social, economic, political and cultural factors favouring the use of violence counterbalanced and often outweighed the desire for peace – just as they have done throughout history.

Peace as a concept, norm and ideal is prominent and pervasive in the historical record from antiquity onwards: it is not an invention of specifically modern, or European, or democratic rhetoric. Nor can one point to any time in antiquity when the concept of peace was invented or gained a new significance: the earliest surviving literature and documents already reveal as keen and articulate an appreciation of peace as one could imagine, short of outright pacifism. No doubt strength of feeling about peace fluctuated, and peaked in periods of protracted and devastating warfare, but there is no sign that attitudes towards peace changed fundamentally in the course of ancient history, or between political regimes or cultural communities. From the western Mediterranean to Mesopotamia and beyond, large territorial kingdoms, small republican city-states, oligarchies and democracies alike regarded peace as the normal and most desirable state of international relations, and as a source of great material and psychological benefits.

If there is a major difference between the ancient and modern world in respect of peace, it lies not so much in the concept itself as in the broader set of ideas about international relations of which it formed a part. The ancient perception of the world as an ordered place, in which communities were bound by ties of kinship, friendship and deference, meant that peace in the sense of mere non-hostility was not the ultimate goal in international relations, but as a first step towards close co-operation and unity in forms ranging from military alliances to 'friendship' and 'brotherhood'. If some modern concepts of peace contain elements absent from ancient usage – harmony, unity and positive co-operation, rather than mere non-hostility – this is not because ancient goals in international relations were limited or shallow. Quite the reverse: ancient societies had a rich vocabulary to describe the kinds of harmonious, co-operative world order to which they aspired; it is the limitations of modern discourse which force the single concept of peace to bear all these meanings.

Bibliography

Adcock, F. and Mosley, D., *Diplomacy in Ancient Greece*, London 1975.
Ager, S., *Interstate Arbitrations in the Greek World, 337–90 BC*, Berkeley 1996.
Arnould, D., Guerre et paix dans la poésie grecque, New York 1981.
Baltrusch, E., *Symmachie und Spondai. Untersuchungen zum griechischen Völkerrecht der archaischen und klassischen Zeit (8.–5. Jahrhundert v. Chr.)*, Berlin 1994.
Bauslaugh, R., *The Concept of Neutrality in Classical Greece*, Berkeley 1991.
Beckman, G., *Hittite Diplomatic Texts*, Atlanta, GA 1996.
Bederman, D. J., *International Law in Antiquity*, Cambridge 2001.
Bravo, B., 'Sulân. Répresailles et justice privée contre des étrangers dans les cités grecques', *ASNP* 10 (1980), 675–987
Chaniotis, A., *War in the Hellenistic World. A social and cultural history*, Oxford and Malden, MA 2005.
de Romilly, J., 'Guerre et paix dans la poésie grecque', in Vernant (ed.) 1968, 207–20
Finley, M., *Ancient History: Evidence and Models*, London 1985.
Gehrke, H.-J., 'Die Griechen und die Rache', *Saeculum* 38 (1987), 121–49.
Gill, C., Postlethwaite, N. and Seaford, R. (eds.), *Reciprocity in Ancient Greece*, Oxford 1998.
Hall, J. *Hellenicity. Between ethnicity and culture*, Chicago 2002.
Hanson, V. D., *The Wars of the Ancient Greeks and Their Invention of Western Military Culture*, London 1999.
Hartmann, A. and Heuser, B. (eds.), *War, Peace and World Orders in European History*, London and New York 2001.
Herman, G., *Ritualised Friendship in the Greek City*, Cambridge 1987.
Hornblower, S., *A Commentary on Thucydides. Vol. II: Books IV–V.24*, Oxford 1996.
Hornblower, S., 'Greeks and Persians: West against East', in Hartmann and Heuser 2001, 48–61.
Jehne, M., *Koine Eirene. Untersuchungen zu den Befreiungs- und Stabilisierungs-bemühungen in den griechischen Poliswelt des 4. Jhdt. v. Chr.*, Stuttgart 1994.
Jones, C., *Kinship Diplomacy in the Ancient World*, Cambridge, MA 1999.
Karavites, P., *Promise-giving and Treaty-making. Homer and the Near East*, Leiden and New York 1992.
Keil, B., 'Eirene', in *Berichte über die Verhandlungen des königlichen sächsischen Gesellschaft der Wissenschaften* 58 (1916).
Kent, R., *Old Persian. Grammar, Texts, Lexicon*, New Haven, CT 1953.
Kuhrt, A., *The Ancient Near East, c. 3000–330 BC*, London and New York 1995.
Lämmer, M. 'Der sogenannte olympische Friede in der griechischen Antike', *Stadion* 8/9 (1982/3), 47–83
Lendon, J. E., 'Homeric vengeance and the outbreak of Greek war', in H. van Wees (ed.) 2000, 1–30.
Lichtheim, M., *Ancient Egyptian Literature. Vol II: The New Kingdom*, Berkeley, CA 1976.
Liverani, M., *International Relations in the Ancient Near East, 1600–1100 BC*, (Basingstoke 2001.
Loenen, D., *Polemos. Een studie over oorlog in de Griekse oudheid*, Amsterdam 1953.
Ma, J., 'Fighting poleis of the hellenistic world', in H. van Wees (ed.) 2000, 337–76
Missiou, A., 'Reciprocal generosity in the foreign affairs of fifth-century Athens and Sparta', in C. Gill et al. (eds.) 1998, 181–97

Mitchell, L., *Greeks Bearing Gifts. The public use of private relationships in the Greek world, 435–323 BC*, Cambridge 1997.

Moran, W. L., *The Amarna Letters*, Baltimore and London 1992.

Oded, B., *War, Peace and Empire: justifications for war in Assyrian royal inscriptions*, Wiesbaden 1992.

Parpola, S. and Watanabe, K., *Neo-Assyrian Treaties and Loyalty Oaths. State Archives of Assyria, Vol. II*, Helsinki 1988.

Piccirilli, L., *Gli arbitrati interstatali greci. Vol. 1*, Pisa 1973.

Raaflaub, K., 'Politics and interstate relations in the world of early Greek poleis', *Antichthon* 31 (1997), 1–27

Raaflaub, K., *The Discovery of Freedom in Ancient Greece*, Chicago 2004.

Rich, J., 'Warfare and external relations in the middle Roman republic', in Hartmann and Heuser 2001, 62–71

Rich, J. and Shipley. G. (eds.), *War and Society in the Roman World*, London 1993.

Ryder, T., *Koine Eirene*, Oxford 1965.

Sidebottom, H., 'Philosophers' attitudes to warfare under the principate', in Rich and Shipley 1993, 195–212

Spiegel, N. *War and peace in Classical Greek Literature*, Jerusalem 1990.

van Wees, H., *Status Warriors: war, violence and society in Homer and history*, Amsterdam 1992.

van Wees, H., *Greek Warfare: myths and realities*, London 2004.

van Wees, H (ed.), *War and Violence in Ancient Greece*, London 2000.

Vernant, J.-P. (ed.), *Problèmes de la guerre en Grèce ancienne*, Paris 1968.

Woolf, G., 'Roman peace', in Rich and Shipley 1993, 171–94.

Zampaglione, G., *The Idea of Peace in Antiquity*, Notre Dame and London 1973.

Christian-Muslim Peacemaking in the Medieval Latin East

Yvonne Friedman

Both medieval Islam and Western Christianity espoused the aspiration to world peace as part of their vision of the apocalyptic era. Each, nevertheless, employed military force against its antagonist, founding institutions aimed at the destruction of its enemy: in Islam, the *jihad,* and in Christianity, the Crusade. The reality, in which the adversaries bonded with each other, engaged in diplomatic negotiations, and signed limited ceasefire agreements, stands in sharp contrast to this hostile ideology and requires explanation.

Muslim law differentiates between intra-Muslim peace, *sulh,* contracted only between Muslim factions, and *hudna,* a temporary ceasefire – peace with the infidel entered into for reasons of expediency alone. The Koran establishes both the compulsory nature of the *jihad* and its collective character (2:216): *jihad* can be carried out by a limited number of individuals and cancelled for the remaining Muslims (Koran 9:112; 4:95). As a collective, not a personal, obligation, *jihad* as fighting allows for many exceptions and this facilitates utilization of loopholes to make peace. Whereas war against the infidel needed no justification, peace or even truce-making required both pretext and explanation.[1] Medieval Islamic legal thought, here exemplified by Ibn Rushd (Averroes) was preoccupied with the circumstances and conditions under which it was permissible to contract a truce:

> The conclusion of truce is considered by some to be permitted from the very outset and without an immediate occasion, provided that the Imam deems it in the interest of the Muslims. Others maintain that it is only allowed when the Muslims are pressed by sheer necessity, such as civil war and the like. As a condition for truce, it may be stipulated that the enemy pay a certain amount of money to the Muslims… Such a stipulation (paying of tribute) however, is not obligatory. Awzā`i even considered

---

1 R. Peters, trans., 'The Chapter on Jihad from Averroes Legal Handbook *Bidāyat al-Mudjtahid*', *Jihad in Medieval and Modern Islam,* Nisaba, Leiden, 1977, vol. 5, 9.

it admissible that the Imam should conclude a truce with the stipulation that the Muslims pay a certain amount to the enemy, should this be forced upon them by emergency, such as civil war and the like. Shafiʿi's opinion is that the Muslims may never give anything to the unbelievers, unless they are in mortal fear of being extinguished, on account of the enemy's superiority or because they are being harassed by disasters.'[2]

Centuries of Muslim warfare and diplomatic relations with the Byzantines led to a practical willingness to limit warfare and enter into treaties and to the development of an intricate web of means of coexistence, which included institutions like *aman*,[3] captive exchanges,[4] and formal diplomacy.[5] Thus, although still idealizing war as the normative relationship with the infidel, medieval Islam had in fact honed the tools with which to make peace. The conditions of treaty-making included the following possible scenarios: (1) from a position of strength either to avoid further bloodshed or occasionally, to buy time to acquire reinforcements and supplies; (2) from a position of parity in order to settle differences for which combat was not desirable; and (3) from a position of weakness in order to make the best of an adverse situation and perhaps gain time for readjustment.[6] During the eighth to tenth centuries, the Byzantine and Abbasid empires often used captive exchanges as an opening and pretext for truce-making. Nor were these endeavours limited to relations with Eastern Christendom alone. The twelfth century saw other Muslim-Christian encounters beside the crusades, many of which ended, or were regulated, by treaties. These ranged from military settlements, including tributary status in Spain, to commercial treaties with Mediterranean powers.[7]

---

2   Ibid., 21.
3   Ibid., 13: 'It is only allowed to slay the enemy on the condition that *aman* has not been granted. There is no dissension about this among Muslims. There is controversy, however, concerning the question who is entitled to grant *aman*. The majority of scholars are of the opinion that free Muslim males are also entitled to grant it, but Ibn Madjishun maintains that in this case, it is subject to authorization of the Imam.' Cf. al-Shaybānī, *Siyar*, trans. M. Khadduri as *The Islamic Law of Nations*, Baltimore, 1966.
4   See my *Encounter between Enemies: Captivity and Ransom in the Latin Kingdom of Jerusalem*, Leiden, 2002, chapter 2; Guemara, 'La liberation et le rachat des captifs: une lecture musulmane', in *La Liberazione dei 'captivi' tra Christianità e Islam*, ed. G. Cipollone, Città del Vaticano, 2000, 333–44.
5   For an example, see al-Tabari, *Ta'rikh al-rusul wa'l-muluk: The History of al-Tabari*, vol. 34, trans. J. Kraemer, Albany, 1989, 168–69. For the Byzantine side, see J. Haldon, '"Blood and Ink": Some Observations on Byzantine Attitudes towards Warfare and Diplomacy', in *Byzantine Diplomacy*, eds J. Shepard and S. Franklin, Aldershot, 1992, 281–94. For the later period see P. M. Holt, *Early Mamluk Diplomacy (1260–1290)*, Leiden, 1995, 3–15.
6   W. B. Bishai, 'Negotiations and Peace Agreements between Muslims and Non-Muslims in Islamic History', in *Medieval and Middle Eastern Studies in Honor of Aziz Suryal Atiya*, ed. S. A. Hanna, Leiden 1972, 50–63 (esp. 51).
7   Alauddin Samarrai, 'Arabs and Latins in the Middle Ages: Enemies, Partners and Scholars', in *Western Views of Islam in Medieval and Early Modern Europe*, eds D. R. Blanks and M. Frassetto,

Western Christianity also exhibited a dichotomy between ideology and practice with respect to war and peace, but its starting point was diametrically opposed to that of Islam. Peace was a religious goal, part of an eschatological program for the world. It belonged to Christian ritual and, in Augustine's eyes, was one of the aims of the City of God.[8] The 'Peace of God' movement, organised and hailed by the church, exemplified Christian ideological adherence to peace, and limitation of warfare. The medieval Western notion of peace encompassed Christians alone, viewing war against the infidel – the crusade – as another facet of peace, if not a prerequisite for it.[9] The church peace councils granted the Church the authority to determine who could employ arms, for what purpose, at whose command, against whom, and when. But this development also suggests that the Church now regarded violence as licit under certain conditions.[10] If crusade is the logical outcome of the Peace of God movement, then Urban II can be viewed as a peacemaking pope, a lukewarm Gregorian reformer who waged a holy war.[11] Thus, crusade could be seen as an act of love in Christian eyes,[12] and the preaching of this act of love included the rallying of forces to a war of extermination against the infidel enemy, employing concepts like the purging and cleansing of the holy places.[13] Although the Church preached peace, the practical outcome was war.

The First Crusaders expected a dichotomous situation of victory or death, with no mercy for the vanquished infidel. On the other hand, they possessed a long tradition of internal peacemaking through treaties and their accompanying ceremonies, such as *satisfactio* and *deditio*,[14] although Koziol notes: 'If rituals like supplication and peacemaking formed a common language throughout northern France, then different regions spoke different dialects.'[15] But this common language was nevertheless part of the crusaders' Western heritage.

Houndmills, 1999, 137–45.

8 Augustine, *The City of God against the Pagans*, with an English translation by W.C. Greene, Loeb Classical Library, London, 1969, 26–28.

9 Many historians have written about the connection between the Peace of God movement and the First Crusade. For a recent synthesis, see T. Mastnak, *Crusading Peace: Christendom, the Muslim World, and Western Political Order*, Berkeley, 2002.

10 Ibid., 10–21.

11 Ibid., 89. Cf. J. Flori, 'De la paix de Dieu à la croisade? Un réexamen', *Crusades* 2 (2003): 1–23, who emphasizes the economic reasons the church had for promoting a peace that would guard their interests.

12 J. Riley-Smith, 'Crusading as an Act of Love', *History* 65 (1980): 177–92.

13 P. Cole, '"O, God, the heathen have come into your inheritance" (Ps. 78.1): The Theme of Religious Pollution in Crusade Documents, 1095–1188', in *Crusaders and Muslims in Twelfth-Century Syria*, ed. M. Shatzmiller, Leiden, 1993, 84–111.

14 G. Althoff, 'Satisfaction: Peculiarities of the Amicable Settlement of Conflicts in the Middle Ages', in *Ordering Medieval Society: Perspectives on Intellectual and Practical Modes of Shaping Social Relations*, ed. B. Jussen, Philadelphia, 2001, 270–84.

15 G. Koziol, *Begging Pardon and Favor: Ritual and Political Order in Early Medieval France*, Ithaca and London, 1992, 15.

Therefore, in facing actual problems of peacemaking – for example accepting the capitulation of a city under siege or signing a ceasefire with a city willing to pay tribute to be left in peace – the crusaders did not encounter a totally unknown situation. Although, ideologically, they saw no need to make peace with the enemy, when they found it profitable to do so they could draw upon their arsenal of European-developed rituals and usages for intra-Christian peace and conflict resolution. Thus, to some extent, like their Muslim foes, peace-loving Christians felt no need to explain the Holy War called by the pope; it was peace that required a pretext and explanation. Actually, the notions of peace and of the need for treaty making were not new; rather, the idea of Holy War was an innovation that placed the crusaders in a position in which peacemaking was not perceived as an option.

The overwhelming novelty of the notion of crusade perhaps explains some of the atrocities of crusader warfare. In addressing the question of treaty-making under such circumstances we must recall that the leaders of the First Crusade were not just charged with religious zeal to free the Holy Land from what they saw as its unlawful inhabitants; they were also down-to-earth military leaders governed by realistic strategic considerations. Therefore, when approached by an enemy willing to surrender under favourable conditions, or proposing a pact seen either as expedient or as forwarding their main goal, it seems that the crusaders' problem was not so much one of overcoming religious-ideological qualms but one of cultural language. The main difficulty inhered in finding a mechanism acceptable to both cultures to ensure that both sides would place trust in, and keep, an agreement. Not simply military, the Muslim-Christian encounter has been rightly defined elsewhere as that of negotiating cultures.[16]

On the assumption that each side in Muslim-Christian encounter fell back on the repertoire of treaty-making with which it was familiar from earlier negotiations, it is pertinent to note a difference in the concept of peace in each camp. Islamic peace was equated with victory; the vanquished side was subjugated and, accordingly, peace and tranquillity ruled in Dar al-Islam. Real peace was not just equated with absence of war; it could be attained only when justice prevailed, namely, upon subjugation of the unbelievers.[17] Signs of subjugation included not only conversion, but also payment of tribute, or submissive gestures such as bowing, kissing the earth in front of the victor, or bringing gifts as a preliminary step to create trust. Intra-Christian peace could include the submission of the vanquished, but it was first and foremost an act of forgiveness, compromise, and eventually even gestures of love. Conflict resolution was achieved not only by one side admitting the other's supremacy: in the Christian setting, peace was signified by an act of friendly association – eating and drinking with the other party – and one outcome was the

---

16   R.I. Burns and P.E. Chevedden, *Negotiating Cultures: Bilingual Surrender Treaties in Muslim-Crusader Spain under James the Conqueror*, Leiden, 1999.
17   L.M. Safi, 'War and Peace in Islam', *The American Journal of Islamic Social Science* 5, no. 1 (1988): 29–57.

return of the letter of *diffidatio*.¹⁸ 'When the war was over, it was over.'¹⁹ Western Christendom had its specific peace gestures that did not work in inter-religious circumstances, such as the kiss of peace.²⁰ In the thirteenth century King Alfonso el Sabio of Spain formulated a blueprint for peace-making that included not only the formal treaty, but also its accompanying gestures, especially the 'kiss of peace':

> 'Men sometimes agree to make peace with one another ... know all persons who see this instrument, that ... So and So ..., and ... So and So ... have mutually agreed to keep peace with one another perpetually with regard to the disagreements, disputes, grudges, and insults, of which they have been guilty toward one another in word and in deed.... And as a mark of the true love and concord which should be preserved between them, they kissed each other before me, notary public, and the witnesses whose names are subscribed to this instrument, and promised and agreed with one another that this peace and concord should forever remain secure, and that they would do nothing against it, or to contravene it, of themselves, or by anyone else either in word, deed or advice, under a penalty of a thousand marks of silver; and whether the penalty is paid or not, this peace and this agreement is to remain forever enduring and valid.'²¹

We have already seen that, for the Muslim side, a pact with the infidel, the ultimate 'other', was by definition temporary and that peace treaties were seen as interwar interludes.²²

Notwithstanding this rather negative notion of peace, the Muslim principalities that the First Crusaders encountered on their way to the Holy Land had a rich tradition of diplomatic relations with Christians, having been a *thughur:* a frontier district between the Muslim and Byzantine empires.²³ During the first two decades of the principality of Antioch (1098–1128) the Muslim powers were forced to cultivate a generally submissive and conciliatory relationship with the Franks. The

---

18 O. Brunner, *Land and Lordship*, trans. H. Kaminsky and J. van Horn Melton, Philadelphia, 1992, 63.
19 Ibid., 90.
20 For the kiss of peace in Western European treaty-making, see K. Petkov, *The Kiss of Peace: Ritual, Self and Society in the High and Late Medieval West*, Leiden, 2003.
21 Alfonso X 'el sabio', *Las Siete Partidas del Rey Don Alfonso el sabio,* Madrid, 1807, trans. S. P. Scott, Chicago 1931, 3, 13, 82.
22 M. Khadduri, 'Sulh', *EI,* 9:845–46. Cf. al-Shaybāni, *Siyar,* trans. Khadduri as *The Islamic law of Nations,* 19.
23 M. Bonner, *Aristocratic Violence and Holy War: Studies in the Jihad and the Arab-Byzantine Frontier,* New Haven, 1996; E. C. Bosworth, 'Byzantium and the Syrian Frontier in the Early Abbasid Period', in *Bilād al-Shām during the Abbasid Period: Proceedings of the Fifth International Conference on the History of Bilād al-Shām,* eds M. Adnan Bakhit and R. Schick, Amman, 1991, 54–62; idem, 'The City of Tarsus and the Arab-Byzantine Frontiers in Early and Middle Abbasid Times', *Oriens* 33 (1992): 268–86.

treaties between them included clauses setting payments of tribute to the Christians and were built on the eleventh-century Iberian precedent of the so-called *Taifa* states and their tributary status.[24] Asbridge sees the difference in willingness to make peace not just as one of political power, but of general outlook: 'It is worth noting that the Latins of Antioch did not share their neighbours' willingness to negotiate or purchase peace in times of crisis. When the principality faced disaster in 1105 or 1119, the Franks did not appear to have even tried to negotiate, relying instead upon military force, risking battle even when they lacked resources and manpower.'[25] But as the balance of power during the first decade of the Latin kingdom and the Syrian principalities usually favoured the Franks, treaties, both of tribute and condominium, were signed and implemented.

When the balance of power shifted, the Franks had to learn to accept that the positions could be reversed. By then a process of acculturation had taught them to accept elements of eastern usage and enabled them, when necessary, to ask for peace. It is, however, illuminating to note William of Tyre's negative reaction to the signing of a treaty placing the Christians on an equal footing with their adversary, Saladin, in 1180, seven years before the great disaster at Hattin: 'The conditions were somewhat humiliating to us, for the truce was concluded on equal terms, with no reservations of importance on our part, a thing which is said never to have happened before.'[26] The Frankish historian and diplomat thought peace-making permissible only when the Franks were the victors, and found an equal status humiliating. This not only marks a shift in the balance of power, but in outlook as well. Saladin sought *jihad* and did not engage in truce making from a position of weakness; rather, his motivation for agreeing to a truce was economic. That such a shift in diplomatic balance is documented only at a rather late date may stem from the Muslim side's ideological preference for demonstrating its need for a truce even when it in fact was not the weaker party.

Analysis of the literary evidence for Muslim-Christian peacemaking contacts from 1099 to 1291 demonstrates which side took the initiative, the role played by emissaries, types of agreements, the language used, treaty terms, and accompanying ceremonies. The starting point for consideration of the details of the peacemaking processes is naturally the agreements themselves, their number, dates, and terms. Using mainly Arabic sources, T. Nakamura charted seventy-two treaties between 1097–1145.[27] More recently, my student Shmuel Nussbaum examined the Latin and

---

24   T. Asbridge, *The Creation of the Principality of Antioch, 1098–1130*, Woodbridge, 2000, 48–9.
25   Ibid., 49–50.
26   *Guillaume de Tyr, Chronique*, ed. R. B. C. Huygens, Corpus Christianorum Continuatio Mediaevalis 63a, Turnhout, 1981, (WT) 22,1: 'humilibus satis quantum ad nos conditionibus, quodque nunquam antea dicitur contigisse, paribus legibus fedus initum est, nichil precipue nostris sibi in ea pactione reservantibus'. English translation: E. A. Babcock and A. C. Krey, *A History of Deeds Done beyond the Sea*, New York, 1943, 447.
27   T. Nakamura, 'Territorial Disputes between Syrian Cities and the Early Crusades: The Struggle for Economic and Political Dominance', in *Beyond the Border: A New Framework for Understand-*

French sources in addition and arrived at 109 treaties in the 1097 to 1291 period.[28] Although there is a large degree of overlap between the two, after combining both tables and consulting the sources, I arrived at an approximate total of 120 treaties over the two-century period. As negotiations failed in eleven cases, the final total is 109. Based on their work, it is possible to point at some preliminary findings, including changes in the way agreements were reached over the course of the two-century period of coexistence. If initial contacts were characterized by oral agreements between the sides regarding surrender or lifting of a siege for monetary recompense, often emphasizing the gestures involved, towards the end of the period we find the sides drawing up formal written agreements, with fixed clauses defining the obligations each assumed.

The two-century span of the Frankish presence in the Latin East can be divided into four parts with respect to the shifting balance of power in Muslim-Frankish relations. The data summarized below relies on my student's research.

1098–1124

This period of overwhelming crusader superiority over the Muslim principalities exhibits a minority of Frankish requests for agreements with the Muslims, only 15 percent of a total of 33 requests attested in the literature, as opposed to Muslim initiation of 46 percent of the agreements. With respect to the remaining 39 percent it was impossible to determine which side initiated the agreement. Nakamura's statistics substantiate this finding. He counted 58 agreements: 29 Muslim initiatives (50%), 15 crusader initiatives, and 11 so-called mutual ones.

1127–1192

During this period, enhanced Muslim military strength, due to unification under the leadership of Zengi, Nur ed-Din, and Saladin, is reflected in a reduction of the number of Muslim-initiated requests for agreements from 46 or 50 percent in the previous period to 35 percent. Frankish initiated requests rose from 15 to 41 percent. A total of 34 agreements are attested for this period.

1193–1250

For the third period, during which the Muslim lands were under Ayyubid rule, the military parity between the sides is reflected in a balanced number of requests to initiate peace agreements. Of the 16 peace-agreement-initiating requests, 38 percent were Muslim-initiated and 31 percent Frankish. In general, periods 2 and 3 were characterized by a relatively even number of ceasefire initiatives.

---

ing the Dynamism of Muslim Societies, Proceedings of an International Symposium, Kyoto, 8–10 October 1999, 126–41.

28 S. Nussbaum, 'Peace Processes between Crusaders and Muslims in the Latin East' (MA thesis, Bar-Ilan University, 2002) (in Hebrew).

1252–1290

For the period of the Mamluk sultanate, during which the Muslims achieved ascendancy, we find the highest degree of Frankish-initiated requests for ceasefires: 77 percent of a total of 26 requests as opposed to only 8 percent of Muslim-initiated requests.

These data clearly demonstrate the correlation between military-political shifts in the balance of power and requests for ceasefires, with the underdog generally seeking cessation of hostilities. Whereas the results for the first and last periods are what we would expect, the state of near equilibrium characterizing the two middle periods does not seem to fit the modern evaluation of the balance of power. With hindsight, the second period is usually seen as one of sharp decline on the Frankish side, and the third period as one of clear Muslim supremacy. Apparently, the picture was different in contemporary eyes or perhaps portrayed differently for religious, or ideological, reasons. Because of their ideology accepting a truce only when absolutely necessary, the Muslims employed formal wording that placed them as the underdog long after they were in fact equal to, or even stronger than, the Franks. Note, for example, Qalqashandi's explanation for the procedure of drafting a truce: 'So the clerk may draw on them for the terms of truces with which he is perhaps unacquainted--God Most High keep us from needing them',[29] thus implying that a truce was a necessary evil even when favourable to the Mamluks. This perhaps sheds light on the discrepancy between the balance of power in the second half of the twelfth century as perceived by modern historians, and as reflected by William of Tyre and statistical analysis. Analysis of the list also enabled elicitation of the factors underlying initiation of ceasefire agreements, highlighting the military one as most prevalent. Not surprisingly, a greater number of treaties are attested both for periods in which one side showed marked superiority, and for periods of intensive warfare. A decisive victory or defeat often led to a treaty or at least a ceasefire. Other factors promoting mutual Muslim-Frankish agreements were: the need for military cooperation in the face of some common enemy, renewal of expired agreements, economic or internal difficulties, such as lack of rainfall, the low level of the Nile, or the weakening of the regime by opposition forces, or simply, the realization that no advantage would ensue from conflict. The economic incentive, such as dividing crops from conquered areas, was probably prominent in the early period, as demonstrated by the treaties between Baldwin I and Tughtigin of Damascus in 1108–9, 1111, and 1113, in which they shared the income from territories held as condominiums.[30]

---

29 *Subh al-a'sha fi sina'at al insha* 14, 71, cited in Holt, *Early Mamluk Diplomacy*, 8.
30 Ibn al-Qalanisi, *Dhayl ta'rikh Dimashq*, trans. H. A. R. Gibb as *The Damascus Chronicle of the Crusades*, London, 1932, 92, 113, 147.

Muslim willingness to enter into agreements was largely conditioned by the pragmatic or political needs of the rulers.[31] In the early period, the leaders of the various principalities acted in their own best interests, as illustrated by what reportedly motivated Shams al-Khilafa, the governor of Ascalon to enter into a truce with Baldwin I in 1111: his being 'more desirous of trading than of fighting and inclined to peaceful and friendly relations and the securing of the safety of travellers'.[32] Albert of Aachen also views trade as a main incentive in the early Muslim treaties with Godfrey of Bouillon.[33]

In the second period, with unification of Syria under Zengi, Nur ed-Din, and Saladin, the religious slogan of *jihad* was used as a power-enhancing mechanism to forward their political aims. Although Saladin fought more intra-Muslim wars to enhance his rule over Egypt and Syria than *jihad* against the Franks, his great victories at Hattin and Jerusalem enabled his propagandists to paint him as the ideal Muslim ruler.[34] During the third period, the Ayyubids entered into many peaceful contacts with the Franks, but now the Franks were the ones taking note of the economic advantages of peace. Thus, with hindsight, William of Tyre saw the breaking of the peace with Egypt (1169) as a mistake:

> 'From a quiet state of peace into what a turbulent and anxious condition has an immoderate desire for possessions plunged us! All the resources of Egypt and its immense wealth served our needs; the frontiers of our realm were safe on that side; there was no enemy to be feared on the south. Our people could enter the territories of Egypt without fear and carry on commerce and trade under advantageous conditions. On their part, the Egyptians brought to the realm foreign riches and strange commodities hitherto unknown to us and, as long as they visited us, were at once an advantage and an honor to us. Moreover, the large sums spent by them every year among us enriched the fiscal treasury and increased the private wealth of individuals. By now, on the contrary, all things have changed for the worse.'[35]

In the Mamluk period, we see almost cynical use of agreements to push the Franks out of the Latin East. The overriding consideration was what would bring greater benefit: war or peace? But, because the religious definition of *hudna* made designa-

---

31   C. Hillenbrand, *The Crusades: Islamic Perspectives*, Edinburgh, 1999, 396.
32   Ibn al-Qalanisi, *Dhayl ta'rikh Dimashq*, trans. Gibb as *Damascus Chronicle of the Crusades*, 109–10.
33   Albert of Aachen, *Historia Hierosolymitana*, ed. and trans. S. B. Edgington, Oxford Medieval Texts, Oxford, 2007, 7.13, 14.
34   See, among others, Baha al-Din Ibn Shadad, *The Rare and Excellent History of Saladin*, trans. D. S. Richards, Aldershot, 2001, 28–32; Imâd ad-Din al-Isfahâni. *Kitāb al-Fath al- Qussi fi' l-Fath al-Qudsi*, trans. H. Massé as *Conquête de la Syrie et de la Palestine par Saladin*, Paris, 1972.
35   WT 20.10.

tion of practical needs an integral part of treaty formulation, the Muslim leader, even when the stronger party, would explicitly state the necessity permitting him to seek peace, a convention the triumphant Baybars included in his treaties. During Baybars' reign, when the Franks repeatedly had to ask for peace, and were, at most, granted an unstable ceasefire, the tone of diplomacy emphasized the Franks' inferior status both in terms of territory and in terms of initiating and paying for the *hudna*. But even then it was necessary to mention the *fidah*, as captive exchanges or ransoming of captives was one of the accepted pretexts to end war. Thus underneath the conventions of treaty-making, we can discern the deep changes in historical circumstances and military balance.

Nonetheless, we must also note that initiation of negotiations was not always a clear-cut sign of objective military inferiority, and that the global political situation, the real reason behind a diplomatic move, sometimes received no mention in the treaty itself. Thus, for example, Ayyubid willingness to extend the *hudna* with the Latin Kingdom in 1204 and to cede Kafr Kanna and Nazareth stemmed not from the balance of power in the Holy Land itself, but rather from preparations for the Fourth Crusade.[36] It may well have seemed expedient for the Muslim side to make concessions to the Franks, which perhaps later proved unnecessary.[37] Thus the Fourth Crusade impacted on the balance of power in the Holy Land and was not a total failure from the perspective of the Holy Land.[38] It may well be that 'the overriding concern of the Latins was no longer making their way to the Holy Land, but consolidating and defending their newly born base in the Levant', but even an 'unholy crusade' was not devoid of strategic value.[39]

Similiarly, Ibn Wasil's explanation that the Egyptian sultan al-Kamil had to cede Jerusalem to Christian rule in 1229 because he had promised it to Frederick II perhaps sounds like a shallow excuse for a move that seemed irrational to local Muslims given the disparity between Frederick's small military presence and dwindling local backing and Ayyubid resources.[40] But to a Muslim leader aware of the danger of Khwarizmian intervention in Syria and the Holy Land, as well as the still unstable division of the Ayyubid Empire between Saladin's heirs, a treaty with the greatest lay power in Christendom might not have seemed quite so outlandish.[41]

---

36 B. Z. Kedar, 'The Fourth's Crusade Second Front', paper delivered at the Sixth Conference of the Society for the Study of the Crusades and the Latin East, Istanbul, 25–29 August 2004.
37 S. Humphreys, *From Saladin to the Mongols*, Albany, 1977, 133–4.
38 For an extreme view, see J. Prawer, *Histoire du Royaume Latin de Jérusalem*, Paris, 1970, vol. 2, 123.
39 D. E. Queller and T. F. Madden, *The Fourth Crusade*, Philadelphia, 1997, x. Witness the long debate on who was to blame for the diversion of the crusade in D. E. Queller and S. J. Stratton, 'A Century of Controversy on the Fourth Crusade', *Studies in Medieval and Renaissance History* 6 (1969): 233–77.
40 Jamal ad-Din Ibn Wasil, *Mufarrij al-Kurub fi akhbar Bany Ayyub*, trans. F. Gabrieli, *Arab Historians of the Crusades*, London, 1969, 269–71.
41 Humphreys, *From Saladin to the Mongols*, 195–204.

Negotiations with Jalal al-Din Khwarizmshah against al-Kamil had already begun under al-Muazzam of Syria in 1226 and, in 1228, when the Khwarizmians threatened Armenia, al-Nasir Daud (the two former rulers' nephew and rival) tried to enter into an alliance with them.[42] Thus, the military balance of power also has to be examined in the larger, and not necessarily local, context.

Cultural mechanisms, such as set conventions and conciliatory gestures, facilitated peace-making. Fruitful, effective negotiations could be fostered by creation of a common cultural language. Comparison of two treaties, one from 1098 – between the ruler of Azaz and Godfrey of Bouillon – and the other from 1167 – between the Caliph of Egypt and the Frankish emissary – shows a process of mutual acculturation, exemplified by the employment of the western ceremony of extending the right hand and the eastern use of gifts. Both cases reflect cultural mediation via outside intervention. In the earlier treaty, a captive Christian wife of the Muslim ruler teaches him western *mores*, instructing him to give Godfrey his right hand rather than to use his preferred eastern method of messengers bringing gifts, a gesture that did not inspire trust on Godfrey's part. Later western sources describe Godfrey as the victorious party, giving gifts as a sign of lordship and supremacy.[43] In the second treaty, the diplomat Hugh of Caesarea forces the caliph to extend his bare hand, contrary to his usage:

> 'Therefore, unless you offer your *bare hand* we shall be obliged to think that, on your part, there is some reservation or lack of sincerity. Finally, with extreme unwillingness, as if it detracted from his majesty, yet with a slight smile, which greatly aggrieved the Egyptians, the caliph put his *uncovered hand* into that of Hugh. He repeated, almost syllable by syllable, the words of Hugh as he dictated the formula of the treaty and swore that he would keep the stipulations thereof in good faith, without fraud or evil intent.'[44]

---

42 See D. Abulafia, *Frederick II: a Medieval Emperor*, 3rd edn, London, 2003, 182–90, who mainly follows Ibn Wasil's account. J.W. Powell, 'Frederick II and the Muslims: The Making of an Historiographical Tradition', in *Iberia and the Mediterranean World of the Middle Ages: Studies in Honor of Robert I. Burns,* ed. L.J. Simon, Leiden, 1995, 261–69) claims that Fredericks's bad reputation in Christian historiography stems from his own propaganda, aimed at redressing this inequality.

43 Y. Friedman, 'Gestures of Conciliation: Peacemaking Endeavors in the Latin East', in *Crusades: Festschrift for B.Z. Kedar,* eds I. Shagrir, J. Riley-Smith, and R. Ellenblum, forthcoming.

44 WT 19,19: '… propterea aut nudam dabis, aut fictum aliquid et minus puritatis habens ex parti tua cogemur opinari". Tunc demum invitus plurimum et quasi maiestati detrahens, subridens tamen, quod multum egre tulerunt Egyptii dexteram suam in manum domini Hugonis nudam prebuit, eundem Hugonem, pactorem formam determinantem, eisdem pene sillabis sequens, tenorem conventorum bona fide, sine fraude et malo ingenio se observaturum contestans.'

The treaty clauses were certainly important, but imposing the gesture was seen as a greater diplomatic victory by the chronicler, William of Tyre, himself an occasional diplomatic envoy.

In September 1192, during the protracted negotiations for a *hudna* between Richard the Lionheart and Saladin, this basically western usage for sealing a treaty is attributed to both sides. Thus Baha al-Din claims that Richard, who was too sick to read the draft, said: 'I have no strength to read this, but I herewith make peace and here is my hand,' and that Saladin said to the Christian envoys: 'These are the limits of the land that will remain in your hands. If you can accept these terms, well and good. I give you my hand on it.'[45] Thus, according to the Muslim chronicler, this gesture had become part of the conventions of treaty-making on both sides.

Notwithstanding this 'victory' of western *mores* of peace-gestures in the twelfth century, I think that careful comparison of the few surviving written treaties and earlier treaties in the West and in the East will demonstrate the greater influence of eastern usage in the Latin East. Such a comparison must, however, take into account the tendency of the victorious side to impose its norms on the text and terms of agreement. For the period for which written texts are extant, this was usually the Muslim party. The opposite appears to have been true in Spain where the Christians were the victors. As we have no extant written treaties from the period when the Franks clearly had the upper hand, it cannot be proved that such was the case in the East. We have seen, however, that in the sphere of nonverbal diplomatic language, the Latins did indeed impose their *mores* on the other side. In the 1268 encounter with Hugh, King of Cyprus (later to become the king of the Latin Kingdom) the Mamluk sultan Baybars instructed his diplomat Ibn 'Abd al-Zahir not to sit lower than the Christian king, who was forced to accept this affront.[46] In this case the gesture was a clear indication of who had the upper hand and could force his cultural language on the opponent.

Gifts were another gesture of conciliation interpreted differently by the Christian and Muslim traditions. In the feudal West gifts functioned to indicate rank, with the stronger party bestowing the gift on the weaker dependent one, usually at the conclusion of negotiations and as part of the sealing of a treaty. In the East gifts were a preliminary step in initiating negotiations and given by the party who started the talks. In 1266, when the besieged garrison at Safad refused his presents, sent to start negotiations 'after the custom of the Saracens', Baybars reacted violently and executed all the Templars after he took the city.[47]

Ratification by oath was another major mechanism of treaty-making. The use of oaths as a means of ensuring that the treaty would be upheld necessitated some knowledge of the enemy's religious tenets and thus, in a way, represents recogni-

---

45 Baha al-Din, *Rare and Excellent History of Saladin*, 229, 230–1.
46 Holt, *Early Mamluk Diplomacy*, 70–1.
47 'Chronique du Templier de Tyr', in *Les Gestes des Chiprois: Recueil de chroniques françaises écrites en orient aux XIIIe et XIVe siècles*, ed. G. Raynaud, Geneva, 1887, 346.

tion of the 'other's' beliefs at the supreme moment of distrust, when assurance was most needed.[48] The texts of these oaths, extant for some of the Mamluk treaties, include a detailed list of the religious beliefs that the oath taker would be willing to abrogate should he fail to keep his promises, as well as a self-imposed penance of thirty pilgrimages. Clearly based on local usage, it was imperative to find a way to make an infidel's oath valid. Only one of the extant oaths cited requires swearing on the Gospels, which was the normal western procedure in oath taking and belonged to the legal procedures of the Latin kingdom.[49]

But can we extrapolate from the detailed late-thirteenth-century texts of oaths to the earlier oaths taken by crusaders and Muslims? Written evidence for the content of early-twelfth-century oaths is not extant, but oath taking on both sides is mentioned in the late twelfth century, during the Third Crusade.[50] However, in relating how Louis IX refused to swear because he would never agree to the clause inserted by renegades: 'He should be as dishonored as a Christian who denies God and his law and in contempt of him, spits on his cross and tramples it underfoot,' Joinville (1250) describes the same kind of pre-formulated, written oaths as the late Mamluk ones. Louis was only persuaded to change his mind by the patriarch of Jerusalem, who was tortured by the Muslims to this end and who promised to take the sin upon himself in addition.[51] The emirs' oath, which included the clause, 'they were to incur the same disgrace as a Saracen who has eaten pork', was checked by Nicole d'Acre, 'a priest who knew their language, and assured him that according to their law they could have devised no oaths that were stronger'.[52] When there was a diplomatic will to compromise, a neutral form could be used, as in the following example from a Latin document from Genoa, clearly translated from Arabic: 'In the name of God the Beneficent, the merciful. May God bless all the Prophets and Have Peace upon them.'[53] This general opening, clearly formulated by a Muslim, could fit any prophets and all three monotheistic religions. The formal language of the oaths, while being a tool to bridge the suspicion between the sides, also made it necessary to learn the other side's religious tenets.

The ransoming of captives is another realm in which we see cultural influence, with Eastern practice influencing the changing *mores* of the Christian side. When the crusaders arrived in the Latin East, they had no institutional framework of ransoming captives; by the end of their sojourn in the East, we find the develop-

---

48   Friedman, 'Gestures of Conciliation'.
49   *Livres des Assises des Bourgeois*, ed. H. Kausler, in *Les Livres des Assises et des usages dou reaume de Jérusalem*, Stuttgart, 1839, par. 236, 273–4.
50   Baha al-Din, *Rare and Excellent History of Saladin*, 229, 231.
51   Jean Sire de Joinville, *Histoire de Saint Louis: Credo et Lettre à Louis X*, ed. and trans. N. de Wailly, Paris, 1874. English translation: M. R. B. Shaw, *Joinville and Villehardouin: Chronicles of the Crusades*, Harmondsworth, 1963, 254–55.
52   Ibid., 254.
53   M. Amari, *Nuovi ricordi arabici su la storia di Genova*, Genova, 1878, doc. I, 1–5, 45–75 (Arabic text: separate pagination, 1–29), cited in Samarrai, 'Arabs and Latins in the Middle Ages', 137–45.

ment of ransoming orders such as the Trinitarians.[54] Ultimately, this may have influenced post-crusade European laws of war. In Spain, as opposed to the Latin East, we see the full-fledged development of laws of war as early as the thirteenth century, as exemplified by *Las siete partidas*. I suggest that the four-century-long Muslim-Christian encounter in Spain represents the culmination of the process of Muslim influence on Christian *mores* of war. In the Latin East, this process was never completed. I also surmise that both arenas of conflict ultimately influenced the emergence of codified laws of war in Western Europe in the fourteenth century.

The need to overcome the cultural gap also enhanced the culture-bridging role played by diplomats. The emergence of a class of diplomats with special privileges and safeguards comprises an important aspect of peacemaking in the Latin East. From the first encounters between the enemies, and until their conclusion, emissaries played a prominent part in preventing hostilities and reaching agreements. In the initial stages, emissaries from each side engaged in preparatory talks, whose outcome often depended on their talents. In this case, too, there existed longstanding traditions of polyglot, skilled diplomats passing between the Muslim and Christian camps, some of them former captives like Hugh of Caesarea, who learned the language and *mores* of the antagonist in captivity. In the East, emissaries were usually chosen from among persons with connections to the ruling elite, at times even members of the royal family. As the diplomat was sometimes expected to identify potential weaknesses in the opposing side during his mission, his astuteness in spying out trends in the enemy camp also played a role in his selection. Prominent diplomats like Saladin's brother al-Adil (Saphadin in Western sources) or the qadi Fahr-a-Din, who negotiated with Frederick II on behalf of al-Kamil, cultivated friendly relationships with the opposing side. A diplomat's political judgment was taken into account, and his influence certainly surpassed that of a simple message bearer.

A well-known instance of the extent to which diplomats could influence the pact making process is the part played by al-Adil and Hubert Walter, bishop of Salisbury, in the negotiations between Saladin and Richard in August 1192. We may well disregard the tearful speech of love and admiration attributed to Saphadin by Richard of Devizes as well as his chronology, but his description of the secret agreement reached without the sick king's knowledge rings true in having al-Adil promise, 'I shall arrange with my brother either for a perpetual peace for you, or at the least for a firm and lasting truce.'[55] The king's sudden recovery placed his ministers in a shaky position, as they had already given and received right hands and agreed to the terms of the treaty with al-Adil. Unaware of this agreement, Richard tried to organise an offensive, which Hubert Walter and Count Henry

---

54 Friedman, *Encounter between Enemies*, 187–200.
55 Richard of Devizes, *The Chronicle of Richard of Devizes of the Time of King Richard the First*, ed. and trans. J.T. Appleby, London, 1963, 75–8.

did their best to sabotage.⁵⁶ When failure made the king willing to negotiate, this provided the negotiators with an opening. To their surprise, or so they claimed, they found that al-Adil, who was supposed to be in Jerusalem with Saladin, was in fact nearby. Instructed on how to speak to Richard, al-Adil obtained a temporary truce ratified by the giving of hands and returned to his brother to arrange his part of the plot. Baha al-Din's description of the same encounter proves that al-Adil's sudden appearance was no chance occurrence; he was in fact waiting to be called.⁵⁷ The *Itinerarium Peregrinorum et Gesta Regis Ricardi* knows nothing of the devious part played by the mediators,⁵⁸ but agrees that the truce initiative came from the crusader side and that the king was presented with a written document of a truce obtained by Saphadin: 'The terms were recorded in writing and read out to King Richard, who approved them,' there presented as the best terms for which Richard could have hoped.⁵⁹

The important role of the diplomats finds corroboration in Baha al-Din's detailed record of the same events. He noted that Richard was presented with a written draft of the truce as a *fait accompli* and referred the finishing touches, including some cardinal terms, to Henry and 'the others'.⁶⁰ Baha al-Din's description of the ceremonial aspects of the treaty, including a delay in the oath taking ceremony, attributed to the fact that the Christians 'do not take an oath after eating' and had eaten that day, may have been a way of gaining time to convince Richard. The mediators were apparently successful in setting international policy behind the backs of the rulers who had sent them to negotiate in their name. Thus the messengers who were only supposed to go between the camps grew in importance and became independent policymakers, using the power bestowed on them by their connections with the other side.

Another important feature of peacemaking was the need to explain the own side why one was entering into an agreement with the enemy. The propaganda associated with Frederick II's treaty with al-Kamil of Egypt (1229) demonstrates each side's felt compulsion to explain the need for compromise over Jerusalem and the expediency of making peace to its coreligionists. Each side claimed that it had not made substantive concessions and that the division of Jerusalem leaving the Temple Mount in Muslim hands, and the rest of the city in Christian hands, was in fact in its favour. Thus al-Kamil claimed: 'We have only ... conceded to them some churches and some ruined houses. The sacred precincts, the venerated Rock and all the other sanctuaries to which we make our pilgrimages remain ours as

---

56   Ibid., 82–83.
57   Baha al-Din, *Rare and Excellent History of Saladin*, 230.
58   *Itinerarium Peregrinorum et Gesta Regis Ricardi*, ed. W. Stubbs, Chronicles and Memorials of the Reign of Richard I, Vol. 1, Rolls Series 38, London, 1864, 6, 27.
59   *Itinerarium Peregrinorum et Gesta Regis Ricardi*, trans. H. J. Nicholson as *Chronicle of the Third Crusade*, Aldershot, 1997, 371–2.
60   Baha al-Din, *Rare and Excellent History of Saladin*, 230–2.

they were; Muslim rites continue to flourish as they did before, and the Muslims have their own governor of the rural provinces and districts.'[61] Frederick claimed that he had not given the Muslims sovereignty over the Temple Mount, only the right to pilgrimage, noting his great territorial achievement in obtaining all the land between Jerusalem and Bethlehem.[62] None of their coreligionists were convinced, but the truce was kept for the stipulated ten years. Similarly, Baha al-Din claimed that the treaty Saladin signed with Richard in 1192 was 'nothing but a providential blessing for him' as he died soon after and without it 'Islam would have been in peril'.[63]

Ultimately, notwithstanding changes in practical peacemaking during the two centuries in the Latin East from oral agreements to more formal written ones and the developing of terms related not only to territories but also to aspects of everyday coexistence – including exchange and ransom of captives and clauses ensuring free trade between the sides – peace still required explanation and apologetics. In the Latin East, the ideal of peace was neither sought nor achieved, but interludes of coexistence were made possible and attained through the development of a shared language, both gestural-ceremonial and formal.

Primary Sources

AA., Albert of Aachen. *Historia Hierosolymitana*, ed. and trans. S. B. Edgington. Oxford Medieval Texts. Oxford: Clarendon 2007.
Alfonso X 'el sabio'. [1807]. *Las Siete Partidas del Rey Don Alfonso el sabio*, trans. S. P. Scott. Chicago: Commerce Clearing House 1931.
Amari, M. 1878. *Nuovi ricordi arabici su la storia di Genova*. Genoa. Cited in Samarrai 1999.
Assises des Bourgeois. Livres des Assises des Bourgeois, ed. H. Kausler, *Les Livres des Assises et des usages dou reaume de Jérusalem*. Stuttgart 1839.
Augustine. *The City of God against the Pagans*, with an English translation by W. C. Greene. Loeb Classical Library. London: William Heinemann 1969.
Baha al-Din Ibn Shadad. *The Rare and Excellent History of Saladin*, trans. D. S. Richards. Aldershot: Ashgate 2001.
Ibn al-Qalanisi. *Dhayl ta'rikh Dimashq*, trans. H. A. R. Gibb as *The Damascus Chronicle of the Crusades*. London: Luzac 1932.
Ibn Rushd. *Jihad in Medieval and Modern Islam: The Chapter on Jihad from Averroes' Legal Handbook* Bidāyat al-Mudjtahid, trans R. Peters. Nisaba, vol. 5. Leiden: Brill 1977.
Ibn Wasil. Jamal ad-Din Ibn Wasil, *Mufarrij al-Kurub fi akhbar Bany Ayyub*, trans. F. Gabrieli as *Arab Historians of the Crusades*. London: Routledge and K. Paul 1969.

---

61   Ibn Wasil, *Mufarrij al-Kurub fi akhbar Bany Ayyub*, trans. F. Gabrieli, *Arab Historians of the Crusades*, 270–1.
62   Roger de Wendower, *The Flowers of History*, ed. H. G. Hewlett, Rolls Series, vol. 84, no. 2, London, 1890, 365–9, trans. E. Peters as *Christian Society and the Crusades 1198–1229*, Philadelphia, 1971, 163–6.
63   Baha al-Din, *Rare and Excellent History of Saladin*, 232.

Imâd ad-Din al-Isfahâni. *Kitāb al-Fath al- Qussi fi' l-Fath al-Qudsi,* trans. H. Massé as *Conquête de la Syrie et de la Palestine par Saladin.* Paris: Libraire Orientaliste Paul Geuthner 1972.

Itinerarium Peregrinorum et Gesta Regis Ricardi, in W. Stubbs (ed.), *Chronicles and Memorials of the Reign of Richard I,* Vol. 1, Rolls Series 38, London. Trans. by H.J. Nicholson as *Chronicle of the Third Crusade,* Aldershot: Ashgate 1997.

Jean Sire de Joinville, *Histoire de Saint Louis: Credo et Lettre à Louis X,* ed. and trans. N. de Wailly, Paris 1874. Trans. M.R.B. Shaw, *Joinville and Villehardouin: Chronicles of the Crusades,* Harmondsworth: Penguin 1963.

Qalqashandi. *Subh al-a'sha fi sina'at al insha.* Cited in P.M. Holt 1995, p. 8.

Richard of Devizes, *The Chronicle of Richard of Devizes of the Time of King Richard the First,* ed. and trans. J.T. Appleby, London: T. Nelson 1963.

Roger de Wendover, *The Flowers of History,* ed. H.R. Hewlett, Rolls Series, vol. 84,2. London 1890.

The Islamic Law of Nations: Shaybāni's Siyar. trans. M. Khadduri Baltimore: Johns Hopkins 1966.

Ta'rikh al-rusul wa'l-muluk: The History of al-Tabari, vol. 34, trans. J. Kraemer. Albany: State University of New York Press 1989.

'Chronique du Templier de Tyr', *Les Gestes des Chîprois: Recueil de chroniques françaises écrites en orient aux XIIIe et XIVe siècles,* ed. G. Raynaud. Geneva 1887.

WT. 1986. *Guillaume de Tyr: Chronique,* ed. R.B.C. Huygens. Corpus Christianorum Continuatio Mediaevalis 63a. Turnhout: Brepols. Trans. E.A. Babcock and A.C. Krey as *A History of Deeds Done beyond the Sea.* New York: Columbia University Press, 1943.

Secondary Sources

Abulafia, D., *Frederick II: A Medieval Emperor,* 3d ed. London: Allen Lane, the Penguin Press 2003.

Asbridge, T., *The Creation of the Principality of Antioch, 1098–1130.* Woodbridge: Boydell and Brewer 2000.

Althoff, G., 'Satisfaction: Peculiarities of the Amicable Settlement of Conflicts in the Middle Ages', in B. Jussen (ed.), *Ordering Medieval Society: Perspectives on Intellectual and Practical Modes of Shaping Social Relations.* Philadelphia: University of Pennsylvania Press 2001, pp. 270–84.

Bishai, W.B., 'Negotiations and Peace Agreements between Muslims and Non-Muslims in Islamic History', in S.A. Hanna (ed.), *Medieval and Middle Eastern Studies in Honor of Aziz Suryal Atiya.* Leiden: Brill 1972, pp. 50–63.

Bonner, M., *Aristocratic Violence and Holy War: Studies in the Jihad and the Arab-Byzantine Frontier.* New Haven: American Oriental Society 1996.

Bosworth, E.C., 'Byzantium and the Syrian Frontier in the Early Abbasid Period', in M. Adnan Bakhit and R. Schick (eds), *Bilād al-Shām during the Abbasid Period: Proceedings of the Fifth International Conference on the History of Bilād al-Shām,* Amman: History of Bilād al-Shām Committee 1991, pp. 54–62.

Id., 'The City of Tarsus and the Arab-Byzantine Frontiers in Early and Middle Abbasid Times', *Oriens* 33, 1992, pp 268–86.

Brunner, O., *Land and Lordship: Structures of Governance in Medieval Austria*, trans. H. Kaminsky and J. van Horn Melton. Philadelphia: University of Pennsylvania Press 1992

Burns, R. I. and P. E. Chevedden, *Negotiating Cultures: Bilingual Surrender Treaties in Muslim-Crusader Spain under James the Conqueror*. Leiden: Brill 1999.

Cole, P., '"O, God, the Heathen Have Come into Your Inheritance" (Ps. 78.1): The Theme of Religious Pollution in Crusade Documents, 1095–1188', in M. Shatzmiller (ed.), *Crusaders and Muslims in Twelfth-Century Syria*. Leiden: Brill 1993, pp. 84–111.

Flori, J., 'De la paix de Dieu à la croisade? Un réexamen', *Crusades* 2, 2003, pp 1–23.

Friedman, Y., *Encounter between Enemies: Captivity and Ransom in the Latin Kingdom of Jerusalem*. Leiden: Brill 2002.

Friedman, Y., 'Gestures of Conciliation: Peacemaking Endeavors in the Latin East', in I. Shagrir, J. Riley-Smith, and R. Ellenblum (eds), *Crusades: Festschrift for B. Z. Kedar* forthcoming

Guemara, R.,'La liberation et le rachat des captifs: une lecture musulmane', in G. Cipollone (ed.), *La Liberazione dei 'captivi' tra Christianità e Islam*. Città del Vaticano: Archivio Segreta Vaticano 2000, pp. 333–44.

Haldon, J., '"Blood and Ink": Some Observations on Byzantine Attitudes towards Warfare and Diplomacy', in J. Shepard and S. Franklin (eds), *Byzantine Diplomacy*. Aldershot: Variorum 1992, pp. 281–94.

Hillenbrand, C., *The Crusades: Islamic Perspectives*. Edinburgh: Edinburgh University Press 1999.

Holt, P. M., *Early Mamluk Diplomacy (1260–1290)*. Leiden: Brill 1995.

Humphreys, S., *From Saladin to the Mongols: The Ayyubids of Damascus*. Albany: State University of New York Press 1977.

Kedar, B. Z., 'The Fourth's Crusade Second Front'. Paper delivered at the Sixth Conference of the Society for the Study of the Crusades and the Latin East, Istanbul, 25–29 August 2004.

Khadduri, M., 'Sulh'. *Encyclopaedia of Islam: New Edition*, 9:845–46. Leiden: Brill 1997.

Koziol, G., *Begging Pardon and Favor: Ritual and Political Order in Early Medieval France*. Ithaca and London: Cornell University Press 1992.

Mastnak, T., *Crusading Peace: Christendom, the Muslim World, and Western Political Order*. Berkeley: University of California Press 2002.

Nakamura, T., 'Territorial Disputes between Syrian Cities and the Early Crusades: The Struggle for Economic and Political Dominance', in *Beyond the Border: A New Framework for Understanding the Dynamism of Muslim Societies: Proceedings of an International Symposium, Kyoto, 8–10 October 1999*.

Nussbaum, S., 'Peace Processes between Crusaders and Muslims in the Latin East', MA thesis. Ramat Gan: Bar-Ilan University 2002.

Petkov, K., *The Kiss of Peace: Ritual, Self and Society in the High and Late Medieval West*. Leiden: Brill 2003.

Prawer, J., *Histoire du Royaume Latin de Jérusalem*, vol. 2. Paris: Centre Nationale de la Recherche Scientifique 1969.

Queller, D. E. and S. J. Stratton, 'A Century of Controversy on the Fourth Crusade', *Studies in Medieval and Renaissance History* 6,1969, pp. 233–77.

Queller, D. E. and T. F. Madden, *The Fourth Crusade: The Conquest of Constantinople*, 2d ed. Philadelphia: University of Pennsylvania Press 1997.

Riley-Smith, J. S. C., 'Crusading as an Act of Love', *History* 65, 1980, pp. 177–92.

Safi, L. M., 'War and Peace in Islam', *The American Journal of Islamic Social Science* 5(1), 1988, pp. 29–57.

Samarrai, A., 'Arabs and Latins in the Middle Ages: Enemies, Partners and Scholars', in D. R. Blanks and M. Frassetto (eds), *Western Views of Islam in Medieval and Early Modern Europe: Perception of Other*. New York: St. Martin's Press 1999, pp. 137–45.

Ideas of Peace in Early Modern Models of International Order: Universal Monarchy and Balance of Power in Comparison

Arno Strohmeyer

Introduction

In Early Modern Times, two models of international order reached outstanding significance: universal monarchy and balance of power.[1] They stood at either end of a broad spectrum spanning the different connecting and organizing principles followed by different European powers during the period from the sixteenth to the eighteenth century. While universal monarchy was based on a relatively high degree of political unity with a lower degree of particularism, the idea of a balance of power was based on the assumption of a variety of powerful states with a low degree of standardisation. However, this contrast cannot be seen in a strict chronological sequence of the concepts concerned. Rather, it is appropriate to think of a long period of parallelism, centred on the seventeenth century. The concept of universal monarchy was drawn from Antiquity and the Middle Ages, and can be seen as in line with Roman and Christian traditions. In the Early Modern Age, mostly it can be diagnosed in the political thought of the sixteenth and seventeenth century.[2] If

---

1   In the Early Modern Age in Europe there were no states in the modern sense. Thus, we may speak of an international order only figuratively
2   See F. Bosbach, *Monarchia universalis: Ein politischer Leitbegriff der frühen Neuzeit*, Göttingen, 1988; J. M. Headley, 'The Demise of Universal Monarchy as a Meaningful Political Idea', in *Imperium/Empire/Reich: Ein Konzept politischer Herrschaft im deutsch-britischen Vergleich: An Anglo-German Comparison of a Concept of Rule*, eds F. Bosbach and H. Hiery, München, 1999, 41–58; C. Kampmann, 'Universalismus und Staatenvielfalt: zur europäischen Identität in der frühen Neuzeit', in *Europa – aber was ist es? Aspekte seiner Identität in interdisziplinärer Sicht*, eds J. A. Schlumberger and Peter Segl, Köln, Weimar, Wien, 1994, 45–76.

we take into consideration the ideas of empire which were connected to the concept of universal monarchy, it would be a discourse spanning the entire period.[3]

The idea of a balance of power – either as an existing international configuration or as a mere concept still to be established between monarchies and polities – derived from different intellectual origins. Its roots are epistemological: the idea of balance has anthropological dimensions and is one of the most widely prevalent models found in all human theorizing. The ancient Greeks extended ideas of balance to matters of foreign policy between their city states.[4] As a concept for organizing the relations between European powers, the idea of a balance was employed for the first time after the end of the Renaissance. Letters of Venetian diplomats from about 1550 serve as early examples of these theoretical reflections.[5] When the model of the balance of power became successful in the second half of the seventeenth century, it owed its triumph mostly to the logic of power in the developing system of states, which consisted of polities whose imparting meaning was increasingly determined by the theory of reason of state and turning away from Christian and ethical norms.[6] Since then, balance of power has been a key concept of early modern thinking about international order.

Starting from this assumption, the following analysis is based on an asynchronous comparison: the ideas of peace in the concepts of universal monarchy during the age of Charles V (1500–1558) and in balance-of-power theories developed in the first half of the eighteenth century. During these periods, each model reached its peak and became the leading idea of international order in Europe.[7] Their basic aim was to solve one fundamental problem of European history: the tension between political particularism and supranational universalism. Apart from this fundamental similarity, there were contextual differences. On the one hand, there was a political culture influenced by humanism and late scholasticism. The bible was serving as a political textbook, and Christian ideas concerning unity and eschatology were important norms standing alongside Roman and canon law. On the other hand, there was a period that was marked by the rationality and

---

3   See J. Muldoon, *Empire and Order: The Concept of Empire, 800–1800*, Basingstoke, London, 1999, 1–20; A. Pagden, *Lords of all the world: Ideologies of Empire in Spain, Britain and France c. 1500–c. 1800*, New Haven-London, 1995, 6; A. Pagden, *Peoples and Empires*, London, 2001, 50–6; D. Armitage, *The Ideological Origins of the British Empire*, Cambridge, 2000, 29–36.
4   See Demosthenes, 'Rede über den Frieden', in *Demosthenes: Politische Reden*, ed. and transl. W. Unte, Stuttgart, 1985, par. 16–17; A. Strohmeyer, *Theorie der Interaktion: Das europäische Gleichgewicht der Kräfte in der frühen Neuzeit*, Wien, Köln, Weimar, 1994, 115f.
5   See H. Kleinschmidt, 'The Balance of Power: An Historical Caveat (I)', *Rekishi jinrui* 19 (1991): 12–30; E. Kaeber, *Die Idee des europäischen Gleichgewichts in der publizistischen Literatur vom 16. bis zur Mitte des 18. Jahrhunderts*, Berlin, 1907, 14–22.
6   See Pagden, *Lords*, 45.
7   The two models have rarely been compared with each other in historical research up to now. One of the few comparisons is drawn by K. Malettke, 'L' équilibre' europeén face à la 'monarchia universalis': Les réactions europeénnes aux ambitions hégémoniques à l'époque moderne', in *L'invention de la diplomatie: Moyen Age – Temps modernes*, ed. L. Bély, Paris, 1998, 47–57.

the mechanistic creeds of enlightenment, the belief in the possibility of rationally organising human existence, and desacralisation. The *raison d'état*, the doctrine of the states' sovereignty, norms of the *Ius Publicum Europaeum* and the idea of convenience were all important influences on international relations.[8] In addition, one must consider the increase in state power from the first half of the sixteenth to the eighteenth century and the formation of a Europe wide system of states.[9]

Concepts of Universal Monarchy in the Age of Charles V

When Charles V was elected head of the Holy Roman Empire in 1519, the debates about universal monarchy, which until then had mostly been on a theoretical level, gained a dimension of practical politics. His vast empire, already including the Austrian hereditary lands, the Netherlands, the Spanish kingdoms, extensive territories in Italy, some bases in Northern Africa, and extensive parts of the New World, was now both dignified and legitimised by his new title of 'Emperor', carrying with it as it did demands of a universal nature. Thus, many contemporaries of Charles V believed that the full realisation of universal monarchy was imminent. As universal monarchy was a very flexible model of rule, which was easily adjustable to diverging interests and goals and which was based on different traditions – the situation in Spain differing from that followed in the Holy Roman Empire, for instance – it is difficult to take an overview of differences in the various systems developed in terms of its general concepts.[10]

These were considerable above all in terms of the political authority of the universal monarch and the spatial dimensions of universal monarchy. Universal monarchy was not a concept of order restricted to Europe. Although it mostly referred to Christendom, it could also be applied to the territory of the *Imperium Romanum*, the Holy Roman Empire, and the ancient-medieval continents Europe, Asia and Africa. It was an exception when authors like the Spanish chronicler Gonzalo Fernández de Oviedo (1478–1557), Charles V's biographer, included the Americas, as most of the New World was not integrated under European rule until the reign of Charles' son Philip II (1555/56 to 1598).[11]

---

8   See H. Duchhardt, 'Interstate war and peace in Early Modern Europe', in *War, Peace and World Orders in European History*, eds A. V. Hartmann and B. Heuser, London, New York, 2001, 185–195.
9   See W. Reinhard, *Geschichte der Staatsgewalt: Eine vergleichende Verfassungsgeschichte Europas von den Anfängen bis zur Gegenwart*, München, 1999.
10 See E. Salvador Esteban, *Carlos V. Emperador de Imperios*, Pamplona, 2001, 31–4; Bosbach, *Monarchia universalis*, 35–45; J. Pérez, 'La idea imperial de Carlos V', in *Carlos V. Europeísmo y universalidad*, eds J. L. Castellano et al., vol. 1, Granada, 2001, 239–250.
11 See Pagden, Lords, 40; H.-J. König, 'Plus ultra – ein Weltreichs- und Eroberungsprogramm? Amerika und Europa in politischen Vorstellungen im Spanien Karls V.', in *Karl V. 1500–1558: Neue Perspektiven seiner Herrschaft in Europa und Übersee*, eds A. Kohler, B. Haider and C. Ottner, Wien, 2002, 197–222.

In its secular sense it was a comprehensive style of government generally granting a single person – in many cases the emperor or the pope – a claim to universal leadership, which could be defined in a disparate way and be valid for some, but not for all crucial sectors of political and social life. This concept had nothing to do with any idea of a homogeneous super-state since it tended to imply no more than a primus inter pares superiority of the universal monarch over other rulers.[12] When Charles V, for instance, captured his strongest adversary, the French king Francis I (1515–1547), in the Battle of Pavia in 1525, he rejected the proposal of the English king Henry VIII (1509–1547) to divide France among themselves. Instead, he released him after signing the Peace of Madrid in 1526, where he presented himself as the highest worldly ruler.[13] The position of the emperor as universal monarch could extend to a pre-eminence covering legislative and juridical competences and the secular leadership of protecting Christendom against the infidels.[14]

In political discourse, universal monarchy and peace were closely connected. How close this connection was can clearly be seen by the criticism of universal monarchy which increased during Charles V's reign. The model's political opponents especially criticised its lack of a positive functional connection to peace. In this way, they were able to doubt the concept as a whole.[15] They claimed, for instance, that a universal monarchy was ungovernable and thus insufficient for peacekeeping, and because of this it was to be rejected. In the same way they denied the legitimacy of the universal monarch as they suspected that he would act almost inevitably as a disturber of peace.[16] So it could be that even those who theoretically spoke in favour of this model rejected it for practical reasons. Antonio de Guevara (about 1480–1545), for instance, chronicler and father confessor of Charles V, called world monarchy the highest rule, divinely ordained, but still rejected it under the prevailing conditions, because, given the princes' conflicting interests, world monarchy could only be achieved by force, which would entail a war for which there was no just reason.[17] Plainly speaking: a universal monarchy without a positive connection to peace lacked legitimacy – opponents and supporters of the concept were in agreement on this.

---

12 See H.-J. König, *Monarchia mundi und res publica Christiana: Die Bedeutung des mittelalterlichen Imperium Romanum für die politische Ideenwelt Kaiser Karls, dargestellt an ausgewählten Beispielen*, Hamburg, 1969, 99–108; H. Pietschmann, 'Imperiale Konzepte im Spanien Karls V.', in *Aspectos históricos y culturales bajo Carlos V.*, ed. C. Strosetzki, Vervuert, 2000, 390–411.
13 Tratado de Madrid, Madrid, 14 January 1526, in *Tratados internacionales de España: Período de la preponderancia española. Carlos V, vol. 3/3: España – Francia (1525–1528)*, ed. P. Mariño, Madrid, 1986, no. 22, 122–172.
14 See Bosbach, *Monarchia universalis*, 54 f.
15 For example Montesquieu, *Réflexions sur la monarchie universelle en Europe*, ed. M. Porret, Genève, 2000.
16 See Bosbach, *Monarchia universalis*, 43–5.
17 See König, *Monarchia mundi*, 108–124.

Models of Balance of Power in the First Half of the Eighteenth Century

Like universal monarchy, the balance of power was an extensive model of international order constructed in a discursive way. Never precisely defined and profoundly changeable, the concept had numerous variants.[18] Three main types can be distinguished for the first half of the eighteenth century, when the balance of power became the leading idea in international relations. On the one hand, it was interpreted as an exact balance in the sense of an equality of power between two powers or groups of powers – mostly the houses of Hapsburg and Bourbon; on the other hand, it was regarded as an order arising from two powers or groups of powers balanced by a third power which had the capacity to 'tip the scales'; Great Britain in particular was often seen in this position. According to a third variant, one state was not allowed to be more powerful than all the others taken together.[19] The basic structures of these three interpretations of the concept of the balance of power can be found as early as the sixteenth century. All three variants shared the principle of neutralising conflicting interests and the rivalry of powers by creating a balanced constellation of common power politics. Those states being included in the model thus were bound together to form a community of interests and a partnership of convenience.

The reference to Europe was much clearer here than in the concept of universal monarchy. Until the mid-seventeenth century, Christendom was a primary frame of reference. Afterwards, it was gradually replaced by the term 'Europe' but not completely dispensed with. In this context, 'Europe' represented the European system of states, which after the Peace of Westphalia in 1648 had found an enduring shape. Particularly in the first half of the eighteenth century, however, the balance theories did not always refer to all members of the system but occasionally only to the most powerful groups among them, like the pentarchy of the five major powers, Great Britain, France, Russia, Prussia, and the Hapsburg Monarchy, which was established in the middle of that century. Small and medium powers were by no means always taken into consideration. It was only after about 1750 that the outer European world and the colonies gained some importance. The Ottoman Empire, which was a part of the European system of states in many ways, tended to remain excluded for religious and cultural reasons. In the sixteenth and seventeenth centuries, the terms 'balance of power' and 'balance of Christendom' were sometimes interchangeable. It was not until the later eighteenth century that a growing number of authors integrated the Ottoman Empire into their balance theories.[20]

---

18 See H. Duchhardt, *Balance of Power und Pentarchie: Internationale Beziehungen 1700–1785*, Paderborn, 1996, 7–19.
19 See Strohmeyer, *Theorie*, 128–134.
20 See A. Strohmeyer, 'Il lungo percorso della Turchia verso l'Europa: l'integrazione del Regno Ottomano nelle teorie dell'equilibrio europeo delle forze', in *Oriente e Occidente tra medioevo ed età moderna: Studi in onore di Geo Pistarino*, 2 vols, ed. L. Balletto, Genova, 1997, vol. 1, 1145–1165.

Like the ideas of universal monarchy, balance of power theories were closely connected to thinking about peace, the problem and possibility of peacekeeping, and the causes and legitimacy of war. However, the connection was understood in a more differentiating way.[21] Those authors who believed in a positive connection and even thought that a state of balance of power between states was essential for peace[22] were contradicted by others claiming that at least for keeping or re-establishing such a balance wars had to be waged.[23] Thus, there were many supporters of these theories who took wars to be an essential part of the equation.[24] Because of this, there were also those who maintained that the balance of power was completely inadequate for the maintenance of peace.[25] Some writers considered subjective disturbances of the balance to be the main cause of war.[26] Around the middle of the eighteenth century, the German cameralist Johann Gottlob von Justi (1717–1771) wrote a polemical paper arguing against the balance of power which among other things is based around this idea.[27] In Immanuel Kant's (1724–1804) opinion the peacekeeping effect inherent in a balance of power was, in any case, a 'mere fantasy'.[28]

Universal Monarchy, Balance of Power and Ideas of Peace

Both the balance of power and universal monarchy touched debates on peace and war within many different contexts. This proves the considerable social range

---

21 For example C.F. Stisser, *Fortsetzung der freimutigen und bescheidenen Erinnerungen wider des berühmten Göttingischen Professors, Herrn Doctor Kahle Abhandlung von der Balance Europens*, Leipzig, 1746, 64 f.
22 For example A. Pecquet, 'L'Esprit des Maximes politiques pour servir de suite à L'Esprit des loix (1757)', in *Theory and Practice of the Balance of Power 1486–1914: Selected European Writings*, ed. M. Wright, London, 1975, 66.
23 For example J.C. Adelung, *Pragmatische Geschichte Europens von dem Ableben Carls VI. an*, 9 vols, Gotha, 1762–1769, vol. 1, 340.
24 For example N.H. Gundling, *Gundlingiana, darinnen allerhand zur Jurisprudenz, Philosophie, Historie, Critic, Litteratur und übrigen Gelehrsamkeit gehörige Sachen abgehandelt werden*, 5. Stück, ("Ob wegen der anwachsenden Macht der Nachbarn man den Degen entblößen könne?"), Halle/Saale, 1716; L.M. Kahle, *Commentatio Iuris Publici de Trutina Europae quae vulgo adpellatur 'Die Balance von Europa'*, Göttingen, 1744.
25 For example C.-I. Castel Abbé de Saint Pierre, *Der Traktat vom ewigen Frieden 1713*, ed. W. Michael, trans. F.v. Oppeln-Bronikowski, Berlin, 1922, 22–24; J.H. Lilienfeld, *Neues Staats-Gebäude In drey Büchern*, Leipzig, 1767, 42; Montesquieu, *Werk von den Gesetzen*, trans. A.G. Kästner, 3 vols, Frankfurt/Main and Leipzig, 1753, vol. 1, 380 f.
26 For example C. D'Avenant, 'The Right of Making War, Peace and Alliances', in *Essays*, C. D'Avenant, London, 1701, 131; N.N., 'Projet d'un nouveau Systéme de l'Europe, Préferable ou Systéme de l'Equilibre entre la Maison de France, et celle d'Autriche', in *Der Europäischen Staats-Cantzley Acht und Achtzigster Theil*, ed. A. Faber, s.l., 1746, 124.
27 See J.H.G. von Justi, *Die Chimäre des Gleichgewichts von Europa*, Altona, 1758.
28 See I. Kant, 'Über den Gemeinspruch: Das mag in der Theorie richtig sein, taugt aber nicht für die Praxis', in *Über Theorie und Praxis*, eds K. Blumenberg et al., Frankfurt/Main, 1967, 86.

of this connection and therefore the fact that it was definitely established within political culture. Mercurino Gattinara's (1465–1530) documents show that concepts of universal monarchy, including ideas of peace, intruded into practical politics. Charles V's influential Great Chancellor, an educated jurist who had built a career in Hapsburg service, was a dedicated supporter of a policy of universal monarchy. He tried again and again to influence the emperor in favour of it. One example is the negotiations for the Peace of Madrid in 1526 dealing with a new organisation of the Hapsburg-French relations.[29]

As early as 1519, just after the emperor had been elected, Gattinara sent a memorandum pointing out to Charles that God had raised him in dignity above all Christian rulers and kings and was now preparing the ground for his legitimate world domination. With this in mind, he regarded Charles as obliged to support Christendom and to help it to achieve general peace.[30] Evidently, this thought was based on the ideas of Dante Alighieri (1265–1321), who in his work on monarchy – one of the most influential political papers in the Late Middle Ages – had made a direct link between the tasks of imperial monarchy and peace. Only in the case of complete peace, said Dante, would mankind be able to develop towards the divinely ordained bliss that was its destiny. The precondition for this was the emperor's power over all mankind.[31]

Models of the balance of power were connected to ideas of peace in the context of political decision-making processes and the actual establishment of peace. The big alliances concluded around 1690 to contain the aggressive foreign policy of Louis XIV were achieved under this slogan. Although the notion of balance in international law did not meet with the same overwhelming and far-reaching response as it did in the writings of publicists and political thinkers,[32] the peace treaty between Great Britain and Spain to end the War of the Spanish Succession, signed at Utrecht in 1713, did contain the aim 'to settle and establish the peace and tranquillity of Christendom by an equal balance of power'.[33] During the following decades, the idea of balance became a 'fundamental constituent of

---

29 See M. Rivero Rodríguez, *Gattinara: Carlos V y el sueño del Imperio*, Madrid, 2005, 129–148; J. M. Headley, 'The Emperor and His Chancellor: Disputes over Empire, Administration and Pope (1519–1529)', in *Carlos V y la quiebra del humanismo político en Europa (1530–1558)*, eds J. Martínez Millán and I. J. Ezquerra Revilla, vol. 1, Madrid, 2001, 21–35; P. Schmidt, 'Monarchia universalis vs. monarchiae universales: El programa imperial de Gattinara y su contestación en Europa', in *Carlos V y la quiebra del humanismo político en Europa 1530–1558*, eds J. Martínez Millán and I. J. Ezquerra Revilla, vol. 1, Madrid, 2001, 115–129.
30 See Gattinara to Charles V., Barcelona, 12 July 1519, in *Quellen zur Geschichte Karls V.*, ed. A. Kohler, Darmstadt, 1990, 59.
31 See Dante Alighieri, *Monarchie*, trans. C. Sauter, Freiburg/Br., 1913, I.4–5.
32 See H. Duchhardt, 'The Missing Balance', *Journal of the History of International Law* 2 (2000): 67–72.
33 Anglo-Spanish Peace Treaty, Utrecht, 13 July 1713, art. V., in *Fontes Historiae Iuris Gentium, vol. 2: 1493–1815*, ed. W. H. Grewe, Berlin, New York, 1988, 231 f. The term 'balance' is also mentioned in the Spanish-Savoyen treaty, concluded in Utrecht on the same day.

the Droit publique d'Europe'[34] finding written expression in further international peace agreements. It can be found for example in the Peace of Vienna in 1735 when France accepted the Pragmatic Sanction organizing the question of succession in the Hapsburg Monarchy.[35]

Ideas of universal monarchy can clearly be found in two peace treaties concluded during the rule of Charles V. The Treaty of Madrid (1526) between the emperor and Francis I obliged the French king to support Charles' journey to Italy, where he was to be crowned emperor. This can be interpreted as the recognition of a legitimate primacy held by the Hapsburg monarch. Charles' claim to leadership also becomes obvious in the article declaring him secular head of Christendom in the war against the infidels.[36] The Treaty of Cambrai (1529), also concluded by Charles V and Francis I, shows a similar choice of words. Ideas of universal monarchy were even integrated into the Peace Treaty of Barcelona, which was signed by the Hapsburg emperor and Pope Clemens VII in the same year.[37]

Another field where the connection of both concepts to ideas of peace can be observed are political tracts and scholarly papers. Several of Charles V's Spanish senior officials and secretaries, for example, employed these media to spread their opinions about universal monarchy – not agreeing with Gattinara at all. Juan Ginés de Sepúlveda (ca. 1489–1573), well known for his disputation with Bartolomé de las Casas on the legitimacy of the Spanish conquests in the New World at Valladolid in 1550/51, published papers connecting universal monarchy with peace, as did representatives of the School of Salamanca, an important base for the development of modern international law.[38]

The combination of both concepts with ideas about peace was particularly clear in political propaganda. When Charles V tried to win the electors' votes in 1519 during his campaign to become head of the empire, he had himself described as a virtuous monarch and the future guarantor of peace in numerous flyers and leaflets.[39] It was strongly announced that only a member of the house of Hapsburg as a universal monarch and emperor would be able to prevent wars and to call disturbers of peace to account.[40] The propagandist utilisation of the balance of power in combination with peace was so intensive during the first half of the eighteenth century that contemporaries were already complaining that this was nothing more than propagandist cover for justifying one's own (warlike) intentions.

---

34 W. Grewe, *Epochen der Völkerrechtsgeschichte*, Baden-Baden, 1984, 328.
35 See M. Sheehan, *The Balance of Power: History and Theory*, London, 1996, 104.
36 See Tratado de Madrid, art. 23, art. 25.
37 See R. Lesaffer, 'Peace Treaties from Lodi to Westphalia', in *Peace Treaties and International Law in European History: From the Late Middle Ages to World War One*, ed. R. Lesaffer, Cambridge, 2004, 31 f.
38 See König, *Monarchia mundi*, 85–98, 108–124.
39 See A. Kohler, *Karl V.: Eine Biographie*, München, 1999, 65 f.
40 See Bosbach, *Monarchia universalis*, 51 f., 73.

One of the most important means of spreading the connection of universal monarchy and peace was monarchical representation of power. Therefore, Charles was presented as an imperial peace-bringer on triumphal arches made on the occasion of his successful Tunis operation in 1535.[41] The same is true for several paintings of the Hapsburg emperor such as Parmigianino's (1503–1540) 'Allegory of Emperor Charles V', which was created around 1530 against the background of Charles coronation as emperor in Bologna,[42] (see table p. 74) Charles, clad in armour, appears in the picture as monarch. In his right hand he holds the staff of command, which is fixed on top of a globe to symbolise his claim to universal power. A winged Victory uses her left hand to crown the emperor with a palm leaf, a symbol of victory, whilst her right hand adorns the globe with an olive branch as a symbol of peace.[43] The famous portrait of Charles on horseback, painted by Titian in 1548 after his victory over the Protestant imperial princes, shows him as the patron of a now pacified Christendom.[44] (see table p. 75) Next to it in the sequence of pictures in Charles V's palace in Granada, a depiction of the emperor's victorious campaigns is combined with allegories of peace.[45]

A reception by broad parts of society is even truer for arguments connecting the balance of power to ideas about peace: in the first half of the eighteenth century a wide-spread distribution started in the media which caught the attention of satirists.[46] Thus, the French author Mirabeau (1715–1789), a physiocrat who voiced his opposition to state intervention in the economy in his works, felt compelled to utter the biting remark that this was a favourite idea of newspapers and coffee houses. He himself regarded it as a dangerous illusion and a fantasy; the cause of numerous wars rather than a contribution to peacekeeping.[47]

What were the features of the ideas of peace integrated in the concepts of universal monarchy? Even if we concentrate on the age of Charles V, this question is not easy to answer as the spectrum of ideas is extremely broad. Depending on context, very different arguments were used. Great variety is therefore one feature. Sometimes an extremely extensive idea of peace can be observed being expressed

---

41   See P. Burke, 'Repräsentation und Re-Präsentation: Die Inszenierung des Kaisers', in *Karl V. 1500–1558 und seine Zeit*, ed. H. Soly, Köln, 2003, 417.
42   See F. Bosbach, 'Selbstauffassung und Selbstdarstellung Karls V. bei der Kaiserkrönung in Bologna', in *Karl V. 1500–1558: Neue Perspektiven seiner Herrschaft in Europa und Übersee*, eds A. Kohler, B. Haider and C. Ottner, Wien, 2002, 99–101.
43   See F. Checa Cremades, 'Das Bild Karls V.', in *Karl V. 1500–1558 und seine Zeit*, ed. H. Soly, 492.
44   See F. Checa Cremades, 'Kunst und Macht in der ersten Hälfte des 16. Jahrhunderts: Karl V. und die Kunst', in *Kaiser Karl V. (1500–1558): Macht und Ohnmacht Europas*, ed. Petra Kruse, Bonn, 2000, 42.
45   See R. Wohlfeil, 'Kriegsheld oder Friedensfürst? Eine Studie zum Bildprogramm des Palastes Karls V. in der Alhambra zu Granada', in *Recht und Reich im Zeitalter der Reformation: Festschrift für Horst Rabe*, ed. C. Roll, 2nd edn, Frankfurt/Main, 1997, 94.
46   See Sheehan, *Balance*, 104.
47   See Mirabeau, *L'Ami des hommes ou traitée la population*, ed. M. Rouxel, Paris, 1883, 557–561.

Table 1: Allegory on Charles V as Ruler of the World
Picture taken from: F. M. Parmigianino, 'Allegory on Charles V as Ruler of the World, 1530', in Kaiser Karl V. (1500–1558): Macht und Ohnmacht Europas, ed. Petra Kruse, Bonn 2000, jacket.

Table 2: Charles V at Mühlberg, 1548
Picture taken from: Tiziano Vecellio di Gregorio (Titian), 'Charles V at Mühlberg, 1548',
in H. Schilling, 'Karl V. und die Religion: Das Ringen um Reinheit und Einheit des
Christentums, in Karl V. 1500–1558 und seine Zeit, ed. H. Soly, Köln 2003, 285–363, 304.

by the term 'general peace'.[48] This meant a condition abstracted from all concrete situations which should span the entire Christian world.[49] But there were also references to 'eternal peace', a concept of peace alluding to medieval moral theology, and to the 'pax Romana'.[50] In the same way a definitely existing or desirable religious or political order could become the focus of attention. Examples of this are creating or maintaining the unity of Christendom or defending it against the infidels.

There was also great variety in the ideas of peace used in theories of balance of power. These ranged from a very abstract and not clearly defined 'general peace', a 'peace for Christendom' and an 'eternal peace' to definite ideas of building a constellation of powers fixed by treaties and designed to prevent wars.[51] Additionally, there were negative definitions like the absence of international tyranny.[52] But a closer definition of content was rare. From this a second feature can be deduced: a certain lack of definition in terminology arising from the fact that peace worked as a norm which did not need any further explanation or exact definition; nobody could speak out against peace as both the chief impulse and ultimate aim of international order. Additionally, this openness gave room for very different interpretations, which could also be favourable to the overall concept.

However, there was more to it than this: peace was often mentioned in one breath with other crucial values that were also functionally connected to the two models. The existing terminological fields allow a more precise interpretation of 'peace'.

Law and justice were associated with universal monarchy particularly often, but there were also combinations that included public welfare, the prevention of wars, and special religious values, among which unity and the protection of Christendom stood out. That is why phrases consisting of two or three nouns like 'peace and order' or 'peace, law, and justice' are typical of the language of the sources. Each of these phrases emphasized a specific meaning of peace and made the links clear. Peace, for example, could be understood as a constant or reconstructed legal system. This interpretation calls to mind the political idea of peace in the Middle Ages.[53] The combination of peace and justice was connected to this, deriving mostly from Christian and Germanic traditions. The universal monarch could hold an important rank, such as being the highest authority concerning secular legal problems,

---

48   F. Bosbach, 'The European Debate on Universal Monarchy', in *Theories of Empire, 1450–1800*, ed. D. Armitage, Aldershot, 1998, 86 f.

49   See W. Janssen, 'Friede', in *Geschichtliche Grundbegriffe: Historisches Lexikon der politisch-sozialen Sprache in Deutschland*, ed. O. Brunner, W. Conze and R. Koselleck, 8 vols, Stuttgart, 1972–1997, vol. 2, 554.

50   See Wohlfeil, Kriegsheld, 94.

51   See Pecquet, L'Esprit, 67; Duke of Berry, 'Renunciation of the Spanish Crown [1718]', in *Theory and Practice of the Balance of Power 1486–1914: Selected European Writings*, ed. M. Wright, London, 1975, 50 f.

52   See Pecquet, L'Esprit, 67.

53   See Janssen, Friede, 553.

being the highest legislator – now and then even direct analogies to Justinian (482–565) were expressed – or being the guarantor of legal security.

The terminological environment of the ideas of peace within the theories of balance of power also shows combinations of crucial values and norms. Therefore, connections to undefined collective terms like *bonum commune* (public welfare) or *tranquillitas* (tranquillity/serenity) were made. The peace ideas in concepts of universal monarchy focused frequently on 'law' and 'justice', whereas in balance theories it was common to mention peace mostly in connection with 'security' and 'freedom' of states. However, this terminological connection was not particularly firm: especially the words 'security' and 'freedom' were frequently used without a direct reference to peace. In addition to that, negative definitions of peace can be found in balance theories in the sense of peace as the absence of war. One can clearly see a move from Christian norms towards changed contemporary values. Primary points of reference were the sovereignty of states, the securing of their existence, increasingly economic factors and the maintenance of the status quo guaranteed by an existing balance or one that was to be established.[54] Of course, this state of affairs was considered to be peace.[55] A consideration of principles of international law was debated. The influence of the early modern development of the states and the formation of a system of sovereign states becomes clear, as the interpretation of peace referred to the relations of several sovereign political communities with equal rights of existence, at least in theory.

A closer look at the way in which the ideas of peace in concepts of universal monarchy and balance of power dealt with 'the other' allows a more detailed explanation of the understanding of peace. Here, universal monarchy proves to be a model of order that was primarily designed for internal peace. Herfried Münkler, political scientist in Berlin, speaks of an 'imperial peace' in this context.[56] As one of its main features, Münkler analyzes the connection to other values and to an imperial mission, which in this case was the battle against the Reformation and the spread of the 'true' Christian faith.[57] In contrast, external wars were not only considered to be a legitimate means of policy but even gave meaning to the model. Crusades against the Ottomans, for example, belonged to the crucial tasks of the universal monarch.[58] Due to this, the pro-Hapsburg propaganda liked to present Charles V as a universal ruler, who accomplishes his mission of acting as the superior protector of the *res publica Christiana* by fighting the Muslims. The magnificent

---

54 See H. Kleinschmidt, 'The Balance of Power: An Historical Caveat (III)', *Rekíshi jinrui* 21 (1993): 3–11.
55 For example D. Defoe, 'A Review of the State of the English Nation [1706]', in *Theory and Practice of the Balance of Power 1486–1914: Selected European Writings*, ed. M. Wright, 48 f.
56 Cf. H. Münkler, *Imperien: Die Logik der Weltherrschaft – vom Alten Rom bis zu den Vereinigten Staaten*, Berlin, 2005, 128–132.
57 Ibid., 132–150.
58 See Bosbach, *Monarchia universalis*, 51.

celebrations in Italy after Charles' successful campaign against the Muslim corsairs in Tunis in 1535 are an appropriate example of this.

This line of thought was aggressive. Juan Ginés de Sepúlveda, for instance, suggested that Charles should establish an order of peace among the Christian princes in order to be able to assemble the powers of Christian Europe for a crusade against Islam.[59] This thought can also be found in somewhat amended form in the terms of the Peace of Madrid, which has already been mentioned.[60] It was claimed that the goal was to (violently) spread the Christian faith and thus to include the infidels in the peace supposedly guaranteed by universal monarchy. In other words, this interpretation of peace did not allow for a society containing followers of a different faith. This idea was influenced by the Christian-Muslim relations in the Middle Ages and particularly dominant in Spain following the *Reconquista* and the struggles with the Ottomans in the Mediterranean.

However, this aggressive potential could also turn against single parts of Christendom if they, like the Protestants in the Holy Roman Empire or Francis I of France stood in the way of a policy which was declared to support universal monarchy and thus were said to disturb peace.[61] Charles V, for example, legitimated his campaigns against the French king by referring to the intended pacification of Italy, which meant the implementation of the values and norms included in the concepts of universal monarchy. This argument was used so often later on that Hugo Grotius (1583–1645) deemed it necessary to place particular emphasis on the injustice of such wars in 1625.[62]

The Ottoman expansion against the Christians in Southeastern Europe and the Mediterranean was accompanied by an ideology of power that showed universalist characteristics. However, Ottoman universalism differed from European ideas of a universal monarchy in many ways. Partly deriving from the honour and status of the East Roman Emperor after the conquest of Constantinople in 1453, it also drew on Islamic prophecies and the Mongolian claim to world domination ascribed to Genghis Khan.[63]

Looking at the theories of the balance of power, a different conclusion is reached. Even among the supporters of these theories there were different opinions concerning the question of whether the international order depending on balance meant a general absence of war. There were extremely controversial debates on the question of whether war was a legitimate resort either to keep the balance or

---

59 See Pietschmann, Konzepte, 405.
60 See Tratado de Madrid, art. 25.
61 See Bosbach, *Monarchia universalis*, 52.
62 See H. Grotius, *De Iure Belli ac Pacis*, Amsterdam, 1651, II/XXII, 13–15.
63 See P. Thorau, 'Von Karl dem Großen zum Frieden von Zsitva Torok: Zum Weltherrschaftsanspruch Sultan Mehmeds II. und dem Wiederaufleben des Zweikaiserproblems nach der Eroberung Konstantinopels', *Historische Zeitschrift* 279 (2004): 309–334.

re-establish a disturbed balance.⁶⁴ Those who said that war could not be excluded as an *ultima ratio* were by no means at variance with the predominant opinion of the scholarly world.⁶⁵ From this perspective it was only a short step to legitimating preventive wars – and this step was taken. The Swiss scholar in international law Emer de Vattel (1714–1767) serves as an example. He held the view that a nation that threatened the freedom of other nations and had intentions of conquest might legitimately be weakened by these other nations by force. The aim of these and other just wars always had to be the restoration of peace, safety and justice. Every good ruler had to obey this rule.⁶⁶

But aggressive potential towards the outer world was not necessary as the European states, which were thought to be united by the principle of balance, did not form even a defensive community against external aggressors, though later balance theories were used to legitimate plans for dividing the Ottoman Empire – and were indeed followed in the case of Poland. In 1807, a series about 'Europe's interest regarding Turkey' was published in the German journal *Minerva*, an enlightened liberal journal specialising in political subjects. It claimed that the Ottoman Empire, which was not acquainted with the principles of the balance of power, owed its continuing existence to the politics of balance pursued by the European states. It was completely wrong to make its preservation into a political axiom and to think that this was the only way to guarantee Europe's safety. On the contrary, it was precisely by its conquest and division that the equilibrium between the European states could be balanced.⁶⁷

Summary

The article is based on an asynchronous comparison: the ideas of peace in concepts of universal monarchy during the age of Charles V (1500–1558) are compared with these ideas in balance-of-power theories developed in the first half of the eighteenth century. During these periods, each model reached its peak and became the leading concept of international order in Europe. In summary it may be said that on both models debates were well connected to prevalent ideas about peace and the problem of securing peace. A positive connection to peace served to legitimise these concepts and is found in tracts and scholarly papers as well as in political propaganda and the symbolic representation of peace. Thus, both models acted as important catalysts for spreading the ideas of peace in early modern

---

64 See C.G. Günther, *Europäisches Völkerrecht in Friedenszeiten nach Vernunft, Verträgen und Herkommen, mit Anwendung auf die teutschen Reichsstände*, 2 vols, Altenburg, 1787.
65 See Duchhardt, Balance of Power, 16.
66 See E. de Vattel, *Le droit des gens ou principes de la loi naturell, appliqués à la conduite et aux affaires des nations et des souverains [1758]*, Tübingen, 1959, III/III par. 49, IV/I par. 3–6.
67 See Anon., 'Das Interesse von Europa in Beziehung auf die Türkey', *Minerva* 62 (1807): 136–139, 331–340, 514–537; 63 (1807): 108–111.

society. Nevertheless, we have to take into consideration that both universal monarchy and balance of power were also delegitimised by some critics as neglecting a positive connection to peace and having a strong connection to war. Particularly intensive discussions referring to this conclusion are found among balance of power theorists.

Universal monarchy was primarily an internal peace order while external wars, especially against the infidels (vide the Crusades), served the purpose of lending legitimacy to the concept. Balance of power theorists did not need such arguments but many of them considered that wars within the system of states, though always subject to debate, were a legitimate means of keeping up or establishing the desired balance.

In both models, the ideas of peace were often deliberately kept unclear. Nevertheless, a connection to other values and norms is obvious. Law and justice, public welfare, and the protection and unity of Christendom are particularly prevalent in debates related to universal monarchy. The theories of balance of power often imply freedom and security of the (major) powers guaranteed either by an existing balance or one that has to be established. Concerning their content, each of the two described models of international order reflects the wide range of the interpretation of peace in their time.

Liberal and Democratic Peace as a Concept in 19th and 20th Century International Relations

GOTTFRIED NIEDHART

The invention of peace on Western terms

The second half of the twentieth century was largely shaped by the East-West conflict with its massive ideological struggle, arms race, quest for superiority as well as real and imagined threats on both sides. Although both super powers used military force, thus indirectly fighting the adversary, they did not go to war against each other. In the end the conflict dissolved peacefully, contrary to many expectations at various stages of the conflict. According to John L. Gaddis this particular outcome of the global struggle can be attributed to three factors. First, due to the existence of nuclear weapons and the mutual ability to annihilate each other war became anachronistic. Second, rather than promoting world revolution the communist type of dictatorship found itself discredited. Third, and intertwined with the second factor, parallel to the global conflict between East and West there was a globalization of democratization. Open societies and market economies proved to be superior to authoritarian systems and command economies.[1] Given "the wave of democratization that has swept the globe," Gaddis does not rule out that democracy might also be planted in the Arab world. Thereby, a lessening of tensions might be achieved.[2] In a much broader sense political scientists, stimulated by Michael Doyle's seminal article,[3] have been engaged in producing a veritable boom of literature on the question how democracy and peace are interrelated. The proponents of the democratic peace theory start from the observation, which

---

1   J.L. Gaddis, *The Cold War. A New History*, New York, 2005, 261 ff. – I am grateful to Martin Kitchen for his editorial assistance.
2   J.L. Gaddis, 'Grand Strategy in the Second Term', *Foreign Affairs* 84 (2005), No. 1, 2–15. See also J.L. Gaddis, 'Das Ende der Tyrannei. Wie die Bush-Doktrin das revolutionäre Ideal der Freiheit wiederbelebt', *Internationale Politik* 64 (2009), No. 1, 70–82.
3   M.W. Doyle, 'Kant, Liberal Legacies and Foreign Affairs', *Philosophy and Public Affairs* 12 (1983), 205–235 and 323–353.

allegedly "comes as close as anything we have to an empirical law in international relations,"[4] "that democracies rarely, if ever, fight each other."[5] The purpose of this paper is to shed some light on the historical dimension of the Democratic Peace theory. In fact, the origins of the Western approach of peace-making can be traced in the late eighteenth century.

The concept of liberal and democratic peace emerged as a critique, firstly of the mercantilist state which regulated economic matters, particularly foreign trade and secondly of the anciens régimes in Europe. The liberal critique was part of the fundamental economic and political change which happened during the second half of the eighteenth century. The European Enlightenment, the Industrial Revolution, the revolutions in North America and France and the reform movement in Britain, signalled the beginning of a new era. With respect to war and peace there was a rethinking which not only reviled war for its terrible human and material costs, but also maintained that the old vicious circle of war and peace could be broken. It was the liberal school of thought which undermined old habits and convictions and sent a truly revolutionary message. Given certain essential preconditions, mankind would no longer find it necessary to go to war. In fact, war would be contrary to the true interests of modern society. The first prerequisite was free trade, the second democracy (or reforms leading to a higher degree of political participation and eventually to democracy). The "invention of peace" happened when the modern Western world began to take shape with its main features a liberal market economy, the trans-national division of labour, parliamentary politics, an open society and democracy.[6] Modern civil society and the trading state could prosper best in a world without war. Given this definition of interest it was only a short step to the belief in a causal nexus between free trade, democracy and peace. Philosophers, political theorists, industrialists, politicians, members of the peace movement, all stressed the relationship between a liberal economy and democracy with peace.

---

[4] J.S. Levy, 'Domestic Politics and War', *Journal of Interdisciplinary History* 18 (1988), 662.
[5] Ch. Lipson, *Reliable Partners. How Democracies Have Made a Separate Peace*, Princeton, 2003, 1. See also M.V. Rasmussen, *The West, Civil Society and the Construction of Peace*, Houndmills, 2003, 40: "Democratic peace theory hypothesised that only democratic states can be at peace with one another and therefore true peace depends on democratisation."
[6] M. Howard, *The Invention of Peace. Reflections on War and International Order*, London, 2000.

No wonder that eventually political scientists too were involved in developing the liberal paradigm,[7] some of them drawing on historical case studies.[8] The main findings of recent research can be summarized in the following, necessarily simplifying, way:

1. Compared with non-democratic states democracies have unique capacities and advantages with respect to non-violent conflict behaviour and to the ability to put their weight on the international system below the threshold of war. Democratic conflict behaviour is different because democracies "have a unique capacity to form effective partnerships that assuage fears, diminish risks, and capture joint benefits"[9] and because democratic norms are "an asset that can be used by democratic leaders to protest and advance their country's interests in international disputes."[10] Furthermore, democracies "are more effective at projecting credible threats *and* credible promises."[11]

2. At the same time the "substantial variation in the conflict behaviour of both democratic and non-democratic states" cannot be overlooked. "At times democratic leaders become as aggressive, if not more so, than non-democratic leaders."[12] As to international cooperation it is "certainly not limited to established democratic states".[13]

---

7   For the purpose of summarizing the state of the art readers and collections of essays were published as well as syntheses. See, e.g., *Debating the Democratic Peace*, eds M.E. Brown, S.M. Lynn-Jones, S.E. Miller, Cambridge, MA. 1996; M.F. Elman, *Paths to Peace: Is Democracy the Answer?* Cambridge, MA. 1997; E.A. Henderson, *Democracy and War. The End of an Illusion?* Boulder 2002; *Demokratien im Krieg*, eds C. Schweitzer, B. Aust, P. Schlotter, Baden-Baden, 2004; *Democratic Wars: Looking at the Dark Side of Democratic Peace*, eds A. Geis, L. Brock, H. Müller, Basinstoke, 2006; B. Barth, *The Democratic Peace Controversy. A Critical Survey*, Oslo: Oslo Files on Defence and Security 1/2008; D. Lektzian and M. Souva, 'A Comparative Theory Test of Democratic Peace Arguments, 1946–2000, *Journal of Peace Research* 46 (2009), No. 1, 17–37.

8   Outstanding examples are J. MacMillan, *On Liberal Peace. Democracy, War and the International Order*, London, 1998; S. Weart, *Never at War. Why Don't Democracies Fight One Another?* New Haven, 1998; P.K. Huth and T.L. Allee, *The Democratic Peace and Territorial Conflict in the 20th Century*, Cambridge, 2002; Lipson, *Reliable Partners*; Rasmussen, *The West*; Ph. Towle, *Democracy and Peacemaking: Negotiations and Debates 1815–1973*, London, 2000; P.J. McDonald and K. Sweeney, 'The Achilles' Heel of Liberal IR Theory? Globalization and Conflict in the Pre-World War I Era', *World Politics* 59 (2006/07), 370–403. See also the introduction to a forum on The History of the Democratic Peace by C. Elman, 'History, Theory, and the Democratic Peace', *International History Review* 23 (2001), 757–766.

9   Lipson, *Reliable Partners*, p. 169.
10 Huth and Allee, *Democratic Peace*, p. 292.
11 Lipson, *Reliable Partners*, p. 180.
12 Huth and Allee, *Democratic Peace*, p. 286 f.
13 Lipson, *Reliable Partners*, p. 188.

So far, there is only very little "multi-disciplinary engagement"[14] across the borderlines between political and historical sciences. But increasingly "historians are looking towards political analysts and their different theories, and how these theories work as experiments within the vast laboratory of history."[15] Historians, much in accordance with political science scholars just quoted, tend to underscore the complexity of the picture and hesitate to idealize democracies and their roles in the context of war and peace: "The link between democracy and peace is not an obvious one, no more than the link between dictators, totalitarianism and war is obvious."[16] Non-democratic regimes may well be interested in avoiding war and peaceful solutions may be the result of calculated risk-taking regardless of the domestic political conditions or the political regimes of the adversaries.[17] Having said this, however, I argue that one cannot conclude from the above differentiation that the democratic peace is a "myth"[18] or that, with respect to peace and war, it does not matter whether a state is a liberal state or not, or whether a state is orientated towards the 'Western' world or not. After all, there is not only the "empirical law" that democracies do not fight each other. One can also maintain that "an international democratic logic has been established" in the course of the 20th century, notwithstanding its violence and wars: "It is obvious that an international democratic logic has been taking shape and been reinforced during the twentieth century."[19]

Since the middle of the 20th century a remarkable development has happened. Certain regions can be identified as zones of peace, notably the European international system.[20] It cannot be ignored that the emergence of such zones is inextricably connected with the trend towards economic interdependence and democracy.[21] From the historian's perspective it is essential to ask for the specific conditions and

14 Proposed by John Macmillan, 'Liberalism and the Democratic Peace', *Revire of International Studies* 30 (2004), 200.
15 R. Frank, 'Political Regimes and Foreign Policies: Attitudes towards War and Peace', in *Foreign Policy and Political Regime*, ed. J. F. Sombra Saraiva, Brasilia, 2003, 65.
16 Frank, Political Regimes, p. 66. See also Jost Dülffer, 'Internationale Geschichte und Historische Friedensforschung' in *Internationale Geschichte*, eds W. Loth and J. Osterhammel, Munich, 2000, p. 261.
17 On this see, e.g., P. W. Schroeder, *The Transformation of European Politics 1763–1848*, Oxford, 1994; J. Dülffer, M. Kröger, R.-H. Wippich eds, *Vermiedene Kriege. Deeskalation von Konflikten der Großmächte zwischen Krimkrieg und Erstem Weltkrieg 1865–1914*, Munich, 1997.
18 Chr. Layne, 'Kant or Cant. The Myth of the Democratic Peace', *International Security* 19 (1994), No. 2, 5–49.
19 Frank, Political Regimes, p. 78, 82.
20 On the emergence of zones of peace D. Senghaas, *Zum irdischen Frieden. Erkenntnisse und Vermutungen*, Frankfurt am Main, 2004, 162 ff.
21 M. W. Doyle, *Ways of War and Peace. Realism, Liberalism, and Socialism*, New York, 1997, 305: "Realist theories can account for aspects of certain periods of international stability. […] But the logic of the balance of power and international hegemony does not explain the separate peace maintained for more than 150 years among states sharing one particular form of governance, liberal principles and institutions."

constellations which can be regarded as significant for the emergence of a discourse of peace and for the implementation of peace in terms of a liberal and democratic peace. However, this article is mainly confined to the concept of this approach and will only touch briefly upon the question how it relates to special interests. Overlooking the last two centuries, two main stages can be distinguished. Firstly, the "invention" of liberal peace at the transition from the 18th to the 19th century. Secondly, the introduction of the concept of democratic peace into international politics during World War I.

Peace through economic interdependence

The reflection on peace and peacekeeping and on whether there might be a chance to avoid violence and war is as old as warfare itself and the writing of the history of war. Towards the close of the 18th century, however, a completely new school of thought evolved. To bring about peace appeared to be a calculable undertaking. Peace was regarded not any longer as a vision for a far distant future, but as a state of affairs which can be achieved (although no time table could be offered). Given the framework and the opportunities of modernity with its revolutionized economy and its political change from Ancien Régime to more open societies, peace became a project much like the increase of wealth or political freedom. Peace was constructed on liberal terms. Ever since the elimination of war rather than its rationalisation has been the concern of the advocates of the liberal paradigm.

Its early promoters were no pacifists. At the same time, however, the prevention of war was regarded as appropriate to the requirements of modern society. Rather than thinking in terms of a zero-sum game, nations appeared to be members of an international society competing with each other to their mutual benefits. Civil society and the modern trading state[22] could best prosper if violence and war were absent on a global scale. Furthermore, free trade was supposed not only to foster prosperity, but also the peaceful conduct of international relations. Immanuel Kant foresaw the inevitability of peaceable interaction between trading states.[23] He did not go as far as Thomas Paine who was more progressive with respect to the idea of democracy.[24] But Kant was convinced that citizens of a "republic" who were able to participate in the process of political decision making would not opt for war. Furthermore, republics would be inclined to overcome international anarchy by establishing a pacific federation. In the last instance, although he had no illu-

---

22 R. Rosecrance, *The Rise of the Trading State: Commerce and Conquest in the Modern World*, New York, 1986.
23 I. Kant, Zum ewigen Frieden. Ein philosophischer Entwurf. Werke, vol. 9, Darmstadt 1983, 226.
24 M. W. Doyle, 'The Voice of the People: Political Theorists on the International Implications of Democracy' in *The Fall of Great Powers. Peace, Stability and Legitimacy*, ed. G. Lundestad, Oslo, 1994, 284.

sions about the long duration of the peace process, Kant developed the notion of a cosmopolitan community.[25]

In the early 19th century there was no experience of a liberal peace in Europe, to say nothing of a democratic peace. On the contrary, the peace settlement which was agreed upon after the Napoleonic wars was largely shaped by traditional elements, even if they were supplemented by the multilateral diplomacy of the Concert of Europe.[26] However, as the Industrial Revolution was progressing the call for free trade became stronger and stronger, particularly in Britain. The free trade activists in the textile industries of Lancashire fought the protectionists and appealed to the public that free trade would lead to an era not only of prosperity, but also of peace. In 1838 the Manchester Chamber of Commerce stressed "the true and peaceful principles of free trade".[27] Shortly before Great Britain finally turned to free trade in 1846 Richard Cobden's message was unambiguous: "I see in the Free Trade principle that which shall act on the moral world as the principle of gravitation in the universe – drawing men together, thrusting aside the antagonism of race, and creed, and language, and uniting us in the bonds of eternal peace. […] I believe that the effect will be to change the face of the world, so as to introduce a system of government entirely distinct from that which now prevails. I believe that the desire and the motive for large and mighty empires; for gigantic armies and great navies – for those materials which are used for the destruction of life and the desolation of the rewards of labour – will die away; I believe that such things will cease to be necessary, or to be used, when man becomes one family, and freely exchanges the fruits of his labour with his brother man. I believe that, if we could be allowed to reappear on this sublunary scene, we should see, at a far distant period, the governing system of this world revert to something like a municipal system; and I believe that the speculative philosopher of a thousand years hence will date the greatest revolution that ever happened in the world's history from the triumph of the principle which we have met here to advocate."[28]

The impact of Cobden's vision on the "pacific theory of international relations" can hardly be overestimated. Cobdenism became a well known term. The Oxford English Dictionary defined it as "a policy of advocating free trade, peace and inter-

---

25 M. Lutz-Bachmann and J. Bohman eds, *Frieden durch Recht. Kants Friedensidee und das Problem einer neuen Weltordnung,* Frankfurt am Main, 1996; O. Höffe ed., *Immanuel Kant. Zum ewigen Frieden,* Berlin, 1995.
26 On this see M. Schulz, *Normen und Praxis. Das europäische Konzert der Großmächte als Sicherheitsrat 1815–1860,* Munich, 2008. See also E. Conze, '"Wer von Europa spricht, hat Unrecht." Aufstieg und Verfall des vertraglichen Multilateralismus im europäischen Statensystem des 19. Jahrhunderts', *Historisches Jahrbuch* 121 (2001), 214–241.
27 Resolution by the Manchester Chamber of Commerce, 20 December 1838. N. McCord ed., *Free Trade. Theory and Practice from Adam Smith to Keynes,* Newton Abbot, 1970, 66.
28 Speech by Cobden in Manchester, 15 January 1846. Ibid., 73 f.

national cooperation".[29] Cobden was an outstanding representative of an international movement that developed the ideas of liberal internationalism.[30] The British peace movement, against the background of the political culture and the economic superiority of Great Britain, played the role of a forerunner. Richard Cobden was by no means a pure idealist. As a textile manufacturer he had vested interests in unhampered international trade. As a member of parliament he fought against the corn laws. As a peace activist he participated in the Universal Peace Congress in Paris in August 1849. There he not only denounced "warlike governments" and the "barbarous system which obstructs commerce, uproots industry, annihilates capital and labour." He also appealed to the merchants, manufacturers, traders, agriculturists and annuitants of civilized Europe" not to subscribe to any war loans: "My object is to promote peace by withholding the sinews of war."[31] The president of the congress was Victor Hugo, who in his key note speech envisaged not only the "United States of Europe", but also a transatlantic zone of peace. According to Hugo the idea of peace was part of the general idea of progress. "A day will come when the only battlefield will be the market open to commerce [...]."[32]

Although he never accepted a government position Cobden was involved in bringing about the Anglo-French commercial treaty of 1860 which liberalized trade between Britain and France. Cobden could rely on the backing by the Chancellor of the Exchequer. Gladstone pointed out to him that the treaty, in his view, was much more than an economic affair: "What I look to is the social good, the benefit to the relations of the two countries, and the effect on the peace of Europe."[33] When he justified the treaty in Parliament he did it not only with respect to the economic advantages. As the dominant economic power in Europe Britain had a vested interest in free trade. Gladstone also underlined the "political character" of the treaty: "The commercial relations of England with France have always borne a political character." Hence, Anglo-French relations were likely to benefit generally from a widening of economic exchange. Gladstone pointed out that trade had not only an international but also a transnational dimension. It contributed to "an union of the Governments" as well as to "an union of the nations". Furthermore, a rapprochement between Britain and France, "those two great nations whose conflicts have often shaken the world," will prove to be "beneficial to the world". A state of "harmony" between Britain and France "will of itself be at all times the most conclusive proof that neither of them can meditate anything which is

---

29 M. Ceadel, *The Origins of War Prevention. The British Peace Movement and International Relations 1730–1854*, Oxford, 1996, 11, 13 f. See also M. Ceadel, 'Cobden and Peace' in *Rethinking Nineteenth-Century Liberalism. Richard Cobden Bicentenary Essays*, eds. A. Howe and S. Morgan, Aldershot, 2006, 189–207.
30 W.H. van der Linden, *The International Peace Movement 1815–1874*, Amsterdam, 1987, 269 ff.
31 Ch. Chatfield and R. Ilukhina eds, *Peace/Mir. An Anthology of Historic Alternatives to War*, Syracuse, NY 1994, 109 f.
32 Ibid., 101.
33 H.C.G. Matthew, *Gladstone. Vol. 1: 1809–1874*, Oxford, 1988, 113.

dangerous to Europe."³⁴ When Prussia entered the Cobden system in 1862 Britain welcomed this step which antagonized Austria but seemed to clear the way for a Prussian supremacy by economic means. A peaceful solution to the struggle for hegemony in Germany would have led to an undisturbed development of the economy in Central Europe and would have served British interests in a liberal European market.³⁵

Peace activists of all kinds were necessarily vague with respect to the time span which was regarded necessary for overcoming the anarchy of the international system and achieving the peace for the 'global village'. Consequently, David Lloyd George did not feel inhibited to repeat Cobden's argument as late as 1908: "Free Trade is a great pacificator. [...] Free Trade is slowly but surely cleaving a path through the dense and dark thicket of armaments to the sunny land of brotherhood amongst the nations."³⁶ The international environment had changed fundamentally since the middle of the 19th century and Great Britain had fought a bitter war in South Africa only a few years before. But Lloyd George was right in pointing out that for decades Britain had not been at war with any major power. In particular, he could have mentioned the North Atlantic zone of peace with the United States and Great Britain as chief actors with great power status. Both did not have identical but, by and large, compatible interests. Since 1812 they had not waged war against one another. It was a long time before the idea of the 'special relationship' became a well known formula, but there was always something special in Anglo-American relations.³⁷ The leading powers of the Western world tried to develop specific procedures in order to avoid force in their bilateral relationships. A meaningful example was the solution of the Venezuela crisis when, in 1895, a conflict over the border between Venezuela and British Guiana arose and the United States intervened on the basis of the Monroe Doctrine. The crisis was resolved by a court of arbitration especially convened for that purpose. What is more important, however, this particular incident led to a general arbitration treaty between the United States and Great Britain in 1897. In the end it was rejected by the U.S. Senate. Nevertheless, it was a remarkable sign of a British-American rapprochement in the sense of a lasting peacable relationship. ³⁸

---

34   McCord, *Free Trade*, 116 f. On Gladstone's approach to international relations see M. Ceadel, 'Gladstone and a Liberal Theory of International Relations' in *Politics and Culture in Victorian Britain. Essays in Memory of Colin Matthew*, eds. P. Ghosh and L. Goldman, Oxford, 2006, 74 ff.

35   G. Metzler, *Großbritannien – Weltmacht in Europa. Handelspolitik im Wandel des europäischen Staatensystems 1856 bis 1871*, Berlin, 1997, 176 ff.

36   Speech in Manchester, 21 April 1908. D. Lloyd George, *Better Times. Speeches*, London, 1910, 43.

37   D. Reynolds, 'Anglo-American Relations Since 1607: Three Historical Paradigms' in *From Enmity to Friendship. Anglo-American Relations in the 19ᵗʰ and 20ᵗʰ Century*, eds U. Lehmkuhl and G. Schmidt, Augsburg, 2005, 13–27.

38   J. Dülffer, Der britisch-amerikanische Schiedsvertrag von 1897 – Ein Modell zur Neugestaltung der internationalen Beziehungen? *Amerikastudien* 27 (1982), 177–202. On the practice of peaceful conflict resolution in American-British relations see also the point made by Klaus Hildebrand who, incidentally, stresses the "Victorian illusions". K. Hildebrand, 'Die viktorianische Illusion.

Similar to Great Britain the United States was engaged in warfare on a limited scale. But the "imperial democracy"[39] was vitally interested in avoiding war on the great power level and preferred "informal" imperialism to new conquests. The U.S. was going to play an active role in the process of internationalism which shaped world politics. The commercial interaction was a significant feature of this process which was expected to contribute to economic growth and societal stability at home and to interdependence and peace internationally. When the Democratic Party won the presidential elections in 1912, Woodrow Wilson stood for a reduction of tariffs. On top of that, the new President took up the Cobdenite link between free trade and peace.[40] Cordell Hull, who at that time was a member of the House of Representatives and was to become Secretary of State in 1933, shared this view and stood out as a proponent of the liberal peace. He was convinced that "one could not separate the idea of commerce from the idea of war and peace" – a conviction to which he hold until the end of his term of office in 1944. Hull regarded "liberal commercial policies" as an "essential foundation of any peace structure."[41] When war came in Europe President Wilson added a new element to the classical liberal approach. He maintained that not only free trade but also the spread of democracy was an essential condition for peace. The United States entered the "Wilsonian century".

New elements in the construction of peace: democracy and international organizations

The First World War was a severe set-back for all sorts of non-governmental internationalism[42] and diplomatic efforts to avoid war.[43] The war changed the international system. With Great Britain in relative decline the United States became the leading Western power. The impact on the Western concept of peace was enormous. During the 19th century, when Britain was the dominant economic power, free trade had been top of the agenda. During World War I and for the rest of the

    Zivilisationsniveau und Kriegsprophylaxe im 19. Jahrhundert' in *Macht und Zeitkritik. Festschrift für Hans-Peter Schwarz zum 65. Geburtstag*, eds P. R. Weilemann, H. J. Küsters and G. Buchstab, Paderborn, 1999, 23 f.

39 E. R. May, *Imperial Democracy. The Emergence of America as a Great Power*, New York, 1973.

40 A. Howe, "Free Trade and the International Order: The Anglo-American Tradition 1846–1946', in *Anglo-American Attitudes. From Revolution to Partnership*, eds F. M. Leventhal and R. Quinault, Aldershot, 2000, 152. On the widespread belief in the civilizing function of trade and for some telling examples of the "liberal optimism about the basically peaceful thrust of commerce" see F. Ninkovich, *The Wilsonian Century. U. S. Foreign Policy since 1900*, Chicago, 1999, 21 ff.

41 C. Hull, Memoirs, vol. 1, New York, 1948, 84. See also ibid., 364 f.

42 M. Herren, *Hintertüren zur Macht. Internationalismus und modernisierungsorientierte Außenpolitik in Belgien, der Schweiz und den USA 1865–1914*, Munich. 2000.

43 J. Dülffer, *Regeln gegen den Krieg? Die Haager Friedenskonferenzen von 1899 und 1907 in der internationalen Politik*, Berlin, 1981; Dülffer, Kröger, Wippich eds, *Vermiedene Kriege*.

20th century there was a more radical approach to the construction of peace on Western terms. Henceforth, the formula 'peace by free trade' was only one side of the peace coin. The other side was 'peace by democracy'.

The central statement in President Wilson's war message of April 2, 1917 was short and unambiguous: "The world must be made safe for democracy." Addressing allies as well as adversaries Wilson dared to announce "the beginning of an age in which it will be insisted that the same standards of conduct and of responsibility for wrong done shall be observed among nations and their governments that are observed among the individual citizens of civilized states." The new age brought to an end "the old, unhappy days when peoples were nowhere consulted by their rulers." It could be conceived as an age without war because "self-governed nations" do not have aggressive designs on their neighbours. Consequently, "a steadfast concert for peace can never be maintained except by a partnership of democratic nations."[44]

Wilson's approach was a complete departure from the tradition of European diplomacy because it implied interference in the internal affairs of other states, and possibly the change of a political regime, by imposing democracy on the war-time enemy as a precondition for concluding peace. This was also a key argument during the Stockholm conference of Socialist parties in 1917. The introduction of democracy in Germany was declared to be a precondition for establishing peace with Germany.[45] When the American President, in January 1918, delivered his famous speech to Congress announcing the Fourteen Points as his "programme of the world's peace", he added a third element. Envisaging a "general association of nations" he proclaimed what recently was called "triangulating peace".[46] According to Wilson peace depended on the triangle with democracy as a crucial factor but only in combination with economic interdependence and membership in international organizations. With regard to the ending of the war Wilson refused to negotiate with the "military party and the men whose creed is imperial domination". Only the "spokesmen" of the "Reichstag majority" would be accepted in any future talks on peace.[47] From the German moderates' point of view it was promising that free trade was a central element in Wilson's statement. In July 1917 the majority parties of the *Reichstag* had already pointed out in their peace resolution that they regarded an "economic peace" as the essential basis for peaceful international relations.[48] At

---

44 W. Wilson, *War and Peace. Presidential Messages, Addresses and Public Papers (1917–1924)*. Eds R. S. Baker and W. E. Dodd, vol. 1, 1927, reprint New York, 1970, 11 f., 14. For a recent account see L. E. Ambrosius, 'Democracy, Peace, and World Order' in *Reconsidering Woodrow Wilson. Progressivism, Internationalism, War, and Peace*, ed. J. M. Cooper Jr., Washington, D. C., 2008, 225–249.

45 W. Geldolf, *Stockholm 1917. Camille Huysmans in de schaduw van titanen*, Antwerpen, 1996.

46 B. Russett and J. R. Oneal, *Triangulating Peace. Democracy, Interdependence, and International Organizations*, New York, 2001.

47 Speech by Wilson to Congress, 8 January 1918. Wilson, *War and Peace*, 159 ff.

48 For the text of the peace resolution G. Mai, *Das Ende des Kaiserreichs. Politik und Kriegführung im Ersten Weltkrieg*, Munich, 1987, 209 f.

the beginning of 1918 the adherents to the liberal school of thought were not in power in Germany. At that time the German leadership enforced a peace on Russia which was the exact opposite to a liberal peace.

The Treaty of Versailles was also far from being a liberal peace treaty too. However, it was a settlement which offered the prospect of peaceful change and the re-integration of Germany into great power diplomacy. At least the United States, together with Great Britain, had a strong interest in revising the peace treaty along liberal lines. The economic peace of the mid-1920s[49] and the admittance of Germany to the League of Nations indicated that the post-war order of Versailles could undergo peaceful change. Commenting on the incipient economic cooperation and political rapprochement of their countries, both the German and the French Foreign Minister, Gustav Stresemann and Aristide Briand, agreed that economic interconnection was a solid foundation for securing peace.[50] They maintained that unhampered economic exchange not only was dependent on peace but also was likely to create peace. During the 1930s, regardless of the turmoil of the Great Depression, the same argument was put forward by the British governments in support of their policy of appeasement. Although confronted by enemies of democracy, market economy, free trade and multilateral diplomacy, Great Britain continued to define its interests as the security of a trading state and pursued a policy of economic appeasement.[51] Trade with and credits for states like Japan, Italy or Germany were regarded as incentives to stay on the course of peace. Hopefully, Nazi Germany could be persuaded to slow down its armaments and to grow more powerful in Europe without going to war. To be sure, Great Britain pursued a double track strategy of peace *and* defence. But the appropriate military reaction to the German challenge came very late. It was delayed because of the imperial overstretch and the resulting British wish to avoid war. But it was also due to the long-standing belief in the pacifying function of economic interdependence.

Very much like the First, the Second World War proved to be a leap forward with respect to the concept of liberal and democratic peace. Again, the United States were all-important. The U.S. leadership not only appealed to the world. It was also prepared to use American money and power. A *Pax Americana* seemed to be the best foundation for world peace. President Franklin D. Roosevelt told the nation in December 1940 that Great Britain must not be left alone: "We must be the great arsenal of democracy".[52] In his annual message to Congress on 6 January

---

49 W. Link, *Die amerikanische Stabilisierungspolitik in Deutschland 1921–1932*, Düsseldorf, 1970; P.O. Cohrs, *The Unfinished Peace after World War I. America, Britain and the Stabilisation of Europe, 1919–1932*, Cambridge, 2006.
50 For a summary of recent research G. Niedhart, *Die Außenpolitik der Weimarer Republik*, 2nd ed. Munich 2006.
51 B.J. Wendt, *Economic Appeasement. Handel und Finanz in der britischen Deutschland-Politik 1933–1939*, Düsseldorf, 1971.
52 Statement by Roosevelt, 29 December 1940 (fireside chat on national security). The Public Papers and Addresses of Franklin D. Roosevelt 1940, New York 1941, 643.

1941, Roosevelt looked forward "to a world founded upon four essential human freedoms".[53] They reflected the basic elements of a liberal order both nationally and internationally. According to Cordell Hull, they "became the basis for our consideration of a future world order." In April 1941 Hull announced that the State Department was working "at the task of creating ultimate conditions of peace and justice."[54] Roosevelt's "Four Freedoms" were popularised by the publisher Henry R. Luce, who edited a number of influential magazines such as *Time* and *Life*. In February 1941, he published a kind of postscript to Roosevelt's recent address. The title of his celebrated essay was: "The American Century". According to Luce, the U. S. had a global destiny. The American century "must be a sharing with all people of our Bill of Rights, our Declaration of Independence, our Constitution. […] We are the inheritors of all the great principles of Western civilization. […] It now becomes our time to be the powerhouse from which the ideals spread throughout the world and do their mysterious work of lifting the life of mankind from the levels of the beasts to what the Psalmist called a little lower than angels."[55]

Finally, in August 1941, these American ideas appear in the key document on a supposedly liberal post-war order. The Atlantic Charter promised a "better future for the world" and looked forward to democratic governments ("the right of all peoples to choose the form of government under which they will live") and free trade ("enjoyment by all states […] of access, on equal terms, to the trade and the raw materials of the world").[56] When the Atlantic Charter was released the United States, although committed to the British cause, was not yet involved in the war. This changed after the Japanese attack on Pearl Harbor and the German declaration of war in December 1941. The structure of the post-war order soon became one of the main topics on the diplomatic level. Eventually, agreement was reached among the Allies on the main institutions: the United Nations, the International Monetary Fund and the World Bank.

The construction of peace on liberal and democratic terms envisaged a global approach. However, it turned out shortly after the war that the Soviet Union felt unable to accept a concept which on the one hand seemed to be useful with respect to the reconstruction of Europe, but which on the other hand served the interests of the United States and other countries of the Western world. Consequently, it was implemented only in Western Europe. The Marshall Plan, the OEEC/OECD, the West European integration and the democratization of West Germany were significant steps in the process of establishing a liberal und democratic zone of peace.

---

53 Ibid., 672.
54 Hull, *Memoirs*, vol. 2, New York, 1948, 1630.
55 A. Brinkley, 'The Concept of an American Century' in *The American Century in Europe*, eds R. L. Moore and M. Vaudagna, Ithaca, 2003, 11.
56 For the text of the Atlantic Charter see The Public Papers and Addresses of Franklin D. Roosevelt 1941, New York 1950, 314 f.

Most important in this success story was the transformation of West Germany into a democratic and civil society closely linked with the West.[57]

The Cold War prevented the liberal and democratic peace concept from becoming an all-European concept. When the East-West conflict entered the period of détente there was a new window of opportunity for expanding the West European zone of peace. Indeed, the *Ostpolitik* of the Federal Republic of Germany envisaged an increase in communication between East and West and aimed at the gradual transformation of the Eastern camp.[58] When détente, in the context of the Conference on Security and Cooperation in Europe, was pursued in a multilateral framework, Western ideas of international behaviour and political order were reluctantly accepted, at least in principle, by the Soviet Union. The CSCE process gradually changed East-West relations and was crucial for bringing the East-West conflict to a peaceful end (although not bringing history to its end).[59] Simultaneously, democracy was making headway, not only in Eastern Europe but also in Latin America[60] Washington, more than ever, regarded itself as the "city upon a hill". The collapse of communism seemed to open the gate for a worldwide march toward democracy and, consequently, peace. Bill Clinton, when campaigning for the presidency in 1991, argued that the future course of international relations depended on "how others govern themselves": "Democracies don't go to war with each other. [...] Democracies don't sponsor terrorist acts against each other. They are more likely to be reliable trading partners, protect the global environment, and abide by international law. Over time, democracy is a stabilizing force."[61] Clearly, Clinton positioned himself as Woodrow Wilson's heir. So did Clinton's successor when he launched not only an ideological crusade but also a war for democracy. Although practising different strategies both Clinton and Bush adhered to the same belief system, maintaining the interconnection of democracy and peace and declaring a liberal order as identical with the interests of the United States.

---

57   M. Zielinski, *Friedensursachen. Genese und konstituierende Bedingungen von Friedensgemein schaften am Beispiel der Bundesrepublik Deutschland und der Entwicklung ihrer Beziehungen zu den USA, Frankreich und den Niederlanden*, Baden-Baden, 1995.

58   See G. Niedhart and Oliver Bange, 'Die "Relikte der Nachkriegszeit" beseitigen. Ostpolitik in der zweiten außenpolitischen Formationsphase der Bundesrepublik Deutschland im Übergang von den Sechziger- zu den Siebzigerjahren', *Archiv für Sozialgeschichte* 44 (2004), 415–448.

59   P. Schlotter, *Die KSZE im Ost-West-Konflikt. Wirkung einer internationalen Institution*, Frankfurt/Main, 1998; D.C. Thomas, *The Helsinki Effect. International Norms, Human Rights, and the Demise of Communism*, Princeton, 2001; A. Wenger, V. Mastny and Chr. Nuenlist eds., *Origins of the European Security System. The Helsinki Process Revisited, 1965–75*, London, 2008.

60   On the interrelationship between the transformation to democracy and foreign policy H. Barrios, *Die Außenpolitik junger Demokratien in Südamerika. Argentinien, Brasilien, Chile und Uruguay*, Opladen, 1999.

61   Clinton in a speech at Georgetown University, 12 December 1991. Quoted by L. Roy, *Die Außenpolitik von Präsident William Jefferson Clinton*, Berlin, 2008, 472.

Conclusion: interests and visions

Many answers have been given to the age-old question how to abolish war and secure peace. The present paper is concerned with an answer which was given when the Western world came into being. Ever since, the liberal approach to the problem of peace and war has competed with the older balance of power concept. The liberal approach stood for modernity and challenged the old world of absolutism and mercantilism. The enlightened citizen participating in democratic politics and the entrepreneur permeating national borders and operating in a global market were supposed to be oriented toward international communication and the division of labour, rather than toward zero-sum games and war. The liberal school of thought envisaged the "bonds of eternal peace" (Cobden) and the "sunny land of brotherhood amongst the nations" (Lloyd George) whereas the realist theory with its pessimistic view of mankind considered that preparedness for war, without necessarily being bellicose, was inevitable. Liberals and realists had different notions of power. Liberals did not want to do without military power. But primarily their focus was on economic and financial power. Giving prominence to soft power, however, did not mean the end of the traditional hierarchy in international relations. On the contrary, the role of the great powers was to persist, even though with a clear preference for informal means of great power policy, for free-trade imperialism.[62] In 19th century Britain the liberal creed and the economic supremacy of the country went hand in hand. However, during the last third of the century severe doubts were voiced whether the *Pax Britannica* could be upheld simply by economic power and the preponderance of the British fleet. Lord Salisbury, Foreign Secretary between 1878 and 1880 and Prime Minister several times after 1885, castigated the optimism of the Manchester school. The Franco-Prussian war taught him the lesson, "that we must drive out the prophets of optimism".[63]

Neither the liberal nor the realist school of thought could prevent the catastrophe of the First World War. Nevertheless, both schools continued to claim the superiority of their approach. While the realists stuck to their well-known convictions, the liberal approach gained momentum. The United States of America decided the outcome of the war militarily and emerged as the dominant financial and economic power. Furthermore, President Wilson saw to it that there was a fresh start of the liberal peace concept. In his Fouteen Points he widened the liberal approach by adding two important components to the concept: democracy as a domestic pre-

---

62 B. Semmel, *The Rise of Free-Trade Imperialism. Classical Political Economy, the Empire of Free Trade and Imperialism 1750–1850*, Cambridge, 1970. See also the classical study Ronald Robinson and John Gallagher, 'The Imperialism of Free Trade', Economic History Review 6 (1953), 1–15.

63 Salisbury in an article for the *Quarterly Review* in January 1871. Chr. Hoyer, *Saisbury und Deutschland. Außenpolitisches Denken und britische Deutschlandpolitik zwischen 1856 und 1880*, Husum, 2008, 99.

requisitefor the renunciation of war and the League of Nations as an international institution dor securing peace. Wilson's triangle with its three interrelated factors (democracy, market economy and free trade, international organization) stood in sharp contrast not only to theadherents of *realpolitik* but also to Lenin's position. Since 1917 two variants of internationalism – liberalism and communism – fought "for the soul of mankind".[64] In the end communism did not succeed but the West could not win over every "soul". Given the low speed of the process of liberalization during the past 200 years this did not come as a surprise. After World War I it proved to be difficult to achieve a democratic transformation in Germany and finally hopes for the establishment of a parliamentary democracy were dashed. Following World War II Roosevelt's vision of a liberal *One World* was frustrated. Although the number of democracies with market economies increased, the liberal paradigm was strictly confined to the Western world with the transatlantic zone of peace as its nucleus. After the dissolution of the East-West conflict the central difficulty which is inherent in the liberal approach still exists. It "rests on the idea of universal progress"[65] but, due to cultural differences and conflicting interests, it is deeply resented in many parts of the world.

This does not suggest that "Kant's project"[66] should be given up. Rather it means that it must not be designed as an ideological crusade or as an attempt to pursue purely selfish economic and political goals. Furthermore, local peculiarities have to be taken into account as well as the time factor. Building peace zones based on the triangle of democracy, economic interdependence and international organizations means to walk on a "long-term path".[67] The protagonists of the liberal paradigm have to give more thought to the problem how the spread of human rights, democracy and a market economy can be accomplished without producing new conflicts. As Mikkel Rasmussen aptly puts it: "Democratic peace theory can explain what happens when the non-democratic state has joined the club, but it cannot describe the process of joining."[68]

---

64 M. P. Leffler, *For the Soul of Mankind. The United States, the Soviet Union, and the Cold War*, New York, 2007. See also M. P. Leffler, *The Specter of Communism: The United States and the Origins of the Cold War, 1917–1953*, New York, 1994.
65 Ninkovich, *Wilsonian Century*, 292.
66 J. Habermas, *Der gespaltene Westen*, Frankfurt am Main, 2004; E.-O. Czempiel, 'Der Friedensbegriff der Friedensforschung' in *Perspektiven der historischen Friedensforschung*, ed. B. Ziemann, Essen, 2002.
67 R. Paris, *At War's End. Building Peace after Civil Conflict*, Cambridge, 2004, 151 ff., 235.
68 Rasmussen, *The West*, 23.

Popes and Peace.
The 'Just War' Doctrine and Humanitarian Intervention in the 20th Century

ALFREDO CANAVERO

One of the most delicate interpretative tasks when studying the history of the Catholic Church in the 20th century is to provide a careful analysis of the inconsistencies between the great doctrinal statements of the Papal Magisterium and the concrete political and diplomatic choices of the Holy See.[1] As Renato Moro has pointed out, "discussing general theoretical statements is not the same as analyzing political and diplomatic choices; [...] examining the Ecclesiastical Magisterium is quite different from studying concrete decisions made by the Catholic Movement in civil society or by the Holy See itself in its international relations."[2] A survey of official papal statements on a given issue can nevertheless be useful if one takes a long view of changes in positions of Catholic leaders in response to changes in the world in which they were living.

An analysis that focuses specifically on the evolution of the attitude of the Holy See regarding a crucial issue such as peace and war in the present age promises therefore to be very interesting. Because of changes in the way wars are fought, the greater involvement of defenseless civilians, the exponential increase in human losses, the destruction resulting from the vastly increased power of modern weapons – which may eventually lead to the annihilation of mankind – and the advent of so-called asymmetric warfare and international terrorism, the traditional doctrine of the Church regarding war has been changing significantly, taking into account the sensibilities of public opinion and the growing attention to the issue of human rights.

---

1 Cf. R. Moro, *I cattolici italiani tra pace e guerra : dall'inizio del secolo al Concilio Vaticano II*, in *Guerra e pace nell'Italia del Novecento. Politica estera, cultura politica e correnti dell'opinione pubblica*, eds. L. Goglia, R. Moro and L. Nuti, Bologna, Il Mulino, 2006, pp. 359–361. Editorial supervision Scott McMurry.
2 *Ivi*, pp. 359–360.

The official doctrine of the Church was for a long time the theory of the "just war", whose origins can be found in the writings of Saint Augustine of Hippo and were later systematized by Saint Thomas.[3] This doctrine did not condemn war categorically; a few conditions (just reason, just cause and right intention) were established for a war to be considered legitimate. The Spanish Dominican Francisco de Vitoria later added a fourth condition: just wars had to be fought with suitable means[4]. Over the centuries several thinkers tried to explain the proper application of the criteria of a just war, but they were not completely successful. For example, Luigi Taparelli D'Azeglio, (1793–1862),[5] a Jesuit, held that the only way to achieve the end of all conflicts was to give the pope the role of an impartial judge presiding over international disputes. However, as this would have required a return to Catholicism in every European country, war continued to be regarded as an unavoidable necessity to restore the right moral order[6].

While the existence of the Papal States and the need to preserve their independence were important factors in Pius IX's actions and policies regarding the issue of war and peace[7], the loss of papal temporal power in 1871 and the ascension of Leo XIII to the papal throne soon led to changes in these areas. The new pope's diplomatic activity aimed at restoring the Holy See to its traditional place on the international stage. His efforts were successful: the German Kaiser and the King of Spain asked him to arbitrate a dispute between their states regarding the Caroline Islands.[8] This request gave the Holy See an opportunity to point out firmly the advantages that would ensue for the whole world if the papacy regained the role of supreme judge in international disputes. This was the concept that Leo XIII (Pecci) emphasized throughout his pontificate and explained well in his allocution *Nostis errorem* published in 1889[9]. This is also why Pope Pecci sought to transform the Holy See into one of the leaders of the Hague Peace Conference in 1899, although his attempt failed because of the opposition of the Italian Government, which feared that he would take advantage of the situation to bring up the Roman Question in the international assembly.[10]

---

3 Cf. Thomas Aquinas, *Summa Theologiae, Secunda Secundae*, quaestion 40 and *Sententia libri politicorum*, II, 14.
4 Cf. F. De Vitoria, *De jure belli*, ed. C. Galli, Roma – Bari, Laterza, 2005.
5 L. Taparelli D'Azeglio, *Saggio teoretico di diritto naturale appoggiato sul fatto*, 5 volumi, Livorno, Mansi, 1845.
6 Concering Taparelli's positions cf. D. Menozzi, *Ideologia di cristianità e pratica della "guerra giusta"*, in *Chiesa e guerra. Dalla "benedizione delle armi" alla "Pacem in terris"*, eds. M. Franzinelli and R. Bottoni, Bologna, Il Mulino, 2005, pp. 94–97.
7 Cf. *ivi*, pp. 98–101.
8 Cf. J.-M. Ticchi, *Aux frontières de la paix. Bons offices, médiations, arbitrages du Saint Siège (1878–1922)*, Roma, Ecole française de Rome, 2002, pp. 61–115.
9 Leo XIII, *Nostis errorem*, allocution during the consistory on February 11th 1889, in *Enchiridion della Pace*, 1, *Pio X – Giovanni XXIII*, Bologna, EDB, 2004, pp. 41–47, particularly p. 45.
10 Cf. J. Dülffer, *Regeln gegen den Krieg? Die Haager Friedenskonferenzen von 1899 und 1907 in der internationalen Politik*, Frankfurt – Berlin, Ullstein, 1981 e J.-M. Ticchi, *Aux frontières de la*

Although in a negative and a far more polemical tone, the same idea was endorsed again during Pius X's (Sarto) papacy. As the Church was no longer exercised temporal power, the pope could only pray to God to prevent the tragedy of war, since "there is nothing left for us to do at the moment."[11] This position was also expressed in Pope Sarto's exhortation to Catholics of the whole world at the outbreak of the First World War.[12]

Facing the enormous catastrophe of the First World War, Benedict XV decided to continue Leo XIII's diplomatic policy, though he preferred to give a traditional interpretation to the deeper causes at the root of the conflict: the war was a punishment for human sins, not for those committed by individuals, but for those of civil communities. As the pontiff pointed out, since governments had decided to ignore "the precepts and practices of Christian wisdom, […] the very foundations of states necessarily began to be shaken." The ultimate result was that "the end of civilization would seem to be at hand."[13] Catholic bishops in many countries supported this idea of the war as punishment for human sins and, in an attempt to justify the participation of their own countries in the war, blamed their enemies for it. Fighting was thus considered a legitimate and morally acceptable act.[14]

Facing a war in which Catholics were fighting Catholics, the pope had to assume an impartial position. The ideal of the Catholic Church was to promote and defend peace, and whenever peace was threatened, its first duty was to urge the belligerents to make peace. As Benedict XV stated in his first encyclical *Ad beatissimi Apostolorum Principis* (November 1st, 1914), war was not the right way to resolve international disputes: "Surely there are other ways and means whereby violations of rights can be rectified."[15] Likewise, on July 28, 1915 (two months after Italy entered the conflict, which was rapidly assuming a global dimension), he urged the warring countries to start peace talks as soon as possible[16]. Benedict XV openly condemned the war, which he eventually defined as a "useless slaughter" in the letter he addressed to the leaders of the belligerent countries on August 1, 1917.[17] Not only did his letter urge peace; it also outlined some conditions that would help preserve peace: simultaneous and mutual reduction of arms, instituting compulsory

---

paix, cit., pp. 201–237.
11 Pius X, *Libenter*, letter to the USA apostolic delegate, June 11th 1911, in *Enchiridion della Pace*, I, cit., p. 81.
12 Pius X, *Dum Europa*, exhortation to the Catholics of the entire world, August 2nd, 1914, *ivi*, p. 81.
13 Benedict XV, *Ad beatissimi apostolorum principis*, encyclical letter, November 1st, 1914, in *Enchiridion della Pace*, I, cit., p. 95.
14 Cf. D. Menozzi, *Ideologia di cristianità e pratica della "guerra giusta"*, cit. p. 118.
15 Benedict XV, *Ad beatissimi apostolorum principis*, cit., in *Enchiridion della Pace*, I, cit., p. 93.
16 Benedict XV, *Allorché fummo chiamati*, apostolic exhortation, June 28th, 1915, *ivi*, pp. 127–129.
17 Benedict XV, *Dés le début*, letter to the heads of the governments at war, August 1st, 1917, *ivi*, p. 153. Concerning the letter, cf. J.M. Ticchi, *Aux frontiéres de la paix*, cit., pp. 368–374.

international arbitration, freedom of communications routes and particularly of the seas, mutual renunciation of claims for war damage and expenditure.[18]

The Triple Entente regarded the pope's intervention as an attempt to aid the Central Powers – and above all the Catholic Austro-Hungarian Empire – after their position had become critical, and this was perceived as undue interference, as a failure of the Holy See to remain absolutely impartial in a conflict that set Catholics against Catholics. But neither did the Central Powers appreciate the pontiff's initiative. Most military chaplains tried to keep it secret, and the Dominican Antonin Sertillanges, an important member of the French clergy, firmly stated his rejection of the pope's efforts in a speech at the Madeleine Church in Paris on December 10, 1917[19]. As a matter of fact, what Benedict XV had proposed was not far from what the American president Wilson was soon to include in his Fourteen Points[20]. As Giorgio Rumi has pointed out, "although the pope was less ideological and closer to universal issues and the president more doctrinaire and aware of the importance of American intervention, both agreed on the necessity of renovating the system of international relations, achieving a just and enduring peace, and replacing the use of force with negotiation and respect for the rights of countries.[21] Unfortunately, the situation was unfavorable for a proper appreciation of the pontiff's efforts.

Benedict XV reaffirmed the necessity of a new international order in remarks he published shortly after the end of the war in his encyclical *Pacem Dei munus pulcherrimum* (May 23, 1920), where he expressed his longing for "one league, or rather a sort of family of peoples, designed both to maintain their own independence and safeguard the order of human society."[22] That was the only way to cut military expenditure without endangering the independence and integrity of each nation. This " League of Nations" had to be based on "Christian law in any of their undertakings, inspired by justice and charity,"[23] so as to create a real brotherhood of peoples, overcome "mutual rivalries and offences", and achieve a real and lasting peace.[24] The pontiff never actually mentioned the real League of Nations. He had put his trust in that organization at first, but his hopes had been disappointed. The Holy See had been excluded from the peace conference at the behest of Italy, and the peace treaties were turning out to be *diktat*, which the defeated countries

---

18 Benedict XV, *Dés le début*, cit., pp. 151–153. Regarding Benedict XV's activity to protect peace, cf. J. F. Pollard, *The Unknown Pope. Benedict XV (1914–1922) and the Pursuit of Peace*, Continuum International Publishing Group, New York 1999. See also *Benedetto XV e la pace – 1918*, ed. G. Rumi, Brescia, Morcelliana, 1990.
19 Cf. A. D. Sertillanges, *La Paix française, discours prononcé le 10 décembre 1917*, Paris-Barcelone, Bloud e Gay, [1918].
20 Cf. G. Rumi, *Benedetto XV e i Quattoridici Punti di Wilson*, in *Ricerche di storia in onore di Franco Della Peruta. Politica e istituzioni*, Milano, Angeli, 1996, pp. 485–496.
21 *Ivi*, p. 493.
22 Benedetto XV, *Pacem, Dei munus*, in *Enchiridion della Pace*, I, cit., p. 205.
23 *Ibidem*.
24 *Ivi*, p. 207.

of the First World War, still banned from the League of Nations, were forced to accept. The result was a precarious peace based on hatred and resentment. Yet Benedict XV did not deny the possibility of a collaboration of the Holy See with the Geneva-based international organization, which, as he was well-aware, had been welcomed by many Catholics.[25] But, as some articles in "Civiltà Cattolica"[26] showed, there were sections of the Roman Curia that seemed to distrust this institution, as it was completely secular and suspected of Masonic influences.

Pius XI was not as well-disposed towards the League of Nations as his predecessor had been. He defined his pontifical programme in the encyclical *Ubi arcano*, in which he stated that no human institution could ever "be as successful in devising a set of international laws which will be as in harmony with world conditions as the Middle Ages were in the possession of that true League of Nations, Christianity"[27]. The only possible peace was in Christ; the tragedy of war and the difficulty of achieving such a condition could be ascribed to the abandoning of Christian principles. Afraid that a peace based on hatred and the power of the strongest would not last long, the pope repeatedly stressed the tragic consequences of war, condemning the arms race and extreme nationalism"[28], "a condition which tends to exhaust national finances, waste the flower of youth, and muddy and poison the very fountainheads of life, physical, intellectual, religious, and moral."[29]

Most of Pius XI's writings during his pontificate bitterly condemned the arms race[30]. By reversing the Latin saying *si vis pacem para bellum*, the pontiff argued that peace could only be achieved if the community worked towards it, invoking and blessing such a condition: *si vis pacem, para pacem*. This was the starting point for him to redefine and limit the theory of just war. Weapons had now become so powerful that both losers and winners would suffer terrible losses, and more than ever it was now necessary to guarantee an enduring peace. The only way to do this was to acknowledge the primacy of Christ the King:

> If, therefore, the rulers of nations wish to preserve their authority, to promote and increase the prosperity of their countries, they will not neglect the public duty of reverence and obedience to the rule of Christ.[31]

---

25 Regarding the Church and the Catholics' attitude towards the League of Nations, cf. D. Menozzi, *Chiesa, pace e guerra nel Novecento. Verso una delegittimazione religiosa dei conflitti*, Bologna, Il Mulino, 2008, pp. 47–76.
26 See for instance E. Rosa, *La pace e la carità sociale nell'enciclica "Pacem Dei"*, in "Civiltà Cattolica" 71 (1920), 2, p. 514.
27 Pius XI, *Ubi arcano*, December 23rd, 1922, in *Enchiridion della Pace*, I, cit., p. 283.
28 *Ivi*, p 271.
29 *Ivi*, p. 265.
30 Cf. for instance Pius XI, *Nova impendet*, encyclical letter, October 2nd, 1931, *ivi*, pp. 372–379.
31 Pius XI, *Quas primas*, encyclical letter, December 11th, 1925, *ivi*, p. 347.

Peace had to be based on charity and international justice, and it implied that economic policy had to respect moral and divine laws, so that every people could have equal access to essential resources on earth. As Pius XI wrote in 1932:

> No leader in public economy, no power of organization will ever be able to bring social conditions to a peaceful solution, unless first in the very field of economics there triumphs moral law based on God and conscience.[32]

Fearing that the world could again experience a disaster like the First World War, a fratricidal conflict among Catholics, Pius XI wrote:

> Men who in every nation pray to the same God for peace on earth will not kindle flames of discord among the peoples; men who turn in prayer to the divine Majesty will not set up in their own countries a craving for domination; nor foster that inordinate love of country which of its own nation makes its own god.[33]

The arms race in the mid 1930s led the pontiff to appeal for peace once again, condemning those who preferred "war to peace" and quoting the passage "Dissipa gentes quae bella volunt"[34] from Psalm 67, which he again referred to a few months later during a secret consistory held on April 1, 1935[35]. Speaking to Catholic nurses on the eve of the Italian invasion of Ethiopia, Pius XI stated that a war whose aim was conquering land could not be a just war. Yet, this seemed far less explicit in the published version – manipulated by Mons. Tardini but almost surely checked by the Pope himself before granting the imprimatur – which seemed ultimately justify the invasion.[36]

Once the war was over, the pontiff could not avoid acknowledging the Italian conquest, and in his opening speech at the World Press Exposition at the Vatican, Pius XI said that the Exposition represented a moment of happiness in harmony "with the triumphant happiness of an entire people, both good and great, for a peace that aimed to and will hopefully be a valid coefficient and the prelude to real

---

32   Pius XI, *Caritate Christi compulsi*, encyclical letter, May 3rd, 1932, *ivi*, p. 401
33   *Ivi*, p. 395.
34   Pius XI, *Discorso al collegio cardinalizio, 24 dicembre 1934*, *ivi*, p. 431.
35   Pius XI, *Pergratus nobis*, allocution at the secret consistory in April 1st, 1935, *ivi*, pp. 441–443.
36   Pius XI, *Discorso alle partecipanti al Congresso internazionale delle infermiere cattoliche*, August 27th, 1935, *ivi*, p. 445. "If the need of expansion is something that must be taken into account, the right of defence has some limits and moderation that must be respected in order for defence to be blameless". On this matter cf. C. F. Casula, *Domenico Tardini (1888–1961): l'azione della Santa Sede nella crisi fra le due guerre mondiali*, Roma, Studium, 1988, pp. 384–386, who has published Tardini's diary. Also see L. Ceci, *Santa Sede e guerra d'Etiopia: a proposito di un discorso di Pio XI*, "Studi Storici", 44 (2003), 2, pp. 511–525 and Ead., *La mancata lettera di Pio XI a Mussolini per fermare l'aggressione all'Etiopia*, "Studi Storici", 48 (2007), 3, pp. 817–840.

European and world peace."³⁷ The League of Nations had been unable to guarantee peace and collective security, so the Holy See had to take cognizance of what had been happened. However, it was often pointed out that the Holy See had missed a chance to re-elaborate and adapt the doctrine of a just war to the times.

It was Eugenio Pacelli, formerly Vatican Secretary of State and Pius XI's designated successor, who had to face the tragedy of the Second World War, which was imminent. At first he adopted a diplomatic position to avoid the outbreak of the war; then he tried to negotiate a solution. The situation was in a way even more critical than that faced by Benedict XV. This war was not simply a war of conquest for colonial dominions (or, at least, this was not its main cause), but a conflict to assert a certain world view and impose it on those unwilling to accept it. The war was a clash between different – and opposite – conceptions of life, and after a few months it was clear that a peace based on a compromise would not be possible as long as Germany was ruled by the Nazi regime. This is why the Holy See, despite some vague attempts to encourage a peaceful solution during the first months of war, which some critics misunderstood and considered to be supporting Germany³⁸, realized it was better to develop other strategies. As Pius XII said to Roosevelt's representative, referring to Nazism but using words that also alluded to Soviet Communism:

> The principles that govern our hopes and our efforts for world peace have deep roots, and we will never approve of, and even less encourage a peace that would benefit those who would undermine Christian principles and persecute religion and the Church.³⁹

Pius XII continued to denounce the war through his encyclicals, speeches and radio messages. The consolatory message he intended to convey was that the pain caused by the war was meant "to purify people through the present-day suffering" which God was allowing in order to cause men to return to him.⁴⁰

Many questions have arisen concerning Pius XII's "silence" on Nazi atrocities and the Holocaust of the European Jews.⁴¹ Yet a careful reading of relevant papal documents shows that he often denounced and condemned those atrocities, although he

---

37 Pius XI, *Siamo ancora*, May 12th, 1936, in *Enchiridion della Pace*, I, cit., p. 451.
38 Pius XII, *Summi pontificatus*, October 20th, 1939, *ivi*, p. 719.
39 Pius XII to M. Taylor, September 22nd, 1942, *Actes et documents du Saint Siege relatifs a la Second Guerre Mondiale*, vol. V, doc. 476, pp. 693–694; also cf. *Sommario delle conversazioni tra Pio XII e Myron Taylor*, Città del Vaticano, September 19th, 22nd and 26th, 1942, in E. Di Nolfo, *Vaticano e Stati Uniti 1939–1952. Dalle carte di Myron C. Taylor*, Milano, Angeli, 1978, p. 184.
40 Pius XII, *In questa solennità*, radio message on the presence of divine providence in human events, June 29th, 1941, in *Enchiridion della Pace*, I, cit., p. 821.
41 On the matter cf. G. Miccoli's well-balanced summary in *I dilemmi e i silenzi di Pio XII. Vaticano, Seconda guerra mondiale e Shoah*, Milano, Rizzoli, 2000. Also see M. L. Napolitano, *Pio XII tra guerra e pace. Profezia e diplomazia di un papa (1939–1945)*, Roma, Città Nuova, 2002.

avoided assigning responsibility. Fearing a severe reaction by the Nazi regime and even more cruel reprisals, the pope resorted to diplomatic measures and avoided explicit – and counterproductive – public protests. For instance, his first encyclical *Summi pontificatus*, published shortly after the German invasion of Poland, alluded to "our dear nation" that "has a right to the world's human and brotherly sympathy" and was expected to rise again "in harmony with the principles of justice and true peace."[42] But Germany was not openly condemned as the aggressor.

The belligerents urged the Holy See to take their respective sides in the conflict. Although officially the Church had to take a neutral position, and this stance was often justified with vague reasons that national governments and churches exploited to justify their involvement in the conflict, it was clear that the Holy See was closer to Western democracies than to the totalitarian states.[43] In radio messages broadcast at Christmas 1941 and 1942 Pius XII not only expressed his longing for a new international order, but he also complained that the laws of war were being ignored,[44] and in 1944 he spoke up for democratic governments.[45] However, the pope's public statements were still cautious and too generic and, as noted earlier, it was easy for each party to claim and use them to their advantage and against their enemies. Thus it has been argued that the pope probably should have adopted a "more prophetic and less diplomatic" approach.[46]

Unable to do anything concrete to restore peace, Pius XII did his best to establish criteria that would keep it once restored. This is exactly what he did in his Christmas speeches and radio messages. In 1939 he outlined five key points for a just peace: ensuring every nation's right to life and independence; mutually agreed disarmament; reforming international relations, taking into account past experience to ensure the faithful observation of international treaties; respect for the real and just needs of all peoples and respect for the rights of ethnic minorities; a sense of proportion and responsibility on the part of governments.[47] Everything would be in vane if, as he stated in his Christmas radio message in 1941, the new international order were not "erected on the steady and immutable foundation of moral law, which the Creator Himself demonstrates through the natural order, and He Himself has engraved it in the heart of man in indelible characters."[48]

---

42   Pius XII, *Summi pontificatus*, October 20th, 1939, *ivi*, p. 719.
43   Cf. P. Pastorelli, *Pio XII e la politica internazionale*, in *Pio XII*, ed. A. Riccardi, Bari, Laterza, 1985, p. 128.
44   Radio messages *Nell'alba e nella luce*, December 24th, 1941, and *Con sempre nuova freschezza*, December 24th, 1942, in *Enchiridion della Pace*, I, cit., pp. 828–839 e 878–895.
45   Radio message *Benignitas et humanitas*, December 24th, 1944, *ivi*, pp. 968–981.
46   Cf. J. Hennesey, *La lotta per la purezza dottrinale di una Chiesa arroccata. Da Leone XIII a Pio XII*, in *Chiesa e papato nel mondo contemporaneo*, eds. G. Alberigo e A. Riccardi, Bari, Laterza, 1990, p. 162.
47   Pius XII, *In questo giorno*, speech to cardinals, bishops and prelates, December 24th, 1939, in *Enchiridion della Pace*, I, cit., pp. 734–743, particularly pp. 739–740.
48   Pius XII, *Nell'alba e nella luce*, cit., p. 834.

It seems as if throughout the war the pontiff was more interested in the creation of an international order that would guarantee a peaceful and prosperous future than in the mere ending of hostilities. Pius XII avoided taking advantage of the situation to condemn the war, for which Hitler was responsible, as unjust according to traditional Catholic doctrine. However, in 1944 he not only affirmed that a war aggression was unacceptable "as a legitimate solution for international disputes,"[49] but he also stated that "the theory of war as a suitable and measured way to solve international conflicts" was now out of date.[50] Thus he implicitly rejected the traditional theory and ended up condemning every war except those fought for purely defensive reasons. The appalling increase in the destructive power of modern arms, especially after the enormous power of the atomic bomb was fully understood, could only reinforce this conviction[51].

In the postwar era Pius XII's biggest concern was Communism, and this often influenced his views. He frequently denounced the tragic situation of the Church in countries that had come under the domination of the Soviet Union. For this reason he was accused of turning the Roman Catholic Church into a tool in the service of the United States and Western polices. Yet he did not soften his severe condemnation of Communism, which lead to the excommunication of all Catholics collaborating in communist organizations (July, 1st 1949). But he also took the opportunity to stress that neither the Communist world nor that part of the world that "loudly declares itself to be 'the free world'" were acting in accordance with the "Christian order," the essential precondition for peace.[52] Only the "Christian conception of a social order" could lead to peace, not the principle of free trade or absolute faith in economic policy. The lack of moral principles in international relations created the conditions for war. As the pope bitterly remarked, "the world is far from the order of God in Christ, which can guarantee a real and lasting peace,"[53] as if God had punished men's separation from Christ with "the scourge of a permanent threat to peace and the distressing nightmare of war."[54]

Although aware of the declining appeal of the Church in contemporary society, Pius XII continued to speak out on the issue of war and peace. The most complete formulation of his view of war dates from 1953, when he spoke to participants at the Fourth International Congress of Penal Law. Modern war, "not determined by an absolute necessity of defence," was a "crime" to be condemned by international criminal law.[55] Unfortunately the actions of "unscrupulous criminals" who did not hesitate to "cause a total war" for their own purposes (and it was evident whom

---

49   Pius XII, *Benignitas et humanitas*, cit., p. 976.
50   *Ivi*, p. 977.
51   Cf. D. Menozzi, *Chiesa, pace e guerra nel Novecento*, cit., pp. 169–177.
52   Pius XII, *Già per la decima terza volta*, Christmas radio message on December 24th, 1951, in *Enchiridion della Pace*, I, p. 1225.
53   *Ivi*, p. 1223.
54   *Ivi*, p. 1221.
55   Pius XII, *Nous croyons*, speech, October 3rd, 1953, *ivi*, p. 1267.

the pope was referring to) allowed resort to defensive measures, but the pope did not clarify whether atomic bombs could be considered such. Once he explained his position about the *jus ad bellum*, Pius XII devoted himself to *jus in bello*, stating that, even in case of "a just and necessary war", not all measures were justifiable, and he provided a detailed list of misdeeds to be sanctioned according to international convention.[56]

Speaking to military doctors a few days later, Pius XII returned to this topic, providing a clear limitation of the right to self-defence:

> Having to defend against injustice is not enough to justify the violence of war. When the damage it causes is incomparably greater than that caused by "tolerated injustice", we may be obliged to "suffer the injustice."[57]

The pope explained that this applied especially to atomic, biological and chemical weapons, which should be banned. He took advantage of further opportunities to explain this in detail, for example in his Christmas radio message in 1955, when he talked about the negative effects of nuclear testing – which had to be stopped – and expressed his longing for a prohibition of atomic weapons and for arms control.[58] But in his next Christmas' message, shortly after the Hungarian Revolution of 1956 and although still referring to the need for arms control, Pius XII did not consider war illegitimate when used as a means "for an effective defence, in the hope of a successful result when unfairly attacked". Under such circumstances, conscientious objection was not acceptable. And he refrained from openly condemning resorting to atomic weapons in such cases.[59]

John XXIII took up the issue of disarmament in his encyclical *Pacem in terris*, which broke with an age-old tradition, as it was not merely addressed to the Catholics but to "all men of good will." When the encyclical was published, the international situation seemed to have eased after tensions caused by crises over Formosa (Taiwan), Berlin and, above all, Cuba, although it was still clear that the world was threatened by the possibility of a nuclear catastrophe. John XXIII is known for having intervened in favor of a peaceful solution to the Cuban Missile Crisis, gaining great support among both Catholics and Communists[60]. Unlike his predecessor, whom the Soviets considered a warmonger close to the American "imperialists," John XXIII was regarded as a man of peace who was leading the Church with impartiality. This is why, along with the diplomatic skills of Cardinal

---

56 *Ivi*, p. 1269.
57 Pius XII, *Arrivés au terme*, speech to the participants to the 15th session of the International Documentation Office of Military Medicine, October 19th, 1953, *ivi*, p. 1299.
58 Pius XII, *Col cuore aperto*, Christmas radio message, December 24th, 1955, *ivi*, pp. 1414–1416.
59 Pius XII, *L'inesauribile mistero*, Christmas radio message, December 23rd, 1956, *ivi*, p. 1456.
60 Cf. G. Fogarty, *L'avvio dell'assemblea*, in *Storia del Concilio Vaticano II*, ed. A. Melloni, Bologna, Il Mulino, 1996, pp. 114–125.

Agostino Casaroli, the Holy See was able to initiate an *Ostpolitik* aimed at the development of relations with the Communist world.

The encyclical *Pacem in terris* (April 11, 1963) was written under these circumstances and edited together with Mons. Pietro Pavan.[61] War was condemned because in the atomic era "it no longer makes sense to maintain that war is a fit instrument with which to repair violations of justice."[62] On the contrary, international disputes had to be dealt with and resolved "under the mastery and guidance of truth, justice, charity and freedom."[63]

Several theologians wondered whether after such an encyclical it was still possible to endorse the old concept of a "just war", whereas others tried to limit its implications.[64] For the first time in a papal encyclical, John XXIII explicitly mentioned the United Nations[65] and praised its role in maintaining and consolidating peace and friendly relations among nations. Moreover, he recognized the importance of the Universal Declaration of Human Rights, which was adopted on December 10, 1948 and was "a step in the right direction, toward a juridical and political ordering of the world community"[66]. The encyclical was a landmark: not only was the Church trying to prevent wars it was also working to create men of peace[67].

However, it was during the Second Vatican Council that Church doctrine concerning war and peace was updated and organically systematized. The entire fifth chapter of the pastoral constitution on *The Church in the Modern World* (*Gaudium et spes*) was dedicated to the promotion of peace and of a community of peoples.[68]

---

61 On the composition and the structure of the encyclical, cf. L. Martini, *L'enciclica* Pacem in terris, in *Chiesa e guerra*, cit., pp. 621–640

62 John XXIII, *Pacem in terris*, in *Enchiridion della Pace*, I, cit., p. 1823. On the problems following the Italian translation published on "L'Osservatore Romano" ("it seems almost impossible to think that the war still aims at restoring the violated rights") which seemed to soften the Latin text ("Alienum est a ratione, bellum iam aptum esse ad violata iura sarcienda") cf. L. Martini, *L'enciclica* Pacem in terris, cit., pp. 624–632 and A. Melloni, Pacem in terris. *Appunti sull'origine*, in *Pacem in terris. Tra azione diplomatica e guerra globale*, ed. A. Giovagnoli, Milano, Guerini, 2003, pp. 141–142. Also cf. the translation proposed by G. Verucci, *Pace e guerra nelle linee dei pontificati di Paolo VI e di Giovanni Paolo II*, in *Chiesa e guerra*, cit., p. 685: "it is absolutely unreasonable to think that the war is employed to restore the violated rights".

63 John XXIII, *Pacem in terris*, in *Enchiridion della Pace*, I, cit., p. 1805.

64 Cf. L. Martini, *L'enciclica* Pacem in terris, cit., pp. 626–632.

65 However, the "United Nations" had been mentioned in the Christmas radio message on December 24th, 1948 (in *Gravi e ad un tempo*, in *Enchiridion della Pace*, I, cit., p. 1139), hoping they would be the "full and pure expression of this international solidarity of peace, deleting from its institutions and statutes every trace of its origin, which has necessarily been a solidarity of war!".

66 John XXIII, *Pacem in terris*, cit., pp. 1829–1831.

67 Cf. John XXIII, *Regi saeculorum*, allocuzione al premio Balzan, *ivi*, p. 1851. Also see M.-F. Furet, *Le désarmement, la paix et le nucléaire*, in *Le Saint Siège dans les relations internationales*, sous la direction de J.-B. D'Onorio, Paris, Les éditions du cerf – Editions Cujas, 1989, pp. 249–250.

68 *Costituzione pastorale sulla Chiesa nel mondo contemporaneo (Gaudium et spes)*, December 7, 1965, in *Sacro Concilio Ecumenico Vaticano II, Costituzioni, decreti, dichiarazioni*, ed. S. Garofalo, Milano, Ancora, 1967, pp. 630–646.

Peace was not simply defined as the "absence of war," but as an order based on justice. As it was explained, "peace is never attained once and for all, but must be built up ceaselessly."[69] It was therefore necessary to get rid of "the age old slavery of war," to declare the absolute banning of war.[70] This would only possible by establishing "some universal public authority acknowledged as such by all [countries] and endowed with the power to safeguard security, regard for justice, and respect for rights [of all nations]."[71] In the meantime it was fundamental to guarantee collective security, strengthen international conventions, limit armaments, especially nuclear arms, which could cause "massive and indiscriminate destruction."[72] It was also necessary to eliminate differences in the standard of living among various countries. This could be achieved easily by limiting armaments expenditure, a real "scandal" and "one of humanity's worst afflictions: "The arms race is an utterly treacherous trap for humanity, and one that ensnares the poor to an intolerable degree."[73] "Any act of war aimed indiscriminately at the destruction of entire cities or extensive areas along with their populations is a crime against God and man itself. It merits unequivocal and unhesitating condemnation."[74] This condemnation also extended to conventional weapons. Nevertheless, some Council fathers tried to soften the pope's declarations.[75]

Paul VI, who succeeded John XXIII in 1963, soon returned to the question of war and peace, approaching the views of the Catholic Church in a more practical way. In his first public message the day after his election (June 22, 1963) he stated that he would struggle to maintain peace among the peoples[76]. He dealt with this matter several times, in the encyclicals *Ecclesiam Suam* (1964), *Mense Maio* (1965), *Christi matri* (1966) and especially *Populorum progressio* (1967), but also in messages, letters and allocutions. The *Enchiridion of Peace* contains 114 statements by Pope Montini concerning peace. As U Thant, the Burmese statesman and Secretary-General of the UN at that time, said, Paul VI seemed to be "obsessed with peace." He did not limit himself to theoretical pronouncements but also started his pastoral trips as a "pilgrim of peace". In 1964 he visited the Middle East and Bombay, the United Nations in October 1965, Fatima and Turkey in 1967, Colombia in 1968, Uganda in 1969, the Philippines, Australia, Indonesia and Sri Lanka in 1970.

What was most striking and significant at the time was the pope's presence at the United Nations General Assembly. Unlike Pius XII, Paul VI expressed neither

---

69   *Ivi*, p. 631.
70   *Ivi*, p. 636.
71   *Ibidem*.
72   *Ivi*, p. 634.
73   *Ivi*, p. 636.
74   *Ivi*, p. 635.
75   Cf. on the matter G. Turbanti, *Il tema della guerra al Concilio Vaticano II*, in *Chiesa e guerra*, cit., particularly pp. 588–595.
76   Paul VI, *Qui fausto die*, radio message, June 22nd, 1963, in *Enchiridion della Pace*, vol. II, *Paolo VI - Giovanni Paolo II*, Bologna, EDB, 2004, p. 1873.

certainties nor condemnations, and he did not appeal to natural or divine right. He did not consider himself a "teacher" in front of the United Nations Assembly, but rather as an "expert in humanity"[77] and willing to give voice to "the poor, the dispossessed, those who suffer, and those who long for justice, dignity of life, freedom, welfare and progress."[78]. Quoting John Kennedy, he solemnly stated: "Never again one against the other, never again!"[79] and "It is peace, peace that must guide the destiny of the peoples and of all humanity!"[80]

In order to achieve real peace it was necessary to eliminate gaps in the different standards of living of each country as well as the "scandal" of glaring inequality. Paul VI held that it was first of all important to "fight against misery and injustice,"[81] to work towards the common good and peace among men and nations. As he observed in *Populorum progressio*, "development is the new name for peace."[82]

As far as institutions were concerned, Paul VI established a specific office within the Holy See – the Pontifical Commission "Iustitia et Pax" – in 1967, which became the Pontifical Council for Justice and Peace in 1988, with the aim of promoting the progress of the poorest countries and encouraging distributive justice among nations. In December of the same year he also declared that January 1st would be celebrated as the World Day for Peace, a day to pray, meditate, study and promote peace in the world. In his annual messages, Paul VI developed a "peace pedagogy" meant to contrast with the culture of war, which he urged every nation to repudiate.[83] He was also known for his numerous initiatives to promote peace, such as the letter he wrote to the governments of the countries fighting in Vietnam in 1965, calling upon them to stop that cruel conflict, a war he often mentioned in his public statements[84] and which he also sought to end through more secret diplomatic activity.[85]

During Paul VI's pontificate, the Holy See worked to expand its diplomatic activity. The number of papal *nunciatures* went from 61 to 109, and of *internunciatures* from 13 to 54, and apostolic delegations were established in almost every country. A permanent Vatican mission was also established at the UN and was soon extended to various specialized UN agencies (after the one at FAO in 1948 and the one at UNESCO in 1951). The Holy See began to take part in international conferences, at

---

77 Paul VI, *Au moment de prendre*, speech at United Nations Assembly, October 4th, 1965, *ivi*, p. 1971.
78 *Ivi*, p. 1973.
79 *Ivi*, p. 1977.
80 *Ibidem*.
81 Paul VI, *Populorum progressio*, March 26th, 1967, *ivi*, p. 2199.
82 *Ibidem*.
83 Cf. J.-Y.Rouxel, *Le Saint Siège su la scène internationale*, Paris, L'Harmattan, 1998, pp. 181–182.
84 The letters have been published in *Enchiridion della Pace*, II, cit., pp. 2072–2079. Cf. A. Saccoman, *La Civiltà Cattolica e la guerra del Vietnam (1965–1973)*, in *Al di là dei confini. Cattolici italiani e vita internazionale*, Milano, Guerini, 2004, pp. 86–87
85 Cf. the documents included in *Foreign Relations of the United States, 1964–1968*, vol. XII, *Western Europe*, Washington, U.S. Government Printing Office, 2001, pp. 636–669.

first only as an observer and then as a full participant. Its presence at the Helsinki Conference on Security and Cooperation in Europe (1973–1975), signed by every European country (except Albania) along with the USA and Canada, was extremely important. Paul VI's strong desire to be part of the conference met with negative reactions from some of his collaborators. To the pope, the conference was not only about defending the principle of religious freedom, which was certainly important; it was also a way to work together with various countries towards peace, in the hope of providing an example that would soon be followed by the whole world.[86]

Peace was the core of John Paul II's pontificate. In his annual messages on the World Day for Peace, the pope firmly condemned resorting to war, stressing the importance of educating the world to peace. His first message was extremely clear:

> Let us pray therefore: Deliver us from war, from hatred, from the destruction of human lives! Do not allow us to kill! Do not allow use of those weapons which serve death and destruction and whose power, range of action, and precision go beyond any limits previously known. Do not allow them to be used ever![87]

Some of the topics John Paul II often broached were the arms race, the necessity of dialogue, the search for peaceful solutions and for a way to eliminate the economic inequalities existing among peoples. In the last years of his pontificate he also promoted a campaign to cancel the debts of the world's poorest nations in order to create better conditions for their development. John Paul II favored a discussion of peace that took into account human dignity and rights. He held responsible for the violation of such rights both Communist regimes, because of their refusal to respect religious freedom, as well as capitalist countries, because of their excessive individualism and their almost exclusive emphasis on the primacy of economic, material factors in human and international relations. He proposed a World Day of Prayer for Peace, inviting representatives of every religion and emphasizing common aspects and their points of contact with Christianity.[88]

Pope Wojitiła did not have to face enormous tragedies comparable to the two world wars, but he had to deal with more than 130 local conflicts. The Holy See often intervened effectively with its good offices. This was possible because of the great popularity and esteem recent pontiffs had been accorded. In some cases, the Holy See was also called upon to resolve disputes, as in its arbitration between Chile and Argentina concerning the possession of some islands in the Beagle Channel

---

86 Cf. Paul VI, *En juin 1973*, letter to Agostino Casaroli, July 25th, 1975, in *Enchiridion della Pace*, II, cit., pp. 2513–2519.
87 John Paul II, *Anno 1979*, homily for the XII World Day of Peace, January 1st, 1979, *ivi*, p. 2607.
88 John Paul II, *In concluding*, speech done in Assisi, October 27th, 1986, in *Enchiridion della Pace*, II, cit., pp. 3172–3182.

(1984).⁸⁹ But there were other cases in which the pope had to take a stand and express his views in his speeches, encyclicals or letters.

As already pointed out in this article, John Paul II deprived "war of any possible religious endorsement."⁹⁰ During the crisis that led to the Gulf War in 1991, the pope firmly condemned both the Iraqi invasion of Kuwait⁹¹ and the war itself:

> Nowadays "humanitarian reasons" demand that we firmly and absolutely banish war and foster peace as a supreme value to which every program and every strategy must be subordinated.⁹²

On January 15, 1991 the pope wrote a letter to the presidents of the USA and Iraq⁹³ proposing a peace conference to eliminate obstacles to peaceful co-existence in the Middle East. He considered the outbreak of war there almost a personal failure, and the only thing he could do was to try to convince the belligerents to end the conflict as soon as possible. During a meeting with cardinals and bishops of the Near and Middle East, he pointed out that the war was not a religious conflict, and there could be no "holy wars", since "the values of love, brotherhood and peace spring from faith in God and require dialogue and a willingness to meet with one's enemies."⁹⁴

The Yugoslav Wars and the conflict in Kosovo were even harder to understand and classify. They were not wars of invasion but conflicts in which populations and ethnic groups were being attacked and deprived of their basic rights in order to achieve what was termed "ethnic cleansing". Traditional international law was inadequate to cope with the crisis. John Paul II appealed for peace several times and he also encouraged humanitarian intervention to put an end to the tragedy. On December 5, 1992, at the opening of the World Conference on Nutrition, he said:

> The conscience of humanity, now supported by humanitarian international law, demands that humanitarian intervention be made mandatory whenever the survival of populations or of entire ethnic groups is seriously

---

89 Cf. G. Montalvo, *Le Saint Siège, médiateur de paix entre l'Argentine et le Chili*, in *La diplomatie de Jean Paul II*, sous la direction de J.-B. D'Onorio, Paris, Les éditions du Cerf, 2000, pp. 203–220 and G. Apollis, *La médiation internationale du Pape Jean-Paul II dans l'affaire du Canal de Beagle*, in *Le Saint Siège dans les relations internationales*, cit., pp. 323–361.
90 G. Miccoli, *Conclusioni*, in *Chiesa e guerra*, cit., p. 727.
91 John Paul II, *L'echange traditionnel*, speech to the members of the diplomatic corps, January 12th, 1991, in *Enchiridion della Pace*, cit., p. 3629.
92 *Ivi*, p. 3631.
93 Message *I am deeply concerned* to Saddam Hussein and *I feel the pressing duty* to George Bush, January 15th, 1991, *ivi*, pp. 3634–3639.
94 John Paul II, *Pemettez moi*, speech to the cardinals and the bishops of the Near and Middle East, March 6th, 1991, *ivi*, p. 3649. On the repudiation of the holy war cf. D. Menozzi, *Chiesa, pace e guerra nel Novecento*, cit., pp. 314–319.

threatened. It is the duty of every nation and the international community.[95]

A new doctrine was being defined, the obligation of the international community to intervene to prevent violations of the rights of whole populations and ethnic groups. Pius XII had already condemned wars of aggression, stressing that the world could not remain indifferent when "a people are victims of aggression." This had legitimized wars of defense, but the pope added that "the solidarity of the family of peoples forbids others to be mere spectators, assuming an attitude of impassive neutrality."[96] This position was reaffirmed during John Paul II's papacy, and the new *Catechism of the Catholic Church* recognized the right of an attacked country to defend itself using arms[97]. Pius XII had simply considered the possibility of aggression among established states, but John Paul II expanded what his predecessor had said to include threats to national minorities and their rights. When negotiations failed to resolve a dispute, if "entire populations are about to fall victim to aggression", the international community was obliged to intervene and disarm the aggressor.[98] This was not simply reaffirmation of the right to self-defense but also a moral obligation for the whole international community[99].

Some critics pointed out that the humanitarian intervention the Holy See appealed for would violate the sovereignty of individual states. The reply was that, as individual countries proclaimed themselves defenders of human rights, those who did not respect such rights excluded themselves from the international community and therefore allowed the international community to intervene to restore justice. This transformed single states into the international community. And such intervention could only be exercised if authorized by international organizations responsible for protecting peace and legality among the various states. Moreover, such intervention would be done to guarantee fundamental rights and the existence of peoples, ethnic groups or populations, and not to affirm the principle of "might makes right" or to expand a nation's territory. Obviously this implied reconsider-

---

95 John Paul II, *J'ai accueilli*, speech, December 5th, 1992, in *Enchiridion della Pace*, II, cit., p. 3893. On the distinction between "humanitarian meddling", which does not imply recurring to the armed forces, and "humanitarian intervention", which can exploit them cf. P. Consorti, *L'avventura senza ritorno. Pace e guerra fra diritto internazionale e magistero pontificio*, Pisa, Edizioni Plus, 2004.

96 Pius XII, *Gravi e ad un tempo*, Christmas radio message, December 24th, 1948, in *Enchiridion della Pace*, I, cit., p. 1140.

97 "A war of aggression is intrinsically immoral. When such a tragedy occurs, the leaders of the assaulted nations have the right and the duty to organize their defense even resorting to arms". *Catechismo della Chiesa Cattolica*, Città del Vaticano, Libreria Editrice Vaticana, 1992, n. 2265. The detailed conditions for the usage of strength are listed in the next point (2309).

98 John Paul II, *Au seuil de l'année 1993*, speech to the member of the diplomatic corps, January 16th, 1993, in *Enchiridion della Pace*, II, cit., p. 3953.

99 Cf. Pontificio Consiglio della Giustizia e della Pace, *Compendio della dottrina sociale della Chiesa*, Città del Vaticano, Libreria Editrice Vaticana, 2005, p. 276.

ing the concept of the state and its absolute sovereignty; the world ought to be considered as a large family based on justice and solidarity and not on bullying competition or the power of the richest and strongest.[100]

This doctrine is still being elaborated, and it requires a more effective international order. Some questions are still open, for instance the relationship between humanitarian intervention and preventive war, particularly with regard to terrorism. As "terrorism is based on contempt for human life" and is therefore "a real crime against humanity," there is a "right to defense against terrorism"[101]. But does this allow preventive war? John Paul II's words to the accredited diplomatic corps at the Vatican in January 2003 – on the eve of the Second Gulf War – seemed to deny such a possibility.[102] This position is thus a further limitation of the idea of a just war, which, albeit only under particular circumstances, is still valid, as well as a step forward "in that tormented process of the religious delegitimizing of war which marked the 20th century."[103]

---

100 Cf. C.M. Martini, *Pace*, in *Dizionario di dottrina sociale della Chiesa. Scienze sociali e Magistero*, edited by the Centro di ricerche per lo studio della dottrina sociale della Chiesa, Milano, Vita e Pensiero 2004, pp. 94–107.
101 John Paul II, *The World Day of Peace*, message for the XXXV Day of Peace, December 8th, 2001, in *Enchiridion della Pace*, II, cit., p. 4607.
102 John Paul II, *Heureuse tradition*, speech to the diplomatic corps, January 13th, 2003, *ivi*, p. 4703: "War can never be considered as a kind of measure to regulate the disputes among the nations. […] War cannot be used, not even to ensure common good, except as the last resort and only respecting rigorous conditions".
103 D. Menozzi, *Chiesa, pace e guerra nel Novecento*, cit., p. 319.

Gandhi, Hindu Traditions, and Twenthieth-Century Indian Political Culture

Sumit Sarkar

On 30 January 1948, Gandhi, the deeply religious Hindu who led the largely non-violent Indian freedom movement against British rule, was murdered for his 'treachery' to the 'Hindu nation' by a very different kind of Hindu, a disciple of the Hindu nationalist ideologue V. D. Savarkar. The intellectual heirs of Savarkar dominated the Indian Government between 1998 and 2004, and though defeated electorally in May 2004, remain a formidable force in Indian political, social and cultural life. Within a few weeks of their coming to power in New Delhi, India was made into a nuclear state. Savarkar's portrait was installed in the hall of Parliament, amidst the pantheon of national heroes, even though he had been an accused in the judicial investigation of Gandhi's murder, and doubts persist about his complicity despite acquittal on the ground of inadequate evidence. And, by a supreme irony, Gandhi's home-state of Gujarat has become the principal laboratory of such 'Hindutva' political culture, as manifested in a state-sponsored bloody anti-Muslim pogrom in 2002 and intermittent persecution of Christians.

My paper will seek to explore a few among the many ramifications of this extremely tangled, paradoxical, and contradictory history, highlighting their linkages with some of the guiding themes suggested for our panel. The title demands a look, first, at the degree to which Gandhian thought was embedded within 'Hindu traditions', and I intend to suggest that understanding of such questions is often simplified or hindered by one or other kind of 'orientalising' homogenisation. More directly relevant for our subject today would be the ways in which the heritage of Gandhian ideology and practices raise the problem of 'self' and 'other(s)'. Here, I shall argue, lay perhaps the most distinctive feature of Gandhian values, the point where they are diametrically opposed to the ways of 'Hindutva'. A second theme would be the question of possible conflicts between the imperatives of 'peace' (in Gandhian terms, non-violence, i.e. *ahimsa*) and political, social, and economic justice. This will require some consideration of the degree of efficacy of Gandhian strategies, geared as they were towards achieving a difficult, shifting balance between rejection of extreme or total confrontations, and bringing about changes in unjust and unequal relationships between Indians and their colonial rulers, as well as between varied sections among Indians themselves. A brief concluding theme will touch upon the abiding appeal of select elements of the Gandhian heritage, even within the sub-continent itself despite the obvious repudiations, and much more so abroad in recent times.

Gandhi's personal piety was beyond question, particularly his deep commitment to certain devotional (*bhakti*) forms of Hinduism. He even insisted that he was a Hindu of the *sanatani* (orthodox) kind, and that the ideals and methods he was propagating comprised the true essence of traditional Hinduism.[1] It has been natural, therefore, to jump to the conclusion that Gandhism was deeply embedded within Hinduism in ways unique to its ethos. This, however, is a totally untenable position, given the immense variety and highly changeable nature of Hindu traditions, so much so that many historians think that speaking of it in the singular prior to the colonial era is itself an error constituted largely by 'Orientalist' ways of constructing the non-West. It is quite unhistorical also to assume that Hindu traditions have been somehow uniquely pacific and non-tolerant, so that Gandhian *ahimsa* (non-violence) embodied its values in a seamless manner. Plurality is not necessarily identical with toleration, given particularly the vast and varied geographical and social spaces of a subcontinent, and the many *sampradayas* (communities, sects) generally termed 'Hindu' have often had quite authoritarian internal disciplinary structures and been mutually hostile occasionally to the point of violence. There has been no lack of violence in Indian history, even apart for the 'quiet' violence of caste oppression. At the level of ideals, too, advocacy of non-violence has been only one among many traditions, and once again claims to any Indian or Hindu exceptionalism need to be rejected. *Ahimsa* was more central to Buddhists or Jains, minority religions swamped or marginalized by Brahmannical Hindu currents in the early centuries of the common era. In the latter, with its hierarchised, fourfold notion of the goals of man as well as of human beings themselves, non-violence might be virtuous for the ascetic or renouncer, but not for the Kshatriya warrior. Gandhi himself was quite clear-sighted about such matters, and once rebuked C. F. Andrews for arguing that non-violence had been central to all major Indian religious texts: 'I see no sign of it in the *Mahabharata* and the *Ramayana*, not even in

---

[1] Though it is possible that such insistence was more common in certain periods of his life and less in others; it would be a serious, though common, mistake to present Gandhi and his ideas as timeless or unchanging. Thus Bhikhu Parekh reminds us that in his early years in South Africa Gandhi had been accused sometimes of being a 'crypto-Christian'. There was a degree of tactical back-tracking, Parekh suggests, during his early years back in India, and in the mid-1920s the highly orthodox Madan Mohan Malaviya was very close to him. This changed quite significantly from the 1930s onwards, with Gandhi insisting on the absolute primacy of ending Untouchability and fighting Hindu-Muslim violence (what in Indian English is called 'communalism'), issues which made many orthodox Hindus oppose him vehemently, eventually to the point of assassination. See B. Parekh, *Colonialism, Tradition and Reform: An Analysis of Gandhi's Political Discourse*, New Delhi, 1989.

my favourite Tulsidas'.[2] Many other aspects of Gandhian thinking and practice were equally in large part non-traditional, notably his total rejection of untouchability (certainly an integral part of most Hindu traditions for many centuries), insistence on the value of service-oriented social activism and manual work for everyone, and extolling of 'feminized' or androgynous ways over conventional masculinity. Parekh suggests that his became 'a way of reforming tradition by traditionalizing reform'.[3] Unlike most reformers, of whom there had been many in the nineteenth century, however, Gandhi seldom used textual exegesis to justify the changes he was advocating without calling them such. His comments on sacred texts were in fact at times remarkably 'modern', rationalistic, and individualistic. In effect, he used his great reputation and saintly aura to pick and choose among them and interpret them by something like an inner light. In a controversy with orthodox groups in 1920–1 that developed over Gandhi's insistence that untouchables had to be admitted to the national schools which had broken away from the official system, he roundly declared that he had little Sanskrit, had read only a few texts in vernacular translations, but was confident about the true method of reading. In that, 'the *shastras* (texts, scriptures) were not above reason', and all authority deserved to be rejected if it conflicted with 'sober reason or the dictates of the heart'.[4]

Gandhi's anti-Westernism has also been somewhat exaggerated. He repeatedly sought to clarify that he was not opposed to everything coming from the West, but only to 'modern', industrial civilization, which he branded as sunk in the worship of money and incorrigibly violent. He admired, and clearly learned from, Christian activist, social service-oriented ethics, despite occasional suspicion about Christian proselytisation. Even within the culture of the chronologically modern West, Gandhi was full of praise for many thinkers, and proclaimed his indebtedness to them, notably Tolstoy, Ruskin, Thoreau and Emerson.[5] And the critique of industrial civilization at the heart of Gandhism clearly owed far more to the modern Western romantic traditions going back to Rousseau, than to anything in Indian thought, ancient or recent. Indian religious revivalists and conservatives generally did not reject the material achievements of the modern West, but claimed that ancient Hindu India had anticipated all such inventions (not excluding aircraft!). Gandhi's was an utterly different take on such questions.

Gandhian thought and praxis is rooted in a rejection of all assumptions of total and irreconcilable difference, Otherness, inevitable and permanent conflict – both between Indians and their British rulers, and among Indian themselves along lines

---

2   Cited in Vidal, *Violence and Truth: A Rajasthani Kingdom Confronts Colonial Authority*, Delhi, 1997, 225.
3   Parekh, *Colonialism*, 225.
4   *Collected Works of Mahatma Gandhi* (henceforth CW), Volume XIX, Delhi, 1964, 328 ('Who is a Sanatani Hindu?', *Navajivan*, 6 February 1921).
5   For a careful analysis of the many sources of Gandhian thought, see Anthony J.Parel's Introduction to Gandhi; A.J. Parel, *Hind Swaraj*, Cambridge, 1997, xxxii-l.

of religious communities, castes, classes, ethnicities, gender. The polar opposite to Gandhism came to be embodied ideologically in most succinct form in Savarkar's *Hindutva (Who Is A Hindu,* 1923) and organizationally in the Rashtriya Swayamsevak Sangh founded in 1925. While at times parading its adherence to the glorious Hindu past, this is in fact as non-traditional – only in a diametrically opposite manner. Central to it is the goal of a Hindu nation and nation-state (*Hindu Rashtra*), which would be quite 'modern' in most ways, but in which only those whose religion, values and culture derive from within India can be true patriots and full citizens. As Savarkar had argued in 1923, only Hindus have an identity of 'fatherland' with 'holy land', and so become superior to Muslims, Christians, and whoever else might have ideals and values that had originated in other lands. And the relations with these Others, in the Hindutva tradition, are conceptualized in terms of inevitable conflict and hostility, a Social Darwinist struggle for existence and mastery.

At stake here, then, are two diametrically opposed ways of dealing with conflict in society, and it is not accidental that the central text of Gandhian thinking, *Hind Swaraj* (1909), was written in significant part as a response to an encounter its author had just had in London with a group of expatriate Hindu nationalists committed to the violent overthrow of British rule through terrorist violence and conspiracy, among whom Savarkar was a leading figure.

Discussions of conflict, violence, and peaceful resolution of tensions, of the kind inevitably generated by any study of Gandhian ideals and methods, need to avoid the twin dangers of excessive specificity and banal generalization. Depending on our values and politics, it has been easy to pick on the conflict and violence generated by one type of oppressive relationship: class and colonial domination, for much of the twentieth century, but nowadays increasingly also ethnicity/race, gender, caste, real or alleged religious injustice. Utopias then get visualized, achievable by radical inversion, transformation, at times extermination, of that one 'basic' structure and its representatives, if need be (at times, even preferably!) through a 'cleansing' phase of violence. Ethical and human questions concerning the methods being used become secondary. Late twentieth-century history, however, has been extremely cruel towards even the most progressive and generous of such hopes, and has highlighted, more and more, even in the best possible cases, the phenomena of victims of violence becoming its perpetrators, the oppressed turning oppressors, the unleashing of cycles of ever-intensifying mutual violence. One does not need to be a pacifist or full-fledged Gandhian today to acknowledge the dire need to problematise such more general issues, move towards a more phenomenological analysis of violence that to some extent would be cross-cultural and across times, and not stop with a discussion of its efficacy or otherwise in a particular situation.

But the opposite, over-generalized extreme also has its problems, for it can degenerate into platitudes about conflict and violence as the inevitable and eternal human condition, passive, mournful contemplation about the pain it always produces, and the reiteration as counterpoint of abstract, moral or spiritual principles that are presumed to be similarly eternal and unchanging. I do not think we can afford to give up the discipline of historical context, while at the same time reaching beyond its specificities to raise wider ethical and philosophical problems. What then gets missed out are the links between conflict, violence, and particular types of oppressive social structures (class, gender and family, caste, colonial and/or racial, etc) that can be conceptually distinguished from each other, but are most often interrelated and interpenetrating in complicated ways. Retaining an awareness of such linkages is vital, because otherwise we might be running away from a recurrent, most vital problem: how non-violence can be kept from degenerating into a defence of the (usually) oppressive status quo, how rather one should seek to combine rejection or at least an uninterrupted critique of violence with building up effective pressures for substantial changes, and, ideally, structural transformations.

Over-generalization can lead also to an elision of a fundamental feature of specifically modern societies: the simultaneous development of forms and levels of violence impossible and unimaginable earlier, and rise of projects, and ultimately movements, for peace and non-violence. The Revolutionary and Napoleonic Wars inaugurated the notion of 'nations in arms': these roughly coincided with Kant's *Project for Perpetual Peace* (1795). The technological dimensions here are very obvious, culminating in thermonuclear and biological weapons that can destroy all life on earth many times over. But of equal importance is the capacity that has really developed only over the last two centuries, one critically related to modern forms of communication (in the widest and most varied sense of that word): the constitution of tightly-bound solidarities ('identities' is the usual term for them today) effectively engulfing large numbers and spaces in often mutually-conflicting ways.

It is in this context, as manifested through the specificities of late-colonial India, that we have to locate Gandhi's life-long efforts to achieve non-violent resolution of conflicts through *ahimsa* and *satyagraha*. Precisely why Gandhi became so concerned with violence is a question that has been, surprisingly, seldom asked. The answer surely lay in the actual and potential violence which he saw around him, or apprehended; violence between Indians and the British, but also notably among Indians themselves. For fundamentally, what was happening was a more-or-less simultaneous consolidation of a series of putative, often conflicting, identities – 'national' (in the sense of anti-colonial), religious, regional, caste, gender, class. And here the specifics of both British rule in India, and a series of developments within India over the late nineteenth and early twentieth century, need to be taken into account.

There is a need to resist the fairly common tendency of blurring the important distinctions between the experiences of colonialism and anti-colonialism in different parts of the erstwhile 'Third World'. The Indian and the African cases, for instance, were in many ways different from each other. What distinguished the subcontinent was the combination of long and stable colonial dominion (across centuries during which Britain and the West also underwent very decisive changes), immense physical and demographic size, and the presence of pre-colonial societies that were exceptionally hierarchised and diversified. The sub-continent never became a settler colony, and the vast disproportion in numbers between the expatriate rulers and indigenous peoples necessitated a shifting pattern of part-accommodations and alliances – unequal but not entirely one-sided – with sections of Indians. Contrary to nationalist dogmas, by no means all Indians suffered equally, or maybe sometimes at all, from British rule, despite unifying factors like racial discrimination and a basic economically exploitative colonial structure. British rule had to rest on adjustments with already-existing power-structures within indigenous societies, and the nationalist appeal could never become universal.

What began emerging in the late colonial era was not just a single, 'natural' or 'inevitable' sense of all-embracing 'national' identity, but a variety of intersecting and often conflicting identities-in-formation. And here what was decisive was not the rather elementary fact of India as a sub-continent having been always a land of great diversities, but a series of processes that cumulatively contributed to a 'hardening' of such identities. Thus late-colonial (and postcolonial) 'modernity' has meant a qualitatively different level of economic, administrative-political, and communicational integration. Concretely, news about a conflict in one locality would have taken months or more to reach a distant part of the subcontinent prior to the late nineteenth century, if it had travelled at all: now it reaches almost instantaneously or within a day or so. Railways and mechanical print, along with the associated flowering of vernacular prose and development of techniques of mechanical reproduction of mass forms of art, enabled the emergence of countrywide 'public spheres' of discussion and mobilization, open for deployment by a wide variety of putative solidarities. Colonial modernity was associated also with the growth of new, or very significantly modified, class structures and formations: agrarian relations characterized by a sharper delineation of property rights, plantation 'coolies' and other uprooted migrant labourers, industrial capitalists and workers. From 1871, Census enumeration encouraged sharper definition of differences between religious, caste, linguistic and regional communities, whose boundaries may have been more inchoate in pre-colonial times, for now the counting of different types of 'heads' demanded sharpened definitions regarding who was what, where one belonged. Soon a numbers game came into existence, regarding jobs, and, with the slow entry of representative politics from the early twentieth century, seats in legislatures. The British Indian legal system carved out separate realms for 'Hindu' and 'Muslim' personal and family law, where cases were supposed to be decided in accordance with religious texts as interpreted by indigenous experts of the two communities. This contributed to a much sharper sense of a uniform Hindu – Muslim disjunction in numerous matters of everyday living than had probably been present earlier.

What needs to be emphasized, however, is that the solidarities-in-formation were not just getting hardened: they were also becoming more potentially more fragile, for simultaneous formation also implied an enormous amount of undercutting. Efforts at consolidating identities through projecting enemy-images of threatening 'other(s)' consequently became a mark of the times, for these were deployed often by dominant or leading groups within the solidarities that were being sought to be cultivated. Thus efforts to build a more unified 'Hinduism' had to confront a simultaneous development of multiple caste identities, for both Brahmannical influence and intermediate-caste and *Dalit* (Untouchable) protest were being strengthened by colonial and postcolonial modernization. *Hindutva*, in one of its key dimensions, can be considered as an effort by some upper-caste groups to ward off possibilities of subordinate-caste breakaways (as well as possibly signs of women's affirmations through an incipient discourse of individual rights, and, by the 1920s and '30s, Left-led labour and peasant movements) through projecting images of Muslims or Christian Others as perpetual threats to the survival of all 'Hindus'. By uniting all Hindus in the name of external threats, they hoped to overcome all internal divisions of caste, gender, or class, without seriously modifying the deeply unjust and hierarchised patterns.

Anti-colonial nationalism also had a not entirely dissimilar hegemonising dimension, for it too sought to subordinate class, gender, and community differences to the higher aim of winning political freedom. The considerable overlaps between nationalism and Hindu communalism in ideas, images, and activists in fact have added greatly to the complexities of Indian politics over the last hundred years. But on the whole strategies of a more accommodating sort, reconciling internal differences through a measure of concessions, became necessary for effective anti-British struggle. This was particularly so for Gandhian nationalism, which with its insistence on non-violent methods alone required sustained mass mobilization on a very large scale for any kind of effective pressures on the rulers. Openness to a degree of social change had to be blended with rejection of extreme goals and methods, in the cause of a 'national unity' which still tended to retain a propertied-cum-high caste tilt.

Some recent work suggests, in addition, a link between Gandhi's appeal and the suppression or breakdown of a series of pre-colonial methods of conflict management in Indian society. These were certainly not always non-violent, but they had often managed to keep conflict and violence within some bounds. They included, besides aristocratic or popular rebellion, methods of peaceful collective petitioning of rulers or other oppressors through sitting down in front of their palaces or seats of authority (what had come to be called *dharna*, a common Indian term today through its revival in the Gandhian era); infliction of suffering on oneself as a means of moral pressure, which could go up to the point of suicide, and mass migration (called in Gujarat *hijrat*) to protest excessive tax burdens (Gandhian peasant nationalism would use that method in the 1930s). British rule, with its drive towards sole control over the right to use violence, systematically suppressed all or most of these forms. What Gandhi did, it has been suggested, is to combine a more intransigent and total rejection of the elements of violence which had entered into many of these old methods, with an effective inversion of the British claim to have ensured law, order, and peace. The systematic beating-up of absolutely peaceful demonstrators revealed that it was the British who were ruling through violence.

And, as we shall see shortly, the same inversion opened up avenues of peaceful but at least partly effective protest against internal acts of oppression, often in areas well beyond the limits of Gandhian practice.[6]

This overall context can help us understand, not so much the emergence of Gandhi as an individual (in many ways highly idiosyncratic), but the great appeal and considerable efficacy of his methods. It is to this question of efficacy of Gandhian *ahimsa* and *satyagraha* that we need to turn now. There can be little reasonable doubt that Gandhi was able to inspire through pioneering methods what in certain periods became a remarkably effective praxis of largely disciplined and non-violent all-India mass struggle. The emphasis throughout on suffering and sacrifice – withdrawal of all forms of voluntary participation in the structures of foreign rule, peaceful violation of select laws followed by mass courting of arrest by tens, sometimes hundreds of thousands of men and women drawn from all strata and regions of the country, remaining totally non-violent in face of brutal police assaults, occasional no-tax campaigns despite attachments of property – all made considerable sense in the context of a disarmed but enormous population. Such methods imparted courage and self-confidence to millions of otherwise humble people, and bred among them a rare sense of superiority over their rulers. It contributed enormously to a crucial loss of hegemony on the side of the rulers. In addition, the Gandhian amalgam of mass, yet controlled struggle fitted in well with the interests and inclinations of large numbers, particularly business groups and relatively better-off peasant strata. Indigenous capitalist and landholding peasants were in fact the two basic sections which nationalism was able to mobilize for the first time under Gandhi. In between big movements, Gandhians in the countryside sought to retain and enhance rural support through programmes of constructive village work. These did not attempt any basic change in landlord-peasant or peasant-landless relationships, but did at their best achieve locally significant, if ultimately marginal, improvements in income and quality of everyday life for the poor (through encouraging hand-spinning and weaving, notably). There are affinities here in attitudes and practices with some strands of contemporary 'grass-roots' work of NGO groups with similar commitments to efforts to stimulate forms of non-violent and autonomous local development.

But the limits and practical failures of Gandhian strategies also cannot be ignored. Despite, or perhaps partly because of his saintly aura and style, Gandhi could often be very undemocratic in his conduct of movements, and insisted on keeping their initiation, content, and calling-offs entirely a matter to be decided by himself. Many came to be disillusioned by his habit of sudden unilateral withdrawal, as well as by an often related hesitation about anti-landlord no-rent campaigns (as distinct from no-revenue, directed against the British government) and a near-total rejection of strikes. These were methods that had nothing inherently 'violent' about

---

[6] D. Vidal, *Violence and Truth*, Chapters 1,9; David Hardiman, *Gandhi in his time and ours*, Delhi, 2003, 41–51.

them, and could have been construed logically as part of the basic emphasis on techniques of peaceful non-cooperation with oppressive forces – but they would of course have adversely affected Indian propertied interests. It is interesting that the grounds on the basis of which the British government in India banned Gandhi's *Hind Swaraj* soon after its publication, despite its very sharp rejection of violence, emphasized the danger of the call for passive resistance and non-cooperation leading to strikes in government offices and disruption of communications.[7] That was a path that Gandhi consistently refused to take, except once in the very special case of Ahmedabad (1918), where he was able to develop close relations with both textile mill owners and workers, both Gujarati, and so effectively mediate between them. Elsewhere, his ideas regarding capitalists becoming 'trustees' for their workers failed to get much support from industrial labour, which leaned much more towards Communists and Socialists during the 1920s and 1930s.

The conception of the Congress as an unificatory umbrella in practice thus seemed to tilt fairly often in the direction of propertied groups. Towards higher castes, too, it has to be added, and suspicions about a Hindu tilt were also common, despite Gandhi's growing insistence on the sinful nature of untouchability, and his sincere life-long plea for Hindu-Muslim unity and brotherhood. Gandhi never quite gave up a basic respect for *varna*, caste hierarchy based on a what he thought was a legitimate division of functions, though insisting that no kind of work was demeaning, and high castes too should do the work considered polluting at least occasionally. He also wanted to keep what he called 'Harijan (his term for untouchables) uplift' primarily the responsibility of repentant upper caste Hindus. A very perceptive *Dalit* (the term untouchables have come to use) intellectual has diagnosed here a fundamental conflict between this Gandhian desire for 'self-purification' of high castes, and the quest for 'self-respect' through autonomous action among increasing numbers of *Dalits*, that came to be embodied from the 1920s in the figure of Ambedkar. *Dalits* in fact were applying to their own relations with their caste oppressors the emphasis on the need for self-emancipation that Gandhi himself had advocated throughout for Indians in connection with the British, as against a demeaning reliance on patronage from above.[8] Again, Gandhi kept on using a predominantly Hindu language and imagery, as notably with regard to the sanctity of cows and the ideal society as 'Ram-rajya', even while emphasiz-

---

7   The official interpreter (the text had been written and published first in Gujarati) in his summary of the book to H. A. Stuart, *Home Secretary*, stated: 'Nowhere the author of the book advocates revolt or the use of physical force against the British Government in India. But he openly advocates passive resistance to subvert British supremacy. If this idea takes hold of the mind of young inexperienced men, it might lead to systematic strikes among Government servants of various classes, as well as Public Works such as Railway, Post, Telegraph, etc. Surely a very dangerous thought to the safety of Government. The sooner it is suppressed the better'. Cited in Parel, *Hind Swaraj*, 5.

8   D. R. Nagaraj, *The Flaming Feet: A Study of the Dalit Movement in India*, Bangalore, 1993, Chapter I ('Self-Purification vs. Self-Respect').

ing throughout the more syncretistic, non-communal aspects of such traditions. This provided a handle for communally-minded Muslims to spread the fear that the triumph of the Gandhian Congress would mean Hindu domination. The fears of both Muslims and *Dalits* were stimulated further by the evident fact that large sections of Congress activists hardly shared Gandhi's non-communal vision, or his deep concerns regarding social injustice with regard to *Dalits*. Many among his followers could not follow the 'double-edged use of Hindu symbolism', the ways in which Gandhi sought to utilize Hindu symbolism to push for reforms from within, and took that language to be uncritically celebratory.[9]

With regard to women and gender questions too, not dissimilar patterns manifested themselves. The Gandhian way achieved an unprecedented mobilization of women, often from very orthodox families who came out on the streets, and even faced police brutality and went to jail, fired with a conviction that it was a kind of Hindu religious duty. But the combination of totally non-traditional actions with a traditionalist language simultaneously energized, and restrained, for in the end patriarchal structures were unaffected or at most marginally weakened, leading to much later feminist criticism.

The biggest failure was obviously in the realm of Hindu-Muslim relations. Despite Gandhi's own passionately sincere efforts, communal tensions and riots grew with the years from the mid-1920s onwards, and culminated in the supreme tragedy of his last years, marked by an incredibly brutal virtual civil war between Hindus and Muslims that accompanied the subcontinent's bloody transition to independence – with-Partition. Gandhi was left deeply saddened man when independence came, and declared himself to have 'run dry of messages' when asked for one by the radio of independent India.

But anything like an overall assessment of the impact of Gandhian techniques needs to take into account also a number of spill-over effects, many of them unintended by him and some which he would have disliked. In the early days of Gandhian nationalism, for instance, and particularly in areas not yet penetrated much by its cadres, all manner of rumours circulated about the Mahatma, imagining him in quasi-millenarian terms, and stimulating very diverse movements with goals and methods vastly different from those envisaged by Gandhi and his disciples. A striking instance was in 1920, when labourers in their thousands left the British-owned tea plantations of Assam, where conditions often amounted to semi-servility, spurred by the rumour that in the coming kingdom of Gandhi they would all get land. Peak-points of Gandhian movements, secondly, were often accompanied, or immediately followed, by a variety of plebeian groups putting forward demands going much beyond Gandhian perspectives, and often agitating for them in ways that he and his disciples emphatically did not favour. Thus, in Midnapur, the district in Bengal where Gandhian nationalism acquired and maintained its great-

---

9   Nagaraj, *Flaming Feet*, 9.

est strength, the nationalist agitations of 1921 and 1930 were quickly followed by sharecroppers' agitation against their employers and refusing payments to them. The local Congress leaders, while opposing such unauthorized extensions, also tried with some success to mediate between sharecroppers and landholders: the logic of Gandhian mass nationalism demanded a degree of accommodation. Regions of marked Gandhian rural activity also saw Gandhian styles and methods being taken over in whole or in part by quite different kinds of agitations, and this has come to be extended over both space and time with the years. For Gandhian struggles had conveyed object lessons in the possibility of unarmed people acquiring the courage and inner strength to withstand often brutal repression, without violence but also without fear. The message could be, and was, applied to other conflict-situations, against landlords or other indigenous oppressors as much as against the foreign rulers. And finally there were the ways in which significant numbers of nationalist activists, disillusioned by Gandhian constraints and sudden withdrawals of movements, eventually turned towards more socially radical, Socialist or Communist ideologies. Midnapur for instance by the mid-century had become one of the main strongholds of the Communists in what was now West Bengal.

Such patterns, finally, help us to understand the continued, and now really world-wide, attraction of Gandhian methods of combining determined but peaceful struggle, non-violence with moves towards a more just world, almost sixty years after the Mahatma had been murdered. In India itself, both official and most oppositional politics has hardly displayed much loyalty to Gandhi. There has been no lack of popular violence, both anti-state and internecine, while the state itself in certain times and regions has been probably much more brutal and repressive than the British most of the time had dared to be, ruling as they did in a situation of vastly disparate racial numbers. Yet Gandhi lives on, often a bit formally, in the frequent use of *dharnas*, hunger-strikes, and peaceful courting of arrest in all manner of movements, right across the political and social spectrum. More significantly, as already mentioned in passing, Gandhian ideas and methods of rural self-help, constructive work, and peaceful agitation, along with a substantial number of ex-Gandhian cadres, have remained an important component of the very large number of 'grass-roots' activists and NGOs that today dot many parts of the Indian countryside. Environmentalist movements, opposed to indiscriminate industrialization, destruction of forests, and construction of big dams displacing large numbers along with ecological hazards, have drawn in particular from Gandhian critiques of industrial society.

We can touch only briefly on the continued impact abroad, but this has very obviously been considerable. Striking instances would include the African National Congress in the early days of its agitation against apartheid, which made considerable use of Gandhian methods of peaceful violation of Pass laws. The brutality of racist repression made the turn to violent methods probably inevitable, but arguably some elements of it returned with the triumph of Mandela, when instead of retaliation, the regime went in for the Truth of Reconciliation Commission. The other well-known instance would of course be the anti-racist civil rights movement in the United States, particularly in the phase of the Students 'Non-violent Coordination Committee' and Martin Luther King. And the biggest of the world's Green parties, that of Germany, had as one of its most inspiring figures a woman deeply influenced by Gandhi: Petra Kelly. In all these and many other ways, the Gandhian legacy lives on, with its perpetual combination of potentials and problems inherent in the quest for balancing maintenance of peace and non-violence with significant moves towards social justice.[10]

---

10 For a very helpful summary and analysis, see Hardiman, *Gandhi in his time*, Chapters 8,9.

Peace-Keeping and Conflict Resolution in Contemporary Africa: Borders, States, Minorities

Pierre Boilley

Since the oppressive colonial period and the wave of independence, contemporary Africa has often been seen as a continent of wrenching cleavages: territorial disputes, conflicting economic interests, confrontations between different cultures, and rebellions against state authority. These sources of recurrent conflict in Africa fall under two general headings: external differences and internal strife.[1] The former, mainly quarrels about borders and territory between nations, have been much fewer than the far more frequent regional, often tribal conflicts within various countries. The latter – often said to be ethnic – have usually stemmed from difficulties at the state level: insufficient or weak control over national territory, unequal access to resources, or the need to develop democracy and citizenship. In the main, they have coincided with a simmering crisis of the "nation-state".

The violence resulting from these conflicts is multiform, as are the procedures used for handling them. The most grievous cases have occurred when the military used force to quell a rebellion or, if opposing forces were of equal strength, the intervention of troops from a neighboring land aggravated the situation. However, methods of conflict management are now being applied more frequently and effectively. We need but think of the suspension of conflicts by the now classical method of placing a peacekeeping force between belligerents, or of the calls for outside mediation, in particular to the International Court of Justice in The Hague (henceforth ICJ).

---

[1] Herein, "conflict" refers to an armed struggle between rival factions. A conflict might be domestic, or it might pit countries against each other. The word does not refer to the violence resulting from a coup d'état or overthrowing a government; nor to the limited, sporadic acts of armed violence related to banditry or clashes between communities. – *Article translated from French by Noal Mellott (CNRS, Paris, France), supervision Scott McMurry.*

The most promising trends in this respect may well be that endogenous methods are now being put to use for conflict resolution. The involvement of traditional chiefs, notables, "resource persons" and civic leaders (sometimes with the assistance of foreign mediators) has helped settle some domestic conflicts by bringing rival groups together for discussions and negotiations. It is worth pointing out that, after the setbacks experienced by the Organization of African Unity (OAU), due to its lack of power to settle conflicts in contemporary Africa, a new approach in the new African Union (AU) now advocates combining older with current forms of conflict resolution.

A "culture of peace" is gradually being developed that brings to mind earlier visions of African unity. We can now observe a range of practices that includes older methods – proven or innovative, and sometimes even exemplary solutions – in particular for handling questions related to national minorities.

African Conflicts: Various Forms of Violence

When creating a typology of the conflicts that have cast a pall over Africa since decolonization, we notice the extreme heterogeneity of these armed struggles and the numerical imbalance between instances of internal and external conflict. Far from the stereotypes that usually present national borders in Africa as absurd and the source of all troubles on the continent, nearly all borders have remained amazingly stable since the 1960s. Border skirmishes are noticeably scarce enough that we should draw attention to this characteristic of Africa's post-colonial history. The main territorial disputes involved Morocco and Algeria in 1963 (the War of the Sands over Tindouf), Mali and Burkina Faso (two "wars" in 1974 and 1985 over Agesher, a narrow strip of land on the border between the two countries), and Chad and Libya (from 1972 to 1994 over the Aouzou Strip). Though similar to a border dispute, the clashes from 1998 to 2000 between Ethiopia and Eritrea can be attributed to the longstanding problems that arose out of the war of independence waged by Eritrea from 1962 to 1991. Since 1992, crises have repeatedly flared up between Nigeria and Cameroon over the potentially oil-rich Bakassi peninsula, but never degenerated into open warfare. What has been called, oddly enough, the "first African world war" – the conflict after 1996 in the Great Lakes region, with all its complications between Congo-Kinshasa, Rwanda, Uganda and Burundi – had as much to do with the power struggle in the former Zaire after the overthrow of Mobutu as with major economic interests, especially in mining. The borders between these countries were not an issue. The conflict in the Western Sahara, a dispute related to decolonization, was and still is about Morocco's southern border only because Morocco simply annexed the Western Sahara. Morocco has refused to recognize the Sahrawi Arab Democratic Republic (SADR), which the international community has not unanimously recognized either.

All other armed conflicts in Africa discussed here – approximately two-thirds of the total – have been domestic. A poorly conducted decolonization process caused some of them, for instance: the war in the Western Sahara, Katanga's secession from the former Belgian Congo (1960–1963), or the first clashes between Ethiopia and Eritrea. In this last case, the Italian colonization of a province that had belonged to Ethiopia for centuries formed the basis of a sense of identity that led to secession and, after a 30-year war (1962–1991), to Eritrean independence. Cold War rivalries complicated decolonization conflicts. In Angola for instance, a civil war from 1975 to 2002 pitted the Popular Movement for the Liberation of Angola (MPLA), which held power with help from the USSR and Cuba after independence in 1975, against the National Union for the Total Independence of Angola (UNITA), which, with South African support, controlled diamond-producing areas. Although the MPLA won the elections organized in 1992, UNITA continued the armed struggle till 1997, then resumed it in 1999 and did not capitulate till April 2002 after its leader, Jonas Savimbi, died. A very similar case was Mozambique. From independence in 1975 till 1992, the Liberation Front of Mozambique (FRELIMO), the Marxist-oriented ruling party in a single-party state, fought the Mozambique National Resistance (RENAMO), which received backing from the South African and US governments.

In other cases, domestic strife has arisen out of competition for power and control over resources, as in Chad, where rebellions have repeatedly broken out since French decolonization, or in Somalia, where warlords have been vying for supremacy over the country and its provinces since the dictator, Mohammed Siad Barre, was overthrown in 1991. We find the same type of conflict in Sierra Leone from 1991 to 1999, Liberia from 1989 to 2003 and Congo-Brazzaville in 1997. Exacerbated by the end of a period of economic growth, the presence of numerous workers who immigrated from neighboring lands, and a disastrous political management of the idea of nationhood (ivoirité), a similar struggle for power was waged in the Ivory Coast after 2002.

Finally, some domestic conflicts in contemporary African states have stemmed from the political or economic disenfranchisement of peripheral peoples to whom access to positions in the government or administration is closed. Conflicts of this type are complicated by cultural differences that can serve as grounds for a sense of solidarity during the struggle. Wrongly said to be "ethnic", these conflicts – their most visible aspect being cultural – are of varying gravity. Under this type, we can place the Biafran secession from Nigeria (1967–1970), the ongoing confrontation between northern and southern Sudan since 1956, the revolt in Casamance, Senegal (1960–2004), intercommunity massacres in Rwanda and Burundi, or even the Tuareg and Moor rebellions in Mali and Niger (1963–1964), then 1990–1996 in Mali, and 1990–2000 in Niger).

Since postcolonial conflicts have taken quite varied forms, there cannot be a single method of conflict resolution. To examine these multiple methods, let us start with outside mediation, international peacekeeping forces and the ICJ. These classical methods have settled certain conflicts and placed others on the back burner while waiting for legal solutions to be worked out.

Outside Mediation and International Intervention

Third-party mediation through recourse to the international court system has been used mainly in classic border disputes. Of the many cases referred to the ICJ, most have been settled thanks to the Court's rulings. One example is the border dispute between Mali and its neighbor Burkina Faso.

The crux of the dispute was the lack of a precisely drawn border between Mali and Burkina Faso (formerly Upper Volta) in the Agesher area, a strip of land 160 km long and, on average, 15 km wide. Granted to Upper Volta but claimed by Mali, it became an object of contention after decolonization. Since the colonial borders represented the administrative bounds between two French colonies, they did not have to be precise. The border had not been clearly staked out; nor was there any geographical description of it. The only source documents were maps that, lacking precision, sometimes contradicted each other.[2] The area has, we should mention, two major natural resources, water and manganese. The strip is crossed by a stream (Beli), and there are several reservoirs there (including the Soum Pool). In the 1960s, the Bureau of Geological and Mining Research (BRGM) discovered a sizeable manganese deposit there. Obviously, this potential source of wealth represented an economic stake for both countries. The first conflict broke out during the great Sahelian drought in 1974, when water, ever scarcer, was a vital issue for nomads with their herds. For economic and human reasons, water resources had to be regulated.

An open conflict over Agesher broke out a second time in 1985. In the night of 29 to 30 December 1985, a cease-fire was signed following mediation by Nigeria and Libya, and under pressure from the African countries that – along with the two belligerents – had signed the Treaty of Non-Aggression, Assistance and Mutual Defense (ANAD). Having lasted less than a week, the war officially came to an end. Besides ending hostilities, the two countries agreed that a delegation of observers should be sent to the field to monitor the cease-fire while a ministerial commission made arrangements for withdrawing troops. Under this agreement, both countries agreed to refer the dispute to the ICJ for a definitive solution. This border dispute ended when both parties officially accepted the ICJ's judgment in December 1986.[3] The ICJ laid down a new border that represented a compromise. Accepted by Burkina Faso and Mali, this international decision definitively settled this dispute, which had lasted a quarter of a century.

---

2 *Atlas des cartes administratives et ethnographiques des colonies de l'AOF*, Paris, 1922; *Atlas des cercles de l'AOF*, Paris, 1926; and *Couverture IGN au 1/20000*, Paris, 1954–1956.
3 Judgement of 22 December 1986 in ICJ Reports 1986, pp. 554–663.

Another example of the same type of conflict resolution arose under more surprising conditions – given the duration and severity of the confrontation as well as its international implications – namely: the settlement of the dispute between Libya and Chad over the Aouzou Strip. Under an agreement signed in 1936 between France and Fascist Italy, the strip was to be ceded to Libya, then under Italian control; but this text was never ratified. On the contrary, a treaty signed between France and Libya in 1955 set the border at its previous bounds. In the late 1960s however, given President Tombalbaye's weak government, Chad soon lost authority other this far northern territory, which became a refuge for dissidents of all stripes. Maneuvering by giving support to various armed political groups one after the other, Colonel Gadhafi gradually edged into this area, potentially rich in uranium and manganese. He finally seized the Aouzou Strip in 1973. In 1982, after taking N'Djamena, Hissene Habré became president of Chad and obtained France's support for taking back the north through an operation (Épervier) mainly intended to counter Gadhafi's foreign policy. Nonetheless, the armed opposition headed by Idriss Déby, who leaned toward Tripoli, seized power in 1990. In September of that year, Chad took the dispute over the Aouzou Strip to the ICJ. In February 1993,[4] the World Court ruled that there were no grounds for questioning the 1955 agreement. Its judgment gave full satisfaction to Chad. Contrary to expectations, Libya complied with the judgment, and evacuated the area.

Another conflict that was very hard to settle was the dispute between Nigeria and Cameroon about the Bakassi peninsula, a tiny borderland near the mouth of the Cross River, a source of conflict between Nigerian and Cameroon since independence. Tensions were always near the boiling point, but never rose higher. Cameroon based its claim to Bakassi on a British-German treaty of 1913, on the outcome of a vote on self-determination in 1960 in the country's English-speaking region, and on General Yakubu Gowon's "Maroua Declaration" in 1975. Under this declaration, which was never ratified, the peninsula was to be handed over to Cameroon in return for its neutrality during the Biafran War. The main stakes were economic: fishing, petroleum and gas deposits offshore and, for Nigeria, access to one of its major ports (Calabar). On 29 March 1994, Cameroon brought the case before the ICJ. The Court ruled in October 2002 that, since the boundary was the one set in the Anglo-German agreement of 11 March 1913, Cameroon had sovereignty over the Bakassi Peninsula. It stated that "Nigeria has the express duty of effecting an immediate and unconditional withdrawal of its troops from the Cameroonian territory in the area of Lake Chad and Bakassi".[5] Nigeria was to complete its evacuation by September 2004. Despite this perfectly clear judgment,

---

4 The framework agreement on the peaceful settlement of the territorial difference between the Great Socialist People's Libyan Arab Jamahiriya and the Republic of Chad. Notified to the Court 31 August 1990/3 September 1990. Judgment of 3 February 1994 in ICJ Reports, 1994, pp. 6–103.

5 Land and maritime boundary between Cameroon and Nigeria, judgment of 10 October 2002, ICJ Reports 2002.

Nigerian authorities dragged their feet[6] before finally accepting the judgment. On the occasion of the ceremony of 14 August 2008 for the withdrawal and transfer of authority in the Bakassi peninsula, UN Secretary-General Ban Ki-Moon declared, "Beginning with the withdrawal of Nigerian troops from Bakassi two years ago and culminating in this ceremony, the case of the Bakassi peninsula proves the viability of a peaceful and legal settlement of border disputes, when it is done with the full support of the international community and in a spirit of mutual respect, good neighbourliness and cooperation."[7]

These three examples are emblematic of conflict resolution through judicial mediation, when parties to the suit abide by the verdict. Note that the rulings were based on colonial treaties, which independent states in Africa have not disputed. Such solutions, though representing a paradigm, do not always work, an example being the Western Sahara, where problems related to decolonization are mixed up with a territorial disputes.

In May 1974, the Polisario Front for the independence of Saguira El-Hamra and Rio de Oro rose up in arms against the colonial power, Spain. As of September 1974, Morocco set its sights on the territory when Spain, in an effort to withdraw, announced its intention to organize a referendum under UN auspices. M. Laraki, the Moroccan minister of Foreign Affairs, stated, "Its fair and correct application [...] should lead to the [Saharan] provinces joining Morocco".[8] To support its argument that the Sahara used to belong to it, Morocco proposed referring the case to the ICJ. The Court issued an advisory opinion a year later, on 16 October 1975.[9] Though recognizing that certain tribes might have owed allegiance to the Moroccan sovereign prior to colonization, the World Court ruled that neither Morocco nor, for that matter, Mauritania had any valid claim to the Saharan territory. Nonetheless, the king of Morocco interpreted the ruling in his favor and called for a peaceful march of Moroccans to occupy their provinces. The Green March of 350.000 volunteers entered the Western Sahara on 6 November.

Unable to use force against the unarmed demonstrators, Spain had to negotiate. On 14 November 1975, it signed the Madrid Agreement with Morocco and Mauritania,[10] which provided for Spanish withdrawal, a temporary tripartite administration and a vote by the population. But three months earlier, King Hassan II and President Ould Daddah had met in Rabat to divide the territory among themselves. As Spanish forces withdrew, the Moroccan and Mauritanian armies took control of the Western Sahara. A border agreement was signed on 14 April 1976. Not having been consulted, the Polisario Front attacked Mauritanian forces,

---

6 S. Smith, "Nigeria refuses to evacuate the peninsula of Bakassi to the advantage of Cameroon", *Le Monde*, 14 September 2004.
7 UN Secretary-General SG/SM/11745 AFR/1737 http://www.un.org/News/Press/docs/2008/sgsm11745.doc.htm.
8 UN AG 39th session A/PV, 2249th meeting, 30/10/74: 88.
9 Western Sahara, advisory opinion, 16 October 1975 in ICJ Reports 1975, p. 12.
10 Ratified by resolution 3458 B (XXXX) of the UN General Assembly.

which collapsed in 1979. Morocco immediately occupied the whole territory and built a wall to seal it off in 1982.

Meanwhile, Algeria was undertaking a diplomatic offensive to obtain recognition for the Polisario Front and the Sahrawi Arab Democratic Republic (SADR). It launched the process for the SADR to join the UN, and managed to obtain a UN resolution on 13 December 1978, whereby the General Assembly recognized the right of the Saharan people to self-determination and independence, and the UN's responsibility for decolonization in this territory.[11] This turned the conflict into an international problem to be managed by the UN. To restore peace, the UN drafted a plan accepted by both Morocco and the Polisario in August 1988. It foresaw granting the population the choice between becoming independent or joining Morocco. Moroccan troops were to be placed under UN supervision, and an international force was to maintain order. The census carried out by Spain in 1974 was to serve as the basis for voter rolls, which a special committee would help update. Ratified unanimously by the Security Council on 29 April 1991, Resolution 690 led to a cease-fire in September 1991 and the deployment of an international peacekeeping force (MINURSO, United Nations Mission for the referendum in the Western Sahara). Nonetheless, more than a decade later, Moroccan intransigence still blocked the referendum, and no end is yet in sight for this conflict. Recourse to an international court is not, as we see, a panacea.

Word Court rulings have a positive effect when parties to a conflict accept them, but encounter a limit, since rulings are not binding. When one of the parties does not accept a ruling, we observe another sort of international intervention, whereby a foreign peacekeeping force is assigned to prevent violence by separating belligerents. This method has been put to use in Africa mainly to mitigate domestic conflicts.

The UN intervened in the newly independent Congo by sending a peacekeeping force. Security Council Resolution 143 set up the United Nations Organization in the Congo (UNOC) on 13 July 1960 in response to disturbances in the country, which faced the secession of Katanga Province, a mutiny in its armed forces and a Belgian military operation. Thanks to the UNOC, which lasted till June 1964, the integrity of the national territory remained intact; and civil war was averted. This was the first on a long list of interventions in Africa. Among the major peacekeeping missions undertaken by the UN without African participation are: the already mentioned MINURSO in Western Sahara; the three versions of UNAVEM (United Nations Angola Verification Mission) that led to the withdrawal of Cuban troops from Angola, the negotiation of the Lusaka Protocol and its application; the deployment of the United Nations Observation Mission in Uganda and Rwanda (MONUOR) in 1993–1994 along with the creation of the United Nations Assistance Mission for Rwanda (MINUAR), which was to supervise application of the Arusha

---

11 UN General Assembly 33rd session. Resolution 33/31 176–177 13/12/1978.

peace agreement signed by Rwanda and the Rwandan Patriotic Front (RPF) but was unable to prevent the genocide (no more than France's Turquoise Operation in 1994). Also to be mentioned among the failures is the deployment of the United Nations Operations in Somalia (ONUSOM I and II) between the rival factions that were tearing the country apart. Unable to achieve its objectives, it had to withdraw in March 1995.

Through UN peacekeeping operations and World Court rulings, the international community often intervened in African conflicts during the thirty years following independence. Our assessment of the results is basically positive. The successes of settling the disputes over Agesher and the Aouzou Strip contrast with the failures of the operations in Somalia and Rwanda. Africans have gradually started intervening themselves in conflicts on their continent, especially since the Economic Community of West African States (ECOWAS) created the Military Observer Group (ECOMOG) in 1990. Since then, nothing has been quite the same. The OAU started assuming a role in conflict resolution along with the UN; and this has continued since, in July 2000 following the Lomé summit, the African Union (AU) replaced the OAU. The AU has decided to set up its own means for conflict resolution. Furthermore, African states have, during the last decade, alleviated some conflicts by resorting to endogenous methods to restore peace.

African arrangements for settling conflicts

The decade of the 1990s was especially noteworthy, not because of an increasing number of conflicts but owing to the many advances made by Africans in assuming responsibility for conflict management on the continent. It began with two domestic conflicts that amazingly ended in an improved integration of rebel populations in the nation-state or even in deepened feelings of nationhood.

The prospects were dire when, in 1990, the Tuareg and Moor rebellions broke out in Mali and Niger. As had happened in 1963–1964, the revolt by nomads rekindled opposition in northern Mali to the central government. The comparison of these two revolts provides insight.

In 1963, Malian authorities occupied the vacancies left by French administrators after decolonization. Unfamiliar with the north, the new administration imposed a Marxist-inspired legislation that the nomads could not stand. It made mistake after mistake, and humiliated locals, some of whom rose up in arms. The Malian army did not bother entering into the complexities of a negotiated solution. It ruthlessly quelled the revolt in the Adagh area. Malian soldiers there had few scruples, and no ties to the area. Many of these soldiers as well as their officers (General Abdullaye Soumaré, chief of staff, and captains Diby Sillas Diarra and Amadou Sissoo) were veterans of the French army and had fought in Indochina or Algeria. To come to grips with elusive rebels operating in an environment that was familiar to them and supported them, Malian forces used classical antiguerilla tactics. They decreed off-limits all the territory from the Algerian border to Kidal, the regional capital. Anyone caught crossing the line they drew would be treated like a rebel and could be killed on the spot without warning. To keep the Tuareg rebels from supplying themselves in food and water, wells were systematically poisoned; and herds, slaughtered. Cut off from its bases, the rebellion was slowly stifled. Of course, this tactic took a toll as blunders were made and hundreds of civilians died. Several witnesses have told about these massacres.[12] The Malian army thus created a vacuum and pursued the rebels over the border into Algeria. It used terror tactics by publically organizing executions. The local commander, Captain Diby Sillas Diarra, earned himself the reputation of bloodthirsty killer. The memory of his acts of savagery and humiliation is still alive in the region. Under these conditions, the rebellion could not last long. On 16 July 1964, the Malian army launched the final engagement with the lone remaining group of rebels in the Timetrin Mountains. The rebellion was crushed, and the whole region was placed under military control. Little was known outside the country about this rebellion. However the orphans of 1963–1964 would become the rebels of the 1990s.

When a new revolt broke out in June 1990, the Malian army tried at first to quell it as it had done thirty years earlier. But times had changed, and lessons had been learned. The Tuareg and Moor rebels were now better trained and armed. Unable to defend itself from surprise attacks, the Malian army encountered setback after setback, losing bases and the weapons there. Given this situation in the north and the democratic opposition arising in the south, General Moussa Traoré, the president and dictator, hurriedly signed the Tamanrasset agreement with the rebels in January 1991. This agreement never took effect. Shortly afterwards, following riots in Bamako from 22 to 25 March 1991, the army ousted Moussa Traoré and set up a transitional committee (Comité Transitoire de Salut Public) under Amadou Toumani Touré's leadership. The rebellion continued with unremitting clashes. The solution to the "northern question" seemed ever farther away since rebel groups did not agree among themselves about how to pursue their movement. Despite this difficult context, the new authorities managed to find solutions.

To reestablish a dialog, the government took two steps: contacting mediators and organizing the Conference on the North. The mediators (the Frenchman Edgar Pisani and the Mauritanian Ahmed Baba Miské) met parties to the conflict, sounded out their intentions, objectives and willingness, and made a report that served as the basis for initial contacts between opposing parties. Following meetings in Paris and Mali, the report was submitted to the transitional government in September 1991. Meanwhile, the national committee charged with organizing the conference was giving thought to a sweeping decentralization that would grant local authorities and peoples more autonomy in the management of their own affairs. In line with endogenous methods of conflict resolution, meetings of reconciliation brought

---

12   Interviews with Iknan Ag Ahmed in Bamako on 10 February 1994 and with Ammera in Paris on 19 June 1992.

together representatives of northern societies (mainly customary chiefs), public authorities and political parties. The Conference on the North, with Algeria as mediator, finally took place in Mopti from 16 to 18 December 1991. It was chaired by Amadou Toumani Touré. All factions in the rebellion were represented; and a panel of the wise, which included leaders of the 1963–1964 movement, served as moderator. This conference aroused interest and sparked debate inside the country.[13] The objective was not to produce an agreement, since the delegations present were not empowered to do so. Instead, the conference was to lay the grounds for further negotiations. The outcome of these negotiations, held in 1992 in Algiers, was a "peace document" known as the "National Pact on the Special Status of the North of Mali".[14] On the occasion of the official signing of the pact in Bamako on 11 April 1992, the representative of Niger, a country managing its own Tuareg rebellion, emphasized this agreement's value as an "example and model"; and the French ambassador, Jean-Didier Roisin, declared from the podium that the pact had "major political significance".[15] This signing raised hopes for peace. Bolder and deeper than the Tamanrasset agreement, the pact was evidence that peoples in the north and rebel combatants had a special status and were willing to accept being part of the Republic of Mali.

In contrast with the 1963–1964 revolt, the parties to the 1990 conflict used both endogenous procedures for negotiation and conflict resolution (which involved customary chiefs, outstanding citizens and the "wise" drawn from civilian society) and, too, classical methods of mediation (foreign mediators, moderators from neighboring countries and "resource persons" in the jargon used in Mali) to reach an exemplary agreement. The integration of rebel combatants for the first time since independence in the uniformed services of the state (i.e., as soldiers, policemen or customs officers), the opening of the north to development projects, broad decentralization and the creation of mixed (government-rebel) "mobile teams" for presenting the agreement to people in the farthest reaches of the countryside, all these actions changed mentalities and led to a genuine integration of former rebels. Without either peacekeeping forces or a UN resolution, Mali, though on the verge of civil war, managed to set an example owing to its national pact for settling a serious, recurrent conflict. This success was demonstrated during the "Flame of Peace" ceremony on 28 March 1996, when thousands of weapons were burned

---

13 See the following articles on this conference: T.B. Maiga, "Conférence spéciale sur le Nord: Ça ne doit pas échouer!", *Les Échos*, 118, 25 October 1991; B. Ouss, "Le Nord: un enjeu stratégique mondial", *Union*, 3, November 1991, p. 2; O. Arrald, "Contributions à la recherche de solutions au Problème du Nord", *Les Échos*, 120, 8 November 1991, p. 4; O.D. Maiga, "Conférence de Tombouctou, un enjeu", *Les Échos*, 120, 8 November 1991, pp. 4–5; T.B. Maiga, "Conférence de Tombouctou. Les raisons du report", *Les Échos*, 121, 12 November 1991, p. 2.

14 Minutes of the third meeting in Algiers (15–25 March 1992) between the government of the Republic of Mali and the United Movements and Fronts of Azawad (MFUA), signed by Zahabi Ould Sidi Mohamed (MFUA), Moussa Diabaté (Mali) and Ahmed Ouyahia (Algeria).

15 C. Gilguy, "La signature du pacte pour la paix et la réconciliation", *Marchés tropicaux*, 17 April 1992.

and the rebel movements disbanded. The same process, played out in Niger but with more difficulty and at a slower pace, ended with a similar ceremony in 1998.

Conflict settlement through negotiations that mix older African methods with classic ones is exceptional. Beyond these examples, attention should be drawn to the fact that Africa has gradually committed itself to maintaining peace and order on the continent. It was, we might say, forced to do so when, as of 1990 and the end of the Cold War, the UN was no longer the inevitable peacekeeping institution. Given the increasing number of domestic conflicts and of potential missions in a world less and less frozen in an East-West pattern, the UN, though remaining a pivotal institution, has been forced to rely on continental or regional organizations, such as the OAU or ECOWAS. These two organizations have responded by setting up organizations for keeping the peace and settling conflicts. On 6 August 1990 for instance, the ECOWAS Standing Mediation Committee decided to set up ECOMOG for monitoring cease-fires; and the OAU, during the 29th ordinary session of the conference of heads of state and of government on 30 June 1993, adopted measures for preventing, managing and settling conflicts.

ECOMOG was set up as part of ECOWAS's peace plan for Liberia.[16] Its role in Liberia was positive, thanks to Nigeria, which, as a major ECOWAS member, put up troops and funds. In September 1993, the UN decided to support this initiative by creating, under Resolution 866, the United Nations Mission in Liberia. UNMIL was responsible for overseeing the peace agreement that, obtained by ECOMOG, was to bring the civil war to an end. For the first time in Africa, a UN mission backed up a peace initiative coming from Africa.

Given this success, ECOMOG's assignment was extended to Sierra Leone in 1997 in an effort to restore Ahmed Tejan Kabbah, the democratically elected president overthrown by a putsch. ECOMOG had to impose an embargo on the new, illegitimate government and try to keep the situation from deteriorating. Once again, Nigeria was on the front line. Its troops laid siege to Freetown in February 1998 and restored the president. The military junta's forces were pushed into the hinterlands. Forming the Revolutionary United Front (RUF), they committed acts of violence and mutilation, but were contained by ECOMOG, once again with the backing of a UN force. As of October 1999, the United Nations Mission in Sierra Leone (UNAMSIL) took over ECOMOG's role under UN Resolution 1270,

The year before, in 1998, ECOMOG had been sent to Guinea-Bissau to intervene in a conflict between factions in the army. Its actions and the pressure exercised by ECOWAS led to signing a peace agreement and forming a national government. In 2003, armed forces from ECOWAS also intervened, along with French forces, in the Ivory Coast. They helped train the United Nations Operation in Côte d'Ivoire (UNOCI). Drawing on the Military Observer Group's failures and suc-

---

16 ECOWAS, *Journal Officiel de la Cedeao*, Bamako peace plan, Volume 21, November 1992, p. 13.

cesses, ECOWAS decided in June 2004 to set up a standing regional force. African states are assuming responsibility for security in the region.

These experiences with domestic conflicts have served as a basis for defining the AU's mission. The AU's Strategic Plan, released in May 2004, declares that Africa must take its security into its own hands: "The establishment of the African Union marked a new phase in African leaders' efforts at promoting peace, security and stability in the continent. In the preamble to the Constitutive Act of the African Union, our heads of state and government declared themselves conscious of the fact that the scourge of conflicts in Africa constitutes a major impediment to the social and economic development of the continent and of the need to promote peace, security and stability as a prerequisite for implementation of the development and integration agenda of the Union."[17] To this end, several institutions have been set up. In July 2002 in Durban, a protocol was adopted for a Peace and Security Council that, modeled on the UN's Security Council, is to intervene directly in African crises. It will be able to deploy a standby peacekeeping force of 15.000 soldiers that is to be created by 2010 out of national contingents. The Council, made up of fifteen UA member states, will put a continental early warning system into operation. Along with it, an advisory Panel of the Wise, made up of five outstanding Africans, has been formed. A "solemn declaration of a common African defense and security policy" was adopted on 28 February 2004; and the fifteen member states of the Council of Peace and Security Council were elected on 15 March. Although – mainly owing to dissensions between the UA and the Libyan president – an African Standby Force has not yet been created, Africa has adopted systems that should help the continent take charge of its own operations of peacekeeping and conflict settlement.

Conclusion

The history of peacekeeping and conflict resolution in Africa since decolonization is short. Forty-five years, in some cases less time, separate the present from the independence of African states. During these decades, Africa has suffered from several conflicts, and the ways of settling them have changed rapidly. By comparison with the violent crushing of the 1963–1964 Tuareg rebellion in Mali or the 1967 secession of Biafra, progress has been made in handling conflicts, evidence of this being both the 1990 revolt of nomads in Mali (and Niger) and the AU's commitment to "ensure effective political-military crisis management aimed at preserving peace

---

17 African Union, *Strategic plan of the African Union Commission*, Volume 1: "Vision and missions of the African Union", May 2004, p. 35.

and strengthening the security of the African continent in all aspects, including the elimination of conflicts".[18]

After decades of French intervention in its "private preserve" and of UN peace-keeping missions from outside the continent – as though Africa did not control its own fate or violence – an awareness gradually arose during the 1990s that has opened the way toward an "Africanization" of peacekeeping operations. This trend should continue if we judge by the AU's declarations. Africa has started using its own methods of conflict resolution, which mix classical mediation with original efforts based on older, endogenous methods. One of the most recent examples is the Panel of the Wise. With no equivalent in other international institutions, this panel clearly stems from an ancestral philosophy of mediation specific to Africa. Might this not be a reason to have hope in the continent's future?

Bibliography

Abi-Saab, G., "La pérennité des frontières en droit international", *Relations internationales*, 64, 1990, pp. 341–349.

Adebajo, A., *Building peace in West Africa: Liberia, Sierra Leone, and Guinea-Bissau*, Boulder, CO: Lynne Rienner Publishers 2002, 192p.

Ayissi, A. N. and United Nations Institute for Disarmament Research, *Coopération pour la paix en Afrique de l'Ouest: agenda pour le XXIème siècle*, New York: United Nations Institute for Disarmament Research 2001, 296p.

Azadon Tiewul, S., "Relations between the United Nations Organization and the Organization of African Unity in the settlement of secessionist conflicts", *Harvard international law journal*, 16, 1975, pp. 259–302.

Bangoura, D. and Observatoire Politique et Stratégique de l'Afrique, *L'Union africaine face aux enjeux de paix, de sécurité et de défense: actes des conférences de l'OPSA, les 18 juin, 13 novembre et 19 décembre 2002, Paris*, Paris: L'Harmattanm 2003, 253p.

Bedjaoui M., "Le règlement pacifique des différends africains", *Annuaire français de Droit international* 1972, pp. 85–99.

Bermejo, R., "Les principes équitables et les délimitations des zones maritimes: analyse des affaires Tunisie/Jamahiriya Arabe Libyenne et du golfe du Maine", *Annuaire de la Haye de droit internationa 1988 l*, pp. 59–110.

Boilley, P., *Les Touaregs Kel Adagh. Dépendances et révoltes: du Soudan français au Mali contemporain*, Paris: Karthala 1999, 644p.

Boilley, P., "La question sahraouie", *Relations internationales et stratégiques*, IRIS/University of Paris-Nord, 13 (spring) 1994, pp. 31–38.

Boilley, P., "Aux origines des conflits dans les zones touarègues et maures", *Relations internationales et stratégiques*, IRIS/University of Paris-Nord, 23 (autumn), 1996, pp. 100–107.

Bourjorl-Flecherb D "Heurs et malheurs de l'uti possidetis. L'intangibilité des frontières africaines", *Revue juridique et politique. Indépendance et coopération*, 1981, pp. 811–835.

---

18 African Union, "Solemn declaration of a common African defense and security policy", Syrte, 2nd AU summit, 28 February 2004

Cabot, J., "Les frontières coloniales de l'Afrique", *Herodote*, 3rd quarter,1978, pp. 114–131.

Carment, D. and Schnabel, A., *Conflict prevention: Path to peace or grand illusion?*, New York: United Nations University Press 2003, 296p.

Cervenka, Z., "The settlement of disputes among members of the Organisation of African Unity", *Verfassung und Recht in Übersee*, 7,1974, pp. 117–138.

Clapham, C., "Guerre et construction de l'État dans la Corne de l'Afrique" in P. Hassner and R. Marchal (eds.), *Guerres et sociétés. États et violence après la guerre froide*, Paris: Karthala 2003, pp. 463–488.

Colletta, N.J., Kostner, M. et al., *Case studies in war-to-peace transition: The demobilization and reintegration of ex-combatants in Ethiopia, Namibia, and Uganda*, Washington, DC: World Bank 1996, 348p.

Commission Régions Africaines en Crise, Fondation Roi Baudouin, et al., *Conflits en Afrique: Analyse des crises et pistes pour une prévention*, Brussels: GRIP Éditions Complexe 1997, 293p.

Commission Nationale Ivoirienne de l'UNESCO, *Conflits actuels et culture de la paix: colloque sous-régional-UNESCO*, Abidjan: Presses Universitaires de Côte d'Ivoire 1997, 455p.

Djiena Wembou, M.C., "A propos du nouveau mécanisme de l'OUA sur les conflits", *Revue générale de Droit international public*, 2, 1994, pp. 377–385.

Dussey, R., *Pour une paix durable en Afrique: plaidoyer pour une conscience africaine des conflits armés*, Abidjan: Éditions Bognini 2002, 323p.

El Ouali, A., "L'uti possidetis ou le non-sens du principe de base de l'OUA pour le règlement des différends territoriaux", *Le mois en Afrique*, 227–228 (December 1984-January 1985), pp. 3–19.

Ela, P.A., *La prévention des conflits en Afrique centrale: prospective pour une culture de la paix*, Paris: Karthala 2001, 218p.

Evans, G.J. and International Crisis Group, *God, oil and country: Changing the logic of war in Sudan*, Brussels: International Crisis Group 2002, 249p.

Gherari, H., "Les frontières maritimes des États africains", *Le mois en Afrique*, February-March 1985, pp. 22–36.

Heinrich, W., *Building the peace: Experiences of collaborative peace-building in Somalia 1993–1996*, Uppsala: Life & Peace Institute 1997, 251p.

Kamto M., "Le mécanisme de l'OUA pour la prévention, la gestion et le règlement des conflits: l'esquisse d'un nouvel instrument régional pour la paix et la sécurité en Afrique", *Arès*, XV-2, 1996, pp. 61–83.

Kohen M.G., "Le règlement des différends territoriaux à la lumière de l'arrêt de la CIJ dans l'affaire Libye/Tchad", *Revue générale de Droit international public*, 2, 1995, pp. 301–334.

Laremont, R.R., *The causes of war and the consequences of peacekeeping in Africa*, Portsmouth, NH: Heinemann 2002, 311p.

Magyar, K.P. and Conteh-Morgan, E., *Peacekeeping in Africa: ECOMOG in Liberia*, New York: Macmillan Press, St. Martin's Press 1998, 191p.

Marchal, R., "Erythrée: la difficile transition civile" in : R. Marchal and C. Messiant (eds.), *Les chemins de la guerre et de la paix. Fins de conflit en Afrique orientale et australe*, Paris: Karthala 1997, pp. 107–156.

Mawété S., *L'éducation pour la paix en Afrique subsaharienne: enjeux et perspectives*, Paris: L'Harmattan 2004, 172p.

Mavungu, M.N., *Le règlement judiciaire des différends interétatiques en Afrique*, Fribourg, CH: Éditions Universitaires 1992, 439p.

Meledje Djedjro, F., "L'OUA et le règlement des conflits", *Afrique Contemporaine*, 180, 1996 (special issue: L'Afrique face aux conflits).
Mgbeoji, I., *Collective insecurity: The Liberian crisis, unilateralism, and global order*, Vancouver: UBC Press, 2003 186p.
Nass, I. A., *A study in internal conflicts: The Liberian crisis and the West African peace initiative*, Enugu, NG: Fourth Dimension Publishers 2000, 354p.
Nzaou, E. P., *Vers la création d'une armée panafricaine*, Paris: L'Harmattan 2004, 180p.
Osaghae, E. E., Onwudiwe, E. et al., *The Nigerian Civil War and its aftermath*, Ibadan, NG: John Archers Publishers 2002, 470p.
Poulton, R. and United Nations Institute for Disarmament Research, *Collaboration internationale et construction de la paix en Afrique de l'Ouest: l'exemple du Mali*, New York: United Nations 1999, 58p.
Sherman, J., *War stories: A memoir of Nigeria and Biafra*, Indianapolis, IN: Mes Verde Press 2002, 122p.
Scherrer, C. P., Ethnic Conflicts Research Project. et al., *Central Africa: Genocide, crisis and change – Peace process in Burundi, normalization in Rwanda, regional war in Congo-DR*, Moers, Institute for Research on Ethnicity and Conflict Resolution 1999, 200p.
Tshiyembe, M., *Géopolitique de paix en Afrique médiane: Angola, Burundi, République Démocratique du Congo, République du Congo, Ouganda, Rwanda*, Paris: L'Harmattan 2003, 220p.
Tvedten, I., *Angola: Struggle for peace and reconstruction*, Boulder, CO: Westview Press 1997, 166p.
Uwazie, E. E., *Conflict resolution and peace education in Africa*, Lanham, MD: Lexington Books 2003, 188p.

Border dispute between Burkina Faso and the Republic of Mali

Compromis entre le gouvernement de la République de Haute-Volta et le Gouvernement de la République du Mali visant à soumettre à une chambre de la CIJ le différend frontalier entre les deux États. Notifié à la Cour le 20 octobre 1983, 7p.
Judgment of 22 December 1986 in ICJ Reports, 1986, pp. 554–663.
Order of 3 April 1985 "Constitution d'une chambre" in ICJ Reports, 1985, pp. 6–8.
Order of 12 April 1985 "Fixation des dates d'expiration du délai pour le dépôt des mémoires" in ICJ Reports, 1985, pp. 10–11.
Order of 3 October 1985 "Fixation des dates d'expiration du délai pour le dépôt des contre-mémoires" in ICJ Reports, 1985, pp. 189–190.
Order of 10 January 1986 "Demandes en indication de mesures conservatoires" in ICJ Reports, 1986, pp. 3–12.
Order of 9 April 1987 "Désignation d'experts" in ICJ Reports, 1987, p. 718.
Decaux, E., "Arrêt de la chambre de la Cour Internationale de Justice dans l'affaire du différend frontalier Burkina Faso/République du Mali (Arrêt du 22 décembre 1986)", *Annuaire français de Droit international* 1986, pp. 215–238.
Gautron, J. C., "Création d'une chambre au sein de la Cour Internationale de Justice, mesures conservatoires et médiation dans le différend frontalier entre le Burkina Faso et le Mali Ordonnance du 10/01/86", *Annuaire français de Droit international* 1986, pp. 192–238.

Quenedec, J. P., "Le règlement du différend frontalier Burkina Faso/Mali par la Cour Internationale de Justice", *Revue juridique et politique. Indépendance et coopération*, January-February, 1, 1988, pp. 29–41.

Singh, G., "Expériences of Burkina Faso v. Mali : Unsuitability of ICJ in settling the use of force cases", *Indian Journal of International Law*, 3/4 (July-December), 1988, pp. 497–505.

Some, G., "Un exemple de conflit frontalier: le différend entre la Haute-Volta et le Mali", *Année africaine*, 1978, pp. 339–370.

Stern, B., "L'affaire du différend frontalier Burkina Faso/Mali", *Journal du Droit international*, 4, 1988, pp. 1177–1184.

Border dispute between Libyan Arab Jamahiriya Jamahiriya and Chad

Accord cadre sur le règlement pacifique du différend territorial entre la Grande Jamahiriya arabe libyenne populaire et socialiste et la République du Tchad. Notifié à la Cour les 31 août 1990/3 septembre 1990.

Judgment of 3 February 1994 in ICJ Reports, 1994, pp. 6–103.

Alibert, C., "L'affaire du Tchad 1980–1985", *Revue générale de Droit international public*, 1, 1986, pp. 345–406.

Order of 26 October 1990, "Fixation de la date d'expiration du délai pour le dépôt des mémoires", *ICJ Reports*, 1990, pp. 149–152.

Order of 26 August 1991, "Fixation de la date d'expiration du délai pour le dépôt des contre-mémoires", *ICJ Reports*, 1991, pp. 44–45.

Order of 14 April 1992, "Fixation de la date d'expiration du délai pour le dépôt des répliques", *ICJ Reports*, 1992, pp. 219–220.

Kamto, M., "Les tentatives de règlement non-juridictionnel du différend territorial tchado-libyen à propos de la bande d'Aouzou", *Revue juridique et politique. Indépendance et coopération*, 45, 1991, pp. 292–304.

Kohen, M. G., "Le règlement des différends territoriaux à la lumière de l'arrêt de la CIJ dans l'affaire Libye/Tchad", *Revue générale de Droit international public*, 2, 1995, pp. 301–334.

Koskenniemi, M., "L'affaire du différend territorial (Jamahiya arabe libyenne c. Tchad) Arrêt de la Cour Internationale de Justice du 3 février 1994", *Annuaire français de Droit international* 1994, pp. 442–464.

Land and maritime boundary between Cameroon and Nigeria

Dossier sur le différend frontalier de la péninsule de BAKASI publié par le Gouvernement de la République du Cameroun, Yaoundé, 1 March 1994, 25p.

Essombe, E. J., "Considération juridiques sur le différend frontalier de la péninsule de Bakasi", *Revue africaine de Droit international et comparé*, March 1995, pp. 98–127.

Garcia, T., "Les mesures conservatoires rendues par la Cour Internationale de Justice, le 15 mars 1996, dans le différend frontalier entre le Cameroun et le Nigeria", *Annuaire français de Droit international* 1996, pp. 409–427.

Njinkeng, J. B., "International dispute settlement: Land and maritime boundary between Cameroon and Nigeria – Origin of the dispute and provisional measures", *Revue africaine de Droit international et comparé*, June 1997, pp. 287–310.

Placca, J.B., "Négociations autour d'un malentendu", Jeune Afrique Économie, 178 (April), 1994, pp. 106–119.

Sall, A., "Actualités des conflits frontaliers en Afrique: L'ordonnance du 15 mars 1996 rendue par la Cour Internationale de Justice dans le différend frontalier entre le Cameroun et le Nigeria", *Revue africaine de Droit international et comparé*, March 1997, pp. 183–194

Sholanke, O., "Delimiting the territorial sea between Nigeria and Cameroon: a rational approach", *International and comparative law quarterly*, 42 (April), 1993, pp. 398–411.

Weiss, T.L., "Migrations et conflits frontaliers. Une relation Nigeria Cameroun contrariée", *Afrique contemporaine*, 180, 1996 (special issue: L'Afrique face aux conflits).

Gender and Violence

War, Violence and Gender – An Introduction

Joanna Bourke and Penny Summerfield

Through the lens of gender – masculinity as well as femininity – military history has been transformed. But simplistic gender binaries are never enough. Gender is not a state, but a relationship. It is always in flux. Class tensions, ethnic friction, generational conflicts, and ideological disputes are always present in the forging of each individual's coming-into-being. This is even true in circumstances of almost unsustainable dread, such as under the weight of military might. The papers in this sub-theme are all meditations on the historical diversity of responses to military violence, and the capacity of individuals to shape themselves and their societies according to a range of possibilities. Five of the essays focus on gender (primarily femininity) and war, while two are meditations on rules concerning the norms of legitimate combat. All seek to unpack cultural meanings of violence. Even as the world around them seemed to be undergoing dramatic (if not revolutionary) changes, men and women have sometimes clung to familiar values and customs and, at other times, used those customs to forge new worlds. After all, the lives that these women and men forged did not abruptly start at the beginning of a conflict, but were created out of materials and ideologies that pre-dated the conflict (and often survived that conflict, too). This point is stated most starkly in Roger Markwick's analysis of the unprecedented mobilisation of Soviet women between 1941 and 1945. The half a million female front-line soldiers of the 1940s were "essentially products of the peacetime Soviet system", in which violence had been legitimised within a largely peasant population. All the papers share Markwick's observation that it is impossible to analyse wartime societies independently of a detailed understanding of earlier decades. Indeed, it is precisely this relentless focus upon broader cultural contexts that enables all participants to question some of the most common dichotomies in the histories of war: in particular, the distinctions between public and private, frontline and home front, victims and perpetrators, and wartime and post-war society.

Victims and Combatants

Without question, war creates victims. Many of these victims were not the ones traditionally targeted according to the "warrior myth". Indeed, civilians were often the victims-of-choice. While only five per cent of deaths in the 1914–18 war were civilian, sixty-six per cent of those who died in the 1939–45 war were civilians. In that conflict, considerably more civilians than military personnel were killed in Belgium, China, France, Greece, Hungary, the Netherlands, Norway, Poland, the Soviet Union, and Yugoslavia. It is startling to recall that even in Britain between 1939 and D-Day (1944), more British civilians had been killed than British servicemen. Charles S. Maier's chapter is a detailed examination of aerial bombardment during the Second World War, yet it is worth reminding ourselves that women were the main casualties. For instance, for every 100 male casualties there were 181 female casualties in Darmstadt, 160 in Hamburg, 136 in Kassel, and 122 in Nuremberg. Around one-fifth of those killed were children under the age of sixteen years and another one-fifth were over the age of sixty.[1] It made mockery of Just War doctrine (as discussed by both Maier and Pieter Lagrou) that insisted on the preservation of the distinction between civilian and military combatants.

Of course, the targeting of civilians was not a modern phenomenon. As Hall and Malcolm point out in the context of medieval Ireland, attacking women was strategic: killing or imprisoning them meant that men were deprived of sustenance (a point not lost in later wars, notably the Anglo-Boer War of 1899–1902, when women and children were forced into concentration camps while their homes and farms were razed to the ground). Pillaging from women in enemy or neutral territory, on the other hand, as in the nineteenth-century Latin American wars discussed by Barbara Potthast, supplied the attacking army. Women were also taken hostage (for instance in Ireland): they could be valuable diplomatic pawns. Violation of the home (or other places of supposed safety, such as churches) in attacks on women, and of women's bodies themselves through rape, had symbolic value as an insult to the masculinity of the enemy: it indicated the enemy's failure to fulfil the unwritten 'gender contract', under which men fought to protect women, who provided them with nurturance. In all conflicts discussed here, there was widespread abduction of women for sexual purposes, and "horizontal collaboration" (and the fear of it) was a dominant theme in occupied territories. Sexual harm was at the heart of propaganda: Paraguayan men were warned against the Brazilian "monkeys" and "black hordes" anxious to rape Paraguayan women (Barbara Potthast) and, in Germany, women were led to expect the mass rapes by "red hordes" and "Bolshevik barbarians" at the end of the Second World War (Roger Markwick). This is a dimension that could be added to Maier's discussion of the reasons that the theme of "German suffering" took so long to emerge within German debates about the Second World

---

1 Hans Rumpf, *The Bombing of Germany*, translated by Edward, London: Fitzgerald, 1963, 160–61.

War. German suffering, including and especially the mass rapes of women in Berlin and elsewhere, was too tightly tied up with the "stain of Nazism", with female collaboration in the crimes of the Holocaust (West and East Germany), and with collaboration with the Soviet Union (East Germany) to be readily admitted. Furthermore, as many women learnt, issues of consent become blurred during times of military violence: what does it mean to say that a starving woman consented to sex with a soldier proffering a loaf of bread, firewood, or shelter?[2] The mere fact of war, further, might have the effect of "lowering the threshold of the exercise of interpersonal violence", as Pieter Lagrou paints out in his chapter. The dynamics of 'premodern' wars have been very much alive in the modern era: bombing has been done both to destroy military production and to demoralise an enemy whose army is unable to protect its civilian population; occupation has been accompanied by violations of all kinds.

Lagrou observes in his chapter that warfare is a "highly codified exercise of violence". As five of the papers point out, however, gender is a crucial part of the code. These papers ask whether women were combatants, and all expose the fictive nature of the distinction between the (male) combatant and (female) non-combatant. Barbara Potthast shows that the campfollowers or *rabonas* of the armies of Bolívar and López in Latin America provided shelter, food, hygiene and nursing care, apparently fulfilling feminine, non-combatant roles. But because they went ahead of the army to set up camp and because they obtained supplies by pillaging, they were armed, and were sometimes aggressors. A mistress who travelled with a general, as Manuela Sáenz did with Bolívar, might be his secretary and quartermaster, but could also be his political adviser and strategist, and accompany him into battle. Women working in the mobile military hospitals of the Balkan and First World Wars, discussed by Jean Quataert, were close to the front line. They were witnesses to violence, and were sometimes themselves under fire: as Tammy Proctor points out, women ambulance drivers in the First World War had to drive through artillery attacks, while Roger Markwick shows that on Eastern Front in the Second World War, Soviet field nurses had to drag the injured, with their weapons, from the battlefield. Yet women serving the military in such roles, as well as others such as clerk, cook, driver, laundress or wireless operator, did not have 'combatant' status.

Those who did were few and far between. Hall and Malcolm cite women acting in the interests of their families of birth by burning down the castles of their marital families and murdering their husbands. They also give the converse example of Dearbhfhorgaill, who led foreign mercenaries against her own kinsfolk in 1315 to advance the cause of her husband. There were female troops in the Mexican Revolution and the Cuban war of independence: the remarkable personal testimony of the Mexican Jesusa Palancares, quoted by Potthast, indicates that she carried

---

2   Anonymous, *A Woman in Berlin: Diary 20 April 1945 to 22 June 1945*, London: Virago, 2005. For a detailed analysis of rape in war, see Joanna Bourke, *Rape. A Cultural History*, London: Virago, 2008.

two guns and fired to kill if enemy soldiers came too close; however, her principal role was of aide-de-camp to her violent husband Pedro, rather than combatant in her own right. Women spies needed to know how to kill, even if their roles were primarily those of courrier or intelligence gatherer. As Proctor argues, such women sometimes thought of themselves as warriors, like the women of *La Dame Blanche*, a British spy ring based in Belgium in the First World War, who considered themselves 'soldiers without uniforms', took an oath of allegiance and were subject to court martial for breaches of discipline. But the identity a woman claimed, and that with which she was endowed by those recording her involvement in war, could be very different things.

The imminence of invasion led to women's involvement in local defence. Markwick shows that on the Eastern front, in 1941, Soviet women took up arms as militia members to defend Moscow and Leningrad, and that in Germany in 1945, as the allies pressed ever closer, women, who had previously been forbidden to bear arms, were recruited to a special infantry battalion to shame male deserters, and were also required to serve in the belatedly formed *Volkssturm* and to engage in house-to-house fighting. In Britain from 1940 to 1943 women demanded to be admitted to the Home Guard as armed members but were resisted by authorities unwilling to abandon the combat taboo completely.[3] In the First World War, the British War Office had recognised the need to recruit women to support combat as auxiliaries, but in the Second they were still determined not to give women combatant roles. Nevertheless, changing technology and labour shortages meant that women were recruited into an increasingly wide range of military roles in many of the participant countries, and the distinction between combatant men and non-combatant women was increasingly difficult to make. Women's involvement in air defences is a good example. Markwick indicates that Soviet women were drafted to anti-aircraft gun sites, where they performed all functions, from June 1941. Women were recruited for the same role in Britain from 1941 to 1943, but the War Office imposed limitations: women (unlike men) had to sign a special letter of consent to indicate that they agreed to handle weapons; and while they operated searchlights, and height and range finders, they were not allowed actually to fire the guns.[4]

The group of women who least ambiguously had combat status were Soviet women recruited to three all-women air regiments in the autumn of 1941, and into the Red Army from the spring of 1942 as snipers. As Markwick shows, the 'night witches' and the Soviet riflewomen were regarded by their Nazi adversaries as 'amazons devoid of femininity': indeed combat was widely seen as unnatu-

---

3 P. Summerfield and C. Peniston-Bird, *Contesting Home Defence: Men, Women and the Home Guard in the Second World War*, Manchester: Manchester University Press, 2009.

4 D'A. Campbell, 'Women in Combat. The World War Two Experience in the U.S., Great Britain, Germany and the Soviet Union', *Journal of Military History*, 57, 1993; G. J. DeGroot, 'Whose Finger on the Trigger? Mixed Anti-Aircraft Batteries and the Female Combat Taboo', *War in History*, 4:4, (1997).

ral and inhuman for women. From medieval Ireland to the Soviet Union in the Second World War, women who engaged in combat were seen as both treacherous and defeminised: they became not only 'men-women' (as they were known in nineteenth-century Latin America), frightening mutants, but also sexual predators, whores who slept with the soldiers with whom they fought. Depictions of the enemy were routinely unflattering: but enemy combatant women were considered especially debased.

Motivations, explanations

Women's motivations for participation in warfare in general, and in combat specifically, are frequently either hidden from history or deeply entangled with the values informing the compiling of the historical record. Three explanations for women's involvement recur in these papers: family, patriotism and coercion.

Women used violence to further the interests of their families in the Irish marches when 'hybridisation', that is social, cultural and ethnic mixing (in which women played a crucial part through intermarriage), was contradicted by efforts to strengthen frontiers. In the Latin American wars of the nineteenth and early twentieth centuries, going to war was an extension of women's customary duty to care for their menfolk: wives who fed and nursed husbands at home must do the same, and in addition load their rifles, on the battlefield. British sisters wanted to serve alongside their brothers in the First World War;[5] and some Soviet women felt the same way in the Second.

Such family reasons for involvement merged into patriotic reasons: revenge for atrocities perpetrated on fellow countrymen as well as family members motivated British[6] as well as Soviet women in the Second World War, as no doubt in other wars. Patriotism, implies Roger Markwick, went deeper for Soviet women than loyalty to the political regime and its leader. But by his own account the two have been difficult to disassociate: the Red Army battle cry 'For Motherland! For Stalin' mobilised women's opposition to the Nazi regime that stood for misogyny as well as imperialism, militarism and anti-Semitism. Whatever the shortcomings of the Soviet regime in these respects, Markwick regards the Soviets as having a profoundly different view of women's place in society from the Nazis.

Coercion took a variety of forms: violent husbands insisted that their wives accompanied them in Latin American wars; the state 'mobilised' women in Britain, Germany and Soviet Russia in the Second World War. Expectations of the continuity of wifely services led to the former; labour shortages were a prime reason for the

---

5 A. Woollacott, 'Sisters and Brothers in Arms: Family, Class and Gendering in World War I Britain' in M.Cooke and A.Woollacott, *Gendering War Talk*, Princeton, Princeton University Press, 1993.

6 P. Summerfield, *Reconstructing Women's Wartime Lives, Discourse and Subjectivity in Oral Histories of the Second World War*, Manchester, Manchester University Press, 1998, chapter 3.

latter. But although the shortage of manpower gave governments compelling reasons to propel women into warfare in the twentieth century, ideology played a huge part in facilitating or impeding the process. National Socialist thinking required Aryan women to be confined to domestic, maternal roles, although women in other social groups could be coerced into war production (including Jewish women, forced female labour from conquered territory, and even, Markwick claims, German mothers if they were working-class). In the last year of war, however, Nazi leaders were sufficiently desperate to contradict their values and draft middle-class Aryan women into war industry and the military.

The German case was only an exaggerated version of the gender-divided worldview of other states: domestic ideology was also strong in the US and Britain, and their governments were sensitive to public opinion, or at any rate to the opinions of Congressmen and Members of Parliament, who were understood to be prepared to tolerate only modest alterations to gender norms. The US and British governments preferred to backfill the spaces left by men sent closer to the front, even when women were more efficient in 'frontline' roles (on anti-aircraft guns and in the Home Guard, for example) than the available men (who were younger, older or less fit than those sent further into battle, and than the women left behind). Such policy-making was essentially irrational in a war situation in which the utmost effectiveness was required in every military role. It was not the product of the self-regulating 'double helix' mechanism proposed by the Higonnets,[7] in which, in spite of changing wartime roles, the esteem accorded men and women always maintained itself in men's favour. It was a case of the deliberate manipulation of wartime options, in order to set limits on wartime alteration to gender relations, because to do otherwise offended dominant values strongly represented in government.

The alternative was to manipulate public opinion, and governments did this with respect to gender when they needed to. Labour shortages bit deeper in Britain than the U.S. and the 'mobilisation' of women was as a result more thorough, even though, as we have seen, combat still marked its limits. Policy-implementation was accompanied by public persuasion. For example, the officially-approved British films *Went the Day Well* (1942) and *The Gentle Sex* (1943), show women learning to kill and not to feel bad about it, in the latter as a member of an anti-aircraft gun battery: although there was public suspicion about the recruitment of women to the women's army auxiliary in which anti-aircraft women served (the A.T.S.), it was not targetted specifically at the 'Ac Ac girls' themselves.

In Britain, the U.S. and, Markwick reminds us, in Germany, the female workforce was stratified by class: mobilisation in Britain extended the customary employment of lower class women in heavy, dirty and sometimes dangerous work, across a wider social range and into types of work associated with male labour. It was customary for Soviet women to be involved in such types of work: it was relatively straight-

---

7   M.R. Higonnet, J. Jensen et al. (eds), *Behind the Lines. Gender and the Two World Wars*, Yale University Press, 1987, pp. 6 and 34.

forward for the Soviet government to include women in heavy industrial war production, in spite of its simultaneous insistence on the importance of motherhood. Nevertheless, as Markwick shows, the authorities were hesitant about women's full military participation in combat, and only undertook it in the context of the ravages of the death toll of 1941–42 on the Red Army. To the Soviets as to the British, Americans and the Germans, women were primarily nurturers, not killers.

The emphasis on family, patriotism and coercion as motivators, omits other reasons women had for going to war. On occasion they involved themselves in order to advance their own causes in the eyes of the government they served: as Quataert shows, Inglis and the members of the Scottish Women's Hospitals did not distinguish their femininity from their patriotic and feminist agenda. These women were determined to ensure that their militant labour on the battlefields would serve a function in ensuring the extension of citizenship rights in the postwar world. In the event, however, they were denied the opportunity to prove their value to their own government: the British War Office would not make use of them, so Inglis put her nationalist, patriotic and feminist project at the disposal of the allies and the Red Cross on the Eastern Front. Nevertheless, Jean Quataert argues that the war helped the cause of suffrage and enabled some women to forge a new sense of female citizenship. Proctor shows that Sarah Aaronsohn, a Zionist Turkish citizen who headed an espionage group working for the British against the Turks in 1917, undertook the role not out of patriotism towards Britain, but in the hope that by doing so the British would be persuaded to help create an independent state of Israel.

Women auxiliaries, nurses and spies were labour forces that governments at war could not do without. The *rabonas* of Latin America performed necessary functions for the armies they served: they would have to be replaced if the generals who wished to get rid of these 'creatures outside society' had their way. As Quataert argues, volunteer medical corps had become a necessary part of British war-making by the early twentieth century: the alternative would have been a state-run military medical service with all the attendant expense. Espionage circuits, which included women, were trained, organised and deployed in occupied countries by the British and other governments in the Second World War. As Proctor suggests, once the war and its associated manpower problems were over, women in such groups were discarded. So too were many servicemen: the difference was that women's service was even less likely than men's to be rewarded with medals, pensions and commemoration.

Finally, what of the selective and distorting process of history making? Hall and Malcolm suggest that the annalists of medieval Ireland disapproved of militant women and so cast them as traitors and wicked counsellors, although these women's exceptionality did at least merit their inclusion in the record. Potthast points out that hostile chroniclers sometimes invented women worriers to suggest the barbarity of the enemy or explain an unexpectedly long campaign, as in the case of the Paraguayan resistance to the allied aggression of Brazil, Argentina and

Uruguay in the 1860s: Argentinian sources suggested that the prolonged fighting was in part due to López' evil deployment of female battalions, which, Potthast tells us, never existed. Patriotism was frequently attributed to women whose participation could otherwise be seen as abnormal. Cuban commemoration of women soldiers motivated by patriotism contributed to the construction of national identity: Potthast, however, sees their involvement as largely forced. Markwick notes that women pilots were excluded from Soviet victory celebrations in 1945, but were put back into the national story in the 1950s as satinised, patriotic heroines. Women mobilised for war had a problem with reputation. Their task was to do 'men's jobs' while maintaining their femininity: if they did the former too well they were defeminised and emasculating; if they did too much of the latter, they demonstrated their inferiority and flaunted their sexuality.

Conclusion

If there had been, historically, no 'gender contract' between the male warrior and the woman nurturer, there would be no need to explain women's participation in war. The resilience of that contract over a long period of time, and in very different historical circumstances, is remarkable. Some of the chapter also demonstrate its internal contradictions. Symbols of the 'motherland' for which wars have been fought, women have been the ostensible objects of protection, yet they have been drawn into the fight: warriors must be nursed and nurtured, and if men are insufficient in number to wage war effectively, women must take their place. The cult of the manly man and the fragile woman is enhanced by war,[8] yet the dynamics of war require social acceptance of women tough enough to take on male roles. State-regulated organisational structures and belief systems, as well as increasingly elaborate technologies of war, enlarge the scale and complexity of warfare, but do not alter the fundamental gender relations. But gender is, of course, not only about women. The area of research perhaps inevitably neglected in these discussions, is the impact of war on men and masculinity. In particular, these papers invite attention to the issue of the fashioning of men's identities in wartime, not just in relation to each other, to the military and to the state, but also in relation to women's participation in warfare, in and out of uniform.

---

8   J. B. Elshtain *Women and War*, Brighton: Harvester 1987.

Beyond the Pale:
Gender and Violence in Ireland, 1169–1603[1]

Dianne Hall and Elizabeth Malcolm

Introduction

Modern Irish political and ethnic divisions have a very long history, stretching back – arguably – to the late twelfth century, when Anglo-Norman adventurers from Wales arrived in the country, invited across the Irish Sea as allies by the deposed Irish king of Leinster, Diarmait Mac Murchada. But this was certainly no Norman Conquest, on a par with that of England a century earlier.[2] The Normans landed in small bands, initially without the approval of their king, and they proceeded to fight both with and against various Irish kingdoms in parts of the south and east. The Ireland to which these Anglo-Norman adventurers came in 1169 was also less united than England in 1066, being fragmented into a large collection of small kingdoms that feuded and raided, and on occasion formed alliances with each other against enemies. Culturally, the Gaelic Irish had much in common, but personal and political rivalries had produced a country with many borders, in which violence was endemic.[3]

Henry II of England, alarmed at the prospect of some of his more troublesome barons establishing an independent base in Ireland, followed them to Dublin in 1171/2 and forced their submission, as well as the submission of a number of Irish rulers. But Henry was too preoccupied with challenges in England and France to

---

1 The research for this paper has been funded by an Australian Research Council grant. Names of people and places are standardised for those well attested; names in quotes are given as in the original. The expression 'beyond the pale' refers to a wooden palisade that was built during the fifteenth century to protect the borders of the English lordship – 'The Pale' – from Gaelic-Irish raids.
2 F.X. Martin, *No Hero in the House: Diarmait Mac Murchada and the Coming of the Normans to Ireland*, O'Donnell Lecture 19, Dublin, 1975.
3 The situation among the Irish in 1169 is summarised by F.J. Byrne, 'The Trembling Sod: Ireland in 1169', in *A New History of Ireland: Volume II. Medieval Ireland*, ed. Art Cosgrove, Oxford, 1987 (new edn, 1993), 1–43.

devote much time to conquering Ireland, although he did designate his younger son, John, 'Lord of Ireland' – a title English monarchs used until 1540. Thus there was no coordinated Norman invasion of Ireland and nor was the whole country brought under English rule. It was not until 1603 – more than four centuries later – that English control was extended throughout Ireland.

From the late twelfth century, however, an English kingdom or lordship was added to the existing Irish kingdoms. Conflict between the English lordship and various Irish kingdoms reinforced the long-standing pattern of endemic warfare. But, the creation of this English lordship introduced cultural frontiers into Ireland where none then existed. Lacking strong central control from England, in time the English lordship itself fragmented into competing dynasties and centres of power. Contrary to modern popular perceptions, late medieval Ireland was never divided rigidly between Irish and English, and the political and cultural frontiers along which the two societies met were not only disordered, but also porous and fluid, to the extent that it is frequently hard to delineate them precisely on a map. While English law, land-holding practices, religious orders and social customs were firmly established from the thirteenth century, these never, before the seventeenth century, prevailed throughout the whole island. There were always large areas that remained under Gaelic-Irish political, legal and cultural control, and, in addition, there were always smaller, shifting areas – contact zones or frontiers – where the two cultures collided, often violently.

The frontiers of medieval Ireland were essentially defined militarily, that is by the 'balance between war and peace'.[4] This was largely how contemporaries identified the major geographical areas of Ireland. English legal documents in particular frequently referred to the 'land of peace' and the 'land of war', noting, for example, that raiders had escaped from the 'land of peace' and were thus beyond the jurisdiction of English law.[5] Engagements involving rival groups of Irish and English occurred primarily in frontier zones, which functioned in similar ways to comparable zones throughout late medieval Europe.[6] Yet these frontiers were not isolated: they impacted, especially via cultural exchange, upon communities, both English and Irish, which did not live in them. For, as well as fighting each other, the Irish and English also inter-married across frontiers, thus connecting and transmitting their different languages, laws and customs. This means that neat ethnic labels, such as Gaelic Irish, Anglo-Norman, Anglo-Irish and Old English, which have made the complexities of late medieval and early modern Irish history more intelligible to

---

[4] B. Smith, 'The Concept of the March in Medieval Ireland: the Case of Uriel', *Proceedings of the Royal Irish Academy* 88 C (1988): 259.

[5] These terms occur throughout such legal sources as the Justiciary Rolls. For an example, see *Calendar of Justiciary Rolls of Ireland, 1295–1303*, ed. J. Mills, Dublin, 1905 [hereafter *Cal. Justic. Rolls Ire.*], 169.

[6] P. M. Duffy, 'The Nature of the Medieval Frontier in Ireland', *Studia Hibernica* 22–23 (1982–3): 38.

modern readers, have at the same time obscured many of the more subtle origins, interactions and divisions that actually existed.[7]

Late medieval Ireland was certainly a volatile place, with communities of Gaelic Irish and Anglo-Irish jostling for power, prestige and wealth, occasionally furthered by alliances, but primarily by means of localised warfare. In addition, Irish lordships continued to pursue their traditional rivalries – violently – among themselves; and even the Anglo-Normans and their descendants, fought with each other, sometimes allied to different Irish lordships, with whom they had inter-married.

Norbert Elias, one of the major twentieth-century theoreticians of violence, identified medieval European societies, up to and including the fifteenth century, as profoundly violent. According to him, 'rapine, pillage and murder were standard practice in the warrior society of this time…The pleasure in killing and torturing others was great, and it was a socially permitted pleasure'. Even the church, argued Elias, being obsessed 'by the thought of death and of what comes after', did not speak out consistently against this 'savagery'. Relations between the sexes, especially in outlying and rural areas, were brutal, being essentially regulated 'by force'. Most knights 'did not behave particularly delicately towards their own wives, or with women of lower rank', both of whom they beat indiscriminately. As a consequence, some women acted little differently from men: the 'lady of the castle' could be a 'virago with a violent temper, lively passions, subjected from her youth to all manner of physical exercise, and taking part in all the pleasures and dangers of the knights around her'.[8]

Late medieval Ireland, with its many warring lordships and lack of central, political control, would appear to offer a fine example of Elias' violent, warrior-based, society, in which cruelty was a virtue, and where clergy and women condoned, if not collaborated in, the bloodshed. Yet, as other medieval historians have recognised, while there is truth in Elias' portrait, many of the complexities and subtleties of the period have been omitted.[9] Violence certainly was highly gendered, as Elias realised, but it was not as unconstrained or as socially acceptable as he suggested. Irish warfare was never anarchic, that is without rules, even if the rules were often

---

7 T. O'Keeffe, 'Concepts of "Castle" and the Construction of Identity in Medieval and Post-Medieval Ireland', *Irish Geography* 34, no. 1 (2001): 80; D. Edwards, 'Collaboration without Anglicisation: the Macgiollapadraig Lordship and Tudor Reform', in *Gaelic Ireland: Land, Lordship and Settlement, c. 1250–1650*, eds P.J. Duffy, D. Edwards and E. Fitzpatrick, Dublin, 2001, 77–97. Names do however have to be used to refer to these various groups. Following current historiographical usage, in this paper the terms used are mainly Anglo-Norman, for the first generations of arrivals from England, Wales and Flanders, and Anglo-Irish or Old English for their descendants. Gaelic Irish will refer to those who were culturally, linguistically and legally considered by themselves and others to be Irish.
8 N. Elias, *The Civilizing Process: Sociogenetic and Psychogenetic Investigations*, trans. E. Jephcott, rev. edn, Oxford and Maldon, MA, 2000, 162–5, 246–7.
9 For an important article that both applies and critiques Elias' theories about medieval violence, see R.W. Kaeuper, 'Chivalry and the "Civilizing Process"', in *Violence in Medieval Society*, ed. R.W. Kaeuper, Woodbridge, 2000, 21–35.

not formally articulated. Women, as Elias pointed out, were not immune from violence, although in theory they should have been, but they experienced it in particular ways that were sometimes different from the experiences of men.

War and Gender

Whereas Elias, writing originally in the 1930s, had stressed the gendered nature of medieval violence, to date few Irish historians have acknowledged gender as a vital tool in analysing Irish warfare between the twelfth and seventeenth centuries. Yet the most obvious characteristic of gendered warfare was readily recognised by contemporary participants: women were not supposed to fight in wars, while men were. In 1317 Domnall Ua Néill wrote a famous 'Remonstrance' to the pope, outlining the reasons for Gaelic-Irish participation in a war against the English:

> 'We are compelled to wage deadly war with them [the English]... preferring under stress of necessity to put ourselves like men to the trial of war in defence of our right, rather than to bear like women their atrocious outrages.'[10]

Thus, in common with other medieval European societies, to the Irish, warfare was gendered male. Women's only role was that of victim, suffering 'atrocious outrages' with resignation, and without responding aggressively.

This rigid gendering of violence meant that the active involvement of women in organised military campaigns, when it occurred – and it did occur – was startling enough to provoke critical comment.[11] Fighting was synonymous with masculinity. Therefore, fighting by women usually impacted negatively on the masculinity of male opponents and also of allies. This is clear from a contemporary account of the actions of Alice of Abervenny, an Anglo-Norman woman, fighting the Irish at the important battle of Baginbun in May 1170:

> 'To a wench they gave
> An axe of tempered steel,
> And she beheaded them all
> And then threw their bodies over the cliff,
> Because she had that day
> Lost her lover in the combat.

---

10 'The Remonstrance of the Irish Princes to Pope John XXII, 1317', in *Irish Historical Documents, 1172–1922*, eds E. Curtis and R.B. McDowell, New York, 1943, 45.
11 For a discussion of general medieval attitudes to women warriors, see M. McLaughlin, 'The Woman Warrior: Gender, Warfare and Society in Medieval Europe', *Women's Studies* 17 (1990): 193–209.

> Alice of Abervenny was her name
> Who served the Irish thus.
> In order to disgrace the Irish
> The knights did this.
> And the Irish of the district
> Were discomfited in this way.'[12]

Alice was obviously not fighting as an ordinary soldier. She had been on the sidelines and was unarmed, until she was given an axe. The presence of women in the trains of pre-modern armies is not often mentioned, but we know that they were there. And in the case of the Anglo-Normans, who originally arrived in Ireland as allies and settlers, as well as soldiers, there is little doubt that women were present among the first groups.[13] But the male Anglo-Norman chronicler gives Alice a very personal motive for wanting to fight: revenge for the killing of her male lover. This interpretation allows Anglo-Norman violence to remain masculine, as Alice's case is exceptional. Nevertheless, her male companions, by giving her an axe when she is maddened by grief, are using her not just to defeat the Irish, but to emasculate them. Any man who could be injured or killed by a woman was 'disgraced', and, indeed, Irish men in the whole district were 'discomfited' by such an event. At the very outset of their campaign against the Irish, the Anglo-Normans were therefore using a woman as a weapon of war, despite war being gendered as exclusively male.

This episode raises questions about attitudes to the intersection of gender and violence displayed in contemporary sources. For instance, was widespread damage to infrastructure and resources, including houses, churches and crops, seen as an inevitable feature of life on a violent frontier? And, in this context, is the explicit mention of violence towards women and children an indicator of the writer's attitude to the perpetrators? There is evidence that this is so, although we must be cautious in the way we interpret the brief and sometimes contradictory sources. Since the main sources, the Irish annals, were written by clerics, it is understandable that the destruction of church buildings and the killing of clergy were considered particularly abhorrent. This is perhaps the reason for the specific report of the burning of the church of Emlagh in 1236, in which were sheltering 'women, children and nuns, among them three priests'.[14] These non-combatants clearly recognised their vulnerability in the face of the attacking forces and sought the best shelter that

---

12 *The Song of Dermot and the Earl*, ed. and trans. G. H. Orpen, Oxford, 1892 (new edn, Felinfach, 1994), 111, lines 1478–89. This portion of the poem is also discussed by Brendan Smith, '"I have nothing but through her": Women and the Conquest of Ireland, 1170–1240', in *Studies on Medieval and Early Modern Women: Pawns or Players?*, eds Ch. Meek and C. Lawless, Dublin, 2003, 49.

13 The question of whether or not the first waves of Anglo-Normans were colonisers has been discussed at length by historians. For an overview see S. Duffy, *Ireland in the Middle Ages*, Houndmills and London, 1997, 57–80.

14 *Annála Connacht*, ed. A. M. Freeman, Dublin, 1944 [hereafter *Ann. Conn.*] date: 1236.

was available, in the supposedly inviolable church building. It would appear that when a writer was keen to emphasise the especially serious nature of destructive attacks, the usual way to do so was to include reference to the killing of women and children, as well as of non-combatant men like clergy. Thus, the willingness of aggressors to attack women, especially if they were sheltering in a church, was taken as a sign of unusual ferocity, beyond that normally accepted by a violent society.

The report in the annals of a sortie in 1315 emphasises the scale and senseless violence of the destruction by noting that: 'an Infinite number of cowes, garrons and sheep were killed by them [the attackers], stripping gentlewomen that could make noe resistance of theire cloathes to theire naked skins: Destroyed and killed without remorse children and Little ones of that jorney'.[15] Here widespread destruction of valuable resources, such as livestock, and the killing of small children are explicitly linked to the humiliation and possible sexual assault of 'gentlewomen', who, it is implied, should not have been treated in this manner. That this level and type of violence was considered by the clerical annalist to be unacceptable is clear from the conclusion to the entry: 'There was not soe much hurt done in them parts before in any man's memory without profitt to the doers thereof'. Such episodes demonstrate that the Irish frontiers, although often very violent places, were not without rules governing the extent and nature of that violence, even if those rule were broken. Elias' characterisation of violence as widely accepted, even by the church, is certainly not borne out by accounts in the Irish annals.

Attacks on elite women were especially repugnant. In the eyes of the annalists, such women obviously deserved respect, and when they did not receive this, it reflected badly on the perpetrators of violence. Elite women are not often described as being outside the protective walls of home or church. Thus, when this protection was breached, it had significant implications for both the male aggressors and the male defenders. Defenders who could not ensure the safety of their women were in grave danger of defeat – and, perhaps even worse, of humiliation. Aggressors able to breach castle walls and kill, injure or capture the women supposedly safe inside had won a symbolic victory, if nothing else. But they also sometimes inspired reprisals. In 1310 Áed Ui Conchobhair led an attack on Maelruanaidh Mac Diarmada, in Clogher castle, during which many women and children were killed. As a consequence Áed himself was killed in a retaliatory raid.[16] This scenario is described frequently in the accounts of warfare contained in the Irish annals. Despite attempts by the church to promote the ideal of protecting women from violence, there is no doubt that killing or capturing the close female relatives of a

---

15 *The Annals of Clonmacnoise, being Annals of Ireland from the Earliest Period to AD 1408, Translated into English, 1637 by Connell Mageoghan*, ed. D. Murphy, Dublin, 1896 [hereafter *Ann. Clon.*], date: 1315.

16 *Annala Rioghachta Eireann: Annals of the Kingdom of Ireland by the Four Masters from the Earliest Period to the Year 1616*, ed. J. Donovan, 7 vols, Dublin, 1851 [hereafter *A. F. M.*] and *Ann. Clon.*, date: 1310.

king or lord had considerable prestige value; and also diplomatic value in communities where the holding and exchange of hostages played a major role in warfare.

Female relatives of key participants in conflicts could be taken hostage and their release used to achieve diplomatic leverage. Such captures usually occurred when defensive dwellings were breached or when women were travelling, and thus more vulnerable. In 1224, for example, William Marshal with his Irish ally, the O'Reilly, besieged a *crannog* (a defended artificial island) on which were sheltering a number of women, including female relatives of William de Lacy. Once the *crannog* was taken, Marshal informed the king that 'within 15 days after' these letters are gone the mother of William would also be prisoner, unless her nephew the King of Connaught return to the King's peace through her'.[17] Clearly Marshal expected the threatened capture of de Lacy's Gaelic-Irish mother, Rose, to force her Irish nephew to support the English against his half-Irish uncle.[18] This episode illustrates, not only the use of captured women to pressurise their male relatives, but also the very complicated marriage alliances that had developed between the Irish and the English within only a few decades of the arrival of the Anglo-Normans. Several years later, a dispute between two members of the Ua Chonchobair family led to the capture of the wife of one of them, who was travelling with her husband when seized. She was then handed over by her Irish captors to the English, presumably to be used as a bargaining tool in their negotiations with her husband, as well as a weapon in the war between two Irish factions.[19]

Rather than violence diminishing at the end of the medieval period, as Elias argued, in Ireland it increased and became more widespread and brutal during the fifteenth century and especially the sixteenth century. Under the Tudors the English embarked on a concerted effort to extend their control throughout the country. A heightened level of anti-Irish feeling was evident among the so-called 'New English', who arrived in increasing numbers from the 1550s onwards. These were soldiers, officials, clergy and adventurers, who considered that their origins as Protestant Englishmen, untainted by generations of intermixing with the Irish, made them superior to those termed the 'Old English', whose families had lived in Ireland for centuries and most of whom had rejected the Protestant Reformation.

Violence intensified, including violence against women and non-combatants. Sixteenth-century English commentators were explicit on this point. One describes how, in 1569, Sir Humphrey Gilbert justified attacking women and burning crops by saying that the men would not fight without their '"Calliackes" [*cailleacha*, old women], or women who milked their "Creates" [*creacha*, herds] and provided their victuals and other necessities. So that the killing of them by the

---

17 *Calendar of Documents Relating to Ireland Preserved in Her Majesty's Public Record Office, London*, eds H.S. Sweetman and G.F. Hancock, 5 vols, London, 1875–86, vol. I, 182–4.
18 J. Lydon, 'The Expansion and Consolidation of the Colony, 1215–54', in *A New History of Ireland: Volume II*, ed. Cosgrove, 156–204.
19 *Ann. Conn.*, date: 1227.

sword was the way to kill the men of war by famine'.[20] These attacks were planned with the gendered nature of warfare in mind. Women were the primary suppliers of food and shelter, though strictly speaking non-combatants. But their supportive roles were so crucial that they themselves became targets. Gilbert, and other English commanders, recognised that killing Irish women was a sure method of defeating Irish men.

As these examples demonstrate, women played important and identifiable roles in the endemic warfare that characterised late medieval Ireland. And this was true whether the warfare was conducted between the Gaelic Irish and the Anglo-Irish, or within the Irish and English communities. But women were not only victims of male violence, they also participated directly and actively themselves in violence, whether it was in the form of warfare or of crime.

Violent Women

Elite women, who took on the role of lord in the absence of their husbands or in defence of family interests, were recognised as assuming masculine duties, but this was an expected part of their function as the wives of rulers.[21] There are numerous instances of women operating within these gendered expectations in late medieval Ireland. In 1315, for example, Áed Ua Domnaill, lord of Tír Conaill (now Donegal), advanced south into Connacht and 'destroyed all that contry by the advice of his wife [Dearbhfhorgaill], the daughter of Magnus o' Connor and [she] came herself with a great route of gallowglasses and took all the spoyles of the churches of Dromkliew without respect of church or churchmen of that place'.[22]

There are a number of ways to read this very interesting episode. By including the information that Áed had invaded Connacht at the urging of his wife, the annalist may, by implication, be criticising his actions. Since Connacht was the territory of the Uí Chonchobair (the O'Connors), the invasion indicates that his marriage had given Áed an interest in internal Uí Chonchobair politics and rivalries. Advising their husbands on matters of war and diplomacy was a recognised, if controversial, avenue for women's involvement in war. But what was striking in this case, and what probably prompted the annalist to record the incident, was the fact that Dearbhfhorgaill not only advised, but actually led the Uí Dhomnaills' fearsome Scottish mercenaries, known as galloglass (Scottish *galloglaigh*, foreign

---

20 T. Churchyard, *A Generall Rehearsall of Warres*, quoted in D. B. Quinn, *The Elizabethans and the Irish*, Ithaca, 1966, 127. Quinn, who was not usually highly critical of the English and had even published an admiring biography of Gilbert, nevertheless titled his chapter on Elizabeth's Irish wars in this book, 'Horror Story'.

21 K. A. Lo Prete, 'Gendering Viragos: Medieval Perceptions of Powerful Women', in *Studies in Medieval and Early Modern Women, 4: Victims or Viragos?*, eds Ch. Meek and C. Lawless, Dublin, 2005, 17–38.

22 *Ann. Clon.*, date: 1315.

soldier), in despoiling the churches of Connacht. The annalist's evident disapproval of these actions may at least in part have been prompted by his clerical status, and so his opposition to attacks on churches. Much later, in 1590, in the same lordship, Ineenduv, the daughter of James Mac Donnell, as part of a campaign to ensure that her son, Hugh Roe, would succeed his father as chieftain of Tír Conaill, arranged a deadly attack on a rival claimant.[23] Women from lordly families, whether Irish or English, could organise and direct violence in the interests of their husbands or sons. Although personally leading bands of soldiers was unusual, it was within the boundaries of recognised female behaviour.

But, like Dearbhfhorgaill, many elite women played crucial roles as advisors, counsellors and translators for their husbands. The language skills of women, who had married across frontiers, could be especially valuable. Yet English sources agreed with Irish ones in deploring the tendency of men to rely upon the advice and aid of women. In fact, the English regarded this as a particular failing of Irishmen, that demonstrated flaws in their masculinity; and such flaws were also to be found among leading Old English families, who had inter-married with the Irish and adopted Irish customs. Such attitudes were very evident during the wars of the late sixteenth century. In 1574, for instance, Sir Henry Sidney, the lord deputy, reported to the privy council in London that the Gaelic-Irish lord of central Ulster, Turlough Luineach O'Neill, who was resisting English demands, was under the influence of 'the lewd counsel of his wife', the Scottish Agnes Campbell.[24] Similarly, Eleanor Butler, the countess of the Old English lordship of Desmond, who was known to advise her rebellious husband, the 15th earl, was considered by English officials to be dangerous. In 1583 she was described as the earl's 'wicked wife', who 'had been the chief trainer of her husband'.[25]

Women who had married across frontiers could experience violence very directly, and sometimes they did not choose to support their husbands with advice, but to turn violence against them. In the frontier zones of late medieval Ireland, as in much of the rest of Europe at the time, skirmishes, raids and even battles tended to be concentrated on strongholds, such as castles, which were centres of military power, but also domestic habitations and so homes to many women.[26] When violence breached castle walls, women were not only caught up in it as victims, but also as witnesses, even participants and, on occasion, as instigators. Women were often present in defended castles because of strategic marriages aimed at establishing peace between some of Ireland's many warring lordships. These marriages across

---

23 *A. F. M.*, date: 1590.
24 *Calendar of State Papers Relating to Ireland, 1574–85*, London, 1860–1911 [hereafter *Cal. S. P. Irel., 1574–85*], 107; see also W. Palmer, 'Gender, Violence and Rebellion in Tudor and early Stuart Ireland', *The Sixteenth Century Journal* 23 (1992): 701.
25 *Cal. S. P. Irel., 1574–85*, 417; see also A. Chamber, *As Wicked as a Woman: Eleanor, Countess of Desmond*, Dublin, 1986.
26 O'Keeffe, 'Concepts of "Castle"', 69–88.

frontiers and borders had inherent dangers and could produce conflicts of loyalty. Some of the women concerned were perhaps never trusted to have replaced loyalty to their father's family with loyalty to their husband's. Women certainly appear on occasion to have used their privileged positions in defended places to facilitate the capture or destruction of the stronghold. In 1266, for instance, Mathgamain Ó Cuiléin was killed in bed with a knife by his own wife, the daughter of MacCarthaig.[27] Female betrayal and violence appears also to have been behind reports of the destruction of Limerick Castle, where 'both stone and wood was burned by one woman in 1413', and the capture of Athlone Castle in 1455, as it was 'taken by the English having been betrayed by a woman who was in it'.[28] Women were believed to be more prone to use tactics, such as betrayal, secret attacks or poisonings, to achieve what 'honest' male fighting could not.

Castles were also the sites of the exercise of public largesse and hospitality, which were vital to the development and maintenance of the delicate weave of personal relationships between lordly families that characterised late medieval Irish politics. Here too women, though rarely mentioned, were centrally important. In 1305 the strands of personal relationships, public hospitality and gendered roles within castles were major factors in the successful ploy used by the Englishman, Sir Piers Bermingham, to rid himself of his troublesome Gaelic-Irish opponents. He invited the Ua Chonchobair Failge to his castle at Carbery in Kildare. Piers had acted as co-sponsor, with Muirchertach Ua Conchobair Failge, at the baptism of Muirchertach's nephew, thus establishing, according to Irish custom, an important personal relationship between the two families. Yet, when all the Ua Chonchobair Failge party, including the child, his father and his uncle, and over twenty followers, were in the castle, Piers ordered that they be killed. This massacre was described by the Gaelic-Irish annalist as both 'deceitful and shameful'. But it was made even worse by the actions of Piers' English-born wife.[29] Expected to help preside over a public display of hospitality and goodwill, she instead stood safely on the battlements of the castle and showed Piers' men where to find the hiding Ua Chonchobair Failge. The actions of both Piers and his wife were condemned in the Gaelic-Irish sources as appalling examples of English treachery, and the Irish were warned never to trust any of the English.[30] Piers had flouted conventions governing war, hospitality and family relationships. In the Irish sources his warrior status – and, indeed, his very status as a man – was implicitly called into question. He could not win in a fair fight, as a man should, instead he resorted to treacherous means, notably employing the secretive wiles of a woman. This episode tells us a great deal about

---

27 *The Annals of Inisfallen (MS Rawlinson B 503)*, ed. S. Mac Airt, Dublin, 1951, date: 1455.
28 A. F. M., dates: 1455, 1413.
29 She is not named but is referred to as *gaillsech Sacsanach*, or English-born foreigner. Dr Hall is grateful to Dr Katharine Simms for correspondence on this point.
30 'The Remonstrance of the Irish Princes to Pope John XXII, 1317', in *Irish Historical Documents, 1172–1922*, eds Curtis and McDowell, 38–45.

what was acceptable and unacceptable violence in late medieval Ireland, as well as something about attitudes to the role of women.

Assessing gendered expectations of violent behaviour in women who were not of the lordly class is, however, much more difficult, largely due to the loss of many of the medieval Irish primary sources.[31] Analysis of legal documents should reveal some of these gendered understandings of criminal violence. Gaelic-Irish law, also known as Brehon law, operated throughout much of the country during the late medieval period. Important Gaelic-Irish and Anglo-Irish families employed *brithemain* or specially trained judges to adjudicate disputes and levy the payment of fines according to carefully differentiated gradings, based on the nature of the injury received and on the status of both victim and perpetrator.[32] While records of few actual cases exist from the late medieval period, there is a wealth of evidence attesting to the extent of the usage of Brehon law with regards to women and physical or verbal violence.[33] In the Irish legal texts women were generally assumed to be non-combatants in warfare, along with priests and children, however the writers and their later glossators, certainly envisioned women perpetrating violent crimes, as the laws mention punishments for women killing by poisoning or arson, and infanticide.[34] The texts recognised in particular the destructive effects of women's speech. A 'sharp-tongued virago', one who had 'fierce words' and a 'sorceress who trafficks in charms' were disqualified from some forms of compensation for injury, along with vagrant women and lunatics.[35]

While frustratingly little survives of Gaelic-Irish legal cases, there are records of criminal cases in the common law sources from the areas of Ireland under English legal jurisdiction. In these sources there are many records of women being accused of violent crimes. Analysis of some of the surviving cases suggests that courts often did not regard women as fully responsible for their actions, or judged their

---

31   Most of the medieval records of the English administration in Ireland preserved into modern times were destroyed in a fire at the Public Record Office, Dublin, caused by the outbreak of the Irish Civil War in 1922. Finding-aids and notes on some of the destroyed records survived the fire and have been used in this analysis. For a discussion of the extent of the losses and the state of the surviving sources for medieval Irish history, see P. Connolly, *Medieval Record Sources*, Maynooth Research Guides for Irish Local History, Dublin, 2002.

32   F. Kelly, *A Guide to Early Irish Law*, Dublin, 1988, 250-60; K. Nicholls, *Gaelic and Gaelicised Ireland in the Middle Ages*, Dublin, 1972, 44-57. The Irish legal texts were written in the early Christian period and were used, copied and commented upon through the medieval period.

33   Kelly, *A Guide to Early Irish Law*, 252-60; see also G. Mac Niocaill, 'Notes on Litigation in Late Irish Law', *Irish Jurist* 2 (1967): 299-307, who points out that there is virtually no information on the prosecution of criminal cases in sixteenth-century Irish sources.

34   '*Sellach*-Text', trans. in Kelly, *A Guide to Early Irish Law*, 352; *Cáin Adomnáin*, trans. M. Ní Dhonnchadha, in *Adomnán at Birr, A.D. 697: Essays in Commemoration of the Law of the Innocents*, ed. T. O'Loughlin, Dublin, 2001, 45. Abortion and infanticide were two of the grounds on which a man could divorce his wife. For the eighth-century text, *Cáin Lánamna*, see *The Field Day Anthology of Irish Writing: Volume IV. Women's Writing and Traditions*, eds Angela Bourke et al., Cork and New York, 2002, 28.

35   D. A. Binchy, 'Bretha Crólige', *Ériu* 12 (1938): 27-9, 35.

disputes to be of less significance than those of men. In 1312, for example, Matilda Baroun alleged that Elena, wife of Laurence de Milltoun, attacked her with four armed men, over a private dispute. Although the court records indicate that the jury agreed the action had occurred, the participants were let off with only a fine.[36]

Yet women could also be convicted of violent crimes without having engaged in violence at all. This was particularly so if they were Irish and living amongst the English, who were clearly suspicious of their Gaelic-Irish neighbours. In frontier zones it was often difficult to distinguish between combatants and non-combatants, and even sometimes between Irish and English. The English authorities partly dealt with this problem by charging those they could arrest with aiding violent men, who had usually been outlawed and so were beyond the reach of the courts. Many women were brought before the courts in the late thirteenth and early fourteenth centuries charged with aiding and abetting family members who had breached English law. In 1311, for example, Fynyna Octouthy and his daughter, Isabella, were charged, convicted and hanged for receiving William and Tayg, who were Fynyna's sons, after they had murdered an English official in Carlow.[37] These women had not committed murder, yet they were judged to be as responsible for the deed because they had helped their male relatives to escape.

Women obviously played significant and sometimes crucial roles in the frontier warfare that characterised late medieval Ireland. They were doubtless victims on many occasions, but to portray them solely as victims, which some of the contemporary sources strove to do, would give a very misleading picture. On occasion, women fought personally; more commonly perhaps, women from lordly families directed fighting men or advised their male relatives on tactics. Such women could also prove significant as hostages. Below the elite level, we can catch glimpses in the scanty sources of women protecting husbands, sons and fathers, even at the cost of their own lives; and also of women providing essential food and shelter for fighting men and, again, as a consequence, becoming targets for violent reprisals.

Conclusion

The frontiers of late medieval Ireland are fascinating places, where relentless and often gruesome violence went hand-in-hand with sophisticated cultural interchange. They might appear, at first glance, to lend credence to Elias' portrait of medieval Europe as a violent and lawless place, dominated by male warrior elites who did little else but fight each other, slaughter their unfortunate prisoners, hunt animals incessantly, and brutalise any women who came near them. Writing from a psychoanalytical point of view, Elias saw this as a society dominated by the primitive 'id'; only from the sixteenth century onwards did the 'super ego', or conscience,

---

36 *Cal. Justic. Rolls Ire., 1308–1314*, 243.
37 Ibid., 233.

begin to make its presence felt in a 'civilizing process' fostered at princely Renaissance courts and later by centralising nation states.[38]

The Irish frontiers were certainly violent places, perhaps more violent than many others at the time, but they were far from anarchic. There were ancient and elaborate law codes in operation, whether Irish Brehon law or English common law, regulating individual behaviour. In addition, we can see from the Irish annals, written by clerics, that the church had very decided opinions as to what was and what was not acceptable in terms of violence. Both the violence and the secular and ecclesiastical rules and expectations impacted heavily upon women, often in distinctive ways.

Some older histories of late medieval Ireland virtually never mention women; it almost appears to be a society wholly composed of men – and elite, violent men at that. The destruction of many sources has certainly made it difficult to study this period of Irish history in great detail. Nevertheless, we will never fully understand either the violence or the complex cultures that characterised this society for over four centuries until we put women into the picture alongside men and explore the gendered nature of life, and death, on the late medieval Irish frontiers.

---

38 Elias, *The Civilizing Process*, 160, 162; see also S. Fontaine, 'The Civilizing Process Revisited: Interview with Norbert Elias', *Theory and Society* 5, no. 2 (1978): 243–53.

Irregular Warfare and the Norms of Legitimate Violence in Twentieth Century Europe*

Pieter Lagrou

Throughout history, warfare has always been a highly codified exercise of violence. In pre-modern societies, war was part of elaborate rituals and the warrior belonged to a distinct category of society. As such, war was a very specific kind of interpersonal violence, between recognized entities – tribes, kingdoms, nations – and subject to a code of honour, regulating the opening and closing of hostilities, lawful and unlawful acts of violence and ways of killing, the treatment of the corpses of killed enemies and of prisoners, norms as to whom was recognized as an adversary and who was not.[1] The latter implied that certain categories – children, the elderly, women, and slaves – were not part of the acts of war, even though they could be considered as spoils of war. Yet, it also implied that codes of honourable warfare only extended to enemies recognized as equals and not, or not in the same form, to barbarians or infidels. The modern era, with the *levée en masse*, massified (mobilised the masses – this is the French Revolution, not Ludendorff!) warfare, but at the same time, this transformation was accompanied by an international effort to codify legitimate forms of warfare, to protect civilian populations, to come to the aid of wounded soldiers, to monitor prisoners of war etc., with the International Red Cross and the various international conventions, such as The Hague Convention of 1907 as its most visible outcome.

The advent of total war in the twentieth century radically challenged these nineteenth century efforts to 'civilize' warfare. The scale of violence increased exponentially from the first to the Second World War, from Verdun to Auschwitz and Hiroshima. With the techniques of mass destruction, the number of victims multiplied and the distinction between soldiers and civilians was blurred. It is often

---

* This article was originally published in Italian under the title: 'La guerra irregolare e le norme della violenza legittima nell'Europa del novecento' in *Crimini e memorie di guerra*, eds L. Baldissara and P. Pezzino, Napoli, 2004), 89–102.

[1] See M. Howard, G. Andreopoulos and M. Shulman (eds), *The Laws of War: Constraints on Warfare in the Western World*, New Haven, 1994.

implied that this mechanical change also affected the behaviour of the belligerents, numbing their sensibilities, lowering the thresholds of the exercise of interpersonal violence, a process described as 'brutalisation'. As a result the norms applying to the forms of legitimate violence and codifying 'honourable warfare' became increasingly irrelevant. In this article I will amend this general assumption on two points. First of all, in the context of generalised transgressions of norms of legitimate violence, particularly against civilians, there was also a partial restoration of codes of honourable warfare in peculiar areas, a counter-current that is indispensable to understand both the attitudes of the belligerents and the events they produced. The use of combat gas or nuclear bombs, to mention only the most obvious examples, triggered fundamental debates and each established new interdictions. Secondly, the observance of the laws of war was based on the anticipation of reciprocity: only those adversaries deemed capable of an honourable behaviour could enjoy the respect of international law. This anticipation was intimately linked to racial imagination, distinguishing civilised adversaries, worthy of respect, and savages, who knew no honour and no rule. This second development explains the first: the partitioning of the world in a civilised and a barbarian sphere, allowed for a partial restoration of norms of honourable warfare in the former, while removing any normativity in the latter. It is a central contention of this paper that this process shows a remarkable continuity all through the century and more particularly, that 1945 did not constitute a major rupture in this mental constellation of modern warfare.

The distinction between soldiers and civilians stands at the heart of the anticipation of reciprocity. If the adversary is suspected of intentionally blurring this distinction, his soldiers forego the protection of the international statute of prisoner of war and his civilian population exposes itself to all forms of retaliation, including mass executions. Central to these accusations, suspicions and outright fantasies are the *Heckenschützen, francs-tireurs, partisans, bandits* or *terrorists*, that is, dishonourable adversaries avoiding the open confrontation of regular army units through secret attacks. The *franc-tireur* is a steadfast archetypal figure of twentieth century warfare, but at first sight, a puzzling inversion occurs on the Western front between the first and the Second World War. In the long controversy over *franc-tireur* activity and German atrocities in reprisal in August 1914 in Belgium and the North of France, the German side insisted on the reality of the partisans' attacks, while the allied side vehemently denied the very existence of it.[2] Apparently, both sides shared a common acceptance of the rule that, had there been *franc-tireur* activity, the reprisals against the civilian population would have been legitimate. During the Second World War, both sides to some extent inversed their roles. The allied nations very much pride themselves on *franc tireur* activity, even where and when such activity was very limited, thus underlining the legitimacy of partisan warfare against invasion and occupation. The German occupier rather plays down

---

2 See J. Horne and A. Kramer, *German Atrocities 1914: A History of Denial*, New Haven, 2001.

the impact of partisan activity and particularly insists on blaming foreign elements for terrorism, thus threatening the entente, based on shared interests and correct behaviour, between the population of occupied West European nations and Nazi Germany.

The newly acquired legitimacy of partisan warfare serves as an illustration for the erosion of the rules of classical warfare under the pressure of total war. It also announces the debates that will divide colonising nations after 1945. How, for example, could France at the same time glorify its own *maquis* fighters, whilst ruthlessly repressing liberation movements in its empire? The figure of the *franc tireur* on the Western Front during the Second World War therefore deserves a closer look.

Let us first of all look at the German side. At the time of the invasion of the Netherlands, Belgium and France, the atrocities of 1914 were on everybody's minds. They had constituted a crucial reference for the behaviour of German troops during the invasion of Poland in September 1939.[3] In May 1940, their memory triggered a massive exodus of millions of civilians, fleeing the advance of the German troops.[4] The German army however was very concerned with its image and tried by all means to present itself as a disciplined, efficient, and even courteous force. The renaissance of chivalric warriors, respectful of the laws of war, was central to the way Nazi Germany represented itself. To some extent, this propaganda was successful, as the civilian population returned swiftly and massively to their homes after the end of the hostilities in mid June. The impression of a courteous and disciplined occupying force also constituted a powerful psychological context that serves to explain the attraction of collaboration and loyal acceptance of the occupation during the second half of 1940 and early 1941. The German occupier even went one step further and turned the accusation of unruly behaviour and atrocities against the defenders. Mayors and civil servants who had fled their municipalities were accused of having irresponsibly abandoned their posts and their constituency at a time when their leadership was most needed and as a result they were fired.[5] In Belgium, the occupier organised a show trial to judge the initiators of the improvised deportation of suspects during the first days of the invasion. In the generalised panic of early May 1940, hundreds of pro-Nazis were rounded up and evacuated by train to internment camps in the South of France, together with German citizens and "apatrids" ("Displaced persons" is a vocabulary of 1945 – here is meant: formerly German citizens stripped of their German nationality by the Nazi State because of their emigration- for the most part German dissidents and Jews. In the midst of the collapse of the French retreat, French soldiers in Abbeville executed a

---

3   Jochen Böhler, *Auftakt zum Vernichtungskrieg: Die Wehrmacht in Polen 1939*, Frankfurt/Main, 2006.
4   See J. Gérard-Libois and J. Gotovitch, *L'an 40: La Belgique occupé*, Brussels, 1971 105–122 ; J. Vidalenc, *L'exode de mai-juin 1940*, Paris, 1957.
5   See B. De Wever, *Greep naar de Macht: Vlaams-Nationalisme en Nieuwe Orde. Het VNV 1933–1945*, Tielt, 1994, 430–1.

convoy of twenty-one Belgian Nazis, among them their leader Joris van Seeveren.[6] In Chartres, the local *préfet*, Jean Moulin, attempted to commit suicide, when the local German commander forced him to sign a document accusing French colonial troops of atrocities actually committed by the *Wehrmacht*.[7]

The *Wehrmacht* did commit atrocities and war crimes during its invasion of the densely populated areas of Belgium and the North of France and the phantom of the *franc tireurs* was still very much part of the mental universe of German soldiers. But it is interesting to observe the German efforts to wipe out all traces of these crimes and the unwillingness to pursue once more the strategy of accusing the local population of unlawful behaviour to justify German exactions. The massacre of Vinkt and Meigem, two villages near Ghent in the North of Belgium are an interesting illustration of this phenomenon.[8] The German troops had crossed the river Lys at one undefended section and rapidly advanced into enemy territory. The Belgian army had held its positions to the left and right of the undefended section and it fired and shelled the German battalion from behind. The rumour of *franc tireur* attacks rapidly spread from the front to the German rear and in the course of three chaotic days preceding the Belgian surrender on 28 May, over one hundred civilians, mostly refugees from other localities, were shot, as well as several prisoners of war evacuated behind the lines. On one of the mass graves, the German army placed a wooden cross with the inscription: 'Soldiers and *franc tireurs*'. The cross was taken into custody by the communal authorities some weeks later, to serve as a proof after the war, but the Germans searched the city hall, confiscated and destroyed it. Looted valuables belonging to some of the murdered civilians were restituted to the communal authorities in March 1943 through the intermediary of the Red Cross. According to the local legend, these had been found on soldiers of Marshall Paulus' sixth army, killed at Stalingrad a few weeks earlier. In 1948, the Belgian *War Crimes Commission* reached the conclusion, on this basis, that the main culprits were dead and it stalled the persecution, but subsequent research revealed that none of the units active in the Lys offensive had been part of the sixth army, and that the atrocities were still very much alive in the regimental memory of the units concerned, among others through a wealth of photographic evidence.

---

6   Belgian officials, most prominently Walter Ganshof van der Meersch, were imprisoned in Brussels but after the charges were dropped in October 1941, they were never brought to trial. Luitenant René Caron and Sergeant Émile-François Mollet of the French army were court-martialled in Paris and executed in April 1942 on the Mont Valérien. See C. Vlaemynck, *Dossier Abbeville*, Leuven, 1977, 147–178.

7   See J. Cordier, *Jean Moulin, l'inconnu du Panthéon. Vol. 2 : Le Choix d'un destin, juin 1936-novembre 1940*, Paris, 1989, 327–334.

8   *Belgique, Commission des crimes de guerre (1944), Les crimes de guerre commis lors de l'invasion du territoire national. Mai 1940. Les massacres de Vinkt*, Liège, 1948, 27. See also P. Taghon, 'Vinkt, Meigem et Deinze: Quand les légendes deviennent des vérités', *Jours de Guerre*, vol. 5, Brussels, 1991, 19–35.

The fantasy of a chivalric war on the Western Front was an integral part of the Nazi vision of a future European order. Hitler's official motivation of his decision to liberate all Dutch prisoners of war is very revealing in this regard. 'In its combat with the Dutch army, the German army has taken all possible precaution to protect the population and spare the country. This German attitude has been in great measure reciprocated both by the Dutch military and by the civilian population. This corresponds to the cultural and moral level of the Dutch people, who are the next of kin of us, Germans. [...] The Dutch soldier has always fought an open and honest battle and he has treated our wounded soldiers and our prisoners consequently. The civilian population has not taken part in the combat and it has acted in accordance with the laws of humanity towards our wounded'.[9] What Hitler did not mention, is that the Dutch army hardly fought a battle, since it capitulated after five days because of the savage aerial bombing of the civilian population of Rotterdam by the *Luftwaffe*. But all Dutch conscripts could return home and the Dutch professional soldiers were liberated on their word of honour that they would abstain from any hostilities against Germany, an oath that only sixty officers of the colonial army refused.[10] Belgian soldiers of Flemish expression were liberated after a language test, while most French speaking prisoners of Belgian and French nationality were held captive for the full length of the war. Even for this group, though, the scrupulous respect of the Geneva conventions, extending even to Jewish or communist prisoners, had a 'chivalric' character, when compared to the systematic massacres and the starving of soviet prisoners of war.[11]

The stark warning the chief of staff Nikolaus von Falkenhorst felt compelled to address to the German troops stationed in Norway on the eve of operation Barbarossa, in June 1941, shows precisely the extent to which the anticipation of reciprocity was rooted in the racial imagination. 'Unlike the chivalric battle to which they have been used in Norway, each officer and each soldier of the army should expect in the war against Russia the most insidious, the most dishonest and least warrior-like behaviour from the Russian commanders. The enemy will revert without scruples to all means of deceit, dissimulation and propaganda and he will not hesitate to commit any crime'.[12] The *Partisanenkrieg* was a reality for German soldiers even before they first set foot on soviet territory.

9 *Enquêtecommissie regeringsbeleid 1940–1945: Verslag houdende de uikomsten van het onderzoek. Deel 8* ^(A en B). *Militair Beleid 1940–1945. Terugkeer naar Nederlands Indië. Verslag en Bijlagen*. La Haye, Staatsdrukkerij- en uitgeverijbedrijf, 1956, 36.
10 Ibid. 37–9.
11 This does not mean that they were not the object of discriminating treatment, in violation of the Geneva convention, including detention in separate quarters and, in some camps for some months, the obligation to wear the yellow star on their uniform. See Y. Durand, *La Captivité. Histoire des Prisonniers de guerre français, 1939–1945*, Paris, 1981, 354–6.
12 G. Ueberschär und W. Wette (eds), *Der deutsche Überfall auf die Sowjetunion: 'Unternehmen Barbarossa' 1941*. Frankfurt/Main, 1997, 262–3.

The savagery of the war on the Eastern Front, when German soldiers received detailed instructions compelling them to violate the Geneva convention, not to speak of their massive participation in the massacres of civilians, reinforced racial stereotypes. From June 1940 through June 1944, there was not a single large-scale military engagement of ground troops on the Western Front. Service in the West was considered as a leave of active combat service or even almost a recuperation holiday and the Western capital cities became chief destinations of military tourism. In the minds of the soldiers stationed there, there was no confusion possible between the local population of Eastern and Western Europe. Next to a dogmatic feeling of racial superiority, German soldiers stationed in France, and particularly in Paris, occasionally expressed vague feelings of cultural inferiority.[13] The idea of a peaceful and courteous coexistence of the occupiers and the occupied, such as expressed, among others, in the resistance novel *Le Silence de la Mer*, corresponded to a certain extent with a social reality.[14]

The absence of large-scale violence was a precious military advantage, since it allowed to occupy large swathes of territory with a minimal investment in German military and civilian personnel. The local occupation authorities did their utmost best to preserve this situation, even at the price of moderate disobedience of orders received from Berlin. Ulrich Herbert's account of the policy of Werner Best, expert in occupation management stationed successively in Paris and Copenhagen, illustrates this perfectly well.[15] When reports of attacks on German military personnel reached Berlin, which they increasingly did by the end of 1941, Adolf Hitler reacted in fits of anger, demanding draconian retaliation. Best, who realised that random retaliation would radicalise the French public, first deported foreign Jews instead of the number of French hostages fixed by the Führer and later substituted them by arrested communists. German propaganda, and that of Vichy, consistently presented the terrorists as foreign elements: East European Jews, Italian or Spanish communists, Armenians. In spite of increasing pressure from Berlin, from 1944 onwards, local authorities resorted to indirect retaliation, through commissioned murders by paramilitary death squads, rather than random retaliation by the German army, such as it was routinely applied, for example, in Serbia, at a rate of 200 to 1 (October 1941). These covert actions, poetically baptised *Aktion Silbertanne* in the Netherlands or even *Aktion Blümchenpflücken* in Norway, allowed the occupier to present the murders as part of a criminal gang war and not the product of the clash between the resistance and German repression. Large scale massacres of

---

13 See, for example, L. Tewes, *Frankreich in der Besatzungszeit 1940–1943: Die Sicht deutscher Augenzeugen*, Bonn, 1998.
14 Vercors, *Le Silence de la mer et autres récits*, Paris, 1951. For a diverging view and a historiographical survey of this question, see A. Meyer, *Die deutsche Besatzung in Frankreich, 1940–1944*, Darmstadt, 2000.
15 U. Herbert, *Best: Biografische Studien über Radikalismus, Weltanschauung und Vernunft, 1903–1989*, Bonn, 1996.

civilian population occurred in Western Europe only after the allied landing, such as in Oradour and Putten. At least in the case of Oradour, where the perpetrators belonged to a division recently transferred from the Eastern Front, a confusion of routine policies in the East with standard practices in the West are a central part of the explanation of these exceptions that in general confirm the rule.[16]

Let us now briefly take a look at the side of the occupied societies. Militant patriotic rhetoric surfaced very early in resistance circles and both in France and in occupied Belgium, major clandestine newspapers and patriotic, non-communist resistance organisations, chose *Franc Tireur* or its Dutch equivalent *De Vrijschutter* as title. These newspapers, however, vigorously condemned the shooting of German soldiers as an irresponsible strategy.[17] The historical reference was not in the first place to 1914, but to 1870 in the French case and for the Belgians even to the freedom fight against the Spanish oppression in the sixteenth century. After the German attack on the Soviet Union, the French communist party called its armed branch *Francs Tireurs et Partisans* – a double reference both to the French revolutionary tradition and to the combat of the Soviet Union. Communist partisans, in France and Belgium in particular, embarked on a radical campaign of terrorist attacks, including German officers and soldiers among its targets, with a peak in France in September-October 1941 and in January-February 1942 in Belgium. The Belgian communists, after a brief spell of radical violence, backed off from targeting the German army in early 1942, after repression almost annihilated the party.[18] In both countries, the shooting of collaborators and the targeting of infrastructure were practised on a large scale, but the killing of uniformed soldiers of the occupying force remained controversial and rather exceptional, including communist ranks. There were pragmatic arguments, namely the terrible price paid by the population at large and the party in particular in German reprisals. There were also ideological reasons. The party engaged in a demoralisation campaign of German soldiers, with German language flyers. In the rhetoric of international worker solidarity, the German conscript, the soldier-citizens could be convinced that this war was not his war. Unlike eliminating a *milicien*, the French fascist volunteer and traitor, targeting German soldiers randomly was not in line with this discourse.

More generally, it seems that in occupied Western Europe, a large majority continued to recognise the legitimate monopoly of violence by the state and its uniformed agents, even if these belonged to a foreign, occupying nation. It is therefore interesting to see the way 'colonel Fabien' is represented in the French communist

---

16 See J.-J. Fouché, *Oradour*, Paris, 2001; M.de Keizer, *Putten : De razzia en de herinnering*, Amsterdam, 1998; J. Weingartner, *Crossroads of death: The Story of the Malmedy Massacre and Trial*, Berkeley, 1979. For a comparison with the Balkans, see L. Droulia and H. Fleischer (eds) *Von Lidice bis Kalavryta: Widerstand und Besatzungsterror*, Berlin, 1999.
17 See, on the choice of the name of the group *Franc Tireur*, J.-P. Lévy (in cooperation with D. Veillon) *Mémoires d'un franc-tireur: Itinéraire d'un résistant, 1940-1944*, Brussels, 1998, 51.
18 See, J. Gotovitch, *Du Rouge au tricolore : Résistance et parti communiste*, Brussels, 1992, 155-194.

tradition.[19] Fabien, the first communist militant to shoot a German officer in a Paris metro station, is always represented with his military grade of 'colonel', and often in his uniform of the French army. His act, as a revolutionary citizen, is retroactively militarised, thereby loosing its *franc tireur* character, of a civilian attacking a soldier. On the level of the representations, even in the French communist ranks, the taboo on the killing of soldiers by civilians outside the context of regular battle still holds parts of its strength. The controversies surrounding the activities of the immigrant brigade of the communist partisans, the FTP-MOI, is another illustration of this continuity.[20] Their bomb attack in Toulouse on a movie theatre attended by German soldiers deeply divided the local resistance and in the post-war commemorations of the communist resistance, the names of the immigrant fighters were carefully erased. This was partly because of the newfound patriotism of the French communist party and its accompanying xenophobic reflexes. For another part, though, it was related to the enduring taboo on the random killing of soldiers outside the context of military engagement. Yet, the French communist party, with its revolutionary ideology and tradition, together with some right-wing ultra-nationalists, for example in Belgium, are among the most radicalised groups, prone to violent action, in Western Europe. When the Dutch Calvinist resistance group *Landelijke Knokploeg (National Commando group* or LKP) envisaged to organise armed robberies of post offices to procure foodstamps for its underground fighters, it first sent an emissary to a professor in constitutional law for an advice on the lawfulness of such action.[21] The reluctance for an all-out attack against the occupying forces was a central trait of the majority of European resistance movements. Special Operations Executive (SOE), for example, not only met with ferocious resistance by the Secret Intelligence Service (SIS), but often also by local resistance groups. For the murder of Heydrich in Prague in June 1942, SOE had to smuggle its own agents into the protectorate, since the local resistance refused to execute the plan, anticipating the indeed frightening reprisals. The hostility of the local population hit by German reprisals in Lydice, in Civitella, in Kalavryta, often turned more against the partisans who had provoked the German furor than against the Germans themselves.[22] In Oradour and Putten, the absence of local partisan activity is strongly underlined in local memories, stressing the arbitrary character of the atrocities, rather than invoking their own heroic contribution to the struggle for liberation. The radicalisation of occupied societies and the escalation of violence in the dynamic of terrorism/counter-terrorism never spiralled entirely out of control

19 See P. Durand. *Qui a tué Fabien?* Paris, 1985.
20 See S. Courteois, D. Peschanksi and A. Rayski, *Le Sang de l'étranger: Les immigrés de la M.O.I dans la Résistance,* Paris, 1989.
21 See C. Hilbrink, *De illegalen: Illegaliteit in Twente en het aangrenzende Salland, 1940–1945,* The Hague, 1989.
22 See S. Farmer, *Oradour : arrêt sur mémoire,* Paris, 1994; L. Paggi, 'Storia di una memoria antipartigiana' in *La memoria del nazismo nell' Europa di oggi,* ed. Leonardo Paggi, Firenze, 1997, 49–80.

in Western Europe. In Denmark, contacts were established between the German governor Best and the local resistance to reach an agreement on limited targets for *demonstrative Sabotagetätigkeit (spectacular but harmless sabotage acts)*, that is, a strategy capable of satisfying British demands for action without threatening the German-Danish entente.[23]

The discourse of racial kinship and shared interest, if not values, somehow even survived into the post-war era and contributed to the European reconciliation. In the non-communist resistance tradition, exemplified by the writings of, among others, Frénay, Vercors or Halin, the idea of 'the other Germany', distinct from the criminal Nazi clique, became a central theme.[24] Odd as it might seem, this tradition identified this 'other Germany' with the conspirators of 20 July 1944, the military aristocracy supposed to personify German traditions of decency, honour, and western civilisation. On the German side, Otto Abetz, German ambassador in Paris during the occupation, devoted his memoirs, published in 1951, to the theme of the 'grand and sincere desire of entente' between the French and German people, forced into a war neither side had wished.[25] Communist terrorists under foreign inspiration tried by all means to disrupt this entente by perpetrating attacks on German soldiers and officers 'precisely in those regions were the relationship between the local population and the occupier were particularly cordial'. Abetz opened his chapter on the resistance with a quote of Alfred de Vigny's *Servitude et Grandeur militaires*: 'In times of civil war and social agitation, some civilians feel they have the right to shoot at the troops who represent the authority. They play this game as if they were on a hunting party, as if the one who wears the uniform were an anonymous being, without father, mother, wife or friend who could weep his death'.[26] Of course, Abets writing is contemporary with the founding of the Federal Republic and the war in Korea, and its French translation in 1953 coincided with the debates on the French amnesty laws and the European Defense Community. German resentment of partisan snipers killing uniformed soldiers resurfaced during the debates on *Wiedergutmachung* with its West European partners through reparation payments to victims of persecution in the years 1958–1962. *Wiedergutmachung* extended to individuals persecuted on the basis of their race, religion or political creed. In the opinion of West Germany's partners, reparation payments should include resistance fighters who were executed or deported to a concentration camp. For German public opinion and the *Bundestag*, however, Nazi persecution and the legitimate repression of terrorist attacks on German troops were entirely different matters and reparation payments to the latter were utterly

---

23   Hebert, *Best*, 382.
24   See P. Lagrou, *The Legacy of Nazi-occupation: Patriotic Memory and National Recovery in Western Europe, 1945–1965,* Cambridge, 2000, 262–291.
25   O. Abetz, *Histoire d'une politique franco-allemande, 1930–1950: Mémoires d'un ambassadeur,* Paris, 1953.
26   Ibid., 305.

unacceptable.²⁷ These sharply differing interpretations would contribute to the final compromise, whereby the Federal Republic paid a lump sum to each national government, leaving it to the national administrations to organise the distribution. It is not a coincidence, therefore, that the infamous Nazi ideologue Carl Schmitt published precisely in 1963 his 'Theory of the Partisan', denouncing the degeneration of concepts of honourable warfare through the legitimisation of partisan warfare as a first step towards 'extermination'.²⁸

The disagreement between the Federal Republic and its Western partners did not occur so much on the legitimacy of partisan war as on the definition of resistance activities. Most resistance movements had contested the lawfulness and the effectiveness of partisan war on the Western Front before the allied landing. Legitimate activities included patriotic propaganda, intelligence, and preparations for the resurrection of a regular army. On this last account, there had even been a significant rapprochement between the French and the German positions, since the German supreme command (OKW) accepted during the Vosges offensive to recognise the Forces Français d'Intérieur (FFI), infantry troops recruited by the resistance, as a regular military formation. Two years earlier in North Africa, it had refused to consider de Gaulle's Free French troops as prisoners of war.

The treatment of the Free French by Rommel's army in North Africa inspired the International Red Cross to submit a proposal to reform the first article of the Geneva Convention on the Protection of Prisoners of War of 1929, from 'members of the armed forces of the belligerent parties' to 'members of the armed forces, whichever the government or authority they claim to belong to'.²⁹ The proposal was discussed on the international conference held in Stockholm in 1948, leading to the renewed Geneva convention of 1949.³⁰ If the Danish government discovered a sudden enthusiasm for partisan warfare, proposing that 'since war of aggression has been declared an international crime by all nations, the resistance by the civilian population should be considered as an act of legitimate defense', most other nations abhorred the idea of inconsiderably extending the protection granted to soldiers to civilians taking up arms.³¹ The national experience during World War II was irrelevant in this regard, since the Soviet Union and France, both self-proclaimed champions (albeit with contrasting legitimacies to their claims) were among the starkest opponents. They were joined by the United States and particularly by the colonial powers, the Netherlands, Belgium, and most of all the United Kingdom.

---

27 See L. Herbst and C. Goschler (eds.), *Wiedergutmachung in der Bundesrepublik Deutschland*, Munich, 1989.
28 C. Schmitt, *Theorie des Partisanen; Zwischenbemerkung zum Begriff des Politischen*, Berlin, 1963.
29 *Rapport du Comité international de la Croix-Rouge sur son activité pendant la seconde guerre mondiale (1er septembre 1939–30 juin 1947) (XVII° conférence internationale de la Croix-Rouge, Stockholm, août 1948)* Genève, 1948, Vol I.
30 P. de la Pradelle, *La conférence diplomatique et les Nouvelles Conventions de Genève du 12 Août 1949,* Paris, 1951.
31 Ibid., 58

The legal clauses proposed in Stockholm displayed an astonishing inventiveness in devising conditions that would apply to the situation of the resistance during World War II, but not to independence movements in the colonies. Resistance movements could be recognised as regular armed forces if they were allied to formal belligerent in an international conflict. The British delegation added a list of additional conditions, such as a formal declaration of war by the resistance movement, effective control by the supreme command over all its units, the existence of radio contact between them, the respect of the international conventions on the treatment of their adversaries.[32]

The extremely restrictive British proposal failed, but the Dutch proposal, limiting the recognition to 'voluntary forces belonging to one of the belligerent parties' was adequate enough to protect the colonial powers from interference with the laws of war in their 'police actions', such as those undertaken in the Dutch Indies at that very time. Full revision of the Geneva conventions, with the extension of protection to national liberation movements, was only adopted in 1977. The conditions enumerated in the 1949 Geneva Convention, namely that such forces should be commanded by a responsible person, have a fixed distinctive sign recognisable at a distance, carry their arms openly, and conduct their operations in accordance with the laws and customs of war, implied that the observance of the rule of war were still based on the anticipation of reciprocity. The field manuals, for example of French troops in Indochina, reveal how strongly these were still rooted in racial stereotype, not fundamentally different from those of General von Falkenhorst.[33]

Beyond the subtleties of international war, a hard core of the mental constellation of modern warfare seems to have survived from the Second World War deep into the Cold War years, namely the division of the world in a civilised, Western sphere, attached to the rules of honourable warfare, mutual respect, and shared values, and a uncivilised sphere of lawless people. To some extent, World War II had not threatened this constellation, but even reinforced it. The 'honourable war' fought by Nazi Germany on the Western Front laid the foundations for post-war reconciliation and the integration of the Federal Republic in the European Community and the North Atlantic Treaty Organisation.[34] The 'Western World' was ready to forget, if not to caution the savage war waged on the Eastern Front, against communists, and Asian hordes. By the same token, the Federal Republic abstained from criticism on the dirty wars fought by France, Britain, the Netherlands and, somewhat later, the United States, against communist and non-European enemies. It is no coincidence that the end of the Cold War has created room for critical retrospection, both for the *Wehrmacht* crimes in Germany and for torture in the Algerian war in France.

---

32   Ibid., 52–54.
33   See the *Manuel à l'usage des combattants d'Extrême-Orient*, published by the État-Major du Corps Expéditionnaire, Forces Armées d'Extrême-Orient, 1949 (courtesy of Alain Ruscio).
34   See, for example, K. Macksey, *The Partisans of Europe in the Second World War*, NY, 1975.

That being said, it would be hypocritical today to pretend that the study of the terrorist as archetypal figure of twentieth century warfare, with all aspects it entails, is of a merely historical interest and that it is entirely unrelated to the challenges brought to us by the incipient twenty-first century. The recent events, from Mazar-i-Sharif over Jenin to Guantanamo Bay, are there to recall that the idea that lawful conduct in war is based on reciprocity, and that a war on terrorism can dispense with the rules of international law, is still as dangerous as ever.[35] As an interpretation of contemporary world affairs, the 'clash of civilisations' is utterly unsatisfactory. As a self-fulfilling prophecy, though, it is highly alarming. The norms of legitimate violence and the boundaries separating honourable combat from the war against barbarians and infidels are still very much at the heart of modern warfare.

---

35 See, for example, 'Israel/Occupied Territories: Jenin War Crimes Investigation Needed' *Human Rights Watch Report Finds Laws of War Violations* (http://hrw.org/press/2002/05/jenin0503.htm) and 'Background Paper on Geneva Conventions and Persons Held by U.S. Forces: Human Rights Watch Press Backgrounder', January 29, 2002 (http://hrw.org/backgrounder/usa/pow-bck.htm).

Female Soldiers and National Heroines in Latin America

Barbara Potthast

Long-standing stereotypes of men as aggressive and war minded, and women as passive, peace-loving creatures[1] have determined our perception of the participants in battles and the make-up of armies over the centuries (Table 3). This holds true for several cultures, but especially so for Catholic Latin America, where deep-rooted veneration of the Virgin Mary and maternity added to the idea. On the other hand, there is the century-old fascination for fighting women like the Amazons, present in Latin American imagination ever since the conquest, or cross-dressing women-soldiers like Catalina de Erauso, better known as "*la monja alférez*", the lieutenant-nun.[2] This tension can be seen in the way the Latin American republics remembered the role of women in the wars that accompanied state and nation building from the independence movement at the beginning of the 19th century to the Mexican Revolution at the beginning of the 20th. In this paper I will argue that women participated in most of the pre-modern armies in several important tasks, but that their contribution in most cases has been neglected. There are some examples, however, where this was not the case and women entered into the collective memory and national identity. Why did these become part of the national master-narrative while others did not? How, in these narratives, has the image of the fighting women been reconciled with the traditional one? In order to answer these questions, I will delve into the motives of these women to participate in the war, the effect on their lives and the public remembrance. I will argue that in

---

1   One of the most prominent formulations of this idea is Margarete Mitscherlich, *Die friedfertige Frau: eine psychoanalytische Untersuchung zur Aggression der Geschlechter*, Frankfurt/M., 1985. For an historical analysis see Sharon McDonald et. al, (ed.), 'Drawing the Lines – Gender, Peace and War: An Introduction', in *Images of Women in Peace and War – Crosscultural and Historical Perspectives*, Basingstoke/Hampshire, 1987, p. 1–26 and Jean Bethke Elshtain, 'Introduction: Beautiful Souls/Just Warriors', *Women and War*, New York, 1987, 3–13.
2   Catherine Davies, Claire, Brewster, Hilary Owen, *South American Independence: Gender, Politics, Text*, Liverpool 2006, p. 131–136, Delia González Afonso, 'Amazonen in der Neuen Welt. Der wiederentdeckte Mythos?', in *asien, afrika, lateinamerika* 22 (1994), 447–460, Juan Gil, *Mitos y utopías del descubrimiento*, Madrid, 1989, vol. 3: *El Dorado*.

Table 3: Peruvian Rabona (Collection Potthast)

collective memory, the women in the armies were either neglected or, if they did enter the pantheon of national heroes, in order to maintain social and familial hierarchies, their image was reduced to the one of a romantic or abnegated lover or mother, no matter whether they had actually fought or had 'only' supplied services for the fighting men. If the deeds of the women were recorded, they were interpreted usually as the outcome of a republican or patriotic spirit, whereas the women themselves were mostly guided (or forced) by traditional gender and family roles. I will base my argument on the examples of the War of Independence in northern South America led by Simón Bolívar at the beginning of the nineteenth century[3], the Cuban Independence Movement[4] and the Paraguayan War[5] in the second half of the century, as well as the Mexican Revolution at the beginning of the twentieth century[6], probably the last example of the massive participation of women in pre-modern armies in Latin America.

If we look at the historiography about wars in nineteenth-century Latin America, we find that they are usually described as eminently military and political affairs; and since women theoretically were excluded from both these spheres, there seemed no need to inquire about their role in them. It is true that most Latin American countries, next to the more prominent male '*próceres*', do know some female heroes, but these are usually described as wives of important men and their contribution to independence seems to have been just that. If it comes to more, they hosted conspirative '*tertulias*', hid one of the conspirators or participated in undercover activities like spying out the enemy or passing information.[7]

Even Manuela Sáenz, the most prominent and most controversial among these 'national heroes', is no exception.[8] Sáenz was the long-time companion of Simón Bolívar, '*el libertador*' (the Liberator) of South America. They met when Bolivar

---

3   1810–1825, see Jaime E. Rodríguez O, *The Independence of Spanish America*, Cambridge, 1998.
4   1868–1878, 1895–1898, see Ada Ferrer, *Insurgent Cuba. Race, Nation and Revolution, 1868–1898*, Chapel Hill/London, 1999.
5   1864–1870, see Thomas L. Whigham, *The Paraguayan War*, Lincoln/London, 2002, Vol. 1: *Causes and Early Conduct*.
6   1910–1917, see Hans Werner Tobler, *Die Mexikanische Revolution. Gesellschaftlicher Wandel und politischer Umbruch, 1876–1940*, Frankfurt/M., 1984, Alan Knight, *The Mexican Revolution*, Cambridge, 1986.
7   Vicente Grez, *Las mujeres de la independencia*, Santiago de Chile, 1966, Inés Quintero, 'Las mujeres de la Independencia: ¿heroínas o transgresoras? El caso de Manuela Sáenz', in *Las mujeres y las naciones. Problemas de inclusión y exclusión*, eds Barbara Potthast and Eugenia Scarzanella, Frankfurt/M./Madrid, 2001, 58–67, Evelyn Cherpak, *The Participation of Women in the Independence Movement in Gran Colombia, 1780–1830*, in *Latin American Women: Historical Perspectives*, ed. Asunción Lavrin, Westport/Conn., 1978, 83–116, here: 85 f., Evelyn Cherpak, 'Las mujeres en la Independencia', in *Las mujeres en la historia de Colombia*, vol. 1, ed. Jorge Toro Velásquez, Santafé de Bogotá, 1995, 219–234, here: 220 f.
8   There is an enormous amount of biographies of different tendencies about Manuela Sáenz, two of the most prominent are Alfonso Rumazo González, *Manuela Sáenz. La libertadora del libertador*. Guayaquil/Quito, 1970 and Victor von Hagen, *Manuela. Manuela Sáenz und Simón Bolívar*, Hamburg/Wien, 1957 (English original: *Four seasons of Manuela*, 1952).

came to liberate Quito, where Sáenz, the illegitimate daughter of a Creole elite mother and a Spanish officer, married to a British merchant twenty years her senior, had joined the independence movement. Together with 110 secular women and 32 nuns she had been awarded the order of the *caballeresas del sol* in Lima, where she had lived temporarily with her husband. Much to the scandal of the upper classes, the widowed Liberator and the married young women entered into an affair that they did not even try to conceal. When Bolívar moved on to free Peru und Upper Peru (later to become Bolivia) Sáenz was his constant companion. She became his political advisor, his secretary and archivist, and she organized the sanitary and alimentary logistics of the insurgent army. It seems that she participated actively in the decisive battle of Ayacucho, but this is one of the many points where historians disagree, since most traditional scholars do not want to admit the fact.[9] Bolívar had already awarded her the title of *capitán*, but when he raised her to *coronel* after that battle, fellow *libertador* Francisco de Santander, by that time vice president of Gran-Colombia, protested. In his defence of the decision, Bolívar not only justified the measure, but also the presence of other women among the troops. He thought them to be necessary not only 'for the tranquillity of the troops' but also because they formed part of the booty that could not be denied to the soldiers.[10] By this, Bolívar alluded on the one hand to the fact that many women were abducted forcefully, indeed were abused by the soldiers; on the other hand he had important services in mind, which these women provided for the armies. But precisely these two aspects were the ones military leaders and historians later on neglected or omitted on purpose.

The presence of women among the troops in the wars of independence and the following civil wars is by now a well documented although mostly still overlooked or unaccepted fact. The example of Sáenz, who was too close to Bolívar and too visible in many decisive moments to be passed by, shows that historians tried to deny her presence at least in important battles, since that – in their view – was somehow detrimental to the glory of the male heroes.

Sáenz certainly is an exceptional figure, but she is a good example because she unites the various roles women could assume in the armies in her person. Gener-

---

For more bibliographical details see Pamela S. Murray, 'Loca' or 'Libertadora'?: Manuela Sáenz in the eyes of history and historians 1900–1990', in *Journal of Latin American Studies* 33, no. 2 (2001), 291–310, Quintero, *Las Mujeres*, Sarah C. Chambers, *Republican Friendship: Manuela Sáenz Writes Women into the Nation, 1835–1856*, in *Hispanic Aamerican Historical Review* 81, no. 2 (2001), 225–257, or Lucia Rojas y Thelen, 'Partizipation der Frauen an der Unabhängigkeitsbewegung in Lateinamerika: Realität und Historiographie am Beispiel von Manuela Sáenz' (Masters Thesis, University of Cologne, 1993).

9   Murray, 'Loca' or 'Libertadora'?, 301–304, Rojas, *Partizipation*, 56–76. In the descriptions of Manuela on the battlefields, the image of the Amazon is invoqued several times.

10 Bolívar to Santander, 17th february 1825, in Manuela Sáenz and Simón Bolívar, *Patriota y amante de usted. Manuela Sáenz y el Libertador. Diarios ineditos con textos de Elena Poniatowska, Miguel Bonasso, Carlos Álvarez, Heinz Dietrich*, eds Heinz Dietrich Stefan et al., México, 1993, 156.

ally, we have to distinguish between two different forms of participation: women who actively took part in combat and those who accompanied the troops in the retinue. Whereas the 'Amazons' have received some attention, the 'camp-followers' usually were not recorded or drew very little attention, from contemporaries as well as from historians. Most descriptions we have are from foreign observers who were already accustomed to modern armies. I will argue here that the presence of the 'service women' was far more important than the one of the women soldiers, but that their participation usually was not motivated by political reasons.

Fighting Women

Let us first take a look at the 'Amazons' (Table 4). During the independence movement, fighting was predominantly male, although we know of a *batería de las mujeres* founded in 1812 in Venezuela. Apart from that, there are, as there always are, stories about individual women who fought in battles, and usually they are described as at least as courageous as the men.[11] Be it during the wars of independence, be it a hundred years later during the Mexican Revolution, these women inevitably were depicted as men-women (or *marimachos* in Mexico), women who not only fought like men but also dressed, swore and sometimes drank like men.[12]

In other cases, the existence of fighting women was exaggerated and used for propaganda reasons, as in the Paraguayan War. During this war, when Paraguay fought against the Triple Alliance of Brazil, Argentina and Uruguay, people were surprised that the country resisted the combined forces for such a long time. For some observers, the reason for this lay in the strong nationalism of the Paraguayans and their unanimous support for the politics of President Francisco Solano López, whereas for the allies the continued resistance was due to the repression of the 'Tyrant López'. In this ideological battle, news about fighting women and even a whole battalion formed by the women of Areguá, a small village close to the capital, which had its own fighting march, were used by López to underline the unconditional support he received by all sectors of the population, even the ones who were not supposed to participate in politics or take up arms. For his enemies, the fact that he even made women fight was further proof of the oppressive, if not satanic character of his rule.[13]

---

11   Emilia Troconis de Veracoechea, *Indias, Esclavas, manutanas y primeras damas*, Caracas, 1990, 143, Cherpak, *Las mujeres*, 93 f., Cherpak, *Participation*, 221 f., Anna Macias, *Against All Odds. The Feminist Movement in Mexico to 1940*, Westport/Conn., 1982, 40–44.

12   Gustavo Casasola, cit. after Macias, *Against All Odds*, 42, Andrés Reséndez Fuentes, Battleground Women: Soldaderas and Female Soldiers in the Mexican Revolution, *The Americas*, 51:4 (1995), 525–553, Elizabeth Salas, 'Soldaderas in the Mexican Militar: Myth and History' (Ph.D. Thesis, University of California: Ann Arbor, 1987), 90–93.

13   The *Baltimore American and Commercial Adviser*, for example, reprinted a report from the <u>Buenos Aires Standard</u> with rumours about women defending the rivers, adding that: 'The guerilla

Table 4: Mexican Soldadera (Collection Potthast)

It is true that the Paraguayan women volunteered to 'take up arms, not only to guard the coast of this place but also to join the army voluntarily,'[14] but most of these proposals were symbolic acts that evolved from the emotional assemblies and from a wish to protect one's own village, though preferably with less aggressive methods than taking up arms. At close examination, however, the existence of women battalions turns out to be mostly propaganda. Notwithstanding some individual cases and the self-defence of women against Triple Alliance soldiers at the end of the war, organized female units never existed in Paraguay.[15]

If we look at the Mexican Revolution or the Cuban struggle for independence, we find a similar pattern. There were a few female troops and some famous '*generalas*' and '*coronelas*',[16] but most women did not go to the battlefield. If they did so, it was as aide-de-camps to their husbands, handing over ammunition or helping to load the rifle. One *soldadera* described her participation in the battlefield like this:

> 'Not many women went into battle; Pedro took me even though he didn't have orders from General Espinos y Córdoba; that's why he made me dress like a man, so they'd look the other way and not report me. [...] Most of the women went into battle for the same reason I did, because their husbands made them; others went because they were trying to be men. But most of them remained behind. [...] I always carried a pistol in my belt, as well as a rifle because a cavalryman carries his rifle on the back of his horse. My job was to load Pedro's Mauser, mine and his; while he'd fire one I'd load the empty one so he could switch back and forth. [...] I was never scared.

---

portion of the campaign – or what is termed here the '*guerra de recursos* [struggle for supplies]' – is entrusted to the women of Paraguay; and reliable data have been received that the troops to the north, near Tranquera Loreto, are exclusively composed of women." The report listed the different tasks performed by women since the outbreak of the war, concluding that "with Satanic power, they are dragged to the front, and placed in the breach to fight the whole Allied army! ... If, as the news goes, the Allies, in attempting to cross the Tebicuarí, have to fight the girls, then the honour of Europe is at stake in at once stopping this horrible war." *Baltimore American and Commercial Adviser*, 26 June 1868.

14 Justice of Peace to Vice-President, Villeta 29 July 1865, Archivo Nacional de Asunción, Sección Histórica 418.

15 Potthast, Barbara, "*Paradies Mohammeds*" oder "*Land der Frauen*"? Zur Rolle der Frau und der Familie in der paraguayischen Gesellschaft im 19. Jahrhundert, Lateinamerikanische Forschungen 21, Köln/Wien/Weimar, 1994, 289–309.

16 Reséndez Fuentes, *Battleground Women*, who gives several examples of fighting women in the different armies that fought in the Revolution, Macias, *Against All Odds*, 39–44, *Las Mujeres en la Revolución Mexicana, 1884–1920*, ed. Instituto Nacional de Estudios Históricos de la Revolución Méxicana, México, 1993, 37–96, for Cuba see Lynn Stoner, *From the House to the Streets. The Cuban Woman's Movement for Legal Reform, 1898–194*, Durham/London, 1991, 18–30, Sabrina Hepke, 'Frauen in der Unabhängigkeitsbewegung Kubas, 1868–1898' (Dipl. Thesis, University of Cologne, 1997), 89–91.

I don't know if I killed anyone. If they were close, I might have. If not, I didn't have any reason to shoot at them.' [17]

Most women did learn to handle a weapon, though, and many photographs of the Revolution show women wearing ammunition belts. This does not always mean, however, that they were active soldiers. The use of arms in most cases was more a measure of self-defence and an expression of the culture of violence that characterized Mexico during the years of the civil war.

Camp Followers

The majority of the women among the troops, were, however, what might be called camp-followers, although this present term implies notions of prostitution or at least sexual relations as an essential part of the reason for their presence.[18] At the beginning of the nineteenth century, however, these women were referred to as 'troperas', (from 'tropa'= troop) or 'vivanderas'(those who provide 'víveres' i.e. food for, but who also live with (= 'viven') the troops) or simply as 'juanas'. In Ecuador they were known as *guarichas* and in Peru as *ravañas* or *rabonas*.[19] Mexicans during the Revolution called them *soldaderas*, a word derived presumably not from the word *soldado,* although these women often were defined simply as 'the Mexican soldier's women'. The word rather was derived from Spanish *soldada*, an old word for *sueldo* = pay, since they were entitled to collect the pay for their husbands in order to provide for them.[20] At the end of the nineteenth century, Cubans called their female independence fighters *mambisas,* a word of African origin, used by the Spaniards to describe a filthy and dishonest person. The freedom fighters, free coloured in their majority, adopted the word and called themselves proudly *mambises* and *mambisas*.[21] The Paraguayans created the word *residenta* for the women who followed the army on their retreat to the north, a word derived from the formula with which these women declared their identity, giving their place of origin and their temporary residence after the evacuation, 'vecina de ... residente en' or '[per-

---

17 Elena Poniatowska, *Here's to you, Jesusa*, New York, 2002 (Spanish original: *Hasta no verte Jesús mío,* 1969), 109/110. See also the chorus of the "corrido de la soldadera" cited below.
18 Majorie Bingham and Susan Cross, *Women in Latin America*, St. Louis Park, 1985, vol. II, 43.
19 Álvaro Tirado Mejía, *Aspectos sociales de las guerras civiles en Colombia*, Bogotá, 1976, 58; Nilsa M. Alzola de Cvitanocich, 'Imagen Tradicional y Realidad de la mujer en el Ámbito Político Argentino (1810–1920)', in *Revista Interamericana de Bibliografía* XXXI (1981), 246–257, here: 256, says, that the origins are to be found in the *mamitas* of the Peruvian Royal army, whereas Salas traces the Meso-American roots. (Salas, *Soldaderas*, 13–36).
20 Salas, *Soldaderas*, 38, Macias, *Against All Odds*, 40f.
21 Stoner, *From the House*, 201f.

manent] inhabitant of ... [now] resident in.'²² As the terms reveal, contemporaries did not stress the sexual or romantic role of the camp followers but other functions.

All these women from different places in Latin America and at different times during this 'long' nineteenth century performed similar tasks: they provided food, they cooked and ironed (if possible), they kept the camps clean, cared for the wounded and consoled the survivors. When medicine was hard to come by, the knowledge of traditional herb medicine by the women also became more and more important.²³

Flora Tristán, a young French Peruvian, left one of the most vivid, although ethnically and socially biased descriptions of the Peruvian *rabonas* she saw in Arequipa in the 1830s:

> 'At the very end of the camp, behind the soldiers' tents, were quartered the *rabonas* with their jumble of cooking-pots and children. Here there were clothes drying and women busy washing or sewing, all making a frightful commotion with their shouting, singing and conversation.
>
> The *rabonas* are the camp-followers of South America. In Peru each soldier takes with him as many women as he likes: some have as many as four. They form a considerable troop, preceding the army by several hours so that they have time to set up camp, obtain food and cook it. To see the female avant-garde set out gives one an immediate idea of what these poor women have to suffer and the dangerous life they lead. The *rabonas* are armed; they load onto mules their cooking-pots, tents and all the rest of the baggage, they drag after them a horde of children of all ages, they whip their mules into a gallop and run along beside them, they climb high mountains, they swim across rivers, carrying one or even two children on their backs. When they arrive at their destination, they choose the best site for the camp, then they unload the mules, erect the tents, feed the children and put them to bed, light the fires and start cooking. If they chance to be near an inhabited place, they go off in a detachment to get supplies; they descend on the village like famished beasts and demand food for the army. When it is given with a good grace they do no harm, but when they are refused they fight like lionesses and their fierce courage overcomes all resistance. Then they sack the village, carry their loot back to the camp and divide it among themselves.

---

22 Potthast, '*Paradies*', 300.
23 Pay-List of the Military Hospital, Cerro León, July – October 1866, Archivo Nacional, Asunción, Sección Nueva Encuadernación 2836, see also George Frederick Masterman, *Siete años de aventuras en el Paraguay*, trans. David Lewis, Buenos Aires, 1870, 110, 120–121, 154, although this British pharmacist was sceptical about the efficacy of these medicines. For Cuba see Hepke, *Frauen*, 42 f.

> These women, who provide for all the needs of the soldier, who wash and mend his clothes, receive no pay and their only reward is the freedom to rob with impunity. They are of Indian race, speak the native language, and do not know a single word of Spanish. The *rabonas* are not married, they belong to nobody and are there for anybody who wants them. They are creatures outside society: they live with the soldiers, eat with them, stop where they stop, are exposed to the same dangers and endure far greater hardships than the men. When the army is on the march it is nearly always on the courage and daring of these women four or five hours ahead of them that it depends for its subsistence, and when one considers that in leading this life of toil and danger they still have the duties of motherhood to fulfil, one is amazed that any of them can endure it … […]
> Several able generals have sought to find a substitute for the service the *rabonas* provide and prevent them from following the army, but the soldiers have always revolted against any such attempt and it has been necessary to yield to them. They are not at all sure that the military administration would be able to provide for their needs, and that is why they refuse to give the *rabonas* up.'[24]

The American journalist John Reed was surprised to see so many women among the rebel armies in Mexico. When he asked one of them who was nursing a baby why she had not stayed at home, she told him that she would have preferred to do so, but her husband had insisted that she must come, with the convincing argument that otherwise he was bound to starve. 'Who shall make my *tortillas* for me but my woman'?[25]

Whereas the normal soldiers relied on the women for food, medical care and emotional comfort, the officials feared that disorder might arise from so many women in the camps. 'Men, women, rum and gunpowder sometimes produced an explosive mixture', writes one modern historian,[26] many contemporary generals would have agreed. A lot of them did not approve of the female presence in the camps, as we have seen in the abovementioned dispute between Santander and Bolívar. The same holds true for the Mexican Revolution. Although several military leaders were not fond of the female presence, all armies had *soldaderas* and female fighters, although each organized their participation in a distinct manner.[27] Other

---

24   Flora Tristan, *Peregrinations of a Pariah*, Trans./ed. Jean Hawkes, Boston, MA, 1987, 179 f. Reséndez Fuentes is one of the few authors who adresses the question of the ethnic origin of the female soldiers and soldaderas in the Mexican Revolution, Reséndez Fuentes, *Battleground Women*, 530/31, 538.
25   John Reed, *Insurgent Mexico*, Berlin, 1978, 45; for a description of the work of the *soldaderas* see also Reséndez Fuentes, *Battleground Women*, 530–547, Poniatowska, *Jesusa*, 64 f.
26   Tirado Mejía, *Aspectos sociales*, 60.
27   Reséndez Fuentes, *Battleground Women* Ana Lau and Carmen Ramos, *Mujeres y revolución, 1900–1917*, México, 1993, 42–45.

generals like Bolívar, López, who also was accompanied onto the battlefields by his mistress, as well as the Cuban insurgents, on the other hand, understood the importance not only of the service of these women, but also of their psychological support for the soldiers. In Paraguay, this can be seen in the last years of the war, when the situation for the army became more and more desperate. Authorities then required women to participate not only as servants but also as dancers, when there were not enough volunteers.[28]

The growing numbers of women in the camps[29] eventually prompted military leaders to establish ranks for women, as we have already seen in the case of Sáenz. In the Paraguayan war camps, *sargentas* (female sergeants) supervised the labour and the life in the camps. In this case, the women lived in separate quarters of the camps, but, as one foreign observer relates with astonishment, at night they were allowed to pass over to the men's part.[30]

This observation did not lead the reporter to think, that most women in the camp were prostitutes in one way or the other, but it does prove that sexual relations did play an important role. The testimonies we have from the Mexican or the Cuban wars reveal just this, but they also reveal a very strict code of behaviour for the women, especially the married ones, as well as extreme jealousy on the side of the men.

> '[The *soldaderas*] accompany the husband or lover on his military marches, carrying a child, a basket filled with clothing, and working utensils. In the abandoned battlefield they carry water to their wounded masters and despoil the dead of their clothing. ... They are jealous and courageous. ... and their moral code has two precepts ... absolute fidelity to and unconditional abnegation for the husband or lover and respect for the officers of the battalion or regiment.'[31]

If women did not adhere to this rule, they were treated cruelly by their men, and rape, mistreatment and wife beating was part of the daily life of many of these

---

28 Potthast, 'Paradies', 281 f.
29 When the US-Army detained forces of the Mexican Federal Army who had crossed the Rio Grande, they captured 3.557 officers and soldiers, 1.256 soldaderas and 554 children, Salas, *Soldaderas*, 118. For the most part, however, the women made up about 20% of the the Federal Army, (ibid. 87). Among the Zapatistas, there were much more women, since, as goes a famous word, the Zapatistas were not an army but a people in arms. During the civil war in Colombia in the 1880ies, an officer reported that after a defeat, he could still count on 900 soldiers and officers, 200 women and 2 000 mules, Tirado Mejía, *Aspectos sociales*, 60.
30 Potthast, 'Paradies', 279–282, Barbara Potthast, 'Protagonists, Victims, and Heroes. Paraguayan Women during the Great War', in '*I die with my country*'. *Perspectives on the Paraguayan War*, eds Hendrik Kraay and Thomas L. Whigham, Lincoln, 2004, 44–60.
31 Julio Guerrero, *La génesis del crimen en México*, 1901, cited in Macias, *Against All Odds*, 41. For Cuba see Hepke, *Frauen*, 42.

women.³² But for many women, life before joining the soldiers had not been much better. The role of physical aggression is described impressively in the life story of Jesusa Palancares, who lived in the Mexican Revolutionary Army most of her youth. Beaten by her own stepmother, she felt obliged to punish her father's lovers when she went to the army with him. Later on she beat and hurt the lovers of her husband in every possible way.³³ Even after the Revolution, beating and aggressive behaviour remained part of her life. Her husband, to whom she got married against her will, was an officer, and when he had to leave for a longer amount of time and left her unprotected, she started frequenting bars. At his return, her husband found her there drinking with other men, and ever since then beat her cruelly until she finally threatened to kill him. The way she tells the story, however, shows that she was conscious about her situation, but had not really overcome traditional gender roles, since she constantly refers to herself as being 'bad'.

> 'Pedro got nicer after I threatened to shoot him. But then I got mean. From the time I was little, I was mean, I was born that way [...] The blessed Revolution gave me self-confidence. When Pedro pushed me over the edge, I thought: I'm going to defend myself or he can just kill me and be done with it.' If I hadn't been mean, I would have let Pedro abuse me until he killed me. But there came a moment when God must have said to me:'Defend yourself.' Because God says: 'the Lord helps those who help themselves.'I heard Him tell me: 'Defend yourself, you've taken enough. Now you start giving it back.' And I took out the gun. After that I said I wouldn't be abused and I've kept my word. I've done such a good job I'm still here to tell you about it.'³⁴

Analysis by Elisabeth Salas of nine life stories, including the one of Jesusa, reveals that 'these women did not always act as stoic and uncomplaining servants'. Their experiences varied considerably and cannot be reduced to either the misery that most contemporary observers saw or the rebellion that some modern analysts like to stress.³⁵ In any case, life in the camps made an adherence to the ideal of the passive, secluded and obedient wife rather difficult, although we have to be aware that this ideal was prominent mostly among the middle and upper classes, whereas lower-class women in Latin America had never been able to live up to

---

32 Especially for the Mexican Revolution we have abundant testomonies of these abuses. See Salas, *Soldaderas*, 87 f., or the story of Elisabetta, recorded by John Reed, who was struck how rapidly and emotionless a *soldadera* passed (or was passed) to another man if hers had died. Reed, *Insurgent Mexico*, 99–109.
33 Poniatowska, *Jesusa*, 66 f., 103 f.
34 Ibid., 101.
35 Salas, *Soldaderas*, 155.

these standards.³⁶ But in the camps women of all classes – be they Manuela Sáenz or a nameless *soldadera* or *rabona* – were forced to transgress the boundaries established for their sex, the physical and spatial ones as well as the symbolic ones. Many women, like the above mentioned *soldadera* Jesusa, not only had to live in situations of constant deprivation, fear and violence during these years, but made aggression and brutality part of their own personality and behaviour.

Dangerous Women

No wonder then that these women made men – especially of the upper classes – fearful of the future gender and family hierarchies, and social stability in general. In addition, the transition from colonial to republican rule also changed notions of honour, status and masculinity.³⁷ This is the reason why the women who accompanied the armies were barred from the collective memories or their role was reinterpreted. In the view of the contemporaries, society rested on a patriarchal model, and the family was its base. The wars of independence, for example, were interpreted constantly in terms of familial relations, with the Spanish crown as the bad father who did not allow his sons to grow and develop, and therefore, his sons had the right to rise against him. This was a dangerous argument, however, since individual sons and daughters might demand the same right. The multiple problems of state and nation building in Latin America, which led to social upheaval and civil wars in most young republics, made the elites worry about the precarious political stability. Thus the patriarchal family had to be invigorated and not to be questioned. Remembering the contributions of the women to the wars of independence, however, would have questioned traditional gender roles and was thus considered dangerous – probably not only by the men but also by the women of the upper classes.³⁸ The same holds true for the Mexican Revolution, where after 10 years of fighting and a precarious political peace, the main aim was to achieve tranquillity – and not to question social and gender hierarchies. In 1925, the Mexican Minister of War considered the *soldaderas* 'the chief cause of vice, illness, crime and disorder' and banned them from the barracks.³⁹ After the fighting

---

36 There is an ongoing debate on the question whether lower class and/or indigenous people had different gender and honour codes than the Spaniards, but this cannot be discussed here. See Steve J. Stern, *The Secret History of Gender: Women, Men, and Power in Late Colonial Mexico*, Chapel Hill et al., 1995, and Potthast, 'Paradies', 185–190.
37 Matthew Brown, 'Adventures, Foreign Women and Masculinity in the Colombian Wars of Independence', in *Feminist Review* 79 (2005), 36–51.
38 A similar development can be seen after the North American and the French Revolution. See Linda Kerber, *Women of the Republic. Intellect and Ideology in Revolutionary America*, Chapel Hill, 1980, Olwen Hufton, *Women and the Limits of Citizenship in the French Revolution*, Toronto, 1992.
39 Cited after Salas, *Soldaderas*, 106.

had stopped, many women – fighters as well as *soldaderas* – demanded pensions in reward for their services, and some of the women veterans received them. But the notion of the *soldaderas* as servants to the soldiers changed, and they came to be considered as wives or relatives –consequently their contribution was equated with housework and thus not subject to compensation.[40]

A similar process occurred in the other countries, and the '*vivanderas*', '*troperas*' and '*rabonas*' were sooner or later forgotten. Where it was impossible to neglect the women, like in the case of Sáenz or the Mexican *soldaderas*, their role was reinterpreted. In the official Venezuelan historiography, Manuela Sáenz was reduced to the passionate lover of Bolívar and her services as a *capitana* were neglected. She was now depicted as an unfortunate illegitimate child, married to a terrible foreign husband, finally leaving her family in pursuit of a greater love – the one to Bolívar and her fatherland.[41] In Mexico, military leaders tried to dismiss the presence of women in the armies as an invention, or stated that they had only participated in the army of the others.[42] In popular culture, the role of the *soldaderas* was reinterpreted too. Popular songs like the '*corrido de la soldadera*' starts every verse with the following lines:

> 'Abnegada soldadera/de tu bien querido Juan/tú le cubres la trinchera/con tus ropas de percal/y le das la cartuchera/cuande se pone a tirar.'[43]
> 'Abnegated soldadera/of your beloved Juan/you cover the trench/with your woven clothes/and you give him the cartridge/when he fires the gun.'

The first two lines then mark the beginning of every verse. By this repetition the adjective '*abnegada*', abnegated, becomes the dominant characteristic of the *soldadera*, and brings her back in line with the sacrificing consort and mother. The famous *corrido* 'La Adelita' remembered the woman as the beloved person who had to stay home, and *las adelitas*, as the *soldaderas* were later called because of this song, inspired romantic novels and films.[44] Some of them, like the famous classic of the so-called novels of the Revolution, *Los de abajo* (The Underdogs) by Manuel Azuela, revealed the cruel and non-heroic sides of the revolution; in his description of the women, however, he fell back to the old stereotypes, by contrasting two women, a prostitute-like Amazon and a sacrificing and mother like angel of mercy.[45] Later on, another novel, *La Negra Angustias*, by Francisco Rojas González, who won the

---

40　Salas, *Soldaderas*, 106–110, Reséndez Fuentes, *Battleground Women*, 546.
41　Quintero, *Las mujeres*, Murray, 'Loca' or 'Libertadora'?, 298–303, see also Chambers, *Republican Friendship*, and Rebecca Earle, 'Rape and the Anxious Republic: Revolutionary Colombia, 1810–1830', in *Hidden Histories of Gender and the State in Latin America*, eds Elizabeth Dore and Maxine Molyneux, 2000, 127–146.
42　Salas, *Soldaderas*, 97.
43　The full text can be consulted in *Las Mujeres en la Revolución Mexicana*, 75.
44　Salas, *Soldaderas*, 208–210.
45　Mariano Azuela, *Los de abajo*, México, 1974, Salas, *Soldaderas*, 194 f.

Premio Nacional de Literatura in 1944, made the problems of the 'unfeminine' role of women during the Revolution and the devastating consequences this had on the families, the major subject of the book. But, even here the Amazon finally finds her true happiness in the role as wife and mother.[46]

In Cuba and Paraguay, on the other hand, the *mambisas* and the *residentas* entered the 'pantheon of the national heroes' without having to deny their contribution to the war, although still reducing them to the role of the mother who sacrifices her husband or companion and her sons to the cause of the nation without doubt or mourning. In this case, the women are the ones who incite the men to fight, and who, in the case of Paraguay, are remembered as those who took up arms to defend themselves, their children and their country, when there were no men left.

As I have argued elsewhere, in the cases of Cuba and Paraguay, these women, who had all trespassed the boundaries of proper behaviour for women, were acceptable because their example helped strengthen the national identity and promote an image of unity in the fight against colonialism or neo-colonialism. In Cuba, women aided in remembering that independence was not only won because of US-American participation in the struggle against Spain, but that it was mainly a fight of the Cubans for their independence. Especially Mariana Grajales, the companion and later wife of Antonio Maceo, the coloured hero of independence, who entered history books as the 'titan de bronce', was useful to symbolize the participation even of the most unfortunate of the Cubans, the Afro-Cuban women, in the movement.[47]

> 'Mariana is remembered today because she was faithful to Cuba and independence. Her motherhood was not only that of the protective, nurturing mother. Hers was the motherhood of total and selfless dedication to a cause, sacrificing home, husband and children to war and making it good. She could become a strong, revolutionary icon, because she symbolised Afro-Cuban resistance. In Afro-Cuban cultures and belief systems, women can lead and commune with the orishas to redress imbalance through ritual and action. A mother exhorting her prodigy to go to war, to kill and to die is within the power and right of a strong woman.
> It is significant that this is how Cubans have chosen to interpret the meaning of Mariana's life. They could have interpreted it otherwise, but instead

---

[46] Francisco Rojas González, *La negra angustias*, 2nd edn, México, 1992, see also the analisis in Salas, *Soldaderas*, 197–99.

[47] Jean Stubbs, 'Social and Political Motherhood of Cuba: Mariana Grajales Cuello', in *Engendering History. Caribbean Women in Historical Perspective*, eds Verene Shepherd, Bridget Brereton and Barbara Bailey, Kingston/London, 1995, 296–317, Barbara Potthast, 'Mujeres, guerra y nacionalismo. Una comparación sobre la función de las heroínas nacionales en Cuba y Paraguay', in *Ciudadanos en la nación*, eds Olga Portuodo Zúñiga and Michael Zeuske Ludwig, Santiago de Cuba, 2002, 161–172. For some interesting aspects of gender and race in this context see K. L. Hoganson, *Fighting for American Manhood: How Gender Politics provoked the Spanish-American and Philippine-American Wars*, New Haven, 1998.

Table 5: Monument for the Paraguayan Residenta (Collection Potthast)

they have recognised and celebrated the resistance of the defiant and heroic mother-leader. What in other cultures and belief systems, both in Cuba and elsewhere, might be considered improper and abusive, was heralded as a virtue. She epitomised the good woman for whom virginity was ultimately less important than self-sufficiency and loyalty to causes beyond her own image and those of husband, father and son.' (Table 5)[48]

Paraguay, which in the 19th century was despised because of its poverty and the strong influence of the indigenous culture in its society, had managed to resist the attacks of its powerful neighbours Brazil and Argentina for almost five years. For this reason, after the war the image of the *residenta* of mestizo or Guaraní origin, helped to give the defeated and destroyed backward country at least one thing it could be proud of – the fame of being a nation of courageous and ferocious fighters.[49] Paraguayan propaganda had already made extensive and skilful use of contemporary gender stereotypes during the war. Bilingual Guaraní and Spanish newspapers directed at the lower classes appealed to the martial and patriarchal values of Paraguayan men when they warned against the Brazilian 'monkeys' and 'black hordes' anxious to rape Paraguayan women.[50] Or they told stories of brave women who defended themselves against jaguars with only a knife, concluding that, 'if Paraguayan women are capable of this, what potent mother's milk to feed the legions of López.'[51] After the war, the women who went with the army and who supposedly took up arms could be used as a proof not only of the courage of the Paraguayan people but also of their nationalism and unity. This image appealed especially to the military, and officers praised the role of the women in their history, mainly emphasizing their role during the war.[52] Long time military dictator Alfred Stroessner finally dedicated a huge monument in the capital to these women.

Whereas Paraguay and Cuba incorporated the Indigenous or African origins of their populations into their national identities at the beginning of the 20th century and thus could accept differing female roles, Peruvian or Mexican Indigenismo tried to better the fate of these groups by assimilating them. Their culture, for this

---

48   Stubbs, *Motherhood*, 313.
49   Barbara Potthast, 'Alterität als nationale Identität. Die Neuformulierung der nationalen Identität in Paraguay nach dem Tripel-Allianz-Krieg', in *Kultur-Diskurs: Kontinuität und Wandel der Diskussion um Identitäten in Lateinamerika im 19. und 20. Jahrhundert*, eds Michael Riekenberg, Stefan Rinke, and Peer Schmidt, Stuttgart, 2001, 239–258.
50   I cannot develop the intersection of gender and race in this context.
51   *Cabichui* (Paso Pucú) 22nd June 1868. See also Potthast, *'Paradies'*, 293, Barbara Potthast, 'Residentas, Destinadas y otras heroínas. El nacionalismo paraguayo y el rol de las mujeres en la guerra de la Triple Alianza', in *Las mujeres y las naciones. Problemas de incluisón y exclusión*, eds Barbara Potthast and Eugenia Scarzanella, Frankfurt/M./Madrid, 2001, 77–92.
52   Ignacio Pane, 'La mujer paraguaya', in *Revista del Instituto Paraguayo*, no. 17 (1899), 161–166, Pastor Urbieta Rojas, *La mujer en el proceso cultural del Paraguay*, Buenos Aires, 1944, Pastor Urbieta Rojas, *La mujer paraguaya (esquema historiográfico)*, Asunción, 1962, Centurión, Carlos R., *La mujer paraguaya a través de la historia*, Asunción, 1962, 91 f.

reason, had to be reprimanded not strengthened or even idealized. This referred not only to language, religious rituals or other cultural practices but also to gender roles that allowed the women – and if it were out of sheer necessity – economic activities outside the house and independent, even violent behaviour. If these values and habits had to be changed, *rabonas* and *vivanderas* came to symbolize the supposed backwardness and criminality of these groups and could not enter the collective national memory. In Paraguay and Cuba, however, things were different and these groups were needed for the construction of a national identity.[53]

'Republican Mothers'[54] or 'Simply Mothers'?

The role as a national symbol makes it difficult to find out what really motivated these women to become part of the armies. If we believe the official Cuban or Paraguayan discourses, the deeds of the *mambisas* or *residentas* were motivated by nothing else but patriotism.[55] The same holds true for some female heroes of the independence period at the beginning of the 19th century, although it is somewhat easier to trace their thoughts because they were mostly upper-class women and left some letters or even diaries that reveal something about their thoughts and their possible motives.[56] Most of the *residentas, mambisas, rabonas* etc. however, were illiterate and left no written documents. The literate men, however, were not interested in writing about these women and it were mostly foreign observers who were struck by their participation in the struggles. But even women writers like Flora Tristan were socially and culturally too far away from the *rabonas* to really inquire about their motives. We have to turn to the Mexican Revolution to find some individual statements like the one of the pregnant woman who was forced to come along by her husband, cited above, or the life story of Jesusa Palancares who went with her father as a young girl, or the stories of women who were abducted by the soldiers in order to serve them. These women definitely had little choice.

---

53 In addition, these countries had been characterized since a long time by a high percentage of informal unions, even higher rates of illegitimate children, and women who worked outside the home and provided for the family. In other words, they were much more used to a different kind of family model than the Peruvian or Mexican elites. For this reason, women who did not fit the Catholic or Victorian gender images, became acceptable as national heroes even to the ruling elite.
54 I borrow this term from Linda Kerber, who analises how the new republican ideal and citizenship was made compatible with traditional gender roles in the USA after Independence. "Republican Mother" did not have to leave their home to serve the country, as did the men. All the women had to do was educate their sons as good citizens and – in the worst case – sacrifice them for the fatherland. Kerber, *Women of the Republic*.
55 Potthast, *Mujeres, guerra y nacionalismo*, Potthast, *Residentas*, Potthast, *Protagonists*.
56 Manuela Sáenz, e.g., left several letters and a diary, although we have to take into account that these women were educated enough to take into account the later publication of their letters or diaries and probably styled themselves after the model they sought most acceptable.

Another Mexican *soldadera* who was asked – by a Northamerican observer – why she participated gave the convincing answer that she was there 'because he is'.[57] In my research on Paraguay I found the custom that already in pre-war times, if a man was enlisted some female member of the family accompanied him to care for his daily needs.[58] If they had to look after the men – be they husband, brother, uncle – already in peacetime, the more so did women feel that they had to care for them in times of war. In that situation, men needed additional care if they were sick or wounded. From these examples we can conclude that for many women their participation in the war was less motivated by political reasons but mostly by traditional gender and family roles. They were the ones who were responsible for the well-being of the male members of the family, be it in peace or in wartime. And if war obliged them to abandon their homes and follow the soldiers to distant and unknown places, they had to extend the range of their activities, spatially as well as functionally. So, in the end, these women were not so much serving their fatherland as they were serving their family.[59] By doing so, they performed a patriotic act, for sure, but this was not their main objective. One could argue that their performance was the extension of their 'private' role into the 'public sphere', but I doubt that the women saw it that way. Besides, the dichotomy of private and public makes little sense in the context wars that so strongly affect the civilian population. We also have to take into consideration that many of these lower-class women, especially the indigenous women in the wars of independence, certainly had a completely different vision of the incipient nation – if they had one at all. This might have been different with many of the Cuban or Paraguayan women in the second half of the 19th century, but still most testimonies from these wars and from the Mexican Revolution prove that their main loyalty was to the men of their families or to their partners and not to the Nation or a political leader. Apart from that, like many soldiers, these women had few options. They were forced either physically or morally to what was expected from them – and that was to look after their men.[60] So, contrary to what upper class men (and women) thought, these women who transgressed the spatial and moral boundaries of their gender, were not threatening gender or family hierarchies, they only adapted their roles to the different circumstances. Gender hierarchies and perceptions of honour had to change with the new republics, but the elites wanted them to change according to their model – and according to existing social hierarchies.

---

57 Reed, *Insurgent Mexico*, 45. For other statements see Reséndez Fuentes, *Battleground Women*.
58 Potthast, '*Paradies*' 130 f.
59 Some of them might also have done this because of the good business opportunities as suppliers of the army. See Potthast, '*Paradies*', 261–271.
60 Potthast, '*Paradies*' 301, Reséndez Fuentes, *Battleground Women*, 532, 540.

Conclusion

Women participated to a greater degree in the struggle for independence and the following wars of the young republics than traditional historiography has accepted, especially in those wars that mobilized a big part of the population like civil wars or wars where the nation was at stake. But they participated in a different way than the episodes of women soldiers or upper-class angels of mercy and discretion depict. Their main contribution to the armies and the war was the work they performed as servants, providers and companions. If they participated in the battles, most of the women had supportive functions, like refilling the magazines of the rifles. Even these subordinate tasks, however, required or had as a consequence the transgression of the limits established in traditional gender roles, and this made ruling elites fearful of the consequences for family and social hierarchies after the wars. Consequently, the images of these 'unfeminine' roles and rebellious behaviours had to be forgotten or reinterpreted. In societies where the camp followers not only belonged to the lower class but also to ethnic minorities who were to be assimilated, the subject was simply dismissed. In countries that wanted to stress the participation of these subordinate groups in order to strengthen national identity, the women were remembered, but mostly as the ones who sacrificed their husbands and sons for the 'national cause'. It was always motherhood and sacrifice, in this case coupled with courage that qualified these women as national heroes. And motherhood or companionship was indeed important to all of these women, but in a different sense. It was the duty of a mother to care for the members of the family, and if these left their homes for the front, in order to be able to fulfil this duty, the women went with them. It was not so much 'republican' but rather 'familial' motherhood that motivated these women.

Women who leave their homes in order to save them are nothing unusual in Latin American history. Even at the end of the 20th century this was a strong motivation for women to step out of their traditional surroundings and roles. The Mothers of the Plaza de Mayo as well as their Chileans adversaries, the women who helped to overthrow Salvador Allende, all were motivated by their roles as mothers and centres of the family in the first instance.

Bibliography

Alzola de Cvitanocich, Nilsa M., 'Imagen Tradicional y Realidad de la mujer en el Ámbito Político Argentino (1810–1920)', in *Revista Interamericana de Bibliografía* XXXI (1981), 246–257.

Azuela, Mariano, *Los de abajo*, México, 1974.

Bingham, Majorie and Cross, Susan, *Women in Latin America*, 2 vols, St. Louis Park, 1985.

Blomberg, Hector Pedro, *Mujeres de la Historia Americana. Heroinas de amor, de la gloria, de la fe, del sacrificio y del milagro*, Buenos Aires, 1933.

Brown, Matthew, 'Adventures, Foreign Women and Masculinity in the Colombian Wars of Independence', in *Feminist Review* 79 (2005), 36–51.
Davies, Catherine/Brewster, Claire/Owen, Hilary, *South American Independence: Gender, Politics, Text*, Liverpool 2006.
Centurión, Carlos R., *La mujer paraguaya a través de la historia*, Asunción, 1962.
Chambers, Sarah C., *Republican Friendship: Manuela Sáenz Writes Women into the Nation, 1835–1856*, in *Hispanic Aamerican Historical Review* 81, no. 2 (2001), 225–257.
Cherpak, Evelyn, *The Participation of Women in the Independence Movement in Gran Colombia, 1780–1830*, in *Latin American Women: Historical Perspectives*, ed. Asunción Lavrin, Westport/Conn., 1978, 83–116.
Cherpak, Evelyn, 'Las mujeres en la Independencia', in *Las mujeres en la historia de Colombia*, vol. 1, ed. Jorge Toro Velásquez, Santafé de Bogotá, 1995, 219–234.
Earle, Rebecca, 'Rape and the Anxious Republic: Revolutionary Colombia, 1810–1830', in *Hidden Histories of Gender and the State in Latin America*, eds Elizabeth Dore and Maxine Molyneux, 2000, 127–146.
Elshtain, Jean Bethke, *Women and War*, New York 1987.
Ferrer, Ada, *Insurgent Cuba. Race, Nation and Revolution, 1868–1898*, Chapel Hill/London, 1999.
Gil, Juan, *Mitos y utopías del descubrimiento*, Madrid, 1989, vol. 3: *El Dorado*.
González Afonso, Delia, 'Amazonen in der Neuen Welt. Der wiederentdeckte Mythos?', in *asien, afrika, lateinamerika* 22 (1994), 447–460.
Grez, Vicente, *Las mujeres de la independencia*, Santiago de Chile, 1966.
Hagen, Victor von, *Manuela. Manuela Sáenz und Simón Bolívar*, Hamburg/Wien, 1957 (English original: *Four seasons of Manuela*,1952).
Helg, Aline, *Our rightful share: the Afro-Cuban struggle for equality, 1886–1912*, Chapel Hill/London, 1995.
Hepke, Sabrina, 'Frauen in der Unabhängigkeitsbewegung Kubas, 1868–1898' (Dipl. Thesis, University of Cologne, 1997).
Hoganson, K.L, *Fighting for American Manhood: How Gender Politics provoked the Spanish-American and Philippine-American Wars*, New Haven, 1998.
Hufton, Olwen, *Women and the Limits of Citizenship in the French Revolution*, Toronto, 1992.
Kerber, Linda, *Women of the Republic. Intellect and Ideology in Revolutionary America*, Chapel Hill, 1980.
Knight, Alan, *The Mexican Revolution*, Cambridge, 1986.
Las Mujeres en la Revolución Mexicana, 1884–1920, ed. Instituto Nacional de Estudios Históricos de la Revolución Méxicana, México, 1993.
Lau, Ana and Ramos, Carmen, *Mujeres y revolución, 1900–1917*, México, 1993.
McDonald, Sharon/Holden, Pat/Ardener, Shirley (ed.), *Images of Women in Peace and War – Crosscultural and Historical Perspectives*, Basingstoke/Hampshire, 1987.
Macias, Anna, *Against All Odds. The Feminist Movement in Mexico to 1940*, Westport/Conn., 1982.
Masterman, George Frederick, *Siete años de aventuras en el Paraguay*, trans. David Lewis, Buenos Aires, 1870.
Mitscherlich, Margarete, *Die friedfertige Frau: eine psychoanalytische Untersuchung zur Aggression der Geschlechter*, Frankfurt/M., 1985.
Murray, Pamela S., "'Loca' or 'Libertadora'?: Manuela Sáenz in the eyes of history and historians 1900–1990', in *Journal of Latin American Studies* 33, no. 2 (2001), 291–310.

Pane, Ignacio, 'La mujer paraguaya', in *Revista del Instituto Paraguayo*, no. 17 (1899), 161–166.

Poniatowska, Elena, *Here's to you, Jesusa*, New York, 2002 (Spanish original: *Hasta no verte Jesús mío*, 1969).

Potthast, Barbara, 'Protagonists, Victims, and Heroes. Paraguayan Women during the Great War', in '*I die with my country*'. *Perspectives on the Paraguayan War*, eds Hendrik Kraay and Thomas L. Whigham, Lincoln, 2004, 44–60.

Potthast, Barbara, 'Mujeres, guerra y nacionalismo. Una comparación sobre la función de las heroínas nacionales en Cuba y Paraguay', in *Ciududunos en la nación*, eds Olga Portuodo Zúñiga and Michael Zeuske Ludwig, Santiago de Cuba, 2002, 161–172.

Potthast, Barbara, '*Residentas, Destinadas* y otras heroinas. El nacionalismo paraguayo y el rol de las mujeres en la guerra de la Triple Alianza', in *Las mujeres y las naciones. Problemas de incluisón y exclusión*, eds Barbara Potthast and Eugenia Scarzanella, Frankfurt/M./Madrid, 2001, 77–92.

Potthast, Barbara, *"Paradies Mohammeds" oder "Land der Frauen"? Zur Rolle der Frau und der Familie in der paraguayischen Gesellschaft im 19. Jahrhundert*, Lateinamerikanische Forschungen 21, Köln/Wien/Weimar, 1994.

Potthast, Barbara, 'Alterität als nationale Identität. Die Neuformulierung der nationalen Identität in Paraguay nach dem Tripel-Allianz-Krieg', in *Kultur-Diskurs: Kontinuität und Wandel der Diskussion um Identitäten in Lateinamerika im 19. und 20. Jahrhundert*, eds Michael Riekenberg, Stefan Rinke, and Peer Schmidt, Stuttgart, 2001, 239–258.

Potthast, Barbara, *Von Müttern und Machos. Eine Geschichte der Frauen in Lateinamerika*. Wuppertal, 2003.

Quintero, Inés, 'Las mujeres de la Independencia: ¿heroínas o transgresoras? El caso de Manuela Sáenz', in *Las mujeres y las naciones. Problemas de inclusión y exclusión*, eds Barbara Potthast and Eugenia Scarzanella, Frankfurt/M./Madrid, 2001, 57–76.

Reed, *Insurgent Mexico*, Berlin, 1978.

Andrés Reséndez Fuentes, 'Battleground Women: Soldaderas and Female Soldiers in the Mexican Revolution', *The Americas*, 51:4 (1995), 525–553.

Rodríguez O, Jaime E., *The Independence of Spanish America*, Cambridge, 1998.

Rojas González, Francisco, *La negra angustias*, 2nd edn, México, 1992.

Rojas y Thelen, Lucia, 'Partizipation der Frauen an der Unabhängigkeitsbewegung in Lateinamerika: Realität und Historiographie am Beispiel von Manuela Sáenz' (Masters Thesis, University of Cologne, 1993).

Rumazo González, Alfonso, *Manuela Sáenz. La libertadora del libertador*. Guayaquil/Quito, 1970.

Sáenz, Manuela and Bolívar, Simón, *Patriota y amante de usted. Manuela Sáenz y el Libertador. Diarios ineditos con textos de Elena Poniatowska, Miguel Bonasso, Carlos Álvarez, Heinz Dietrich*, eds Heinz Dietrich Stefan et al., México, 1993.

Salas, Elizabeth, 'Soldaderas in the Mexican Militar: Myth and History' (Ph.D. Thesis, University of California: Ann Arbor, 1987).

Stern, Steve J., *The Secret History of Gender: Women, Men, and Power in Late Colonial Mexico*, Chapel Hill et al., 1995.

Stoner, Lynn, *From the House to the Streets. The Cuban Woman's Movement for Legal Reform, 1898–194*, Durham/London, 1991.

Stubbs, Jean, 'Social and Political Motherhood of Cuba: Mariana Grajales Cuello', in *Engendering History. Caribbean Women in Historical Perspective*, eds Verene Shepherd, Bridget Brereton and Barbara Bailey, Kingston/London, 1995, 296–317.

Tirado Mejía, Álvaro, *Aspectos sociales de las guerras civiles en Colombia*, Bogotá, 1976.
Tobler, Hans Werner, *Die Mexikanische Revolution. Gesellschaftlicher Wandel und politischer Umbruch, 1876–1940*, Frankfurt/M., 1984.
Tristan, Flora, *Peregrinations of a Pariah*, Trans./ed. Jean Hawkes, Boston, MA, 1987.
Troconis de Veracoechea, Ermilia, *Indias, Esclavas, manutanas y primeras damas*, Caracas, 1990.
Urbieta Rojas, Pastor, *La mujer en el proceso cultural del Paraguay*, Buenos Aires, 1944.
Urbieta Rojas, Pastor, *La mujer paraguaya (esquema historiográfico)*, Asunción, 1962.
Whigham, Thomas L., *The Paraguayan War*, Lincoln/London, 2002, Vol. 1: *Causes and Early Conduct*, Lincoln, 2002.

Between the Lines:
Female Auxiliaries, Resistors, and Spies in the First World War

Tammy Proctor

Scholars in recent years have given increasing attention to the role of women in times of war, and excellent studies provide a comprehensive picture of female participation, both physical and ideological, in the war effort on "home fronts."[1] These home fronts, so named to be a companion to the male sphere of battle fronts, have dominated popular and scholarly understandings of civilians' role in twentieth century warfare. As men fought in the lines of trenches of World War I, women did their part "behind the lines" as support staff who were uneasy occupants of this martial culture. Women were, and remain, crucial to modern warfare, yet they are most often designated as outsiders to war – as reluctant recruits in time of need. This elaborate formulation of male combatant and female non-combatant helps motivate men to fight for the protection of non-combatants and justifies massive military expenditure and militarization of societies to support the necessity of war. As Cynthia Enloe has noted in her work, "all military work – not just work done by women – is organised on the basis of gender."[2] War makes real men, but it can do so only if women are ideologically separate from the combat that defines the masculine war experience.

This gendered organization of wartime societies was increasingly apparent in the First World War, the first war where multiple states had the capability of mobilizing mass numbers of people and institutions for military purposes. A study of propaganda alone from 1914–1918 yields a wealth of information on the gendering of war, with women's images used to sell war to men. Add to that campaigns to force men to be "real men" with white feathers for cowardice, and the gendered rhetoric

---

1 One such work is M. Higonnet, S. Michel, J. Jenson, and M. Collins Weitz (eds), *Behind the Lines: Gender and the Two World Wars*, New Haven and London: Yale University Press, 1987.
2 C. Enloe, *Does Khaki Become You? The Militarisation of Women's Lives*, London: South End Press, 1983, 175.

of war seems inescapable.³ In some ways, even feminist scholars concerned with "gendering the war" have played into the militarization process by focusing their efforts on the somewhat elaborate and in many ways false dichotomy of "home" and "battle" fronts. Using these formulations obscures both the people who do not fit neatly into these categories, and it bolsters the idea that these are real and separate worlds. Again, to cite Enloe, "Acquisition of manpower has required an elaborate gender ideology and social structure … [and] has necessitated that the public believe that wars are fought on something considered the 'battle front' and supported on something called the 'home front.'"⁴

This paper takes issue with the neat division between home and battle front and examines the women who fall between the lines, those caught in occupied zones or in front-line areas during World War I. Although I explicitly focus on such women, I would also like to suggest that these are only the more obvious ways in which the fiction of the male combatant and female non-combatant breaks down. Susan Grayzel and other historians have also begun picking apart this division, and Grayzel notes that although "the idea of separate fronts helped to maintain the status quo of gender identities …" the "boundaries erected between home and war fronts were often porous."⁵ For women in occupied territory, their homes were war fronts, and although there were nuances to individual behaviors, most had no real choice but to participate in some way, either by passively accepting occupation or by actively resisting it. In addition to those women swept up by war through invasion, I consider female volunteers who put themselves deliberately in the front lines through auxiliary work. In both cases, these women at war threatened the carefully constructed notion that war was men's work and that soldiering was something best left to them. Because the women undermined this ideology, the post-war commemoration of their service had to be repackaged to fit the appropriate gender roles assigned to them in wartime.

Women and War

Although the twenty-first century media most often portrays women in combat situations as a recent experiment, in fact, war has never been an exclusively male enterprise. Not only were women often victims of marauding armies of history,

---

3 N. Gullace, 'The Blood of Our Sons': Men, Women and the Regenotiation of British Citizenship During the Great War, New York: Palgrave Macmillan, 2002, 73–98.
4 Enloe, Does Khaki Become You?, 211.
5 S. Grayzel, Women's Identities at War: Gender, Motherhood, and Politics in Britain and France During the First World War, Chapel Hill and London: University of North Carolina Press, 1999, 11. See also K. Hagemann and S. Schüler-Springorum (eds), Home/Front: The Military, War and Gender in Twentieth-Century Germany, Oxford/New York: Berg, 2002, and H. McCartney, Citizen Soldiers: The Liverpool Territorials in the First World War, Cambridge: Cambridge University Press, 2005.

some also disguised themselves as men to fight as soldiers. More commonly, however, females became members of the military as wives, sutlers, prostitutes and servants. It was a common sight in European armies of the past to see women guarding baggage, carrying water, or selling spirits at battle fronts, and military wives were paid to cook, clean, sew, nurse and do laundry for regiments from at least the seventeenth century to the late nineteenth century. For example, British army regulations mandated the number of "official" wives allowed to accompany regiments, but many more "unofficial" women also traveled with armies in the field.[6] In fact, as Holly Mayer found in her study of camp followers and the American Revolution, the British Army legitimized women's presence "on the strength" by paying them for their work and subjecting them to military justice. As Mayer noted, "Women were ineligible for military service but not for service to the military."[7]

However, as the military professionalized in Europe in the nineteenth century and began to change its image, female "camp followers" were increasingly pushed out of their traditional roles as the armies incorporated such labor directly into formal battalions and services. Historian Barton Hacker describes the process in this way, "As armies became more professional and bureaucratic – they became, in fact, more exclusively military – they also became more exclusively male, as striking parallel to the contemporary masculinization of medicine ... By the time of the First World War the once integral place of women in Western armies had faded from memory."[8] Hacker astutely points out that as professional history was emerging as a field in the late nineteenth century, women had already been purged from many armies, so they were virtually invisible to the military historians chronicling the wars of the past.[9]

Part of the reason for professionalizing armies was to make them more efficient and to provide better central control. Stricter military codes emerged with more standardized regulations and the men and women civilians who had served in various capacities were excluded. Non-combatant services increasingly fell to army battalions created for that purpose, while women's participation in army life became confined to sexual and familial services.[10] When women volunteered for service in 1914, they did so as part of a much different military structure, and the women of

---

6   S. Hendrix, "In the Army: Women, Camp Followers and Gender Roles in the British Army in the French and Indian Wars, 1755–1765, in G. DeGroot and C. Peniston-Bird (eds), *A Soldier and a Woman: Sexual Integration in the Military*, Harlow, Essex: Pearson Education Limited, 2000, 35, 38; M. Trustram, *Women of the Regiment: Marriage and the Victorian Army*, Cambridge: Cambridge University Press,1984, 2–3; N. St John, *Judy O'Grady and the Colonel's Lady*, London: Brassey's Defence Publishers, 1988, 1, 11–12.
7   H. Mayer, *Belonging to the Army: Camp Followers and Community during the American Revolution*, Columbia: University of South Carolina Press, 1996, 6–8, 122.
8   B. Hacker, "Women and Military Institutions in Early Modern Europe: A Reconnaissance," *Signs: Journal of Women in Culture and Society*, 6(4), 1981, 676, 681.
9   Hacker, "Women and Military Institutions ...," 645.
10 Trustram, *Women of the Regiment*, 3, 12–13.

occupied territories faced different challenges from these armies than they might have a hundred years earlier.

When the war began in early August 1914, the first women drawn into the conflict were those inhabiting zones through which armies moved and sometimes occupied. Floods of refugees picked up what belongings they could take and relocated to other parts of their own countries or to other nations. In Belgium, tens of thousands of people fled to the coastal areas and the Netherlands during the first three weeks of the war, and by 1915, more than two hundred fifty thousand Belgian refugees were in Britain.[11] Likewise, millions of refugees on the Eastern Front left Galicia and Bukovina for the cities of Austria (such as Vienna) by 1915, while Russians, Poles, Armenians, and Ukrainians moved east to escape danger.[12] Those who remained in occupied territory faced what was to be a long period of economic difficulty and in some cases, surveillance, forced labor, and deportation. In the northern French city of Lille, for instance, the Germans deported about twenty thousand women and young girls for forced labor in the countryside.[13] For the millions caught up in the 1915 Russian retreat or the Armenian genocide, the war meant starvation and death.[14]

In occupied territories, women were in a particularly precarious position because of the sexual overtones. Women were seen as "available" to soldiers, a stereotype they found it difficult to dispute. Women's proximity to occupying forces also complicated matters, since their complicity was often assumed when women worked as servants for enemy troops, billeted them, or served them in cafes and shops. While men might be classified as war profiteers, women were often depicted as "intimate" collaborators. Certainly women did serve as prostitutes both in towns close to the front lines and in occupied territories, but women faced suspicion of "horizontal" collaboration through their mere presence in areas frequented by soldiers. Ute Daniel notes that "the sexual behavior of the entire civilian population became the object of police intervention and surveillance" especially in occupation zones, since the spread of venereal disease was considered an attack on military effectiveness.[15]

11 D. Bilton, *The Home Front in the Great War: Aspects of the Conflict 1914–1918*, Barnsley: Leo Cooper, 2002, 217; P. Cahalan, *Belgian Refugee Relief in England during the Great War*, New York & London: Garland Publishing, 1982.
12 P. Gatrell, *A Whole Empire Walking: Refugees in Russia during World War I*, Bloomington: Indiana University Press, 1999, 15–20.
13 A. Becker, *Oubliés de la grande guerre*, Paris: Éditions Noêsis 1998, 68–69.
14 J. Horne and A. Kramer, *German Atrocities, 1914: A History of Denial*, New Haven and London: Yale University Press, 2001, 84.
15 U. Daniel, *The War From Within: German Working-Class Women in the First World War*, Oxford and New York: Berg, 1997, 140–143.

Woman and Resistance

One example of the dilemma of the occupied woman is Marthe Cnockaert, a young woman trained prior to the war as a nurse. She walked the thin line between collaborator and resistor in Belgium by working for the Germans as a nurse and helping her parents maintain a café for German soldiers, while in her spare time she worked as a spy for the British. This ambivalent and dangerous position is symbolized by the two medals she won during the war: a German Iron Cross for nursing and a British War Medal for espionage. Often women such as Cnockaert had to choose between the roles of "victims of German aggression or sordid sexual collaborators" – their resistance, heroism, and courage lost in the postwar reassertion of proper roles for women.[16]

In 1914, however, resistance looked like the only option for some women caught in combat and occupation zones. Sophie de Schaepdrijver estimates that "By December 1914, nine-tenths of Belgium was under German occupation," and she notes the country became "virtually sealed territory" with the erection in 1915 of a "10 foot high, 50,000 volt electric fence" around the occupation zone.[17] People faced regulation of most aspects of their daily lives and as the war progressed, the food shortages and morale-crushing presence of occupying forces increased their hardships. One French woman documented some of the problems in her wartime "black journal": "(30 January 1915) Bread very poor in quality ... (14 February 1915) No Lenten fast this year, since every day is necessarily a fast day ... (3 April 1915) Easter. No bells ringing ... (4 April 1915)."[18] Indeed one important resistance activity for men and women was food smuggling. A Brussels woman noted in her diary for Oct 3, 1917: "I saw 4 poor women, being marched to the police station, by a Boche sous-officier. For carrying potatoes, small quantities. It appears that the confiscated potatoes are sold to the alimentation, the price is given to those who arrested the carriers, who, besides losing their precious wares, are fined one mark per kilo, of what they were smuggling."[19]

Resistance efforts in occupied areas were varied and dangerous. Many women in Belgium and Northern France became involved almost immediately in efforts to hide and move Allied soldiers separated from their units or downed Allied airmen. Louise Thuliez records her scorn at German promises to shoot those helping

---

16 T. Proctor, *Female Intelligence: Women and Espionage in the First World War*, New York and London: New York University Press, 2003,143.
17 S. de Schaepdrijver, "Occupation, Propaganda, and the Idea of Belgium," in A. Roshwald and R. Stites, (eds), *European Culture in the Great War: The Arts, Entertainment, and Propaganda, 1914–1918*, Cambridge: Cambridge University Press, 1999, 269, 271.
18 Madame Delahaye-Théry, "Cahiers Noirs," in H. McPhail, *The Long Silence: Civilian Life under the German Occupation of Northern France, 1914–1918*, London and New York: IB Tauris, 2001, 58–59.
19 Anonymous female author, "Local Gossip and 'side-shows' of the war during the German occupation of Belgium" unpublished diary, Documentariecentrum Ieper.

Allied soldiers, and notes that they began organizing escape services from Northern France through Belgium to the Netherlands in fall 1914.[20] Using their peculiar advantages, in particular the tendency among military authorities to downplay the threat that women posed, women offered their houses as hiding places, served as couriers and messengers for escape networks, and forged documents. One such network was led by Vicomtesse Gabrielle de Monge, a 31-year-old aristocrat from Ohey, and staffed by women of all ages, young boys, and elderly men. The service ran successfully from November 1914 to its capture by German authorities in April 1916, and it was responsible for transporting nearly four hundred soldiers to neutral territory.[21]

Another such network gained fame in 1915, when one of its principal participants, British nurse Edith Cavell, was executed by the Germans. Her death in October of that year not only publicized the activities of such resistance groups, with their male and female participation, but it also provided a powerful propaganda image for Britain and its allies. Cavell was not depicted as a courageous resistor to German occupation, but as a murdered martyr, a victim of German barbarism. Despite the fact that she and thirty-five other people (including thirteen women) had been caught after a year of successfully running an escape network, the media trumpeted instead Cavell's martyrdom. Robert Underwood Johnson's poem in the *New York Times* captures the essence of this transformation:

> Room mid the martyrs for a deathless name!
> Till yesterday, in her how few could know
> Black War's white angel, succoring friend and foe –
> Whose pure heart harbored neither hate nor blame
> When Need or Pity made its sovereign claim.
> Today she is the world's![22]

Cavell's active role in the war is completely absent in this gendered account of her nurturing, maternal figure, and the poem mirrors postcard images of her kneeling, praying, or collapsed on the ground in front of a murderous looking German officer. "In the weeks after her death, Cavell was transformed from an active resister to a passive pawn, providing a powerful story for women in wartime and a motivating force to men."[23]

Like Cavell, other women resistors from the First World War have been lost to history, either reinscribed as victims or forgotten entirely. In Belgium alone, thousands of women participated in resistance activities as diverse as espionage, running

---

20 L. Thuliez, *Condamnée à Mort*, Paris: Flammarion, 1933, 23–30.
21 Imperial War Museum, La Dame Blanche Box 2, Folder 11 "Service de Passage" (Nov. 1914-April 1916).
22 Robert Underwood Johnson, "Edith Cavell," *New York Times* (24 October 1915).
23 Proctor, *Female Intelligence*, 106.

escape networks, smuggling, running underground presses, or sabotage. Marthe Cnockaert was finally captured and imprisoned in 1916 after dynamiting a supply depot, while national heroine, Gabrielle Petit, was a useful British spy for almost two years before her execution. The countless women who were never captured faded into obscurity with the armistice, and some never received any medals or recognition for their service to Belgium.

Two particular examples provide a window into the important activities in which women engaged during the war in occupied Belgium, Luxembourg, and northern France. First, in espionage networks, women were a crucial component because of surveillance and heightened official suspicion of male agents. In *La Dame Blanche*, a British espionage network headquartered in Liège, the male leaders purposefully created a "shadow executive" council of women who could run the espionage service unassisted should the men be arrested or deported. For the eight men who served on the supreme council, there were seven women designed to take their places in any emergency. All seven women already occupied positions of importance in the organization as battalion commanders, couriers, members of the Secretary-General, etc., but they were cross-trained in other duties just in case.[24] The second example concerns the working of the clandestine newspaper, *La Libre Belgique*, and *Le Mot du Soldat*, an underground postal service that transmitted letters to and from the Belgian army to families in occupied territory. Again, women were an invaluable part of these organizations, especially as distributors, and so their role in the "cultural resistance" to occupation was also important.[25]

In both espionage and cultural resistance networks, women were integral and active to the success of such endeavors. As with times of revolution, occupation by enemy armies breaks down the militarized gender dynamic of home/front and creates the necessity of women's participation in their own protection. Occupation can also spur patriotic resistance, with women feeling the same antagonism toward their captors as men. Many women involved in resistance activities conceptualized themselves as soldiers, albeit unconventional ones. Consistently these women describe their "service" in terms of soldiering, noting that they were just doing their duty, being patriotic, or answering their country's call. For the agents of *La Dame Blanche*, the title of soldier was a required one as the network was organized along military lines as a sort of British Observation Corps, and LDB included an oath of allegiance and the possibility of court martial. Called "soldiers without uniforms" by one member, Jeanne Delwaide, the women of *La Dame Blanche* took their military role seriously, but their very existence as a British auxiliary army threatened the notion of men's unique place at the front in the postwar. Most members received

---

24 Archives Generale du Royaume (AGR), P/212 Service Patriotique, 1 November 1918.
25 De Schaepdrijver, 272, and D. De Weerdt, *De Vrouwen van de Eerste Wereldoorlog*, Gent: Stichting Mens en Kultur, 1993, 148–153.

postwar payments and British War Medals, but they were not celebrated significantly in postwar commemoration either in Belgium or Britain.[26]

In addition to women's patriotic mobilization against enemy occupation as in Belgium, many females joined nationalist movements that affected the war itself, but which had as their goals larger changes. Well-known examples of this phenomenon are the women revolutionaries such as Constance Markiewicz (Ireland), Rosa Luxemburg (Germany), or Alexandra Kollontai (Russia). Less famous perhaps, but equally as instructive, was the experience of men and women in colonized areas drawn into the war experience. Such nationalists sought to use wartime service to sway European authorities to look more kindly on their causes, just as European authorities tried to exploit nationalist movements for their own ends during the war by using promises of postwar settlements.

One of the most fascinating of these nationalist organizations to emerge in the war in the Mediterranean is the NILI espionage ring, which is an acronym for *Netzach Israel lo Ishakare*, or the Eternity of Israel will not lie.[27] This British intelligence group was created in Palestine by a Zionist family, the Aaronsohns, and their friends. Most of its members were under thirty years old and nominally, at least, enemy combatants (Turkish citizens), but they offered their services to the British because they saw Britain as the best hope for the creation of a Jewish independent state in Palestine. Although the network began gathering information in 1915, they could not establish contact with the British and a safe transmission system until 1917, when the service was headed by Sarah Aaronsohn, the 26-year-old sister of NILI's founder, Aaron. Sarah's war service was motivated by the Zionist cause but also by her disgust over Turkish atrocities against Armenians, which she witnessed in fall 1915 when she deserted her husband in Constantinople in order to return to Zikhron Ya'akov, her home village.[28]

Like the women in occupied territory, Sarah took many risks and saw herself as a soldier for a larger cause, in this case, Zionism. Beyond her espionage activities, she was responsible for running her brother's international agricultural station in Athlit and for funneling American funds into Palestine for famine relief and Zionist activism. When the network was captured finally in October 1917, Sarah was tortured by the Turks and forced to watch her father's torture before she tricked her captors and committed suicide. As with the women of Belgium involved in resistance activities, Sarah conceptualized herself as a warrior, writing in her farewell note: "we have died as warriors … we have striven, we have paved a road of

---

26 Proctor, *Female Intelligence*, 75–98.
27 A. Verrier (ed), *Agents of Empire: Anglo-Zionist Intelligence Operations 1915–1919, Brigadier Walter Gribbon, Aaron Aaronsohn and the NILI Ring*, London: Brassey's, 1995, 320n1.
28 Y. Auron, *The Banality of Indifference: Zionism and the Armenian Genocide*, New Brunswick/London: Transaction Publishers,2000, 162, 176–177; H. V. F. Winstone, *The Illicit Adventure*, London: Jonathan Cape, 1982, 226–229; Verrier, *Agents of Empire*, 143–146; and A. Engle, *The NILI Spies*, London: The Hogarth Press, 1959, 38, 62, 86, 100–110.

right, and happiness for the Nation ..."²⁹ Her motivation is clear here – nationalism. In other accounts of her death by NILI members imprisoned next to the room where she was tortured, her bravery is clear: "She cursed her tormentors in French, Yiddish, and Arabic. Sarah would repeat certain phrases over and over during the long hours of torture: they would get nothing form her; don't think that because she is a woman she will ask her torturers for mercy or beg; she had no partners in her activity."³⁰

For Sarah Aaronsohn and others like her, war service was a means to a larger end. In her case, she could help fight the tragedy visited upon the Armenian population while perhaps freeing Jews from Turkish rule and establishing a Jewish homeland. However, like Edith Cavell, Gabrielle Petit, and other heroines of the period, she has been commemorated as a victim in the fight for Zionism, a blood sacrifice, rather than as the warrior she believed herself to be.

Women Auxiliaries

With the women of Belgium, northern France, Palestine, and other occupied areas, resistance was a choice, but it was one made more "natural" by the circumstances in which they found themselves. Living between the lines meant having to assume new roles and to declare loyalties in a way that women in non-occupied zones did not. Yet women at the "home" fronts still volunteered, sometimes in large numbers, to place themselves in danger in combat or occupation zones. These women auxiliaries also undermine notions of an ideological separation between home and war fronts, suggesting that imaginatively and literally, women harbored many of the same ambitions for war service, patriotism, heroism and adventure as the men who enlisted in armies. Indeed, perhaps they too had little choice but to take an active interest in the war, given that rationing, air raids, censorship, VD legislation, and other wartime changes altered their lives. Nicole Dombrowski describes this process as the incorporation of women into war, as they are "enlisted into military conflicts with or without their consent."³¹ Through the gendering of war itself, women are drawn into the process of militarization and its propaganda, despite official ideological insistence that war is for men. In short, women involved in war could "disrupt the concept of war as a masculine activity [and] they could also pose a threat to the home front as a female domain."³² Yet the manpower shortage in

---

29 Verrier, *Agents of Empire*, 13.
30 Auron, *The Banality of Indifference*, 180.
31 N. Dombrowski (ed), *Women and War in the Twentieth Century: Enlisted With or Without Consent*, New York and London: Garland Publishing, 1999, 4.
32 J. Bourke, *An Intimate History of Killing: Face-to-Face Killing in Twentieth-Century Warfare*, Great Britain: Granta Books, 1999, 328.

World War I and the desire of women themselves to get involved insured that the lines were blurred between the feminine home and the male war front.

Like their camp follower sisters of the past, women attached themselves to the military in a variety of wartime positions, some in formal auxiliary organizations and others in private charitable activities or through prostitution and/or commerce. One of the most celebrated roles of women in the war was in the medical services, and women served as doctors, nurses, nurses' aides, and ambulance drivers throughout the four years. Female doctors who sought to volunteer often faced discrimination from military authorities, and several British efforts were privately organized such as the Scottish Women's Hospitals. When Elsie Inglis approached the British War Office about staffing a hospital with women in 1914, she was turned down without much of a hearing, but she got favorable responses from other governments desperate for medical care.[33] Like Ingliss, American Mary Borden took matters into her own hands even before the United States entered the war, and using her own money established a "frontline surgical unit under French military command in the Belgian zone."[34] Likewise, British women Elsie Knocker and Mairi Chisholm ran a surgical unit on the Western Front, while their countrywoman, Mabel St. Clair Stobart organized a hospital in Antwerp in 1914.[35]

Many other women provided auxiliary service through nursing, which was considered a traditional and non-threatening role for females seeking to help the war effort. In France, the government mobilized more than twenty thousand Red Cross-trained nurses in 1914, but they were quickly overwhelmed with casualties and had to seek volunteers, and eventually more than sixty thousand women served as nurses.[36] As in France, in Germany, Red Cross nurses were immediately called up for war service in 1914 and a call for women to volunteer for nursing training was also issued.[37] In Britain, Army nurses were supplemented by the use of Voluntary Aid Detachments of middle-class females with little practical nursing training. These women were deployed to home front hospitals as well as to theatres of war in France and the Mediterranean, and some nurses were even sent to inspect prisoner of war camps.[38]

---

33 M. Krippner, *The Quality of Mercy: Women at War, Serbia 1915–1918*, Newton Abbot and London: David and Charles, 1980, 10, 29.
34 M. Higonnet (ed), *Nurses at the Front: Writing the Wounds of the Great War*, Boston: Northeastern University Press, 2001, viii, ix.
35 Higonnet, *Nurses at the Front*, x, and Krippner, *The Quality of Mercy*, 19.
36 M. Darrow, *French Women and the First World War: War Stories of the Home Front*, Oxford and New York: Berg, 2000, 137–141.
37 B. Schönberger, "Motherly Heroines and Adventurous Girls: Red Cross Nurses and Women Army Auxiliaries in the First World War," in Hagemann, *Home/Front*, 89.
38 A. Summers, *Angel and Citizens: British Women as Military Nurses*, London: Routledge and Kegan Paul, 1988, and A. Rachamimov, *POWs and the Great War: Captivity on the Eastern Front*, Oxford: Berg, 2002, 172–180.

For many women, in fact, volunteer nursing was much more grueling than what they had expected. As British VAD Vera Brittain recorded after the war, "What did profoundly trouble and humiliate me was my colossal ignorance of the simplest domestic operations ... most of [the VADs] came to the hospital expecting to hold the patients' hands and smooth their pillows while the regular nurses fetched and carried everything that looked or smelt disagreeable."[39] Women ambulance drivers also found themselves in the midst of artillery attacks in the dead of night, risking their lives as surely as their male soldier relations. Perhaps most the most astonishing thing about these ambulance corps is that they were often composed of volunteers who paid for the privilege of such work.[40] Young women from good families rolled along in ambulances between field hospitals for the whole course of the war. In her fictional account, Helen Zenna Smith described the experience: "Trainloads of broken human beings: half-mad men pleading to be put out of their misery; torn and bleeding and crazed men pitifully obeying orders like a herd of senseless cattle, dumbly, pitifully straggling in the wrong direction ..."[41] These women were certainly not separate from the experience of war – such hazardous occupations brought women right into the war front, placing them squarely within the combat framework, despite their official designation as "non-combatants."

The other non-combatant women drawn into duties on or near the fronts were the members of service auxiliary corps created during the First World War. These corps differed in timing, numbers, and scope according to national needs and political realities, but many European countries tried some form of women's auxiliary army. In most cases, these women were drawn from working-class and lower middle-class backgrounds, in opposition to the predominantly middle- and upper-class women in nursing and ambulance corps. These auxiliaries performed a variety of support duties to free men for front-line duty. The twenty-thousand German female auxiliaries replaced male soldiers in occupied zones, while approximately eighty thousand British auxiliaries worked as cooks, laundresses, and drivers, staffed dispensaries, and performed clerical tasks.[42] Although much different that the women soldiers of World War II, women's corps briefly became fighting units in Russia during 1917–1918 as the country's cohesion was shattered by revolution.[43] As a contemporary British observer of these women's auxiliaries noted at the time, "The whole question of the civilian population has taken on a different aspect

---

39 V. Brittain, *Testament of Youth*, New York: Penguin, 1989, 165–167.
40 J. Marcus, "Afterword: Corpus/Corps/Corpses: Writing the Body in/at War," in H. Smith, *Not So Quiet ... Stepdaughters of War*, New York: The Feminist Press, 1989, 243.
41 Smith, *Not So Quiet*, 29.
42 Schönberger, "Motherly Heroines," 91; N. Loring Goldman and R. Stites, "Great Britain and the World Wars," in N. Loring Goldman (ed.), *Female Soldiers – Combatants or Noncombatants? Historical and Contemporary Perspectives*, Westport, CT: Greenwood Press, 1982, 29; and F. Tennyson Jesse, *The Sword of Deborah*, New York: George H. Doran Company, 1919, 27.
43 L. Stoff, "They Fought for Russia: Female Soldiers of the First World War," in DeGroot and Peniston, *A Soldier and A Woman*, 66–82.

since the outbreak of the war … but the sub-division labeled 'Women' has perhaps undergone more revision than any."[44]

In addition to women hired for work by governmental organizations, women placed themselves squarely in the line of fire for charitable purposes and for private enterprises. Some women served as international observers for the Red Cross, others helped with relief efforts in distributing food to refugees, and still other women staffed entertainment centers near the front for organizations such as the Salvation Army and YWCA. One African-American volunteer in a French canteen for soldiers described in a postwar account the services women offered to soldiers at the front: "Over the canteen in France, the woman became a trusted guardian of that home back in America. To her were revealed its joys and sorrows. Because of that same loneliness – that loss of background – the soldier poured out to the canteen worker his deepest and dearest memories and dreams."[45]

Women also made it to the front as workers for private companies, most notably as clerical support and as journalists. Female reporters had to work hard to gain access to the front lines, often using subterfuge to get into the trenches. *Saturday Evening Post* reporter Mary Roberts Rinehart described for neutral Americans conditions at the front in 1915:

> As of the trenches, many have written of the stenches of this war. But the odor of that beautiful lagoon was horrible. I do not care to emphasize it. It is one of the things best forgotten. But any lingering belief I may have had in the grandeur and glory of war died that night beside that silver lake – died of an odor, and will never live again.[46]

Roberts joined other female reporters who managed to get close enough to the front to report on its conditions. The well-known writer, Colette, wrote her account of Verdun in early 1915, explaining her voluntary foray into this zone: "I have arrived, and I will try to remain here, a voluntary prisoner … I am wild to hear about everything, to shudder, and to hope."[47] Women such as Colette and Rinehart traveled to the trenches seeking an authentic experience of the war and that they could then document for home audiences.

---

44 Jesse, *The Sword of Deborah*, 93.
45 A. Hunton, "Over the Canteen in France," in S. Grayzel, *Women and the First World War*, London: Longman, 2002, 132.
46 M. Roberts Rinehart, "No Man's Land," *Saturday Evening Post* (8 May 1915), in M.R. Higonnet (ed), *Lines of Fire: Women Writers of World War I*, New York: Penguin, 1999, 137.
47 Colette, "Verdun," *Le Matin* (December 1914-January 1915), in Higonnet, *Lines of Fire*, 133.

Conclusion

Yet despite all these varied participatory roles for women in the war effort at the fronts and in occupied zones, there remained (and remains today) a divide between women and war, and women's wartime service has not been remembered or commemorated in the way that men's was. Scholars reiterate this point when discussing World War I, writing, "Women might serve but never soldier," and "The military was perfectly happy to have the services of women ... but not enthralled with having women in service."[48] As with camp followers of the past, often portrayed as parasites clinging uselessly to the military, women in World War I service were "used by militaries to solve their nagging problems of 'manpower' availability, quality, health, morale, and readiness," and then quietly discarded.[49] The roles they played – nurses, cooks, spies, drivers, merchants, prostitutes – are the same tasks they have been performing for armies for hundreds of years. The difference, by 1914, is that they are performing these roles under the auspices of a professionalized armed forces institution, where their services can be more closely controlled. Women were integrated into the war effort but in carefully designed "auxiliary" roles as "replacements" or "diluted" labor, and their feminized uniforms were symbols of their continued "apartness" from the war experience. In this way, women functioned as the important symbol of home that was to be protected by the male soldier, boosting morale and ensuring compliance, while simultaneously providing labor, sometimes unpaid, for the war effort.

---

48   J. Tuten, "Germany and the World Wars," in Goldman, *Female Soldiers,* 50, and Goldman, "Great Britain and the World Wars," 28.
49   C. Enloe, *Maneuvers: The International Politics of Militarizing Women's Lives,* Berkeley and London: University of California Press, 2000, 44.

Gendered Medical Services in Red Cross Field Hospitals during the First Balkan War and World War I*

Jean H. Quataert

Gender analysis has transformed the writing on warfare, one of the oldest topics in the field of history. Through its critical lens, it has reworked the old adage that "war is men's business." On the one hand, it takes seriously the connections between masculinity and warfare, demonstrating, for example, the place of war in the construction of masculine identity and the historic ties between soldiering and male citizenship. On the other, it helps erode the simply polarities behind the war story as a masculine preserve: the separation of home and front, civilian and combatant, and indeed, even peace and war as two distinct moments in time. As both real and symbolic figures, women consistently have been drawn into war's orbit.[1] As the extreme of organized violence, war's many phases (from preparation to fighting to the so-called "normalcy" of peace time) have profound, if often unanticipated, consequences for gender power relations.

This chapter examines the dangerous, front-line work of British volunteers in the mobile field hospitals following the armies to the battlefields during the First Balkan War and the Serbian campaigns of World War I. These hospitals (originally called ambulances) were part of the "Geneva idea" providing medical aid to wounded and sick soldiers on and near the battlefield under an internationally recognized sign of neutrality, the Red Cross and, by 1878, Red Crescent. With passage of the Geneva Conventions in 1864, volunteer medical service increasingly

---

* I want to thank the German Marshall Fund, USA for supporting this research under a Senior Research Fellowship, 2001–2002. I am not a trained British historian and come to this topic through my new interest in the implementations of early humanitarian law in Europe's continental and colonial wars from 1864 to 1921. In addition, I thank the organizers of the sub-theme "War, Gender, and Violence," for including my paper in the panel at the 20th International Meeting of Historical Sciences, Sydney, 3–9, July 2005 and for the exchange of ideas with the other member of the panel and the audience.

1 Stefan Dudink, Karen Hagemann and John Tosh, eds, *Masculinities in Politics and War: Gendering Modern History*, Manchester, 2004 and Miriam Cooke, *Women and the War Story*, Berkeley, 1996.

had been sanctioned by member states' military forces; the volunteer movement was incorporated into international law formally in the revisions to the Geneva Conventions in 1906.

Transnational mobilization around the Conventions and its volunteer personnel represented an early international humanitarian crusade, with the wounded enemy soldier as symbol of suffering humanity. Reflecting the transition to "people's wars," Europe's ruling elites – from members of dynastic courts to high military officers to elected officials and prominent philanthropists – proposed new multilateral treaty law to safeguard Europe's manpower and convince an interested public that the state provided the most up-to-date scientific medical care to the conscript or volunteer soldier. If the original architects of the Geneva Conventions spoke about this medical branch using the male gender, the operational development of volunteer field hospital care proved more complicated. Its gendered forms were connected to larger domestic and international changes in the later nineteenth century: the competition for empire, the medicalization of society, the feminist struggle for rights and equal educational opportunities as well as new gendered understandings of citizenship and duty. The field hospital, therefore, becomes a rewarding site to examine the connections between war, politics and gender and address the links between the battlefield and the social groups sponsoring the hospital unit at home. In operation, furthermore, these hospitals were makeshift liminal spaces, witnesses to violence and places of refuge from it. They both challenged gender and cultural stereotypes and confirmed many of them at the same time.

The chapter provides a close reading of the concrete operations of two British field hospitals, an analysis, which, however, is set against wider socio-political changes helping underwrite the work of the men and women who volunteered for Red Cross service.[2] One is the thirty-eight all-male unit of surgeons, dressers and orderlies under the command of Major E. T. F. Birrell (surgeon) sent by the British Red Cross Society to Kirk Kilise near the Çatalca line (the last defense line before Istanbul) between the Bulgarians and Ottomans during the First Balkan War (October 18, 1912-May 30, 1913). The second is the all-woman units of the Scottish Women's Hospitals consisting of roughly twenty-four surgeons, nurses, orderlies, drivers and mechanics under Dr. Elsie Inglis working in 1915 in the north of Serbia near the Rumanian border until their capture and internment by the Austrians and Germans in Kruschevatz in November. Repatriated to England as was required by international law, the units were reconstituted in August 1916 and assigned to the Russian Red Cross to support a Serbian division under Russian arms until the

---

2 The main sources are found in the British Red Cross Archives, London, England, "Report on the British Red Cross Society's Services for Bulgaria. Balkan War, November 1912 to January 1913," by Major E. T. F. Birrell, Royal Army Medical Corps. Late Commandant, British Red Cross Society for Bulgaria, London, April 18, 1913, typed script (hereafter BRCA, "Report") and The Women's Library, London, England, Scottish Women's Hospitals Archives, GB/106/2/SWHA (hereafter WL, SWHA).

Revolutions of 1917 disrupted all foreign medical activities. According to standard historical chronology the units were operating in two distinct wars but the conflicts reflected a common origin and tragic logic: the crisis of the Ottoman succession as the large empire was forced to retreat in the Balkans, resulting in ethnic and national rivalries over self-determination and territorial borders. Separated by time and place (even if bounded by the vague but evocative notion of the Balkans), other ties indirectly linked the two units. At his headquarters in Bulgaria, Birrell had been supported by the British Women's Sick and Wounded Convoy Corps, the organizational model for the subsequent formation of the Scottish Women's Hospitals once Britain declared war on the Central Powers in August, 1914.[3]

The units also shared a number of important characteristics that offer a distinct perspective on wartime. First, under the Geneva sign, both ministered to soldiers not of their own nationality: Birrell to Bulgarians fighting Ottomans in former Ottoman territory and Inglis to Serbian soldiers opposing the German and Austrian advances on the Western front. In the former case, Britain was neutral; in the latter, Britain was a major belligerent nation and ally of Serbia. Second and somewhat atypical, the hospitals were comprised of all-male and all-female staff. Appreciably, the same-sex character of the two hospitals skirted the many tensions that existed between staff nurses and ward orderlies but gender itself proved to be both a significant bond and a source of serious disruption. Third, each commander in charge of the units wrote extensive reports to the sponsoring organization back home; in addition, Inglis sent weekly letters to her coordinating board. The reports are detailed and rich documents describing the work of getting to, setting up, and running the hospital. These are unique commentaries on warfare, combining medical perspectives with newer understandings of international law, and infused with the deep nationalist prejudices of the day. They represent alternatives to the typical war narratives, whether soldiers' first-hand accounts of their own war experiences, the views of the occupying armies or even those of photojournalists. Read against other contemporary accounts, they also are important for what they do not say.

Record-keeping was an essential element of the whole medical enterprise, part of the reciprocity between medical training, technological breakthroughs, and pharmaceutical advances back home that were continuously refined through their implementation on the ground in the wars. The practical lessons from treating wounded soldiers at the front impacted medical teaching in the large army hospitals of the sponsoring nation. No wonder that Major Birrell was explicitly instructed to keep "a daily order book" of all the persons admitted to the hospital, tabulating types of wounds, numbers of sick, nature of illnesses and the death rates as well as "any [other] incidents of importance." Although subjected to censorship, the British medical personnel also sent and received letters from home. These exchanges – as those later between frontline soldiers and their families in World War I – kept

---

3   BRCA, "Report," p. 29 and John B. Allcock and Antonia Young, eds., *Black Lambs and Grey Falcons: Women Travellers in the Balkans*, Huddersfield, 1991.

up the connection between the home and the front during the war. In addition, there were a series of activities at home that continuously supported the medical unit abroad, including extensive publicity of its work by excerpting sections of the reports in newspapers for public consumption in an effort to garner popular support. After all, these Red Cross hospitals, as volunteer units, relied on private funds to pay for equipment, instruments, supplies, stock and salary. In the case of the Scottish Women's Hospitals during World War I, coordinators set up "sewing parties" in multiple venues throughout the country to procure blankets, clothing, bandages and other vital necessities.[4]

Running Field Hospitals: Male and Female Experiences

The organization and role of the mobile hospital under Major Birrell reflected decades of testing on the ground. British volunteer societies had been raising money to aid foreign soldiers in wars in which Britain was strictly neutral since the Franco-German war of 1870–71. Under Red Cross wisdom, such "valuable" neutral aid was an essential part of the "necessities of civilized warfare," as a retrospective account of the work of the British National Aid Society (the forerunner to the British Red Cross Society) put it in 1877 – a hallmark of the march of civilized society itself, although the term is a complicated one, used by the Great Powers to justify imperial conquests and wars against 'primitive' and 'uncivilized' peoples.[5] As with other state parties to the Conventions, over time the organization of civilian volunteers developed in tandem with changing army medical services for British sailors and soldiers; tested by fire, trained volunteer medical corps became a "necessary" part of British war making in its drive for empire. By 1880, the National Aid Society was training a small staff of lady nurses at its own expense "for service in every future war"; by 1885, the staff was incorporated into the Army Nursing Corps. The disasters of the Boer War (1899–1902) – protracted guerrilla conflicts, excessively high death rates, and scandalous conditions for the sick and wounded soldiers due to the spread of diseases – led to a major reorganization of the military and volunteer medical services along lines of territorial defense. The National Aid Society became the British Red Cross Society in 1905 and, while still voluntary and private, developed increasingly close ties to the Army Medical Department and the Imperial War Office. The Admiralty and War Office made the British Red Cross Society responsible for all Red Cross activities in the empire; in wars directly involving

---

4   WL,SWHA, GB/106/2/SWH/A10/1–2, circular letters, April 30, 1915.
5   BRCA, *Report of the Operations of the British National Society for Aid to the Sick and Wounded in War during the Turco-Servian War, 1876*, London, 1877, p. 5.

Britain, all volunteer offers of assistance, furthermore, had to be channeled through the Society to the Imperial War Office.[6]

After negotiating with both belligerent countries in 1912 as was the custom, the British Red Cross Society sent Birrell's unit out to aid the Bulgarian soldiers. Despite years of alternative practice, it officially consisted of only men, reflecting unresolved ambivalences about women in front-line medical service, an issue that had been brought home by the shifting fortunes of guerrilla warfare during the Boer War, which all but obliterated the once solid divide between base and front hospital. Development of the volunteer medical services, however, had produced its own gender hierarchy, even as it opened new public roles for women in patriotic defense of the nation and empire. Nurses were strictly subordinated to doctors (as in civilian life proper), although as of 1905 they were made powerful authorities on the hospital wards.

Appreciably, Birrell's world conformed to the self-evident maleness of military service, even if hierarchically organized, tightly disciplined and fraught with its own tensions. This hegemonic understanding is reflected in the Red Cross records of its many activities in colonial and continental wars. Reports speak of the "big fellows," the "men of the battery," and of "a fine set of men"; they also repeatedly remark on their "competen[cy]." As Birrell makes clear, his staff consisted of "old soldier types" (of veterans), who previously had served in the army. The men were under strict contract, required to obey all the orders of Red Cross directors and military authorities of the state in which they were working, and organized hierarchically, although the dresser rank was confusing, Birrell confesses in his longer summary report: "they messed with the officers but traveled second class, as did the men." He also admits that "few of the dressers had sufficient hospital experience to be of much service," although did not recommend substituting trained nursing sisters in the future. Advocates for women nurses back home argued precisely the point about professional competency. Importantly, Birrell was given considerable authority by the Bulgarian military commanders: "in cases of urgent necessity" he could requisition food, transport, and billets "either from a community or from individuals." Traveling to the front lines, at one point the unit was billeted in the "Greek quarter" of a small town, Birrell writes. This first hand commentary captures the multi-ethnic character of the Ottoman state, diluted subsequently by the massacres and population exchanges after World War I and later by nationalist mythmaking in the Ottoman successor states.[7] The unit flew the British as well as Bulgarian and Geneva flags.

---

6   A. K. Loyd, "Introduction," *An Outline of the History of the British Red Cross Society from Its Foundation in 1870 to the Outbreak of the War in 1914*, London, 1917, p. 24.

7   National Army Museum, London England, 7710–52-1 Record of Service of J. Edward, CBMD, ERCP, Lt. Col and Hon. Col. RAMC (Volunteers), letter copy, 1885; BRCA, "Report…Turco-Servian War," pp. 9, 19 and "Report," p. 40. For the biases in the national historiographies of

The organization of the Scottish Women's Hospitals, too, reflected decades of social change that increasingly drew middle class women into professional life. Pressed by vocal feminist advocates, the leaders of the army and the Red Cross had reluctantly agreed to train and utilize women nurses, beginning with the southern African colonial wars (the Zulu and Sekhukhune campaigns). By 1877, other feminists pushed successfully to open medical training to women. Here, too, gender stereotypes both facilitated and accompanied the shifts. As the reports from the field make clear, nurses "inculcate cleanliness and order" and bring "brightness to sufferers as only women can." According to a nursing journal in 1901, reflecting the dominant professional self-understanding, the nurse extends her influence because of her "increasing knowledge, her unfailing gentleness, her consistent unobtrusiveness, her womanly tact [and] her reckless devotion to duty...[8] And, yet, in their daily routine, the women of Inglis' hospitals expanded their competency well beyond these overused and normative tropes.

The all-women units consisted of four doctors, ten nurses (those "fully trained" professionals who completed a three-year stint at a hospital), six dressers (senior medical students or VADs – members of the Voluntary Aid Detachment, part of the territorial defense system emerging after 1909), two house and kitchen orderlies and also an administrator, clerk as well as car and lorry drivers.[9] Take for example the career of Dr. Anette Benson, who was appointed the Chief Medical Officer of Inglis' Unit. Benson had studied math and science at Newnham College at Oxford, which opened its doors to women in 1879, and attended the London (Royal Free Hospital) medical school for women. After holding a few positions in London, in 1894 she went to India to head the Cama Hospital in Bombay, "the only civil hospital ... entirely staffed by medical women." Her biography is similar to other doctors' career paths, women who also ended up working in parts of the Empire before returning to London to do their 'bit' in wartime patriotic service. Take also Miss Geraldine Hedges, trained at Wilders Garage, Wellingford, who served as transport officer in Russia and Salonica or Miss Spencer Daniell, who offered her car (an Austin) to the hospital. The assessment notes that she "did not have much experience driving but will give the next two months to learn thoroughly all running repairs...." The interviewer adds: "Sounded quite in earnest and dependable." Of Miss Green, a cook: "her heath is extremely good, her passport is ready; she

---

the Balkan states and Turkey see Donald Quataert, *The Ottoman Empire, 1700–1922*, 2nd edition, Cambridge, 2005, pp. 174–194.

8   BRCA, *Report of the Operations of the British National Society for Aid to the Sick and Wounded in War during the Servo-Bulgarian War, 1885, 1886*, London, n.d., p. 16; HRH, the Princess of Wales' Branch of the National Aid Society (Soudan and Egypt), *Report, 1885–1886*, np, nd, p. 9. Also, "The Nurse in the Twentieth Century," *The Hospital* Nursing Mirror, London, January 5, 1901.

9   WL, SWHA, GB/106/2/SWH/A/10/1–2, circular letters, October 1914.

has traveled a great deal in Central Europe, has stayed considerable time in Egypt, Constantinople, Warsaw and Croatia and speaks a little Croatian"[10]

The Serbian units of the Scottish Women's Hospital were part of a wider complex of medical services that also operated on the western front in France and Belgium. Raised by the National Union of Women's Suffrage Societies, they were a vital component of a feminist agenda that was not pacifist but rather committed to showcasing women's multiple talents – what they called "this great body of expert women." Theirs was a patriotic enterprise "useful for both country and Suffrage." The explicit linkage to a future reform of the parliamentary franchise was so central to the mission that the leadership threatened to pull out of the Serbian Relief Committee unless it openly publicized the hospitals' ties to the suffrage question. Inglis herself reflected a cautious and moderate feminism, calculated to bring home to men how important women are in public life. "So much of our work is done where men can't see it," she writes. "They'll see every bit of this." The work equally was in the defense of Britain, designed to help "cement alliances with other powers in the cause of right," as a pamphlet defining the hospitals' goals records. It adds a feminist chord to this nationalist call: the group would "prove to our allies that women like men of the empire know that alliance means 'help in terms of need.'" Repeatedly shunned by the War Office ("young men straight from universities were sent out but women who were first rate surgeons … refused," Inglis complained at one point), the Scottish Women's Hospitals ended up working under Serbian (and French and Belgian) Red Cross auspices.[11] Thus, it was international sanction and transnational contacts that authorized this British nationalist, patriotic and feminist project. Dr. Inglis, as Major Birrell, acquired considerable authority as commander of the unit. Indeed, unlike he who could not convince Bulgarian officials to move his unit closer to the front, at one point in September 1916 she successfully negotiated with a high Russian army doctor in Odessa for a location directly at the battlefield.

Field Hospitals and War Narratives

The reports of Drs. Birrell and Inglis make clear that the first order of business of the hospital was to handle the devastating effects of war on men's bodies. The rhythm of hospital life, indeed, was dictated by the fortunes on the battlefield. Violence was all around them – and even a number of staff was killed in the confusion of shifting battle lines. Birrell describes the continuous sound of heavy fire nearby at Edirne and the use of searchlights throughout the night; Inglis notes the "boom of distant cannons" at the bombarding of Belgrade. Birrell recounts passing corpses

---

10   WL, SWHA, GB 106/2/SWH C/5/2/1, individual staff biographies, C/5/2/5, Miss Geraldine Hedges and A9/1, correspondence, general, August 4, 1914.
11   Ibid., A,16/1, December 14, 1916.

lying on the ground after combat. He also records an obvious war crime: "this man had been killed later evidently by a bullet in the upper part of his chest, probably at close quarters." While too often caught up in war propaganda, medical witnesses nonetheless helped introduce the reading public to the new legal taxonomy of crimes, atrocities, and victims that followed codification of the laws of war at the Hague Congresses in 1899 and 1907.[12]

Major Birrell is graphic in shattering the so-called heroic myths of war. Dr. Inglis, by contrast, maintains a greater distance on male suffering even when describing a horrendous battle in which the Serb division held the line – while the Russians and Rumanians to their left and right fled – but at a considerable cost of Serbian life. Of 15,000 troops, only 7,000 survived: "no one could imagine what conditions the Serbs were in after the fight," she writes cryptically. In another context, she acknowledges that "one does not see much of the glamour of war from this end; it was terrible to have these broken men pouring in." But in the same breath, she explains their deaths in the name of Serbian national self-determination.[13] By implication, she reinforces the modernist linkage between war, nationhood, and male sacrifice that underpinned men's citizenship rights. Birrell minces few words in describing the conditions of the wounded. His depictions are graphic, only part of which are quoted here:

> many wounded on arrival were greatly exhausted, silent, their clothes muddy and ragged, their dressing pus-stained and sometimes dripping with discharge; a few with severe injuries seemed dazed, others had lost self-control and whimpered and moaned when spoken to.[14]

As Red Cross personnel, arguably, each accepted war as an inevitable part of modern political life. As a male, Birrell, perhaps, felt able to provide an unfettered view, arguably for the eyes of his superiors alone. Stretching gender norms already, Inglis found strength in nationalist myths. She was part of a feminist wing that promoted the expansion of British imperial power, by armed force if necessary. Through the example of her war work, she aimed to integrate women into the nation as citizens with equal rights *and* responsibilities.

Both Birrell and Inglis also were witnesses to the civilian costs of war. They describe the long lines of refugees, hungry, cold, and fearful, fleeing the enemy

---

12 A. Pearce Higgins, *The Hague Peace Conference and Other International Conferences Concerning the Laws and Usages of War. Tests of Conventions with Commentaries*, Cambridge, 1909.

13 Her view contrasts starkly with the conclusions drawn by a commission of experts sent by the Carnegie Endowment for International Peace in 1913 to "inquire into the causes and conduct of the Balkan wars." The authors decry the "megalomania of the nationalist ideal" which left little room for reason or compromise, *The Other Balkan Wars: A 1913 Carnegie Endowment Inquiry in Retrospect with a New Introduction and Reflections on the Present Conflict*, ed. George F. Kennan, Washington, D.C., 1993, p. 11.

14 BRCA, *Report*, Chapter IV, Condition of the Wounded, p. 26.

armies as well as semi-deserted villages, the "empty homes burnt and gutted," observes Birrell movingly.[15] Originally, the Geneva Conventions made no mention of civilian populations; the agreements were about wounded soldiers' needs and not those of civilians. However, the confused situation on the ground during war helped transform sentiments rewriting international law. Initially the Red Cross units and hospitals on their own initiative began to aid civilians such as refugees and displaced persons first on an ad hoc and piecemeal basis. This expansion began with the many challenges of dealing with the refugees pouring into Istanbul during the Russo-Ottoman war (1877–78). In the same war, field hospital personnel started to help all wounded, "though they were not properly socalled combatants."[16] Similarly, during the first typhus scourge in Serbia, Inglis' unit had nursed civilians as well as soldiers. By 1915, Inglis was involved in a multi-layered war, with villages and train stations subject to aerial bombings that took the lives of civilians and not just soldiers. Ironically, as the laws of war sought to differentiate between soldiers and civilians, the industrialization of modern warfare increasingly blurred the lines. The on-going revisions of the Geneva Conventions worked to strengthen the legal safeguards on civilian life and property in wartime.

The situation was similar with prisoners of war, who also were not mentioned in the original articles of the Geneva Convention. Here, too, the real-life experiences of wartime led to new articles defining and safeguarding prisoner of war status, including provisions for captured Red Cross medical personnel. Articles 9, 12–15 of the Revised Geneva Conventions of 1906 declared that the Red Cross personnel in enemy hands were not prisoners; they were to be "protected and respected," allowed to continue their work and, if no longer needed, were to be sent back to their army or country by a route "compatible with military exigencies." During the winter offense on Belgrade in November 1915, several units of Dr. Inglis' Serbian outfit remained behind and were taken prisoners by the Germans and Austrians; in Inglis' case, the Germans requisitioned her hospital, so she and her staff set up shop in a nearby location. She continued to minister to sick Serbian soldiers under foreign occupation for four months. During this time all communication back home ceased so the personnel's whereabouts became a matter of grave public concern. Implementing the Geneva Conventions' protections, the group was freed and sent to Zurich, Switzerland. Here, they were hailed by the Entente allies as that "heroic band of women," (but remember, the War Office had shunned their offers of assistance) and transformed into symbols of courage and sacrifice for the war effort. Back in England for a while, Dr. Inglis used this extensive publicity to campaign for Serbian national independence. She organized "throughout the country" commemorations of the Kosovo battle of June 28, 1389, when the Ottomans had

---

15 BRCA, *Report*, p. 11.
16 International Committee of the Red Cross Archives, AF 19, Turquie, 1/120 Alif to Moynier, Constantinople, 14 March 1878 and BRCA, Princess of Wales Branch, *Report*, Kenneth Barrington to Lady Roseberg, Tambut (Egypt), April 26, 1885.

nearly killed him." He did, in fact, die a week later. Birrell offers only one example in the whole chapter, arguably drawing more on the stereotypes and rumors that had circulated during the Boer War when much of the blame for the high death rates of British soldiers had been placed on society women doubling as nurses – instead of where it belonged, on the generals responsible for the (mis)conduct of a war fought by irregular tactics and for the sorry state of military medical services.[20]

Birrell's long overview report nonetheless draws attention to the important roles of women in this presumably "all male" unit. In Belgrade, the British hospital took on three women translators (Miss Dimetrieff, Miss Economoff and Miss Haskell), who proved to be indispensable for the successful operations of the unit. For example, billeted in the dark at one point on the way to the front, the women's language skills were needed to round up all the men dispersed in numerous houses. As his report also shows, they brought order to a disorderly gender situation that required men take up many of the so-called women's tasks of cooking, cleaning, laundering and sweeping. With no irony intended, Birrell writes that "one of the men acted as hospital washerman; he could not, however, cope with the work," and much of the laundry subsequently was outsourced to other hospitals at the base camp. There also was the matter of washing the floors. Birrell explains, "as there appears to be no prospect of obtaining women servants for the purpose," the British men after two days turned the task over to Bulgarian militiamen, lower down on the masculine hierarchy. Eventually Miss Haskell supervised these Bulgarian workers. In time, the women translators took over running the non-medical tasks of the hospital: they oversaw the Bulgarian workers, employed eight to ten "Turkish charwomen" from neighboring villages ("result very satisfactory"), engaged domestic servants for all manner of work, arranged "sewing parties" as in England for the women in the nearby villages to procure pillowcases, blankets, mattresses and "sleeping units," oversaw the preparation of the patients' food (it continued to be done by "our personnel," notes Birrell) and helped the patients "about their letters." After his hostile jibe at female nursing, which he claims had disrupted medical life, Birrell admits that the women "proved invaluable" to the smooth functioning of the hospital. In his view, they had instituted a proper gender order for its collective work.

The Scottish Women's Hospitals employed only women doctors, nurses and dressers. However, handling contradictory gender notions was also a constant balancing act for the personnel. These women operated in presumably earlier unimaginably harsh and trying conditions to prove their mettle for country and Womanhood. They also were determined to represent themselves as proper women. This task, for example, included organizing a "Family Dress Competition" on the ship sailing to Russia. Most importantly, it meant holding the units to the strictest moral

---

20 Ibid, p. 35. Similar hostilities are found in other Red Cross records in Geneva, for example, *Sanitäres über den türkisch-montenegrisch-servischen Feldzug i. J. 1876*, Separat Abdruck aus der Deutschen militairärztlichen Zeitschrift von 1877, p. 47, which contains an attack on Russian women doctors.

and sexual standards (in stark contrast to the men under Birrell's command) that alone made possible access to the wounded male body. At one point, under the strain of war work, one of the transport staff apparently had a nervous breakdown. Interestingly, it took the form of gender reversal: "she is going about dressed like a man, sitting in restaurants, smoking and talking to anybody and everybody," writes Inglis in a letter marked confidential so that it would not come to the attention of the public. She was also seen flirting and allowing men to touch her arm. In the short run, the situation did not improve. Slightly more than a week later, Inglis adds "she is still going about dressed in knickers with a Russian soldier's cap on, flourishing a whip and with a revolver and cartridges."[21] The behavior caused Inglis great worry – personal anguish about the fate of the woman, to be sure, (Inglis tried to have her sent home) but also serious concern about "our reputation." The centrality of sexual propriety – measured by dress, demeanor, and speech – to the actual work of the hospital, becomes clear in the letters. She tolerated no cursing, a "reprehensible habit," and at one point felt the need to vigilantly patrol the girls to prevent flirting ("we got a different type of girl," she writes in a reference to their working class not middle class backgrounds). A stronger indication of this powerful moral sense was her decision, when working under foreign occupation, not to treat women for venereal disease. She writes in retrospect that the decision was difficult, given "our modern version of the solidarity of womanhood," but "to have taken over the work would have been to encourage vice and that we could not do."[22] Safeguarding women's sexual purity appears key for the successful functioning of the units – for their own internal discipline and for the wider public reception.

Yet, at times, the women staff had very different understandings about "what was and was not women's work." The fate of the women drivers of cars was at the center of this controversy. Two of the staff – Miss Knox and Miss Henderson – wanted to use men for the job. In her letter reporting the difficulty back home, Inglis responds, "We should never have any Scottish Women's Hospitals at all if they and their sort, dear things, had been listened to. How they would have disapproved of Florence Nightingale's little band!" Secretly, however, the two had approached the English Consul and, to Inglis' dismay, he had wired home that "it would be 'criminal' to send out women." For Inglis, the conflict was about the central purposes of the hospitals. "The first object," she reminds the coordinating board back in London, "was to care for the wounded and the second was to do it through a woman's organization, managed and officered by women." But she was equally angry at the Consul's action, taken without consulting her. She levels her own gender charge: "he never would have done it if a man has been head of these hospitals; imagine him wiring home about the armored cars without consulting

---

21　WL, SWHA, GB/106/2/SWH/C/3, Correspondence Dr. Elsie Inglis to Lady Ashmore, File 4,5, November 3 and 12, 1916.
22　Ibid., C/2a, reports, VI, Galatz, December 19, 1916 and Elsie Inglis, "The Tragedy of Serbia: II – in the Hands of the Enemy," *The Englishwoman*, 30, 90, June 1916, p. 201.

Commander Gregory; wiring to the Red Cross about the personnel of the British Red Cross units without talking it over with …"²³ Dr. Inglis made sure that women continued to man the cars.

Everyday Observations and Cultural Misconceptions

The medical personnel traveling to and from the front lines were witnesses to life around them. Their reports are filled with seemingly objective descriptions of villages and local customs, at times even of the flora, fauna and natural geography of the area. They describe the construction of the huts and the "flocks of sheep, herd swine and fowl" as well as the ubiquitous ox wagon ("every bullock in Bulgaria does the work of two soldiers," writes Birrell). A staff of Dr. Inglis describes a village market. They also write in detail about the dress of the common people and militiamen around them.

Embedded in the writings, however, are cultural biases and tensions, partly reflecting the filer through which the authors look at the world: the professionally trained medical eye. Each devotes considerable space to the many tasks insuring cleanliness and sanitation, of utmost importance to the success of the hospital to be sure. Inglis rightly calls the sanitation needs her "most important department" but then adds an interesting comment. "We dug into the ground the rubbish, emptied the overflowing cesspools, built incinerators, and cleaned, and cleaned, and cleaned. That is an Englishman's job all over the world," describing, in effect, one of the presumed English traits that authorized the expansion of empire. The contrast of their own hygienic standards with the filthy conditions of the original surroundings is marked in both accounts. Birrell writes with undisguised disgust about the dreadful state of the Turkish bathrooms and is equally condescending about the Bulgarians: "despite all attempts to prevent it, they continue to use the urinals for their water needs." And, at moments of extreme frustration, Inglis reverts to cultural and gender stereotypes. Unhappy with a Serbian doctor who had dressed down one of her staff, she describes her response: "I said to Dr. H[averfield], it is so silly to quarrel with these poor little men, peasants in the last generation."²⁴ These comments highlight differences with others and affirm an identity rooted in assumptions about their higher level of social and moral development.

Birrell offers an additional insight into the scientific role of the field hospitals beyond the obvious medical one. These institutions also took part in larger international scientific projects to explore the geographic, geological, and ethnographic complexion of the world, although they were less focused on these efforts than the scientific expeditions financed and sent out, for example, to catalogue the life and material culture of peoples around the globe. The fruits of these ethnographic

---

23 WL, SWHA, GB/106/2/SHW/A 17/1, June 12, 1917.
24 Ibid, C/3, File 5, November 12, 1916.

explorations were filling up the new national and provincial museums in the urban centers of the West.[25] Mere byproducts, the hospitals' investigations were not without wider scientific importance. As Birrell recounts in Chapter X, the specimens of forty-four blastings from the ridge of the battle zone in Kirk Kilise were sent off to Mr. Lang of the Geological Department of the British Museum for analysis. They were found to be compact organic limestone of the Tertiary era. He writes that the organisms recognizable to the naked eye were corals. Interestingly, in the midst of war, the project of mapping the geological history of the world continued.

Conclusion

As this chapter demonstrates, the mobile field hospital is a valuable and underutilized site to explore the reciprocal influences between war, gender and politics. It connects the battlefield to its host society, continuously bringing war into peacetime routines and deepening the interconnections in times of armed conflict. With its ties to the international Red Cross movement, it holds considerable promise for new transnational histories, as glimpsed in the debt the Scottish Women's Hospitals owed foreign Red Cross societies. Its operational development, furthermore, opened new venues for women's participation in public life, providing ammunition for the feminist efforts to gain greater educational opportunities and, ultimately, full citizenship. But these reform advances were matched and constrained by larger medical and military structures that subordinated women to male authority. The exceptions, as Inglis' Scottish Women's Hospitals, are valuable but somewhat fleeting counter narratives. Women physicians did not gain adequate recognition in the medical profession as a whole after the war.

This history of medical volunteers nonetheless offers new perspectives into the question of postwar gender politics. Undeniably in Britain, the expanded war services of men and women powerfully pushed the cause of adult suffrage (manhood suffrage was granted in 1918 while women's full political citizenship had to wait until 1928). This new world of formal citizenship belies any simple notion of postwar *re*-construction, a peacetime reimposition of old gender assumptions that returned women to domestic roles and men to their rightful place in social, economic and political life. Rather, women and men, drawing on their wartime experiences, confronted the many challenges of the postwar era as active and creative agents.

The emergence of the International League of Red Cross Societies founded to coordinate a new global public health and nursing training program in 1919 is a graphic case in point. Drawing partly on the work of the Scottish Women's Hospitals, which had taken over public health needs on the island of Corsica for the

---

25 H. Glenn Penny, *Objects of Culture: Ethnology and Ethnographic Museums in Imperial Germany*, Chapel Hill, 2002.

French toward the end of the war, the project created an influential role for women in the form of an independent Nursing Division.[26] At the same time, this agency extended the official limitations placed on women's medical opportunities into the expanding international arena. Developing directly out of the war, the leaders set the Division's operative methods according to their understanding of the wider psychological impact of war on the nursing profession itself – exploiting its "rich harvest of experience." In a 1920 article, Alice Fitzgerald, an American- trained nurse who served in 1916 with the British Expeditionary Force and later headed the League's Department of Nursing, captures the assumptions guiding the international nursing movement. The war had caused a real "upheaval" in the nursing profession, she writes; nurses "who had seen service in foreign countries" now "can't return to their former ways of living." Despite "speaking different tongues [and]… possessing varied education and training…" they "all belong to one large international group," with a renewed sense of responsibility toward weaker members, "not from superior knowledge but [out of] sympathetic understanding." To make the operations effective, Fitzgerald acknowledges that nurses had to gain a "thorough" understanding of other people and their values, customs, traditions, and history. Two interrelated tasks would follow from this precondition: one, to send out a large contingent of nurses to promote the most modern methods of medical care abroad and, two, to dispatch a smaller group to work with local people to gradually "raise nursing [training] and hospital standards."[27] In daily practice, however, the project rested on too simple a set of assumptions, belied by the very reports that I have examined in this chapter. It posited an objective fount of knowledge unmediated by cultural, gender and national differences. While there is, of course, no inevitable "clash of cultures," international work requires constant negotiations drawing in multiple perspectives and vantage points. It would take the new commitment to universal human rights after 1945 to provide the possibility of envisioning fruitful cross-cultural dialogues, which are fundamental to the difficult but ultimately laudable goal of a non-ethnocentric universalism.[28]

---

26 International Federation of Red Cross and Red Crescent Societies, Geneva Switzerland, Box 12468. Nursing-Bureau, Box 16501. Complete Proceedings of the Cannes Conference. Cannes, Minutes, p. 208.
27 Alice Fitzgerald, "International Mind in Nursing," *International Journal of Public Health*, l, 1, July 1920, pp. 65–68.
28 Bhikhu Parekh, "Non-ethnocentric Universalism," in *Human Rights in Global Politics*, eds. Tim Dunne and Nicholas J. Wheeler, Cambridge, 1999, pp. 128–159.

Women, War and 'Totalitarianism': The Soviet and Nazi Experiences Compared[*]

Roger D. Markwick

Some 800,000 Soviet women saw military service in defence of their 'Motherland' against Hitler's onslaught during the Great Patriotic War, 1941–45. Half a million of these women actually joined the Red Army; either they volunteered or they were mobilised. Women field nurses, partisans, snipers, anti-aircraft gunners and fighter pilots became models of Soviet heroism. Female participation in military conflict on such a scale is historically unique. In stark contrast to all other combatant countries in the Second World War, in particular National Socialist Germany, Soviet women took on roles that were generally regarded as the exclusive domain of males: from heavy industrial work to front-line combat.

In contrast, Nazi Germany, the Soviet Union's mortal enemy, was reluctant to mobilise women for the home front let alone combat, even for total war. In Nazi doctrine, women were not only relegated to '*Kinder, Küche, Kirche*' but also to reproducing the future generations of Aryan, male warriors. In the Nazi 'racial state' biology was supposed to determine women's destiny. In reality, however, under the pressure of military retreat and the threat of defeat, German women were increasingly drawn into the war effort, although very rarely as combatants. In the militarist ideology of Nazism, warfare was seen as the exclusive prerogative of males.

This chapter compares the role of women in the Soviet and Nazi war efforts during the Second World War. Despite the seeming symmetry of these two draconian, so-called totalitarian states, official policy and popular attitudes towards the participation of women in their respective war efforts as a whole and in front-line combat in particular differed markedly. A particular objective of the chapter is to examine what it was about Soviet state, society and culture that motivated or required women to assume fighting roles that were anathema to Nazism.

---

[*] Research for this paper was supported by an Australian Research Council Discovery Project grant: 'Women, War and the Stalinist State, 1941–45'. Particular thanks to Martin Janecek and John Mitchell for assistance with German language sources.

The making of the 'frontovichki'

The young women 'frontovichki' who went to war in the 1940s were essentially products of the peacetime Stalinist system of the 1930s. The majority of the 18 to 20 year-old, 'front generation' who went to war between June 1941 and May 1945 knew nothing else but the massive social transformations that came in the wake of Stalin's forced collectivisation of agriculture and forced-marched industrialisation and the political indoctrination that accompanied it.[1]

During the 1930s decade of shock industrialisation and urbanisation which engulfed the Soviet Union, the *Komsomol*, the Communist Party Youth Organisation, was key to organising youth and instilling in them loyalty to the Soviet party and state. The *Komsomol* exhorted young women to participate as fully as men in production and social life: 'Women to the tractor!', 'Women take up flying!' were among the watchwords of the 1930s.[2] The rise of fascism and fear of 'imperialist' war gave rise to a growing 'militarisation of society' with Soviet youth of both sexes encouraged to acquire para-military skills, although only boys were encouraged to pursue military careers. *Osoaviakhim* (The Society for Cooperation in Defence and Aviation and Chemical Development), the key organisation charged with providing military training for civilians, initiated a network of military-sporting groups in every enterprise and institution. Close cooperation from the mid-1930s on between *Osoaviakhim* and the *Komsomol* soon saw paramilitary skills and sports become the favourite recreational activity of millions of youth.[3] Girls were subjected to a 'barrage of visual propaganda' that depicted women flying, shooting, parachuting, excelling at sport and physical culture, often under the benign gaze of Stalin, 'Ready for Labour and Defence' against alleged enemies, within and without.[4]

Encouragement of women to train in the military arts by no means erased gender roles. On the contrary, a reassertion of marriage and family as social ideals in the 1930s necessarily re-emphasised distinct social roles for the sexes. But continued mass female participation in the Soviet industrialization drive, and commitment to the (Soviet) nation and Stalin, generated self-conceptions of Soviet womanhood that were a hybrid of pre-revolutionary and Soviet values of family, marriage and nation. In these circumstances, the generation of *'frontovichki'* that went to the front in the 1940s combined a sentimental, 'feminine' commitment to marriage,

---

1   E. S. Senyavskaya, *1941–1945 Frontovoe pokolenie. Istoriko-psikhologicheskoe issledovanie*, Moscow, 1995, 77.
2   E. S. Seniavskaya, 'Zhenskie sud'by skvoz' prizmu voennoi tsenzury', *Voenno-istoricheskii arkhiv*, No. 7 (22), 2001, 81.
3   Andrea Moll-Sawatzki, 'Dobrovol'no na front? Molodye zhenshchiny mezhdu motivatsiei i mobilizatsiei', in *Mascha + Nina + Katuscha: Frauen in der Roten Armee 1941–45 zhenschiny-voennosluzhashchie*, ed. Peter Jahn, Berlin-Karlshorst, 2002, 21–2.
4   Alison Rowley, 'Ready for Work and Defense: Visual Propaganda and Soviet Women's Military Preparedness in the 1930s', *Minerva: Quarterly Report on Women and the Military*, Fall-Winter 2000, 3–12.

motherhood and Motherland with an inherent, passionate belief that they were 'strong women' and equal partners in the heroic Soviet project with men.[5]

Accordingly, Soviet women gave a feminine twist to the 'militarisation of mass consciousness' entailed in Stalin's forced march to 'socialism in one country' amidst 'capitalist encirclement'. The resultant Soviet idea gripped the popular imagination, fuelling a mentality of patriotic, 'heroic-romantic self sacrifice' for their Soviet Motherland.[6] With the German invasion in June 1941, these were the values that motivated thousands of young women to volunteer for the front, with little idea of what Hitler's 'war of annihilation' would mean – not least for women.

Motivations

Patriotism, fighting for the Motherland [*rodina*], was almost invariably the fundamental motivation for women volunteering for the front. The official Red Army battle cry was 'For the Motherland! For Stalin!' (*Za rodinu! Za Stalina!*).[7] Whether or not Stalin's name was often invoked, the cry signified not only love of their land, but also pride in and identification with the social achievements of the Soviet Union. But patriotic, political motivations also gelled with personal and family reasons for women taking up arms.[8] In September 1941 a young Leningrad woman begged the Komsomol to send her into the army, having graduated as a nurse, because her two brothers and her husband – antiaircraft gunner, pilot and tank driver – were at the front. 'And this means my place is at the front', she implored,[9] an appeal to family ties which also implied equality of the sexes.

Such positive motivations for fighting were reinforced by negative reactions to the mass atrocities of the German-fascist invaders. Revenge increasingly came to the fore from 1942 on as the genocidal nature of German warfare became common knowledge; 'sacred vengeance' fuelled by cries to 'kill a German'.[10] But it did not take much propaganda to instil such sentiments. Real life and death were the root causes. Witnessing the fate of Soviet prisoners of war, the most intense mass killing in human history,[11] was enough to drive one young woman into the partisans:

---

5   Sheila Fitzpatrick and Yuri Slezkine, eds, *In the Shadow of Revolution: Life Stories of Russian women from 1917 to the Second World War*, Princeton, New Jersey, 2000, 9.
6   Senyavskaya, *1941–1945*, 72–3, 75.
7   Ibid., 132.
8   Susanne Conze and Beate Fieseler, 'Soviet Women as "Comrades-in-Arms": A Blind Spot in the History of the War', in *The People's War: Responses to World War II in the Soviet Union*, ed. Robert W. Thurston and Bernd Bonwetsch, Urbana and Chicago, 2000, 224.
9   Murmantseva, *Sovetskie zhenshchiny*, 121.
10 Catherine Merridale, *Night of Stone: Death and Memory in Russia*, London, 2001, 282–3.
11 'Case Study: Soviet Prisoners-of-War (POWs), 1941–42', *Gendercide Watch*, http://www.gendercide.org/case_soviet.html

> Immediately I learned how to hate! How dare they trespass on our land! Who are they...? Where from? So much blood and death did I see on the roads... Our prisoners... A column had passed, leaving hundreds lying on the road. Starving, exhausted, they had fallen... They executed them. Like dogs...[12]

Mobilising Soviet women

The mobilisation of women for the Soviet war effort proceeded through two phases. The day after the Axis invasion on 22 June 1941, women doctors, nurses and medical orderlies were mobilised for military duty in accordance with the 1939 Law on Universal Military Service.[13] This was followed in spring 1942 by a far more concerted government effort to compensate for the haemorrhaging of the routed Red Army. By the end of 1941, more than four million of its original five million men were dead or captured.[14] The accelerated participation of women in traditional male work, including military service, freed up men for the front line. As the war bogged down into a titanic military contest, 'a [female] patriotic movement to master male professions became a mass phenomenon'.[15] But in the first instance, it was not manpower shortages that motivated women to want to take up arms. Mass desire by women to volunteer was a popular process, triggered by aggressive war.

Within 24 hours of the German invasion, thousands of Soviet women flocked to meetings and military recruiting posts 'begging, demanding and crying' to be sent to the front, arms in hand.[16] In the major cities, Communist Party and Komsomol offices and military commissariats were besieged by young women determined to take on a combat role.[17] Women who volunteered, however, were rejected by the recruiting officers: 'There are enough men. War is not women's business', went the refrain.[18]

Such sentiments reflected the views of the Soviet political and military hierarchies that war was a purely masculine vocation. Women were nurturers – not killers. Wartime propaganda posters were unambiguous: 'Men into battle, women to the labour front'. The communist party newspaper *Pravda* depicted combat as an exclusively male affair. The official expectation, and the reality for the overwhelming majority of women, was that they should carry the primary burden on the home front, in the family, agriculture and industry, freeing up men for the front.

---

12 Svetlana Aleksievich, *U voiny – ne zhenskoe litso*, revised, complete edition, Moscow, 2004, 62.
13 *Pravda*, 1 September 1939.
14 Senyavskaya, *1941–1945*, 77.
15 Murmantseva, *Sovetskie zhenshchiny*, 24.
16 Aleksievich, *U voiny*, 42.
17 Murmantseva, *Sovetskie zhenshchiny*, 120
18 Polina Gelman, *O boiakh, pozhaishchakh i druz'iakh-tovarishchakh ...*, Moscow, 1995, 7.

Spurred on by patriotic appeals, reinforced in 1942 by compulsory labour decrees, women did carry the burden, participating in the workforce on an even broader basis than ever before. By 1943 the female industrial workforce had peaked at 53 per cent, by which time women were 73 per cent of the collective farm workforce.[19] Women were therefore the backbone of wartime production, often engaged in the most arduous, traditionally male occupations: from mining to railway construction.

The popular clamour by women for direct participation in the Red Army was resisted by state and party authorities. Nevertheless, they adopted a number of resolutions mobilising women for service. The State Committee of Defence [GKO], the war cabinet set up on 30 June 1941, passed decrees admitting women into the air defence, military transport and communications.[20] However by August, the dire military situation saw the GKO covertly include women as it prepared to introduce compulsory 'Universal Military Training' [*Vsevobuch*].[21] Women were also accepted as volunteers, mainly as medical aids, for the militia, formed in Moscow and Leningrad in the early the months of the war as the *Wehrmacht* threatened these cities. With rudimentary military training and weapons, facing the most lethal military in Europe, hundreds of women were condemned to a virtual death sentence.[22] Nevertheless, women were still not accepted as frontline combatants. Thousands of women, however, flocked to train as nurses, the traditional role for women in war, many in the hope that nursing would open the way to the front. Elena Yakovleva, a nurse assigned to a hospital after receiving a mere three months training, 'deserted' to the frontline in February 1942.[23]

The singular exception to the official prohibition on women combatants in the Red Army was Stalin's secret decree of 8 October 1941 authorising the formation of three women's air regiments.[24] The record-breaking navigator Marina Raskova had personally and successfully lobbied Stalin, who, like his air-force commanders, opposed women fighting, to form the three regiments, including the famous all-female night bomber regiment, which became known by the contemptuous sobriquet German soldiers gave them: 'night witches'; a sobriquet these female flyers themselves embraced with ironic pride. A unique phenomenon in the annals of

---

19   Susanne Conze, 'Stalinistische Frauenpolitik in den vierziger Jahren', in *Stalinismus: Neue Forschungen und Konzepte*, ed. Stefan Plaggenborg, Berlin, 1998, 295; V. T. Aniskov, *Krest'ianstvo protiv fashizma 1941–1945: Istoriia i psikhologiia podviga*, Moscow, 2003, 87.
20   Murmantseva, *Sovetskie zhenshchiny*, 122
21   Russian State Archive of Social-Political History – Youth [RGASPI-M, 1/7/3, 1–10, reverse.
22   Richard Overy, *The Dictators: Hitler's Germany and Stalin's Russia*, New York, 2004, 516 and photo 30.
23   Aleksievich, *U voiny*, 49.
24   'Prikaz o sformirovanii zhenskikh aviatsionnykh polkov VVS krasnoi armii', *Russkii Arkhiv. Velikaia Otechestvennaia*, T. 13, 2 (2), Moscow, 1997, 112–13.

air warfare, these predominantly female regiments produced a total of 30 women Heroes of the Soviet Union – the highest Soviet military award.[25]

It seems that Stalin's prime motivation for secretly deploying women flyers was to channel the demands of educated women to fight, not to propagandise Soviet women's achievements and certainly not to challenge gender roles in either the military or Soviet society at large. Their planes and weaponry were generally outdated and their numbers, a total of 400, miniscule. Nevertheless, the pride that the women took in their military achievements, for many at the cost of their lives, was real. But these achievements came despite the male military hierarchy, not because of it.[26] As Galina Dokutovich, a 'night witches' navigator, noted in her diary, 27 May 1943, three months before her death: '…We achieved the right to be equal in battle. And when we achieved this, we showed that we could be in the front ranks of the warriors.'[27]

In spring 1942, the second phase of women's mobilisation was launched by Soviet authorities, desperate to compensate for massive male casualties. In March and again in October 1942, the GKO decreed the mobilisation of women, without children and not engaged in essential military production, for active service. Officially, this was not conscription; women remained 'volunteers'. Female recruitment, although not coerced, was tantamount to 'self-mobilization,' achieved through a combination of mass propaganda and mobilization.[28] Faced with seeming defeat, the ruthless Stalinist state mobilised its 'inexhaustible' human reserves, as Stalin put it, including women.[29] Again, the Komsomol was the primary organiser. It mobilised half a million women, 200,000 of whom were Komsomol members. 70 per cent of the women mobilised by the Komsomol entered active service in the army. Another 1,000 Komsomol and communist party members were recruited for political work within female units in the military.[30] At the height of their participation rate, 1943, women formed eight per cent of the Red Army.[31] The bulk of these served on the so-called 'second front': especially in the medical services (nurses and doctors), in supply and logistics (cooks, laundresses), in communications and administration (wireless operators and typists), and transport (drivers). Given the savagery of the war, these were often front line jobs, particularly for field nurses who were required to drag the wounded together with their weapons from the

---

25   Reina Pennington, *Wings, Women and War: Soviet Airwomen in World War II Combat*, Kansas, 2001, 2.
26   Ibid., 65–9.
27   Belarus State Museum of the History of the Great Patriotic War [BGMIVOV], KP- 36792, 124.
28   Dietrich Beyrau, 'Mekhanizmy samomobilizatsii i propaganda v gody vtoroi mirovoi voiny,' *Sovetskaya propaganda v gody Velikoi Otechestvennoi voiny: "Kommunikatsiya ubezhdeniia" i mobilizatsionnye mekhanizmy*, ed. A. Ia. Livshin, I. B. Orlov, Moscow, 2007, 26–30.
29   Beate Fieseler, 'Zhenshchiny na voine: nenapissania istoriia', *Mascha + Nina + Katuscha*, 12.
30   Murmantseva, *Sovetskie zhenshchiny*, 123
31   Conze and Fieseler, 'Soviet Women', 212.

field, often under direct fire. Accordingly, casualty rates among Soviet nurses were extremely high.³²

Other than in the medical services, the largest number of women was deployed in anti-aircraft defence, including as gunners where they directly engaged and were exposed to hostile enemy aircraft. In March and October 1942, the GKO decreed the mass recruitment of women for anti-aircraft defence. Under the auspices of the Komsomol, between April 1942 and May 1945, 300,000 women were mobilised. In some cases, women constituted 80 to 100 per cent of the anti-aircraft detachments, including 8,000 who served in the charnel house of Stalingrad.³³ 'The first page of the Stalingrad defence', the Soviet writer Vasily Grossman observed, was written by volunteer women anti-aircraft gunners, 'barely out of high school'.³⁴

In one other field were women specifically trained and ordained by the Soviet state to kill: sniping. At the behest of the GKO, a women's sniper 'movement', which began in 1942 with the training of female snipers at the front, was put on a formal basis. A 21 May 1943 decree established the Central Women's School for Sniper Training, which over the next two years graduated 1061 snipers and 407 instructors.³⁵ Although initially greeted by their male comrades with a mixture of 'rapture' at the prospect of female company and 'scepticism' about their ability as snipers, during the gruelling two year march on Berlin these women proved themselves to be just as 'hardy and bold' as the men and their equal as fighters. Their lethal sharp shooting dispatched thousands of *Wehrmacht* officers and men. Major General Morozov, 'the father of the sniper movement', attributed superior female marksmanship to the fact that 'a woman's hand is more sensitive than is a man's. Therefore when a woman is shooting, her index finger pulls the trigger more smoothly and purposefully'.³⁶ Innate feminine characteristics, so it seems, predisposed women to surgical killing.

Only in one other arena did women take up arms from the first phase of the war: partisans behind enemy lines. A total of 28,500 women became *partizanki*, 9.8 per cent of the partisan forces. The image of the pretty *partizanka* became one of the defining models of the Soviet heroine. The archetypal female hero was an 18-year old Komsomol *partizanka*, Zoya Kosmodemyanskaya, who was captured, tortured and hung in November 1941 just outside Moscow. Immortalised as the Soviet 'Joan of Arc', for her martyrdom rather than her military prowess, 'Zoya' became a powerful mobilising icon, disseminated through the appeals of her suf-

---

32 Fieseler, 'Zhenshchiny na voine', 11, 14.
33 Yu. N. Ivanova, *Khrabreishie iz prekrasnykh. Zhenshchiny rossi v voinakh*, Moscow, 2002, 150–54.
34 Cited in Antony Beevor, *Stalingrad*, London, 1999, 98, 106.
35 Ivanova, *Khrabreishie*, 150–51.
36 N. A. Iakovskaia, 'Byla takaia rota', *Voenno-istoricheskoi arkhiv*, No. 10, 2000, 38–83, 48.

fering mother who urged the Soviet people to revenge her 'Zoya [who] met death like a true man, a fighter, a communist'.[37]

In fact, it was the mother image and women on the home front, rather than female soldiers, who predominated in the Soviet propaganda arsenal. Even when in 1942–43 woman combatants became quite prominent in Soviet newspapers, the focus was only on a few heroic women, thereby downplaying mass participation of women in the military, 'masking the fact that hundreds of thousands of women were actually in the front lines… The Soviet state never considered combat women a desirable mass movement or an integral part of the Red Army.'[38]

Soviet women in combat

In reality, despite the cult of the mother as mobiliser, many mothers were aghast when they realised their daughters had taken up arms, most of whom did so without the slightest knowledge of the horror that they were to confront. The Stalin generation were educated in the belief that they should be prepared to 'die for their Motherland'. 'In death they expected life'. What they were not prepared for was killing for the Motherland. But Hitler's war gave them no other option. A woman sniper vividly recollected her traumatic transition to trained assassin. On her first real 'hunt' she baulked at shooting a German officer: 'My hands began to shake, my whole body quaked with terror… It was one thing to hate fascism another to kill an individual human being.'[39]

But this was war, and of extraordinary ferocity. Blood and gore abounded: from the brutal butchery of amputations in earthen hospitals to the stench of scorched flesh. 'Even blood burns', a nurse realised. Hand-to-hand fighting was inhuman 'horror'. The sight of death came as a shock; even more disturbing if the dead were women. 'Hatred' of the enemy it seems was particularly necessary for women, as opposed to men, to kill.[40] Hitler's war gave these women plenty of reasons to hate and to kill. In letters home shortly before her death, the renowned sniper, Natasha Kovshova (1920–42), who became a Hero of the Soviet Union, evinced no feminine flinching from killing: 'My hatred for the cursed fascist beast grows stronger everyday; with every battle … I will shoot the vermin point blank. I will pump bullet after bullet into their foul skulls, stuffed with insane thoughts about our Moscow and of ruling over us, a free, proud and bold people.'[41]

---

37 Rosalinde Sartorti, 'On the Making of Heroes, Heroines, and Saints', in *Culture and Entertainment in Wartime Russia*, ed. Richard Stites, Bloomington and Indianapolis, 1995, 176–93.
38 Conze and Fieseler, 'Soviet Women', 218, 221–22.
39 Aleksievich, *U voiny*, 27–32, 42–3, 63.
40 Ibid., 66, 76, 107, 131, 139.
41 Kovshova, N., Pisma s fronta iz kollektsii Tsentral'nogo muzeya Vooruzhennykh sil [Letters from the front from the collection of the Central Museum of the Armed Forces], 30 July 1942 and undated, Vol. I, 116, 120.

Notwithstanding their capacity for ruthlessness, these women soldiers never lost a sense of themselves as women. On the contrary, war seems to have reinforced their sense of female identity. Women, suggests the Belarus oral historian Svetlana Aleksievich, saw war through 'other eyes'. Even in throwing themselves into combat, these women adhered to the conventional conviction that 'to hate and kill' did not come naturally to women. Yet these young women soldiers, many still in their late teens, seemed to have been able to surmount any contradiction they felt between a sense of themselves as women and their role as combatants. Concerns about such a contradiction were more likely to be expressed by male officers or worried parents – reflecting those of the Soviet state. Female identity was certainly reinforced by male military leaders: 'You are the most beautiful women in the world', declared a male commander to the night-bombers, 'because real beauty resides not in made-up eye-brows and lips but in that great inner drive with which you fight for the freedom of our Motherland'.[42] Female soldiers certainly maintained a strong sense of themselves as women in terms of their appearance, their leisure activities, and their relations with men. The military great coat was 'heavy' and 'masculine' while military boots produced an unflattering gait. Most feared disfigurement or maiming more than death itself.[43]

Women soldiers were acutely aware that they had entered into a predominantly male world. With the exception of the air regiments, women were scattered throughout male units. There was little privacy and they suffered personal shame in relation to their toilet and menstruation, although often their periods stopped due to the shock of combat, leaving many fearful they would never have children. Most seemed wary of men, in a society in which even a kiss could be construed as a sign of eternal love. Yet others became the 'mobile field wife' (*PPZh: pokhodno-polevaia zhena*) of officers, because this offered some comforts and companionship, shielded them from the dangers of battle and afforded some protection from predatory male soldiers; soldiers feared dying never having known sexual relations.[44] But there was also coercion and harassment within some military units, leading to desertions. 'Better to die from a fascist bullet ... than through this scoundrel who humiliates us,' declared one woman when an officer threatened to shoot her.[45] A desperate cry from a young woman who would have been only too aware of the barbarism the Nazis reserved for Soviet women soldiers.

---

42   I. Rakobol'skaya, N. Kravtsova, *Nas nazyvali nochnymi ved'mami Tak voeval zhenskii 46-i gvardeiskii polk nochnykh bombardirovshchikov*, Moscow, 2002, 38.
43   Aleksievich, *U voiny*, 155, 188.
44   Ibid., 17, 162–3, 197, 232–3.
45   RGVA [Russian State Military Archive], 38694/1/42, 42.

'Bolshevik rifle women'

'Bolshevik beasts' and 'amazons devoid of femininity' were amongst the lurid epithets the *Wehrmacht* coined to depict the 'ferocious' Soviet 'riflewomen' [*Flintenweiber*] they encountered on the Eastern front. The German military were aghast. In the inferno of Stalingrad, 'female beasts', they alleged, treacherously shot them in the back.[46] In keeping with the Nazi view that Slavs in general were 'sub-humans', women soldiers were 'crafty, inhuman creatures'.[47]

In keeping also with Hitler's injunction that the Eastern Front was a 'war of annihilation' in which the summary execution of Jews, Communist commissars and partisans was obligatory,[48] no quarter was to be given to the captured 'cruel', 'Jewish rifle woman', particularly female partisans. Few were taken prisoner. *Wehrmacht* directives required they be executed immediately. Field Marshall von Reichenau's notorious order for 'The conduct of armed forces in the East', issued 10 October 1941, complained that these 'degenerate women' were being taken prisoner rather than immediately executed. They were to be summarily 'shot'. This ruthless, criminal fanaticism explains why, with the exception of a few hundred medical personnel, there were hardly any Soviet females in German prisoner of war camps.[49] It explains too why Red Army women preferred to save the 'last bullet' for themselves rather than be captured. Neither the wounded nor the dead were spared desecration, including sexual. A captured 18-year-old nurse was found with 'her eyes gouged out, her breasts cut off … impaled on a stake'. Such was the visceral fear, ferocity and hatred which women warriors provoked in the Nazified *Wehrmacht*. To the Nazi mind, *Flintenweiber* were 'not women but monsters – Russian fanatics' that embodied the unnatural barbarism of Bolshevism.[50]

Nazi attitudes to women

Wehrmacht animosity on the battlefield towards Soviet *Flintenweiber* was an extension of National Socialist and extreme-right German attitudes towards women entrenched well before Nazism came to power in January 1933. 'Degenerate', 'Marxist, Jewish, cosmopolitan women's rights advocates' along with 'treasonous' Social

---

46 Beevor, *Stalingrad*, 66.
47 Claudia Freitag, 'Trofei 'baba s ruzh'em'. Zhenschiny-krasnoarmeitsi v nemetskoi plenu', *Mascha + Nina + Katuscha*, 32–3.
48 'Hitler's Speech to the Commander-in-Chief of the Armed Forces on ideological warfare in Russia, 30 March 1941', in *Nazism 1919–1945: a documentary reader*, eds J. Noakes and G. Pridham, Exeter, 1983–1998, 619–20.
49 Freitag, 'Trofei 'baba s ruzh'em'', 33–6.
50 Aleksievich, *U voiny*, 129.

Democrats were blamed for Germany's ignominious defeat in 1918.[51] The Nazis equated Bolshevism with the destruction of the family. Fearful of the spectre of Bolshevism, middle-class, particularly urban, Protestant, women voted for National Socialism almost as strongly as their male counterparts. In doing so, they were repudiating a Weimar republic not only discredited by the humiliation of Versailles but also by its association with challenges to traditional gender roles. 'Emancipation from emancipation' was the reaction of many conventional, middle class women who effectively called for 'virile patriarchy' to shield their mythologised conceptions of motherhood from the chaotic depredations of modern, capitalist Germany. They yearned for a 'living room' (*Lebensraum*) in which all women could harmoniously pursue their interests as 'mother, consumer, homemaker, producer and churchgoer'.[52] The Nazis offered them such a *Lebensraum*, thereby fraudulently enlisting such women into their real, ultimate goal: conquering 'living space' in the Soviet Union.

The Nazis championed the traditional concerns of the middle-class women's movement: 'motherhood, racial hygiene, social health, and eugenics'.[53] Accordingly, National-Socialist women, a mere six per cent of the party membership in January 1933, willingly embraced an ancillary role to the militarist misogyny of the male Nazi leadership, who monopolised the public sphere of politics. Adolf Hitler would later ban women from holding any high office.[54] There was certainly no Nazi 'Krupskaya' (Lenin's wife), let alone any attempt to draw women into the workforce as the Soviets had done.

On the contrary, for the first four years of their tyranny, the Nazis aggressively propagandised motherhood and domesticity, having by 1936 succeeded in subordinating all women's organisations to the Nazified state. Five million, overwhelmingly middle-class, women made up the mass Women's Bureau (*Frauenwerk*), while the two million strong National Socialist Women's Association (*NS Frauenschaft*) was the preserve of the Nazi female elect.[55] Membership of the League of German Girls (*BDM*), soared from a mere 19,200 in 1932 to more than 1.5 million by 1939. But a clear sexual division of labour was inherent in Nazi doctrine and organization. Whereas the Soviets had one youth organisation, the Komsomol, Nazi Germany had separate organisations for girls and boys. The *BDM* exhorted girls to 'Be Faithful, Be Pure, Be German!', while boys in the Hitler Youth were exhorted to 'Live Faithfully, Fight Bravely and Die Laughing!' The Nazified education system was

---

51 Renate Bridenthal, Atina Grossmann and Marion Kaplan, eds, *When Biology became Destiny: Women in Weimar and Nazi Germany*, New York, 1984, 18.
52 Claudia Koonz, *Mothers in the Fatherland: Women, the Family and Nazi Politics*, New York, 1987, 4, 13.
53 Bridenthal, Grossmann and Kaplan, eds., *When Biology became Destiny*, 22.
54 Koonz, *Mothers in the Fatherland*, 207.
55 Ibid., 188; Koonz, 'The 'Woman Question' in Authoritarian Regimes', in *Becoming Visible: Women in European History*, third edition, ed. Renate Bridenthal, Susan Mosher Stuard and Merry E. Wiesner, Boston, New York, 1998, 476.

crucial to producing not only feminine girls and virile boys but also inculcating the immutability of biological difference: 'Germanic life of the future will be two absolute axioms', declared the Nazi woman educationist Auguste Reber-Gruber in 1934, 'the laws concerning race and the laws regulating the polarity between the sexes.'[56]

Like almost all European governments, the Nazis were concerned to reverse downward demographic trends that were steepest in highly industrialised Germany. True to their militarist discourse, the Nazis fought a 'battle for births'.[57] To an unparalleled degree, their militant pro-natalism was justified by a crude biological determinism. In Joseph Goebbels' vulgar formulation: 'The mission of woman is to be beautiful and to bring children into the world … the female prettifies herself for her mate and hatches the eggs for him.'[58] Nazism imparted a particularly militarist, eugenicist twist to the traditional division of labour between men and women. As Hitler put it in his speech to the *NS Frauenschaft* in September 1934: 'What the man gives in courage on the battlefield, the woman gives in eternal self-sacrifice, in eternal pain and suffering. Every child that woman brings into the world is a battle, a battle waged for the existence of her people.'[59] Such a polarised sexual division of labour, a sharp contrast to Stalin's Soviet Union, was in keeping with Nazism's militarist origins, doctrines, organisation and objectives. But it ran up against the reality of the Nazi state's rearmament for aggressive war.

This conflict between ideals and reality became evident in the first instance in relation to female participation in the workforce. On taking power, the Nazis implemented a series of measures intended to drive women out of the work force and into the home. But in reality female labour remained an essential component of the German workforce, and increasingly so with the elimination of unemployment and then the shift to rearmament from 1936 on.[60] Between 1936 and 1939, the number of women in the workforce actually increased from 11.6 million to 14.6 million.[61] The regime achieved this by its discriminatory recruitment of working-class mothers less than 35 years of age, despite its ostensible commitment to the sanctity of German motherhood. Middle-class women were never obliged to work.[62] Without demurring, the *Frauenwerk* now prepared women to consider it their duty to enter the work force. Even military service for women was considered. In the gender *apartheid* of Nazism, 'subordination' was the only role for women.[63] Yet remarkably, in such a repressive state, coercive measures were never used to mobilise German women.

---

56 Koonz, *Mothers in the Fatherland*, 195–6, 204–5.
57 Bridenthal, Grossmann and Kaplan, eds, *When Biology became Destiny*, 23.
58 Cited in Noakes and Pridham, eds, *Nazism 1919–1945*, 363.
59 Cited in Ibid., 364.
60 Overy, *The Dictators*, 508.
61 Bridenthal, Grossmann and Kaplan, eds, *When Biology became Destiny*, 25.
62 Elizabeth D. Heineman, 'Whose Mothers? Generational Difference, War, and the Nazi Cult of Motherhood', *Journal of Women's History*, 12 (Winter 2001), 4, 138–63, 139–40.
63 Koonz, *Mothers in the Fatherland*, 200.

The German home front

War in September 1939 brought even greater demands for women's labour. Yet, despite a massive campaign under the slogan 'Women Help to Bring on Victory', few obliged. In marked contrast to the Soviet Union, where many women clamoured to contribute to the war effort, German women generally reacted to the outbreak of war with mute dread.[64] They baulked at contributing anything. Indeed, as a result of the payment of generous allowances to military families, 300,000 women actually left the workforce in the first four months of the war.[65] The regime therefore had recourse to drafting working-class women into the poorest paid, least skilled, occupations, particularly the armaments industry.[66]

The demands for female labour became even more urgent as the *Blitzkrieg* of Barbarossa stalled outside Moscow in December 1941. Mindful of the war weariness, particularly among women, that had detonated the November 1918 revolution, Hitler had been reluctant to impose the ruthless austerity that total war required, although even before 1939 he had imposed 'exceptional levels of military preparedness and economic diversion'.[67] Despite the concessions that had been made to female employment since 1936, he personally opposed total female labour mobilisation in good part on the grounds that it would be detrimental to their childbearing capacities. Göring, distinguishing between thoroughbreds and workhorses, argued that genetically superior middle-class women should be encouraged to breed. Finally, however, after defeat at Stalingrad in January 1943 necessitated a declaration of 'total war', Hitler relented, signing a 'Decree on the General Mobilisation of Men and Women for the Defence of the Reich'. But it was dubbed a 'rubber' decree, there were so many exemptions. Society women regarded it as 'Bolshevist'.[68] As late as May 1944, by which time even middle-class mothers were required to register for work, Germany's female workforce had grown a mere 1.2 per cent since the pre-war period.[69] German women continued to be forbidden from working in heavy industries, such as mining. Although in the face of defeat in mid-1944 Germany instituted emergency mobilisation of some women, such as domestic servants, it was too little too late. As long as possible, Hitler persisted in his personal opposition to the mobilisation of women, more precisely respectable middle-class women, even though this conflicted with the rational requirements of a state engaged in a life and death struggle.

---

64 Gerda Szepansky, '*Blitzmaedel*', '*Heldenmutter*', '*Kreigwitwe*' *Frauenleben im Zweiten Weltkrieg*, Frankfurt, 1986, 13.
65 Martin Kitchen, *Nazi Germany at War*, London and New York, 1995, 135–6.
66 Koonz, *Mothers in the Fatherland*, 198; Szepansky, '*Blitzmaedel*', 12–13.
67 Overy, *The Dictators*, 504.
68 Kitchen, *Nazi Germany*, 138–9.
69 Heineman, 'Whose Mothers?', 141–3; Conze and Fieseler, 'Soviet Women', 218.

Instead of mobilising German women en masse, Germany turned to forced female labour, mainly drawn from the conquered peoples of the Soviet Union: so-called '*Ostarbeiterinnen*'. Hitler believed sturdy Slav women were more suited to arduous labour than lithe limbed *Frauen*.[70] By 1942, one million women endured forced labour, including Jewish women from SS concentration camps who slaved under the most inhumane conditions in heavy industry.[71] Whereas in the Soviet Union women took on the heaviest of industrial work, such occupations were anathema to Nazi conceptions of German womanhood. But racism overrode gender considerations in pursuit of wartime production and profits, in a capitalist economy.

'Hero mothers' and 'lightning girls'

In stark contrast to its Soviet adversary, the sexual division of labour prescribed by the Nazis generally precluded women's full participation in the military. Women were, however, enlisted in propaganda. The woman ammunition worker who had invested all her strength on the Home Front was now hailed as a 'valiant little soldier'. But it was chiefly as 'Hero mothers' that women contributed to the aggressive war on the Eastern Front, in two senses: firstly, that she sacrificed her son 'for the Fuehrer, for the People and the Patriotic' and, secondly, that she raised her son to be a hero.[72]

But just as Nazism's commitment to motherhood could be opportunist, so too could its commitment to women serving in the military. While Nazism idealised war making as the ultimate manifestation of masculinity, some 500,000 women were drafted into the Auxiliary Military Service (*Kriegshilfsdienst*), which in mid-1941 extended their service to 12 months. The demand for women rose dramatically with the enormous losses on the Eastern Front. Most were conscripted into military administration and communications, as typists, telephonists and radio operators – nicknamed 'lightning girls' due to the insignia on their uniforms. From 1943 on, as in the Soviet Union, women began to replace men as searchlight operators or anti-aircraft gun assistants. But unlike Red Army women, German women auxiliaries had no military status; they were merely designated as 'Military retinue' (*Wehrmachtgefolge*), forbidden to carry or fire weapons.[73] 'The German woman', declared Hitler, should 'not be stuck in a women's battalion and put on the guns like the Soviets'.[74]

---

70 Kitchen, *Nazi Germany*, 142–3, 147–8.
71 Szepansky, '*Blitzmaedel*', 13.
72 Ibid., 13–14.
73 *Mascha + Nina + Katuscha*, 172.
74 Ursula von Gersdorff, *Frauen im Kriegsdienst 1914–1945*, Stuttgart, 1969, 72.

Imminent defeat at the hands of the Red Army, however, brought a complete about face on German women serving in the military. A separate 'Women's Army Auxiliary Corps' (*Wehrmachthelferinnenkorps*) was to be formed under Hitler's further decree of July 1944 for 'Total War'. Compulsory service for all women aged 17 to 55 was declared. Suddenly it became an 'honour' for women to serve in war. In February 1945 Hitler himself authorised the formation of a 'women's battalion'. Now arguing that a women's battalion would have a positive effect on male morale, he declared privately, 'Whether girls or women is entirely irrelevant: everybody must be called up'.[75] From 1945 on, women could be forced to serve in the newly formed, pitifully armed and trained, Home Guard (*Volkssturm*). No longer was combat an exclusive male prerogative: the rocket-propelled grenade was the 'ideal weapon in a woman's hand'. Now, for the first time, German women confronted the gruesome reality of combat. Desperate Nazi propaganda further terrified a population that faced a vengeful army that seemed to embody their nightmare of Bolshevik barbarism: rape and violence would be the fate of thousands of German women.[76] But by now the masculinist facade of Nazism had collapsed. German men no longer seemed all-powerful in the eyes of German women.[77]

Aftermath

German women were made to pay the price of an aggressive, genocidal war that took the lives of 3.5 million German men; the women were left to pick up the remnants of their lives amid the rubble. But Nazism had never seriously challenged their gender role. On the contrary, its ubermasculinist, militarist discourse had reinforced feminine identity. It was otherwise for Soviet women who had stormed, or been assigned to, the ultimate masculine bastion: military combat. Stalin's party-state, having deployed and endorsed women taking up arms, albeit reluctantly under the twin pressures of popular pressure and military necessity, even before victory moved to return women to more acceptable roles; they were relegated to the double-burden of the industrial home front and to overcoming the demographic crisis wrought by a genocidal, total war. There were to be no careers for women in the Red Army. The radical 'expansion of gender roles' afforded by the Great Patriotic War proved 'temporary'.[78] Women soldiers quickly became invisible. They did not begin to reappear until the Khrushchev era, when they were mythologised and sentimentalised in official, censored publications as one-dimensional heroines. But their idealised image during and then long after the war conflicted with the actual experiences of many female veterans. Tainted with reputations as officers' 'whores',

---

75 Ibid., 71–2.
76 Szepansky, 'Blitzmaedel', 15–16.
77 Antony Beevor, *The Down Fall*, London, 2003.
78 Pennington, *Wings, Women and War*, 153.

many were too ashamed to don their medals.[79] And when women veterans did resurface, in their memoirs, in histories, in Victory Day marches, only the survivors and martyrs were immortalised and venerated. The disfigured, the deserters, the drunken, the pregnant, and the 'amoral' remained hidden in the archives. The human dimension of Red Army women's challenge to gender roles was thereby safely contained within acceptable Soviet limits.

Conclusion

It is a commonplace that the Soviet-Nazi conflict was a clash of two repressive, totalitarian states that were mirror images of one another, and that this explains the extraordinary ferocity of the Eastern Front.[80] Yet the experiences of Soviet and German women at war invites another perspective. Motivated by a crude biological determinism, Nazism set out to make absolute the gendered division of labour, putting in place a purely 'masculine state'[81] in which German women were supposed to breed on the home front while the Teutonic warriors waged war. But the attempt to sustain this sexist, pre-industrial dystopia in the most highly industrialised, militarised state in Europe buckled in the face of 'total war' and 'total defeat'. In the end, Nazi doctrine on women proved to be as superficial as its pretensions to a peculiarly 'National Socialism'.

The issue of gender was one of the great divides between Soviet socialism, even in its Stalinist form, and German fascism. Stalin's Soviet Union, although it had retreated from the radical gender equality and sexual liberation of the first decade of the revolution, still retained a substantial commitment to the equality of men and women. Unlike Nazism, the Soviet Communist Party adhered to a crude Marxist conviction that socio-economic development, not biology, was the key to equality between the sexes. Stalin's super-industrialising state therefore actively promoted the role of women in production, reproduction and the acquisition of para-military skills – a triple burden.

The Stalin generation of young Soviet women who went to war, either voluntarily or mobilised, was the product and beneficiary of an industrialising, urbanising, revolution from above, with which they powerfully identified. The ruthless Stalin regime had given many young women from a largely peasant background an unprecedented opportunity to throw themselves into social and productive life which many would fight to the death to defend. When Nazism confronted Bolshe-

---

79 Barbara Alpern Engel and Anastasia Posadskaya-Vanderbeck, eds, *Voices of Women in Soviet History*, Boulder, Colorado, 1997, 179.
80 This is certainly the underlying argument of Beevor, *Stalingrad* and *Berlin*. For a critique of totalitarianism see Roger D. Markwick, 'Communism: Fascism's "other"?' in *The Oxford Handbook of Fascism*, ed. Richard Bosworth, Oxford and New York, 2009, 339–61.
81 Von Gersdorff, *Frauen im Kriegsdienst*, 39.

vik 'rifle women' on the Eastern Front it was a lethal clash between two radically conflicting conceptions of the place of women in society, despite the seeming symmetry of these two 'totalitarian' dictatorships.

Targeting the City:
Debates and Silences over Aerial Bombing since World War II

Charles S. Maier

The Moral Issues in Context

For many years the debates over the atomic bombing of Hiroshima and Nagasaki obscured debate over the 'conventional' bombings during and even before the Second World War. A certain tacit consensus prevailed: the German bombings of Madrid in the autumn of 1936, of Guernica, of Warsaw and of Rotterdam, the London Blitz and the bombing of Coventry, which gutted St. Michael's Cathedral, were all reprehensible, whereas the more extensive allied air attacks on Italian and German cities (with Dresden perhaps an exception) and then on Japanese urban centres (including the massive 1945 assault on Tokyo that may have taken 100–125,000 lives) were legitimate military recourses. The massive attacks on northern French cities in 1944, far more destructive than German bombardment in 1940, have also been largely accepted as legitimate war efforts.

To be sure, the German attacks were condemned because even if the German war effort might be deemed legitimate (usually so considered only by Germans), the Luftwaffe's bombings often seemed gratuitous and excessive, designed just to terrorize and demoralize civilian populations. The attack on the Basque city served little military purpose, and victory was already in hand when Warsaw and Rotterdam were bombed. What about allied bombing, however? Even if they might be as violent as German attacks, they were often defended as a necessary means to a worthy end. In short, for a long while, most post-war debate over means was subordinated to a consideration of ends: Allied victory was a worthy end that justified the very means which was condemned when in the Service of Axis victory – an unworthy end.

What has happened, of course, was that the debate over means, which seemed to have been silent for so long, has now re-emerged. This paper looks at both the context of the debate and the issues involved. By the nature of the subject it must involve an analysis of moral questions as well as a historical account.

Actually the discussion over means is a two-fold debate although often a rather muddled one. War is an evil and recognized as such, but there are lesser and greater evils, and there has been general agreement in the West that the evil should be minimized. This sets restraints on the recourse to war *(ius ad bellum)* and to the waging of a war once it is deemed necessary *(ius in bello)*. The concept of 'necessity' is usually the license to resort to war and to undertake means in war that are harmful – but necessity remains a subjective standard. And even necessity has been ruled out as an excuse for bringing harm to civilians in some cases by international agreement, although the agreement is often not honoured.

War involves a means-end calculation in several ways. Just war doctrine suggests both that the recourse to war must observe certain criteria, and so must the conduct of a war already decided upon. Waging war cleanly will cause death and destruction and so the recourse to war – codified as the *ius ad bellum* – must be a last resort and must be undertaken only if the good achieved can outweigh the harm that will arise. The second sphere in which war is to be limited is by setting restraints on its conduct, that is by observing *ius in bello*. At the heart of these restraints are two major moral priorities: first, preservation of the distinction between civilians and military combatants; second – and again, as in the case of the recourse to war – the invocation of proportionality as a standard. The harm done should not be disproportionate to the good supposedly achieved. An aggrieved state should not go to war lightly and once in war should not employ a level of violence that seems disproportionate to the provocation. Now many military men, such as General Sherman, have cogently argued that harsh measures used in waging war make war more unlikely.

But many measures in war also ran afoul of the other underlying moral priority laid down for the conduct of war: the distinction between combatants and civilians and by extension the distinction between combatants not yet disarmed and those rendered harmless by capture. In brief: don not kill civilians and don not murder prisoners of war. The question of killing soldiers clearly bent on mass retreat has fallen into a greyer area. (The American air attacks on the disabled and fleeing columns of the Iraqi army in the Gulf War of 1991 caused some qualms here, but not such as to become a major theme of discussion in the United States. Americans don not really believe themselves capable of war crimes. When they occur they remain the exception that proves the rule.) Intentional destruction of civilian property has also found condemnation, but of far less intense a degree.

Although the distinction between civilian and combatant has often been erased, it has been recognized since Antiquity. Thucydides narrates how the morality of the Greek armies degenerated in the Peloponnesian War. The Melian dialogue and the repression of Mytilene suggest that male civilians were deemed at least potential soldiers; but remember, too, how shocking appeared the Thracian attack on Mycalessus, where soldiers 'sacked the houses and temples and butchered the inhabitants, sparing neither youth nor age, but killing all they fell in with, one after the other, children and women, and even bests of burden … in particular they attacked a boys' school, the largest that there was in the place, into which the children had just gone, and massacred them all.'[1] Tacitus's *Annals* are filled with such accounts: slaughter after overcoming a besieged city remained commonplace way into the Thirty Years War of the seventeenth Century. Still, it was generally recognized as wrong in some fundamental way and that recognition lay at the base of what was claimed to be 'natural law' or developed as 'international law'. Eighteenth Century theory and practice in Europe attempted to reimpose the firewall between civilians and combatants, not without some military men complaining that this just made war more likely.

What has made the issue more difficult in modern times, however, was that the modern technology of warfare has tended to erase once again the distinction between civilians and soldiers. The blurring has occurred, though, from both sides, as it were. On the one hand, the technology of weaponry made it harder to limit destruction and casualties. The use of submarines and torpedoes in World War I presented this argument in acute form. For a submarine to give notice of attack was to render it highly vulnerable and far less effective. In this situation the Allies did not contest the fact that it would be impractical for a submarine to surface, ask the passengers or crew of a vessel to take to the life boats and only then destroy or capture the target ship. The allies just said that the recourse to attack without warning on ships carrying civilians was illegitimate. The German retort that the Allied blockade (formally counter to the rules of war that allowed close blockade at a harbour mouth, but not the interdiction of sea routes at a remote distance) also killed civilians never quite had the same power, since effects were indirect and hard to visualize as an immediate and direct consequence.[2] (The same disjunction of cause and effect has also attended the debate on economic sanctions against Iraq or other offending governments: Are sanctions that attack a population as a whole justified against dictatorial regimes that supposedly keep their populations in thrall?) By 1918, moreover, the outlines of war from the air were becoming clear enough, above all with Zeppelin raids over London that the question of civilian harm had to be considered.

Considering the issues raised by aerial bombing in general, debate has often centred not on the degree to which military necessity might justify harm done to civilians, but on the question whether military necessity really came into play. In other words, even if one suspended the issue of taking civilian casualties in stride, might not victory be possible without such cruelties. Debate over use of the Hiroshima bomb, and even more the Nagasaki bomb has usually focused on the issue of their necessity to conclude the war. Was either needed to compel the

---

1   Thucydides, *The Peloponnesian Wars*, XXI, 29. – An earlier version was published as: "Targeting the City: Debates and Silences about the aerial bombing of World War II."*International Review of the Red Cross*, vol. 857, No. 859 (September 2005): 429–444.
2   G. Best, *Humanity in Warfare: The Modern History of the International Law of Armed Conflicts*, London, 1983.

Japanese surrender? At least, did those advocating its use believe it was necessary to compel surrender without a great expenditure of American lives?[3] Was the second bomb equally necessary? Might a greater interval have been allowed?

But, of course, a major reason that civilians have become (or became) a target is that modern technology makes civilians instrumental in warfare. The growing dependence of warfare on society as a whole – especially the role of labour in arming a nation – rendered the civilian-combatant distinction questionable. Modern warfare was so dependent upon war production at sites remote from the fighting that the concept of a front line tended to seem irrelevant. Surely, a belligerent nation was entitled to destroy the industrial capacity of its adversary since that seemed so integral to the military effort. But was it entitled to attack the civilians who worked in such production facilities? As is well-known the doctrine of 'collateral damage' was put forward first among British air strategists to cope with this issue. Civilian casualties had to be accepted as a by-product of attacks on physical plants used for war production or even related civilian production.

No earlier dilemma had required the same splitting of hairs. In the Franco-Spanish war of the early nineteenth Century and the Franco-Prussian war of 1870–71, the issue of non-uniformed guerrillas had arisen. Prussian military insisted that such guerrillas or *franc-tireurs* lost any protection due to combatants taken prisoners of war, but could be executed out of hand. Subsequent Geneva and Hague Conferences attempted not to shield the irregular soldier as such, but to establish guidelines for differentiating the legitimate militia from the *franc-tireur*, essentially by insisting on some visual insignia and the open, not concealed carrying of weapons.[4] They were not civilians – rather they were more akin to spies, who also did not announce their presence, and thus could be rightfully executed on discovery. Not surprisingly, hard-bitten commanders in such wars often took action without undue precision. And in 1914 the fear of *franc tireurs* led to massive German atrocities in Belgium.[5] In World War II, however, the guerrilla fighter became the partisan, deserving of recognition as a combatant in the eyes of his British or American allies, but meriting execution in the eyes of the occupying force. Since some German commanders resorted to civilian reprisals as well as

---

3   Barton J. Bernstein has sorted out much of the argumentation in many essays. Of course, quantitative issues then intrude. How many lives would have had to be saved: The Stimson-Bundy claim was that the atomic bomb was believed to forestall an invasion of Honshu, planned for 1946, and which might have cost 'a million lives'. The argument was refined – for the first invasion planned for the fall of 1945 would probably have taken place in Shikoku, a smaller island, with a smaller number of estimated casualties. On the other hand, when those objecting to the bomb have suggested that no invasion was really necessary, defenders of the bomb's use suggest that a blockade of Japan would probably have cost more Japanese lives than did the bomb itself. See McGeorge Bundy's reflective weighing of the issues in Mc G. Bundy, *Danger and Survival: Choices about the Bomb in the First Fifty Years*, New York, 1988.
4   Best, *Humanity in Warfare*, 190–200.
5   See J. Horne and A. Kramer, *German Atrocities, 1914: A History of Denial*, New Haven, 2001.

executions of captured partisans (General Kesselring in Italy was a notable example for a western front), this issue soon cast even the fate of partisans in the shade. After World War II, new guidelines drafted in 1949 extended similar protection to resistance fighters, and in recent decades even paramilitary fighters have asked for similar recognition.

Nonetheless, reprisal policy remains at the heart of guerrilla war because it seems to emerge from that 'necessity', which remains despite all the conventions the underlying justification of violence. Guerrilla warfare, as practiced by World War II partisans and as perfected in colonial struggles after the Second World War, deliberately involved the civilian base as a resource. It was a war either to recruit (by conviction or coercion) civilian support for the partisan cause or to make such support too costly. The theory of guerrilla warfare, which French authorities zealously studied from Chinese and Vietminh writings, basically urged that the distinction between people and army be erased.[6]

It is the co-involvement of civilians that unites the guerrilla or partisan issue with that of aerial bombardment. Still, there were differences. Partisans after all acted with putative intent to kill or wound. They took to the field or the forest.[7] But what were the rights and wrongs of bombing civilians (and their families) who merely took to the factories? Bombing did not introduce this issue: bombardment had originated with shelling, and the British had made famous the idea of 'Copenhagening' in 1807 – naval bombardment of a neutral city – but by the end of World War I, the possibilities of bombing were recognized and doctrines for use had to be developed. Another Hague Conference in 1923 contributed Draft Rules for aerial bombardment that would have prohibited the bombardment of civilian populations not in the 'immediate neighborhood of land forces'. They incurred objections and were never ratified, although clearly on the table as guidelines whose rejection had to be argued for. Neville Chamberlain in 1938, American airforce generals through much of the war seemed to show sympathy (although by 1944 American practice seemed as ruthless as British). British advocates of the new weapon, however, did not want to be trammelled. Air Marshall Hugh Trenchard's championing of the new war aim, and finally Arthur ('Bomber') Harris's conviction that precisely the bombing of civilian centres could win the war for Britain are the best known examples. In 1928 Trenchard argued that one might seek to 'terrorise munitions workers (men and women) into absenting themselves from work' but that the indiscriminate bombing of a city for the sole purpose of terrorising the civilian population was 'illegitimate.'[8] This distinction proved

---

6   Besides Best, see H. Münkler (ed.), *Der Partisan: Theorie, Strategie, Gestalt*, Opladen, 1990; Münkler, *Die neuen Kriege*, Reinbek, 2002.
7   See H. Münkler (ed.), *Der Partisan*, for a series of essays on theories of revolutionary and partisan war.
8   Best, 274; Ch. Webster and N. Frankland, *The Strategic Air Offensive against Germany, 1939–1945*, 4 vols., London, 1961, IV, 71–76.

far too fragile to retain as a maxim of strategy. By early in the war, the British moved on to define (along Trenchard's lines) the idea of collateral damage. But collateral damage was the up-to-date version of what Scholastic just-war doctrine had sanctioned as 'double effect.' If despite care to minimize civilian casualties (and such care was necessary to render the procedure acceptable), civilians were still injured or killed to secure a legitimate military end – and there was no dissent that wiping out enemy industrial capacity was a legitimate objective – this was acceptable within the more general injunction to observe proportionality.[9]

Proportionality, it should be stressed, remained a criterion needed to justify both the recourse to war and the conduct of war. It linked *ius ad bellum* and *ius in bello*. But what guidance did it actually provide especially when the results were not so clearly decisive as proponents such as Harris or Lord Cherwell promised? There is no scope here for a survey of the statements and the strategies of the air wars. It is general knowledge that by 1945, Churchill himself had some doubts and that until a few years ago Arthur Harris was deprived of the honours bestowed on the air warriors themselves. Long before, however, two judgments became commonly accepted: that the Americans somehow had clung to precision bombing as a strategy and were less morally obtuse than the British, at least in Europe; second that the bombing was not really effective in achieving its goals.

Both these Statements can be contested, however. It is true that with the important exception of General Hap Arnold and his junior officer, Curtis ('Bomb them back to the Stone Age') LeMay, transferred to oversee the bombing of Japan in 1944–45, American military doctrine did not argue that civilian bombing as such might produce a rapid end to the conflict. The U.S. clung to shrouding large-scale bombing with particular industrial or strategic objectives. Nonetheless, American bombers did participate in the Dresden raids and continued bombing targets until close to the last weeks of the war, at a time when it was clear that they could play little strategic role. In theory, disruption of rail communication could justify almost any attack; but in fact, it seems, the prevailing emotion was that no target should remain unspared. This was an argument of potential resistance implicitly made. It no longer claimed that civilian morale would collapse. It just proceeded on the assumption that the more destruction, the sooner the collapse. Americans, too, studied how to achieve the happy result of firestorms such as ravaged Hamburg. And Americans, of course, pursued an air war on Japan that took cities as targetable units. The United States chose weapons – incendiary bombs – designed to start wide-spread devastation of urban areas, understanding that both civilians and artistic monuments must fall victim to this destruction.

The issue of efficacy was opened up by the famous results of the United States Strategic Bombing Survey, whose members – especially John Kenneth Galbraith –

---

[9] S. A. Garrett, *Ethics and Airpower in World War II: The British Bombing of German Cities*, New York, 1993, 142–4; also M. Walzer, *Just and Unjust Wars: A Moral Argument with Historical Illustrations*, New York, 1977.

argued that bombing had achieved far less of an impact than had been claimed. Germany's industrial production continued to increase until the fall of 1944; railroads and even factory sheds were quickly repaired; morale was not seriously impaired. But these minimizing judgments were also politically motivated and recent assessments, such as Overy's challenge the view. The last year of the war brought attacks of unprecedented intensity and a vicious circle of industrial collapse for the Third Reich: Germany was relying on synthetic oil from hydrogenation for three quarters of her consumption. But this was already short rations and the 'oil offensive' cost Germany 90 percent of her synthetic production between May and September 1944.[10] Destroying rail lines precluded adequate fuel transportation and thus the capacity to use a defensive air force, which rendered Allied bombing all the more effective, thus destroying more fuel supplies, etc., etc. And intuitively it seems incredible to think that the massive and continuous attacks on a crowded urban country did not cut into transportation and production. We cannot test the counter-factual – what would German production have achieved without the bombing? German production declined only from the second half of 1944, and part of the downturn followed once Romanian oil sources were finally overrun by Soviet troops. Still, to think of bombing as counter-productive seems as simplistic a conclusion as to believe it alone could have defeated the Third Reich. It was a costly strategy – airmen were not easily replaced and 140,000 British and American died in the attacks while 21,000 planes were lost. It had costs in the Pacific theatre, too – less in terms of bombers succumbing to defending fighters, for Japan was largely denuded of defence, than in terms of the lives and efforts needed to capture the island bases from which the planes could reach the home islands. Nonetheless, with less tonnage, bombing took its terrible toll, even before Americans used their two nuclear weapons.

Perhaps it is useful to separate the arguments for bombing used before D-Day from those afterward. Between 1940 and 1942, Britain could bring no counterforce to areas outside of North Africa unless it was by air. Military 'necessity' usually remains a highly subjective factor. But Churchill believed, and I think correctly, that it was important for the UK to inflict damage on the foe during a period it had been forced out of the continent, its troops in Africa remained hard-pressed, and it stood without a major ally until June 1941. Once Russia entered the war, bombing allowed the British to claim that they, too, were contributing positively to the defeat of Hitler. As Overy points out, however, Churchill's turn to bombing in 1942 was provoked by Stalin's taunts about Allied inaction with respect to a second front, and it came just at a point when it seemed as if it was wasteful and diversionary from a better use of airpower.[11] Dresden, too, was probably attacked

---

10 The various reports of the U.S. Strategic Bombing Survey became available from October 1945 on; see J.K. Galbraith, *A Life in Our Times: Memoirs*, Boston, 1981; Richard Overy, *Why the Allies Won*, New York, 1995, 230–2.

11 Overy, *Why the Allies Won*, 103–4.

largely because the Soviets complained Britain and the United States were not contributing proportionally in the winter of 1945 to the forthcoming land battles within Germany.

The arguments for bombing, however, were not officially developed early on in terms of morale and retaliation. They followed the more tortuous course of reasoning about the permissible civilian casualties that were permissible to set back German war industry. Although Harris and others thought terror as such was permissible because it must weaken the enemy's will, the Allies did not officially accept such a justification. Nonetheless, the earlier notions of collateral damage themselves proved sufficiently elastic – any industrial or transport capacity contributed to the German and Japanese war efforts. How much devastation was allowable? Even God was willing to allow innocent victims in targeting Sodom and Gomorrah for incendiary attacks. Once the tide had turned, violence was ingrained and the capacity to inflict damage – but largely indiscriminate damage – had been vastly enhanced. Only Hitler and Goebbels were frank enough to declare that their attacks in the latter stages of the war were frankly designed as counter-terrorist. The V-1 and V-2 were so named for the German word 'Vergeltung', or reprisal or retaliation. But they could not win hat battle.

The German Debate and the Issue of Taboos

In retrospect what is striking about the post-war German discussion of these issues was the relative absence of political reproach except among right-radical circles, at least until a few years ago. Dresden, for all the implicit reproach in the discussion, never became a Hiroshima. Of course, the numbers – despite propagandistic inflation – were lower: 35,000 not 70–100,000.[12] The reasons are not hard to find. West Germany remained dependent on the British and Americans for its post-war

---

12 The toll at Dresden quickly became a politicized estimate. For a while the figure of 100,000 was offered as a round number and then tolls of 135,000, rising up over time to a quarter million were given credence by David Irving in *The Destruction of Dresden* (1963), who finally seemed to settle for a hundred thousand. It suited the Communist regime to accept such an approximate tally, but more careful estimates revised the number downward. At the entrance to the restored Zwinger, the East German plaque still stands with its take on the history of the Second World War: 'destruction of the inner city of Dresden', by Anglo-American air forces in February 1945, 'liberation' of Dresden from the fascists by the armies of the Soviet Union in May 1945, and reconstruction of the baroque masterpiece by the German workers and peasant state. For the first scholarly re-evaluation see G. Bergander, *Dresden im Luftkrieg*, Köln, 1977, who estimated 40,000 and for the most recent evaluation (between 25 and 40,000) see F. Taylor, *Dresden: Tuesday. February 13. 1945*, New York, 2004, 443–8 with its discussion of how casualty figures became inflated. [Editors note: A recent research program by the City of Dresden, headed by Rolf-Dieter Müller und presented at Dresden during the Historikertag of 2008 estimates between 18,000 and 25,000 death – http://hsozkult.geschichte.hu-berlin.de/tagungsberichte/id=2403, Jost Dülffer.]

security against the Warsaw Pact. To take up German suffering seemed for many 'good' post-war Germans tainted by neo-Nazi politics. It might be acceptable for the Japanese to play the role of unique victims because of the atomic bombing, but indeed that had involved a new and terrible weapon. And even the Japanese did not harp on the equally destructive conventional bombing attack on Tokyo in April 1945.

Still, debate was renewed a few years ago and along two separate tracks. First of all, the issue of German victims re-emerged, most sensationally in a work by Jörg Friedrich, *Der Brand: Deutschland im Bombenkrieg 1940–1945* ('The Fire: Germany in the Bombing War'). Alongside this arose the question of whether post-war German culture had 'repressed' any sustained discussions of victimhood, as was claimed most notably by the late literary scholar and novelist W. G. Sebald in his Zürich lectures published as 'Air War and Literature'. Relatedly, Günter Grass published his novel *Im Krebsgang* ('Crab's Walk'), which focused on the torpedoing of a German liner carrying 9,000 refugees in the Baltic as they were being evacuated from the Soviet course of invasion.[13] None of these authors could be suspected of neo-Nazi tendencies: Friedrich had written about German war crimes; Grass was a maverick leftist; Sebold had written melancholy tales of German-Jewish refugees and the impact of persecution on their later lives. Obviously all were moved by the numbers (half a million killed in the air war; 9,000 on the unfortunate ship) and needed to let the dead finally have a voice. Friedrich's is an effort to describe the bombing war from the viewpoint of those bombed, which it does with unsparing description. It has broken through what was a virtual taboo about open discussion of the roughly half a million German civilian deaths in the Anglo-American bombardment of 1940–45 as well as the physical destruction of cities and cultural treasures. Let us separate the book from the problem or problems it raises. At the emotional centre of his account, Friedrich insists on incendiary bombing: death by burning in melting asphalt, by baking in cellars, by asphyxiation through carbon monoxide and deprivation of oxygen. There is no shortage of large explosive bombs and the effect of explosive shock on the human frame, he also gives due credit to guidance systems, and the marking of targets by flares, but the real technological protagonist remains the incendiary stick, dropped by thousands, burning through the roofs of Gothic and Renaissance landmarks as well as private housing. He describes the shrivelled or carbonized remnants of victims being brought in baskets for burial, the destruction of families, the efforts at civil defence and dispersal of children (which the population hated). He points out that as much destruction followed during the last year of the war as in all the years before: devastating raids not just on railroads

---

13 J. Friedrich, *Der Brand: Deutschland im Bombenkrieg 1940–1945*, Munich, 2002; W. G. Sebald, 'Air War and Literature' ['Luftkrieg und Literatur'], 2001, now included in his *On the Natural History of Destruction,* trans. Anthea Bell, New York, 2003; G. Grass, *Im Krebsgang*, Göttingen, 2002;

or return visits to towns smashed repeatedly before, but on cities from Dresden to Würzburg, and Potsdam, whose destruction seemed called for mainly by the fact that they had been previously spared.

Although the book focuses primarily on British bombing, American readers will recall the devastating accounts of the Tokyo raid of March 9/10, 1945 and the toll as our B-29s roamed virtually unopposed over Japanese cities from November 1944, delivering incendiary weapons with sometimes even greater human costs on wooden housing. Billy Mitchell, the American pioneer of naval bombing, had recognized this as early as the 1920s, when he described the Japanese cities as 'the greatest aerial targets the world has ever seen...'[14]

The Friedrich book offended many Germans (and *a fortiori*, Anglo-American readers) by its inflammatory language which borrowed the rhetoric used for the Final Solution, including the terminology of the Holocaust.[15] But I wonder whether we Anglo-American readers for whom the Second World War remains above all our most righteous military cause do not draw too much comfort from the flaws that are documented. (And so, too, may those German readers who fear the apologetics implicit in the work.) Sebald's thesis of literary repression is also flawed. In the early post-war period, as Volker Hage's collection, shows, accounts of bomb-

---

14 Cited in R. Rhodes, *Downfall: The End of the Imperial Japanese Empire*, New York, 1999, 48.
15 See excellent reviews submitted to the H-German network by Joerg Arnold and Douglas Peifer, 4 Nov., 2003, which appropriately address, I believe, the strengths and weaknesses of this work – Peifer's with more emphasis on the military and political issues, Arnold with greater emphasis on the moral and conceptual problems. Others have also indicated the deficiencies of the book as a scholarly source. See for instance Hans Boogs's list of errors in his contribution to L. Kettenacker (ed.), *Ein Volk von Opfern? Die neue Debatte um den Bombenkrieg 1940–45*, Berlin, 2003. Obviously many issues are in contention in this debate. The most parochial issues are those that concern historians qua historians. To what extent can the historian merely report or dissect the differing positions without engaging his own sense of moral judgment. Second, what sort of rhetoric is legitimate in a historical account? If a particular vocabulary becomes associated with what is agreed is egregious atrocity (such as the antiseptic language used by the Germans in carrying out the 'final solution') is it illegitimate to use that language for other situations? Is 'tasteless' a category that makes sense for historical writing? Saul Friedlaender sought to take up this issue from the other side when he questioned Nazi Kitsch – the deliberate effort to evoke the aesthetic dimensions of fascism and Nazism. (See S. Friedlaender, *Reflections of Nazism: An Essay on Kitsch and Death*, New York, 1984. We know the phenomenon from films (*Syberberg*, and *The Night Porter*), novels (Alain Tournier's *Roi d'Aulnes* or *Erl-Koenig*). Friedrich's book suggests that the historian cannot rest content with a history of lived experience, no matter how important it may be to convey that experience. Television and cinema and the society's preoccupation with victims' testimony have suggested us that history is sterile without the evocation of experience, but history cannot be just the excavation of experience – old pictures, sad songs, diary snatches, and the like. To rely on these is our version of a pathetic fallacy. It is appropriate to convey testimony, indeed, I think, often a duty. But doing justice to the witness is not the same as writing history. It may be the beginning or the end of historical reflection, but is a different sort of exercise. No history perhaps without memory, but no history that does not discipline memory.

ing and urban destruction did appear.[16] But they were not sustained in important essays or novels. No German dialogue with the issues emerged, such as the Germans themselves generated for their own war crimes and genocide. As Peifer rightly notes, there was in fact a large though often specialized literature on this theme. More than an outright taboo, there has been an inhibition against producing or citing material about German suffering as such. Yes, we have had surveys of the air war – the ones written by the victors and the important scholarly work of the Freiburg military historians.[17] But such works rarely dwell on the experience of being bombed. Commentators have also raised the question why non-neo-Nazi Germans did not write this history so graphically before or why it has not been more openly discussed before. The answer offered by Hans-Ulrich Wehler and others is that they were acutely aware that their regime bore the responsibility for the war and committed even larger scale killing, outright murder in which each and every death inflicted was intentional. Some Germans, I believe, were silent not merely because they could not process the deaths, but because they really did understand where the chain of murderous warfare began. 'No oaths of revenge against the allied bombers. In a certain sense we felt a solidarity with them; they would destroy that system that we ourselves ... had erected but which we did not have the strength to overthrow', Peter Wapnewski writes.[18] Even Friedrich, who is outraged, writes: 'The destruction of the cities helped the cause of eliminating Himmler and his adherents, who had taken hostage these places, this history and this humanity, all Germany and all Europe.' But it was also Germany, too, which had taken these hostages, 'whether through violence, approval, or anger, out of equanimity or impotence. A different Germany was nothing but hypothetical – a would- or might-have-been.' But he goes on to say that it is also hypothetical to ask whether the fire might have been unnecessary. 'Did Hildesheim have to be destroyed for its railroad Station? Was this the reason, was there really any reason? Did those who set the fires intentionally and in anger want to win at any price, or was this the price that had to be paid for their victory? Certainly this was their effort. If this represents no tragedy as part of the allies' history, was their total success the same for the history of the Germans?'[19]

We can safely compartmentalize the book as flawed, but we cannot seriously deal with the issues if we merely object to inflammatory language or lack of balance. Friedrich does understand that after the defeat in the West, there seemed no choice for the British but to strike at the enemy with whatever weapons were

16 V. Hage, *Zeugen der Zerstoerung: Die Literaten und der Luftkrieg*, Frankfurt, 2003.
17 On the German side, H. Boog, G. Krebs, D. Vogel, *Das Deutsche Reich in der Defensive: Strategischer Luftkrieg in Europa, Krieg im Westen und in Ostasien 1943–1944/45*, Stuttgart 2001; see O. Groehler, *Bombenkrieg gegen Deutschland*, Berlin, 1990. From the Anglo-American perspective, Noble and Frankland, *Strategic Air Offensive against Germany*, and Wesley Frank Craven and J. Lea Cate, *The Army Airforces in World War II*, 7 vols., Chicago, 1951.
18 In L. Kettenacker (ed.), *Ein Volk von Opfern*, 122.
19 Friedrich, *Der Brand*, 217–8.

available. If the British were not to come to terms, what other offensive weapon did they have? Could any democratic statesman not have pursued this strategy? Still, was there not a point where it changed – as Arthur Harris said it ought – from a purposeful pursuit of targets, whether railroads or industry – to moral bombing? As Friedrich understands, the air war became one of *Vergeltung* or retribution, carried out by the British far beyond the measure of destruction they had absorbed (just as American *Vergeltung* against Japan vastly overshadowed the toll at Pearl Harbor that was so often cited as justification). Retribution fed the air war as much as strategy. The weapons that Goebbels promised would change the balance were named outright as 'Vergeltungs' or 'V weapons', and Peter Wapnewski's recollection notwithstanding, many Germans impatiently awaited them.

The contentious issue is not just military success. The American Strategic Bombing Surveys disputed the success of the strategy early on and emphasized how quickly the Germans could protect or repair their production facilities. Still, we no longer simply dismiss the bombing as ineffective. By the summer and autumn of 1944, the war machine was largely broken. Air defences were becoming ineffective, production began to fall sharply. Surely, argue its historian defenders, the tonnage rained from the air brought about that collapse. To which critics can respond that the Russian conquest of the Romanian oil fields was also a critical set back for the Germans. Furthermore, that while so-called precision bombing was not precise, the Allies did not have to embrace city bombing so indiscriminately. I personally think that the bombing can be credited with another success: the demonstrated hopelessness of the Nazi defence had something to do with the fact that after WW II three was no real revanchist movement, no defiant nationalism. But, again, defeat without immolation might also have achieved an equal post-war success. No, the issue remains the price of success, and that is always debated, and must be debated by historians as well as actors.

The Anglo-American Non-Debate and the Issue of Reprisal

What is striking about these debates is, I believe, first the fact that they did not evoke a stronger resonance in Germany. For all the cries about the German proclivity to victimization, the bombing issue has hardly become a major or burning political subject. It has not claimed public sympathy or consciousness the way the Hiroshima attack has done in Japan. The German civic culture abandoned the *tu quoque* attitude it still largely maintained through the 1950s. Yes, for a long while, there were many stories of victimization – especially among refugees from East Prussia, the territories taken by post-1945 Poland, and the Sudetenland. Friedrich's book can be seen as a continuation of with this strand of self-pitying and often rightwing apologetics, but in fact non-Germans are willing to listen to this narrative with a sympathy that was excluded except on the far Right until recently. Vaclav Havel's expression of regret at the Sudeten expulsions was a conspicuous case in point. Nonetheless, Friedrich's book and the related series of memoirs and commentaries in the press did not unleash any widespread effort to claim a moral equivalence of German war crimes and allied bombing. I believe that this is due to the fact that there remains deep-seated recognition that one cannot indulge in a sort of moral bookkeeping that sets off one set of atrocities with even what might be considered another. The recent celebration of 8 May (V-E Day), 2005 demonstrates even more that the Germans are willing to forswear any political exploitation of the air-war issue. A few years ago, Germans often tended to say that their country could not celebrate May 8 as a day of liberation since it simultaneously marked a catastrophic national defeat. In this most recent commemoration, at Moscow and elsewhere, this reserved stance had completely changed: Germans participated as Germans who could welcome the results of 8 May, 1945, without reserve. The political culture that allows this overcoming of conventional national feeling is not one that will sustain the undercurrents raised by Jörg Friedrich. Jürgen Habermas could be proud: constitutional patriotism has prevailed even in united Germany.

But equally striking, I believe, is the absence of discussion in the United States (if not Great Britain). American political culture allows, I think far less tolerant examination of earlier failings in World War II – at least not yet. True, Americans have engaged in national expiation about Indians, African-American slavery, lynching, and segregation, about the internment of West-Coast Japanese-Americans in World War II. But the 'good war' is still too fresh or too necessary to subject to the same emotional scrutiny. The fate of the Enola Gay exhibit in 1995 – flawed as the explanatory material might have been – revealed the great resistance to this sort of scrutiny.[20] In fact, Hiroshima and Nagasaki can be questioned and discussed, but the conventional air war remains beyond widespread popular re-evaluation. The recent histories of America's bombers, expecially Stephen Ambrose's history of B-24 'Liberator' raids is cast in the heroic mold. Thomas Childers' moving study, which evidently inspired Ambrose (though he never acknowledged it), of his uncle's B-24 war, *Wings of Morning*, likewise did not seek to question the rationale for bombing raids through April 1945.[21] Childers, however, was explicitly writing a book about subjective experience – the very dangerous one that ordinary Americans undertook on orders – and he has promised a counterpart volume on the experience of the war from the ground. But no one has suggested that if American soldiers are supposed to resist immoral orders, or commanders are punishable for giving them, that any aspect of the air war should fall under this moral category.

---

20 T. Childers, *Wings of Morning: The Story of the Last American Bomber Shot down over Germany in World War II*, Reading. MA, 1995; St. E. Ambrose, *The Wild Blue: The Men and Boys who Flew the B-24s over Germany*, New York, 2001.

21 See P. Nobile (ed.), *Judgment at the Smithsonian: Smithsonian Script by the Curators at the National Air and Space Museum*, New York, 1995. The 'Afterword' by Barton J. Bernstein is a valuable summary of the debates since 1945.

What the air-war discussions reveal – the German, the British, and the American alike – is that much of the discussion about the legitimacy or 'just war' justification of massive aerial bombardment was beside the point. In large-scale national wars, even in the case where societies are under totalitarian control and citizens are not thought to have influence over their rulers, reprisal became an accepted recourse. (It certainly became an acceptable recourse during the Cold War when massive retaliation rested on 'mutual assured destruction' and second-strike or counter-city strategy were largely accepted until the 1980s, when the consensus about nuclear deterrence started unravelling.) But such reprisal must be stochastic or actuarial. What remains unacceptable is the targeting of individual civilians. What is acceptable is reprisal with the statistical certainty that a given percentage of civilians must be killed thereby. Ultimately those of us who would accept the air war say that under certain conditions it may be necessary to burn babies. Even if we are not explicitly targeting babies we all live with statistics enough to know that our historically mediated choice will kill those whom no theory of a society at war can plausibly claim have opted for war. Vengeance is mine, supposedly sayeth the Lord. Vengeance, though, is also ours – including civilian deaths so long as these victims are not personally selected. This remains curious. Why is it more acceptable to accept that, say, 5 percent of a city of half a million will be killed (25,000) so long as we do not specify which 5 percent, but that shooting 50 hostages out of hand is unacceptable? Nonetheless, it is. Whether bombing, blockade, radiation deaths or the like, the non-specified death is more acceptable than the specified death. And why is it more tolerable to accept massive city bombing with the statistical certainty of innocent victims as a means of warfare but to reject the terrorism that purposely kills innocent civilians as a pawn in political answer. There are two possible answers – neither very satisfactory. Terrorism is specifically intended to kill innocents; city bombing merely accepts their death. The historian, of course, is not an ethicist. But how robust a distinction does this really amount to? The second is that evil regimes hold their own citizens up as hostages and are as responsible for the death of 'innocents' as are those who seek to defeat them. Well, this sounds good, but it does not diminish the complicity of the bombers. At what age did one become a Nazi or even a supporter? Surely not under four or five or six or ... or ... or. Readers expect historians (legitimately I think) to take a surrogate responsibility for approval or disapproval of their protagonists' hard choices. To say that Friedrich's *Fire* is flawed by lack of balance or inflammatory language cannot get us off the hook. As good liberals, we might plausibly argue that our statesmen and pilots could have killed fewer babies, or non-combatants, and probably that is where most of us are left after reading his book. Still, at the end I am forced to confront inconsistencies and beliefs that I would rather avoid. *Ius in bello* remains at best an asymptotic guideline, never fully to be achieved.

Universality and Identity

In terms of war and peace, it is particularly essential to think of human beings both as universal beings, and as belonging individually to specific groups with different identities. The universality of war can no more be contested than the universality of peace. They both reveal a fundamental human ambivalence. The universality of war demonstrates both the universality of human aggression – *homo homini lupus* (Plaute's 'man is a wolf to other men,' later used by Hobbes) – and the human will to assert the primacy of its group's identity. But in the name of this identity, people are prepared either to wage war or to make peace with the enemy, depending on whether a balance of power is organised or whether the power struggle is favourable or not. The universality of a desire for peace reveals, on the contrary, a common need for openness to the idea of 'otherness' and an aspiration towards universality. But this need is not only altruistic, it may also arouse the temptation to impose on others universal values which, in fact, derive from its own identity, and this desire to 'universalise' others to one's own image can transform what was the desire for peace into a desire for 'pacification by war'. In this way, the ideal of universality leads as much to peace as to war, and the defence of identity leads as much to the risk of war as to the possibility of peace. It is the way the ambivalence between identity and 'otherness' operates which determines war or peace, and which turns the war and peace duo into an inseparable couple.

The cities of Ancient Greece are too often presented as absolute enemies, considering war between themselves as a necessity, despite their common language, religion and culture. Hans Van Wees shows that, on the contrary, these cities were fully committed to the universal aspiration for peace, and which prevailed over the desire for war. Was it more 'natural' for the Greeks to declare war on the 'Absolute Other' (the Persian), considered to be the absolute 'barbarian'? This is certainly the case. However, this absolute 'otherness' can be used to serve an ideological purpose. Athens happened to affirm the extreme difference between the Greeks and the 'Great Barbarian' when she intended to assert better her democratic superiority over certain Greek cities where some institutions were still close to oriental despotism[2]. The imperial ideal can be a way of thinking war simultaneously in terms of conquest and of 'pacification'. Peace, once the conquest is achieved, is in fact the continuation of war by other, supposedly peaceful, means: the imperial power imposes its peace on competing identities; through imperial peace the Romans saw themselves as spreading universal civilisation, with the granting of citizenship (*civis romanus sum*). The peace may nonetheless be accepted and appreciated for what it was. Arno Stromeyer explains that in modern times, the aspiration towards a universal monarchy, as expressed by Charles V, was embodied in the use of the notion of civilisation as the peaceful union of all Christians against the Great Turk,

---

2 Yvon Thébert, "Réflexions sur l'utilisation du concept d'Etranger: évolution de l'image du Barbare à Athènes à l'époque classique", *Diogène*, 112 (1980), p. 90–115.

a dimension which went beyond Europe and spread through the rest of the world at the time of the conquest and forced conversion to Christianity of North and South America.

The emergence of modern states gave rise to a radically different view based on the balance of power, the rejection of hegemony among these states and the wariness of tyrannical or imperial universality. Yet this did not mean that they denied the universality of the values that united them. The balance of power was not a simple mechanical equilibrium, it could be also an organic balance, an agreement based on a shared civilisation, shared ideas and visions of the world, either 'reactionary' (the Holy Alliance after 1815) or democratic (the Locarno System from 1925 to 1932)[3]. During and after decolonisation, nationalist movements and later the new independent states took on board part of the concept of universality that the colonial powers had wanted to teach them. Sumit Sarkar tells us that Gandhi was not only an heir to the Hindu tradition, he had read Tolstoy. After his death, Gandhi's vision was also a source of inspiration for Martin Luther King and Nelson Mandela. In the same vein, Pierre Boilley explains how the African states in their peace-building processes refer back both to universal institutions (the International Court of Justice or the UNO) and to the Wise Men of their own traditions. With regard to culture and peace, there is no contradiction between universality and identity in this process of appropriation and cultural transfer.

The universality-identity dialectic becomes more difficult to discern with the introduction of gender analysis, when comparing the representations and attitudes of war and peace of both men and women. Their perception of war is not necessarily different. There is no masculine warrior identity or feminine pacifist identity. Women accept war and they go to war. The difference lies rather in the roles assigned, with warriors on one side, and the nurturing mothers or nurses on the other. When war requires women to become more involved and even to fight, everyone accepts this new situation, including the men, at least those who belong to the same side. The enemy, on the contrary, derides these furious Amazons, questioning their femininity or demonising them as 'whores' sharing the beds of their fellow warriors. But, after the war, the stereotypes and images remain: the courage of the women who fought on the front is not necessarily underlined and people prefer to remember traditional male and female roles.

Most certainly, assigned identities have more impact than experienced identities. War or peace strategists should not disregard these experienced identities on either side. Ignoring them can lead to errors or inefficiency.

---

3   Jean Bérenger and Georges-Henri Soutou (eds), *L'Ordre européen du XVIe au XX siècle*, Paris, PUPS, 1998.

Identity and Legitimacy

If in wartime, group solidarity enables one side to transcend the differences between men and women, social groups, different opinions and different cultures, it is because the warrior event is experienced as a 'community of destiny'. This works well if the society involved in the military conflict considers the conflict to be legitimate. The belief in war as legitimate is one of its main strengths, and is as least as important as the arms and armament plans. We can only ask our own people to risk their lives if they are convinced in themselves of the necessity of self-sacrifice. The link between legitimacy and identity is obvious: the defence of group identity – the family, the homeland – is the easiest to explain and legitimise. This is why aggressors ultimately run a risk. They may have the benefit of surprise, but the defender has the superiority of legitimacy, and thus motivation and self-sacrifice. In 1941–1945 the Red Army, men and women alike mobilised in great numbers and authentically experienced the war as a 'great patriotic war'. This patriotism, aroused by the Nazi aggression probably carried more weight than the will to defend the Communist regime (Roger Markwick). This does not mean that all aggressors were necessarily defeated in the past, but it is worth noting that in the 20th century all the tyrant conquerors, without exception, lost both the war and their conquests, even if it took some time to make them return their ill-acquired gains.

The Christian concept of "just war" applies mainly against aggression. To this "just cause" which gives the *jus ad bellum*, Francisco de Vitoria added a condition pertaining to the *jus in bello:* 'the war has to be fought by proper means'. With the Crusades, a just war became a 'Holy War' and this was a fundamental change. Christian identity and Muslim identity confronted each other in the name of God, in the name of the Absolute. The war against the 'Infidel' thus became the norm and had to finish in total victory. It aimed at overcoming the enemy not because of the danger he represented or what he 'had done', but in the name of what he 'was'. This did not mean that there were no truces and peace-treaties (Yvonne Friedman). But they were only settled for a time, whereas between Christians (or Muslims) peace was the norm, had to be continually sought after, and for a long time. During the 20th century, the Church no longer invoked "just wars". War appeared as the evil. It was only during the Yugoslavian conflicts that the Church reverted to raising the question of the 'just war' more clearly, because of the horrors of ethnic cleansing and the new issues at stake in humanitarian war. Yet in 2003, all Churches condemned the war in Iraq as being 'immoral, illegal, and ill-advised'. In short, beyond theses various stances, the debate on 'just war' has returned to the forefront at the end of the 20th century and at the beginning of the 21st century.

The legitimacy of war against an aggressor is an old concept. But, there is another ancient law in the history of humanity. All military occupations create an occupying-occupied relationship, the relationship of the weak to the strong in which the weak draw their strength and the strong meet their weakness. Occupation creates or reinforces both identities and legitimacy. The English occupation during the Hundred Years' War, the French occupation under Napoleon, and the Israeli occupation since 1967, have all, in turn, revealed the French, Italian, German and Palestinian political identities.

The relation between identity and otherness is necessarily a part of the thought process concerning the war and peace duo. In many cases, the maxim of the Palestinian intellectual, Elias Sanbar applies: "To wage war is to hurt the enemy, to be at peace is to hurt oneself"[4]. Hurting others illegitimately is a means of making them stronger, of giving them the opportunity to give meaning to the ultimate sacrifice. And accepting peace is to a certain extent to recognise in the other what one has refused to recognise until then. It entails working on oneself and changing one's way of being. In principle, it should be easier for democracies. But is it really that simple?

Legitimacy and Democracy

Democracy engenders its own legitimacy. Will the spread of democracy throughout the world create a global system of legitimate causes outlawing war? Gottfried Niedhart analyses the emergence of two concepts since the 18th century: 'liberal peace' and 'democratic peace'. The former considers that peace stems from the development of trade, helped by the setting up and generalisation of free trade. From Kant to Cobden, one finds the idea that trading nations establish their relations on peace, not war. The second concept, 'democratic peace', owes much to Kant who advocated the generalisation of Republics in order to guarantee a real and lasting peace – not just the absence of war but a true state of general concord. War was only worthwhile for Kings and Princes, who sent others into battle while they continued to hunt and engage in courtly pleasures. On the contrary, the citizens of a Republic would not be as keen to declare war because they would have to pay for it and to fight for themselves. Kant did not like the word 'democracy' because to him it represented the tyrannical and bloody demagogy of the French Jacobins of 1793–1794, and he preferred the concept of a 'Republic' based on rights, citizenship and the separation of powers. In the 20th century, the word 'democracy' no longer has such a bad reputation and the Kantian principle becomes 'democracies do not wage war against one another'. There is occasionally scepticism about this statement[5]. Britain attacked the United States in 1812, but was Britain a democracy then? France and Britain were at war with Germany in 1914–1918, but was the Second Reich a democracy? One may argue indefinitely on this issue.

---

4   Elias Sanbar, "Un spectre hante Israël …", *Le Monde*, 25 january 2001.
5   See Jost Dülffer, "Are Democracies Really more Peaceful? Democratic Peace Theory Revisited", in Boris Barth and Rolf Hobson (ed.), *The Democratic Peace theory revisited*, New York, Oxford 2009 forthcoming.

If there is a debate on the possibility or impossibility of war between democracies, there is no discussion on the ability of democratic states to go to war: they are involved in most of them. They are capable of "democratic" imperialism at the expense of non democratic countries. Indeed, the predominant tendency of the 20th century for democratic states was to go to war in support of rights against authoritarian regimes (World War I, even if this democratic claim was not the cause of the war, but was expressed once the war started) or totalitarian (World War II) regimes. But their war 'idealism' was tempered by a strategic 'realism': during these conflicts, they entered into alliances with the autocratic Russian Tsar or with Stalin's totalitarian USSR. Often selfish and cruel, democratic states used their wealth and their industrial superiority to engage in an asymmetrical war. As they are accountable to public opinion for the number of deaths of their own subjects, they must conduct the conflict so that as many lives as possible of their own troops are preserved, while inflicting permanent damage on the enemy, in order to make it give up the fight as quickly as possible. From this point of view, aerial warfare is very practical for rich democratic states, because it spares more human lives of the bombers and it terrifies the targeted enemy.

Even if these calculations have proved to be somewhat illusive and even if aerial warfare alone has never lead to a decisive result (Kosovo in 1999 being the only exception), the bombings in Germany in 1943–1945 and in Vietnam in 1965–1969 are nonetheless significant examples of this asymmetrical vision of war. Charles Maier raises an interesting question concerning the aerial bombings on German towns which inflicted severe losses on the civilian population: because they generally claim to respect *jus ad bellum* and only go to war when absolutely necessary, are democracies still entitled to transgress *jus in bello* in order to put an end as rapidly as possible to a war they are not responsible for? Must a just war in its ends also be just in its means? In any case, it is important to note a certain evolution. The 'Zero Killed' war, or an OK War exclusively on one's own side, is an older concept for the United States. As their military intervention takes place at a distance, it is harder for them to accept heavy sacrifices than for Europeans who were for a long time involved in wars to defend their homeland. In the second half of the 20th century, the thresholds of European sensitivity moved closer to that of the Americans. Then, recently, since the 1990s, with the globalisation of media coverage, the emotional shock of war images and the growing popularity of humanitarian aid, the idea of the symmetrical 'Zero Killed' war – in other words on both sides, including civilians on the enemy side – came onto the agenda, despite the fact that it seems difficult to actually apply this principle.

Thus democratic states go to war, and, what is more, they fight cruel wars. Let us come back to the 20th century trend: democracies do not go to war *with one another*. It may of course be argued that there are many factors other than the democratic one to be considered: welfare, social justice, cultural change with the mass-consumption society, etc[6]. Nonetheless, because of this trend, it is tempting for democracies to do all that is possible to spread democracy throughout the world and to try to attain the Kantian ideal of perpetual peace. Gottfried Niedhart reminds us that Woodrow Wilson and Franklin Roosevelt had this perspective in mind. Does this mean that the American neoconservatives who pushed for the intervention in Iraq in 2003 were Wilsonian? No, because Wilsonianism and neoconservatism diverge completely on one essential matter. Wilson, as a lawyer, knew the difference between justice and law. Peace cannot last when it is based on justice only and not on law. In this sense, Wilson was influenced by the whole movement which had started to emerge at the end of the 19th century around 'peace based on law' (la "paix par le droit") and which inspired the idea of the League of Nations[7]. This legal approach can be found in Franklin Roosevelt and his successors, hence the importance of the role given to the UN which adopted a multilateral approach. Later, when the UN was blocked by the veto of undemocratic powers, the source of legitimacy came from a general democratic consensus (Korea 1950, Koweit 1991, Bosnia 1994–1995, Kosovo 1999), which was not obtained in 2003. Neither was it in 1956, when Britain and France attacked Egypt after the nationalisation of the Suez Canal. Nasser did not endanger the world order, as did Hitler – to whom he was falsely compared –, and the war against him contributed to the unification of the Arab world and the Third World countries against the Western world. At that time, the French and British made an intellectual error, whereas the Americans showed more wisdom. Assuredly, when democracies wage war against dictators only when they endanger international peace (1939–1945, 1950, 1991), the principles of legitimacy and efficiency, based on democratic consensus, are more likely to be reconciled. International democratisation means democratisation of the international system and, if necessary, war against warmongers, but not war against all dictatorships.

The spreading of democracy after 1945 has been the consequence of the defeat of dictatorships (*jus post bellum*), but not the motivation for entering into war (*jus ad bellum*). The democratisation of Japan and Germany was not the cause of World War II. It certainly owed a lot to the occupation by the victorious Western allies, but it owed even more to the internal political forces in the countries where there had been either a previous democratic tradition (the Weimar Republic), or a liberal tradition (Japan in the 1920s). It is a mistake to believe that free elections alone will make a democracy. A 'demos' must initially exist, i.e. a community with sufficient solidarity so that the minority accepts the law of the majority, where citizens vote not for what they "are" (Sunnites, Shi'ites, Kurds), but for what they "want".

---

6   See Jost Dülffer, *ibidem*.
7   Jean-Michel Guieu, *Le rameau et le glaive. Les militants français pour la SDN*, Paris, Presses de Sciences Po, 2008.

Should we draw the conclusion that *pax democratica* is impossible, because democracy cannot be established everywhere and is reserved for only the happy few? No, we simply need to re-read what the previous chapters tell us about the 'universality-identity' duo. The universal quality in mankind makes the advent of democracy possible everywhere, in all civilisations. But this may take time and the shortest way is certainly not through constraint from an outside power. The 'end of history' which Fukuyama has evoked,[8] that is the reign of democracy and peace everywhere, is therefore not imminent. On the other hand, Samuel Huntington's formula 'the clash of civilisations'[9] and his idea of a clash between the democratic *West* and the undemocratic *Rest* of the world are completely unsuitable, unless this becomes a self-fulfilling prophecy. In fact, every civilisation, including the Western one, has its share of barbarism, and has clearly demonstrated this both in the past and the present. The 'clash' can only occur if the most barbarian part seizes power in each civilisation (with its fundamentalists and its intolerance), in the name of a narrow 'essentialist' vision of culture and tradition. If there is to be a clash, it will be a 'clash of barbarisms': not a *cultural clash*, but a *political clash* between radicals instrumentalising culture.

To guard against this clash of barbarisms, to fight against all forms of fundamentalism, one certainly needs to refer to the identity-legitimacy-democracy trilogy also mentioned in this book. Wars against identities must be avoided: identities must be respected, must be appeased, must be taken into account in the state-building and demos-building process. Therefore, if democratic states have to go to war, it must in no way resemble a crusade. The purpose of history is to combat Manicheism and understand complexity. It may prove in the end that to think in terms of complexity with regard to war and peace is less complicated and less dangerous in its consequences than over-simplification.

[8] Francis Fukuyama, *The End of History and the Last Man*, New York 1992.
[9] Samuel P. Huntington, *Clash of Civilizations and the Remaking of World Order*, New York 1996.

Authors

Joan Beaumont, Dean of Arts and Sciences, The Australian National University, Canberra, Australia

Pierre Boilley, Professor of History, Centre d'Études des Mondes Africains (CEMAf) Université Paris 1 Panthéon – Sorbonne, France

Joanna Bourke, Professor of History, Birkbeck College, London, Great Britain

Alfredo Canavero, Professor, Dipartimento di Scienze della Storia e della Documentazion Storica, Università degli Studi di Milano Storici, Italy

Jost Dülffer, Professor of Modern History, Historisches Seminar I, Universität zu Köln, Germany

Robert Frank, Professor, Centre de recherches et d'histoire de l'Europe centrale contemporaine, Université Paris I – Panthéon – Sorbonne, France

Yvonne Friedman, Professor, Martin (Szusz) Department of Land of Israel Studies and Archaeology, Bar-Ilan University, Israel

Dianne Hall, Dr, School of Historical Studies, University of Melbourne, Australia

Pieter Lagrou, Professor, Départment de Sciences Politique, Université Libre de Bruxelles, Brussels, Belgium

Charles S. Maier, Professor, Center for European Studies, History Department, Harvard University, Cambridge, U.S.A.

Elizabeth Malcolm, Professor, School of Historical Studies, University of Melbourne, Australia

Roger Markwick, Senior Lecturer, Faculty of Education and Arts, School of Humanities and Social Science, University of Newcastle, Australia

Gottfried Niedhart, Professor, Historisches Institut, Universität Mannheim, Germany

Barbara Potthast, Professor, Abteilung für Ibero-Amerikanische Geschichte, Historisches Seminar I, Universität zu Köln, Germany

Tammy Proctor, Professor, History Department, Wittenberg University, Springfield, OH, U.S.A.

Jean H. Quataert, Professor, Department of History, State University of New York, Binghampton, N.Y., U.S.A.

Sumit Sarkar, Professor, Department of History, Delhi University, Delhi, India

Arno Strohmeyer, Professor, Geschichte, Fachbereich Kultur- und Gesellschaftswissenschaften, Salzburg, Austria

Penny Summerfield, Professor, School of Arts, History and Cultures, University of Manchester, Great Britain

Hans van Wees, Professor, History Department, University College London, Great Britain

Index of Names

A

Aaronsohn, Sarah 153, 212, 213
Abetz, Otto 177
Áed Ua Domnaill 162
Áed Ui Conchobair 160
Al-Adil (Saphadin) 58, 59
Albert of Aachen 53
Aleksievich, Svetlana 243
Alexander (King of Macedonia) 28
Alfonso el Sabio (King of Castile) 49
Al-Gadhafi, Muammar 131
Alice of Abervenny 158, 159
Alighieri, Dante 19, 71
Al-Kamil 17, 54, 55, 58, 59
Al-Muazzam 55
Al-Nasir Daud 55
Ambrose, Stephen 265
Andrews, C. F. 116
Aristophanes 11
Arnold, Henry H. (Hap) 258
Asbridge, Tom 50
Augustine of Hippo 47, 98
Augustus (C. Julius Caesar A., Roman Emperor) 35
Azuela, Manuel 194

B

Baba Miské, Ahmed 135
Baha al-Din 56, 59, 60
Baldwin I 52, 53
Ban Ki-Moon 132
Baroun, Matilda 166
Baybars 54, 56
Benedict XV (Pope) 99–101, 103
Benson, Anette 224
Bermingham, Sir Piers 164
Best, Werner 174, 177
Birrell, E. T. F. (Major) 220–223, 225–232
Boilley, Pierre 18, 20, 23, 269
Bolívar, Simón 149, 183–184, 190–191, 194
Borden, Mary 214
Briand, Aristide 91
Brittain, Vera 215

Bush, George W. 93, 267
Butler, Eleanor 163

C

Campbell, Agnes 163
Canavero, Alfredo 18, 20, 24
Casaroli, Agostino 107
Cavell, Edith 210, 213
Chamberlain, Neville 257
Charles V (Emperor) 19, 22, 66–68, 71–75, 77–79, 268
Cherwell, Lord (Frederick Lindemann) 258
Childers, Thomas 265
Chisholm, Mairi 214
Churchill, Winston S. 258, 259
Cicero, M. Tullius C. 28, 35
Clausewitz, Carl von 11
Clemens VII (Pope) 72
Clinton, William Jefferson 93
Cnockaert, Marthe 209, 211
Cobden, Richard 85–89, 94, 271
Colette (Sidonie-Gabrielle C.) 216

D

D'Azeglio, Luigi Taparelli 98
Daniell, Spencer 224
Dante, see Alighieri
Dearbhfhorgaill 149, 162, 163
Déby, Idriss 131
Delwaide, Jeanne 211
Diarmait Mach Murchada 155, 160
Dokutovich, Galina 240
Dombrowski, Nicole 213
Domnall Ua Néill 158
Doyle, Michael W. 81

E

Elias, Norbert 157, 158, 160, 161, 167
Emerson, Ralph Waldo 20, 117
Enloe, Cynthia 205, 206
Erauso, Catalina de 181
Esarhaddon 32
Espinos y Córdoba (general) 187

F

Fahr-a-Din 58
Falkenhorst, Nikolaus von 173, 179
Fernández de Oviedo, Gonzalo 67
Fisch, Jörg 17
Fitzgerald, Alice 233
Francis I (King of France) 68, 72, 78
Frederick II (Emperor) 17, 54, 58–60
Frénay, Henri 177
Friedman, Yvonne 17, 19, 21, 22, 270
Friedrich, Jörg 261–266

G

Gaddis, John Lewis 81
Galbraith, John Kenneth 258
Galtung, Johan 20
Gandhi, Mohandas Karamchand 16, 18, 20, 21, 23, 24, 115–126, 269
Gattinara, Mercurino Arborio di 71, 72
Genghis Khan 78
Gilbert, Sir Humphrey 161, 162
Gladstone, William Ewart 87, 88
Godfrey of Bouillon 22, 53, 55
Goebbels, Joseph 246, 260, 264
Göring, Hermann 247
Gowon, Yakubu 131
Grajales, Mariana 95
Grass, Günter 261
Grayzel, Susan 206
Grotius, Hugo 78
Guevara, Antonio de 68

H

Habermas, Jürgen 11, 265
Habré, Hissene 131
Hacker, Barton 297
Hage, Volker 262
Halin, Édouard 177
Hall, Dianne 148, 149, 153
Harris, Arthur 257, 258, 260, 264
Hassan II (King of Morocco) 132
Hattushili III 30, 31, 37
Havel, Vaclav 264
Hedges, Geraldine 224
Henry II (King of England) 155
Henry VIII (King of England) 68

Herbert, Ulrich 174
Herodotus 27, 33, 36, 38
Hesiod 26
Himmler, Heinrich 263
Hitler, Adolf 9, 23, 105, 173, 174, 235, 237, 242, 244–249, 259, 260, 273, 278
Hobbes, Thomas 26, 268
Homer 27, 33
Howard, Michael 18
Hubert Walter (Bishop of Salisbury) 58
Hugh of Caesarea 55, 58
Hugh of Cyprus 56
Hugo, Victor 87
Hull, Cordell 89, 92
Hussein, Saddam 9, 267

I

Ibn Abd al-Zahir 56
Ibn Rushd (Averroes) 45
Ibn Wasil 54
Inglis, Elsie 153, 210, 210, 211, 224–228, 230–232

J

Jalal al-Din Khwarizmshah 55
Joan of Arc 241
John (King of England) 56
John Paul II (Pope) 110–113
John XXIII (Pope) 106–108
Justi, Johann Gottlieb v. 70
Justinian (Byzantine Emperor) 77

K

Kant, Immanuel 10, 11, 23, 70, 85, 86, 95, 119, 271, 273
Kelly, Petra 126
Kennedy, John Fitzgerald 109
Kesselring, Albert 257
Khrushchev, Nikita S. 249
King, Martin Luther 126, 269
Knocker, Elsie 214
Kollontai, Alexandra 212
Kosmodemyanskaya, Zoya 241
Kovshova, Natasha 242
Koziol, Geoffrey 47
Krupskaya, Nadezhda 245

L

Lagrou, Pieter 148, 149
Laraki, Ahmed 132
Las Casas, Bartolomé de 72
LeMay, Curtis 258
Lenin, Vladimir I. 95, 245
Leo XIII (Pope) 98, 99
Livy (Titus Livius) 34
Lloyd George, David 88, 94
López, Francisco Solano 149, 154, 185, 191, 197
Louis IX (King of France) 57
Louis XIV (King of France) 71
Luce, Henry R. 92
Ludendorff, Erich 169
Luxemburg, Rosa 212

M

MacDonnell, James 163
Maceo, Antonio 195
Maelruanaidh Mac Diarmada 155, 160
Magnus o'Connor 162
Maier, Charles S. 148, 272
Malcolm, Elizabeth 148, 149, 153
Mandela, Nelson 125, 269
Markiewicz, Constance 212
Markwick, Roger 147–155, 270
Mayer, Holly 207
Merneptah 25, 36
Milltoun, Laurence and Elena de 166
Mirabeau, Marquis de (Victor de Riqueti) 73
Mitchell, William (Billy) 262
Monge, Gabrielle de 210
Moro, Renato 97
Morozov (Major General) 241
Moulin, Jean 172
Münkler, Herfried 77

N

Nakamura, T. 50, 51
Nasser, Gamal Abdel 273
Nicole d'Acre 57
Niedhart, Gottfried 18–20, 271, 273
Nightingale, Florence 230
Nur ed-Din 51, 53
Nussbaum, Shmuel 50

O

Ó Cuiléin, Mathgamain 164
O'Reilly 161
Octouthy, Fynyna and Isabella, family 166
Ouldh Daddah, Ahmed 132
Overy, Richard 259

P

Paine, Thomas 85
Palancares, Jesusa 149, 192, 198
Parekh, Bhikhu Chotalal 116, 117
Parmigianino (Girolamo Francesco Maria Mazzola) 23, 73, 74
Paul VI (Pope) 108–110
Paulus, Friedrich 72
Pavan, Pietro 107
Peifer, Douglas 262, 263
Pericles 21
Petit, Gabrielle 211, 213
Philipp II (King of Spain) 67
Pisani, Edgar 135
Pius IX (Pope) 98
Pius X (Pope) 99
Pius XI (Pope) 101–103
Pius XII (Pope) 103–106, 108, 112
Plato 11, 29
Plaute (Titus Maccius Plautus) 268
Pliny (C. Plinius Secundus) 36
Polybius 30, 40
Potthast, Barbara 148, 149, 153, 154
Proctor, Tammy 149, 150, 153

Q

Qalqashandhi 52
Quataert, Jean H. 149, 153

R

Ramesses II (Ramses II) 31, 37
Raskova, Marina 239
Rasmussen, Mikkel 95
Reber-Gruber, Auguste 246
Reed, John 190, 192
Reichenau, Walter von 244
Richard of Devizes 58
Richard the Lionheart (King of England) 22, 56

Roberts Rinehart, Mary 216
Roe, Hugh 163
Roisin, Jean-Didier 136
Rojas Gonzalez, Francisco 194
Rommel, Erwin 178
Roosevelt, Franklin Delano 9, 91, 92, 95, 103, 273
Rumi, Giorgio 100
Ruskin, John 117

S

Sáenz, Manuela 149, 183, 184, 191, 193, 194, 198
Saladin 22, 50, 51
Salas, Elisabeth, 53, 54, 56, 58–60
Salisbury, Marquess of (Robert Gascoyne-Cecil) 94
Sanbar, Elias 271
Sarkar, Sumit 18, 20, 21, 23, 269
Savarkar, Vinayak Damodar 20, 23, 115, 118
Savimbi, Jonas 129
Schaepdrijver, Sophie de 209
Schmitt, Carl 177
Sebald, Winfried Georg (W. G.) 261, 262
Sepúlveda, Juan Ginés de 72, 78
Sertillanges, Antonin 100
Shams al-Khilafa 53
Siad Barre, Mohammed 129
Sidney, Sir Henry 163
Sillas Diarra, Diby 134, 135
Sissoo, Amadou 134
Soumaré, Abdullaye 134
Spinoza, Baruch de 11
St. Clair Stobart, Mabel 214
Stalin, Joseph 51, 236, 237, 239–242, 244, 246, 249, 250, 259, 272
Stresemann, Gustav 91
Strohmeyer, Arno 17, 19, 22

T

Tacitus (P. Cornelius T.) 36, 255
Thomas Aquinas 98
Thoreau, David Henri 20, 117
Thucydides 19, 21, 26, 29, 38, 39, 254

Timaeaus 30
Tír Conaill (Donegal) 162, 163
Titian (Tiziano Vecellio) 73, 75
Tolstoy, Leo 20, 117, 26
Tombalbaye, Ngarta 131
Toumani Touré, Amadou 135, 136
Traoré, Moussa 135
Trenchard, Hugh 257, 258
Tristán, Flora 189, 198
Tughtigin of Damascus 52
Tukulti-Ninurta I. 29

U

U Thant 108
Ua Chonchobair (family) 161, 162, 164
Underwood Johnson, Robert 210
Urban II (Pope) 47

V

van Wees, Hans 17, 21, 268
Vattel, Emer de 79
Vercors (Jean Bruller) 177
Vigny, Alfred de 177
Virgil (P. Vergilius Maro) 35

W

Wapnewski, Peter 263, 264
Wehler, Hans-Ulrich 263
William de Lacy 161
William Marshal 161, 166
William of Tyre 50, 52, 53, 56
Wilson, Woodrow 9, 89, 90, 93–95, 100, 273

X

Xenophon 29, 33

Z

Zengi 51, 53
Zenna Smith, Helen 215
Ziegler, Karl-Heinz 18

Veröffentlichungen
des Arbeitskreises Historische Friedensforschung

Karl Holl/Wolfram Wette (Hg.), Pazifismus in der Weimarer Republik. Beiträge zur historischen Friedensforschung, Paderborn 1981

Jost Dülffer/Karl Holl (Hg.), Bereit zum Krieg. Kriegsmentalität im wilhelminischen Deutschland 1890–1914. Beiträge zur historischen Friedensforschung, Göttingen 1986

Gottfried Niedhart/Dieter Riesenberger (Hg.), Lernen aus dem Krieg? Deutsche Nachkriegszeiten 1918 und 1945. Beiträge zur Historischen Friedensforschung, München 1992

Jost Dülffer (Hg.), Parlamentarische und öffentliche Kontrolle von Rüstung in Deutschland 1700–1970. Beiträge zur Historischen Friedensforschung, Düsseldorf 1992

Detlef Bald (Hg.), Rüstungsbestimmte Geschichte und das Problem der Konversion in Deutschland im 20. Jahrhundert (Jahrbuch für Historische Friedensforschung, Bd. 1), Münster. Hamburg 1993

Arnold Sywottek (Hg.), Der Kalte Krieg – Vorspiel zum Frieden? (Jahrbuch für Historische Friedensforschung, Bd. 2), Münster 1994

Jost Dülffer (Hg.), Kriegsbereitschaft und Friedensordnung in Deutschland 1800–1914 (Jahrbuch für Historische Friedensforschung, Bd. 3), Münster 1995

Andreas Gestrich (Hg.), Gewalt im Krieg. Ausübung, Erfahrung und Verweigerung von Gewalt in Kriegen des 20. Jahrhunderts (Jahrbuch für Historische Friedensforschung, Bd. 4), Münster 1996

Andreas Gestrich/Bernd Ulrich/Gottfried Niedhart (Hg.), Gewaltfreiheit. Pazifistische Konzepte im 19. und 20. Jahrhundert (Jahrbuch für Historische Friedensforschung, Bd. 5), Münster 1996

Friedhelm Boll (Hg.), Volksreligiosität und Kriegserleben (Jahrbuch für Historische Friedensforschung, Bd. 6), Münster 1997

Stig Förster/Gerhard Hirschfeld (Hg.), Genozid in der modernen Geschichte (Jahrbuch für Historische Friedensforschung, Bd. 7), Münster 1999

Wette, Wolfram (Hg.), Militarismus in Deutschland 1871 bis 1945. Zeitgenössische Analysen und Kritik (Jahrbuch für Historische Friedensforschung, Bd. 8), Münster 1999

Thomas Kühne (Hg.), Von der Kriegskultur zur Friedenskultur? Zum Mentalitätswandel in Deutschland seit 1945 (Jahrbuch für Historische Friedensforschung, Bd. 9), Münster 2000

Benjamin Ziemann (Hg.), Perspektiven der Historischen Friedensforschung, Essen: Klartext Verlag 2002 (Frieden und Krieg. Beiträge zur Historischen Friedensforschung, Bd. 1)

Thomas Kühne/Peter Gleichmann (Hg.), Massenhaftes Töten. Kriege und Genozide im 20. Jahrhundert, Essen: Klartext Verlag 2004 (Frieden und Krieg. Beiträge zur Historischen Friedensforschung, Bd. 2)

Christian Jansen (Hg.), Der Bürger als Soldat. Die Militarisierung europäischer Gesellschaften im langen 19. Jahrhundert: ein internationaler Vergleich, Essen: Klartext Verlag 2003 (Frieden und Krieg. Beiträge zur Historischen Friedensforschung, Bd. 3)

Detlef Bald (Hg.), Schwellen überschreiten. Friedensarbeit und Friedensforschung. Festschrift für Dirk Heinrichs, Essen: Klartext Verlag 2005 (Frieden und Krieg. Beiträge zur Historischen Friedensforschung, Bd. 4)

Jennifer A. Davy/Karen Hagemann/Ute Kätzel (Hg.), Frieden – Gewalt – Geschlecht. Friedens- und Konfliktforschung als Geschlechterforschung, Essen: Klartext Verlag 2005 (Frieden und Krieg. Beiträge zur Historischen Friedensforschung, Bd. 5)

Thomas Kater (Hg.), „Der Friede ist keine leere Idee ..." Bilder und Vorstellungen vom Frieden am Beginn der politischen Moderne, Essen: Klartext Verlag 2006 (Frieden und Krieg. Beiträge zur Historischen Friedensforschung, Bd. 6)

Corinna Hauswedell (Hg.), Deeskalation von Gewaltkonflikten seit 1945, Essen: Klartext Verlag 2006 (Frieden und Krieg. Beiträge zur Historischen Friedensforschung, Bd. 7)

Benjamin Ziemann (Hg.), Peace Movements in Western Europe, Japan and the USA during the Cold War, Essen: Klartext Verlag 2007 (Frieden und Krieg. Beiträge zur Historischen Friedensforschung, Bd. 8)

Kirsten Zirkel, Vom Militaristen zum Pazifisten. General Berthold von Deimling – eine politische Biographie, Essen: Klartext Verlag 2008 (Frieden und Krieg. Beiträge zur Historischen Friedensforschung, Bd. 9)

Christine Brocks, Die bunte Welt der Krieges. Bildpostkarten aus dem Ersten Weltkrieg 1914–1918, Essen: Klartext Verlag 2008 (Frieden und Krieg. Beiträge zur Historischen Friedensforschung, Bd. 10)

Detlef Bald/Wolfram Wette (Hg.), Alternativen zur Wiederbewaffnung. Friedenskonzeptionen in Westdeutschland 1945–1955, Essen: Klartext Verlag 2008 (Frieden und Krieg. Beiträge zur Historischen Friedensforschung, Bd. 11)

Helke Stadtland (Hg.), „Friede auf Erden". Religiöse Semantiken und Konzepte des Friedens im 20. Jahrhundert, Essen: Klartext Verlag 2009 (Frieden und Krieg. Beiträge zu Historischen Friedensforschung, Bd. 12)

Lothar Wieland (Hg.), Aus der Zeit ohne Armee. Ehemalige Wehrmachtoffiziere im Umfeld des Pazifisten Fritz Küster, Essen: Klartext Verlag 2009 (Frieden und Krieg. Beiträge zu Historischen Friedensforschung, Bd. 13)

Jost Dülffer, Robert Frank (Eds.), War, Peace and Gender from Antiquity to the Present. Cross-Cultural Perspectives, Essen: Klartext Verlag 2009 (Frieden und Krieg. Beiträge zu Historischen Friedensforschung, Bd. 14)